T0248390

Marse

A Psychological Portrait of the Southern Slave Master and His Legacy of White Supremacy

H. D. Kirkpatrick

Prometheus Books

Guilford, Connecticut

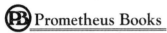 Prometheus Books

An imprint of Globe Pequot, the trade division of
The Rowman & Littlefield Publishing Group, Inc.
4501 Forbes Blvd., Ste. 200
Lanham, MD 20706
www.rowman.com

Distributed by NATIONAL BOOK NETWORK

British Library Cataloguing in Publication Information Available

Library of Congress Cataloging-in-Publication Data

Names: Kirkpatrick, H. D. (Hugh DeArmond), II, 1948– author.
Title: Marse : a psychological portrait of the southern slave master and
  his legacy of white supremacy / H.D. Kirkpatrick.
Description: Lanham, MD : Prometheus, [2022] | Includes bibliographical
  references and index. | Summary: "Written by a clinical and forensic
  psychologist, Marse: A Psychological Portrait of the Southern Slave Master
  and His Legacy of White Supremacy focuses on the white men who
  composed the southern planter class. The book is a psychological autopsy
  of the mind and slaveholding behavior that helps explain the enduring
  roots of white supremacy and the hidden wound of racist slavery that
  continues to affect all Americans today"— Provided by publisher.
Identifiers: LCCN 2021023134 (print) | LCCN 2021023135 (ebook) | ISBN
  9781633887572 (cloth) | ISBN 9781633887589 (epub)
Subjects: LCSH: Slaveholders—Southern States—History—19th century. |
  Slaveholders—Southern States—Psychology. | Plantation life—Southern
  States—History—19th century. | Slavery—Southern States—History—19th
  century. | Slavery—Southern States—Psychological aspects. |
  Slavery—Religious aspects—Christianity. | Slave trade—Southern
  States—History—19th century. | Elite (Social sciences)—Southern
  States—History—19th century. | Southern States—Race relations. |
  Southern States—Social conditions—19th century.
Classification: LCC F213 .K57 2022 (print) | LCC F213 (ebook) | DDC
  306.3/620975—dc23
LC record available at https://lccn.loc.gov/2021023134
LC ebook record available at https://lccn.loc.gov/2021023135

To the Kirkpatricks
All of us

Contents

Foreword

When H. D. Kirkpatrick learned that his North Carolina ancestors had owned enslaved people for generations, the family myth of a past as pastoral dairy yeomen shattered. The man who told him about his family's history, when they reconnected after forty years, was Jimmie Lee Kirkpatrick, who had been a Black football hero at their Charlotte high school. Back then, Jimmie Lee had always called H. D. "Cuz." Now it turned out that Jimmie Lee could actually be his cousin.

But this book is not the story of how H. D. and Jimmie Kirkpatrick found each other and their ancestors, or how the two of them became like family, although they did.

Instead, it's an answer to H. D.'s first question after his discovery. He didn't ask why those white Kirkpatricks became slaveholders. Historians could tell him that, with explanations including economic forces, labor supply, and Christian paternalism, and he read them all. Historians could also teach him what slavery was like, how it grew, and where it dominated the land and politics. But academic histories usually avoid exploration of the first question that popped into H. D.'s mind: "How does a man justify to himself that owning another human being as property is morally and ethically acceptable?"

H. D. later found that W. E. B. Du Bois had wondered the same thing. Du Bois wrote that "the psychological effect upon [the white master] was fatal. The mere fact that a man could be, under the law, the actual master of the mind and body of human beings had to have disastrous effects." But Du Bois's concerns lay elsewhere, and he never systematically explored those effects. Eugene Genovese came closest in *The World the Slaveholders Made*, but his explanations followed the economic imperatives of plantation slavery. Michael O'Brien followed the intellectual twists and turns that slave owners used to enable themselves to own other human beings in the magisterial two-volume book *Conjectures of Order*. H. D. realized that if he wanted an answer to his question, he would have to answer it himself.

Hugh DeArmond Kirkpatrick is a forensic psychologist. He spent forty years testifying in court on issues such as defendants' "likely state of mind" when they committed crimes. Enslavement was a crime, one that masters committed not just once but on a daily basis, year after year. Kirkpatrick combed secondary and primary material; this book is an apt historiography of the historical literature on slavery, using those works and the slaveholders' own words and actions to unearth their psychology.

He discovered that "the capacity to reach an emotional place in oneself that justifies owning another person seems insidiously complex." Here he untangles that complexity in eleven chapters, using forensic methods to explore and classify the psychological mechanisms that slave owners used to enable them to justify their crimes and, often, even to see themselves as benevolent Christians. He argues that slaveholding was not simply a "peculiar institution"; rather, it created psychopathologies in individuals, families, and, ultimately, the collective Confederacy.

L. P. Hartley wrote, "The past is a foreign country. They do things differently there." If so, we might be skeptical about applying twenty-first-century psychological analysis to nineteenth-century people. As an undergraduate psychology major who didn't experience a jot of cognitive dissonance when I abandoned the field to earn a history PhD, I harbored a few doubts as well. However, Kirkpatrick's pairing of history with his rigorous application of forensic psychological methods is always intriguing and convincing. Nineteenth-century people experienced cognitive dissonance too. For example, when the Presbyterian General Assembly took a vote in 1797 on the question "Is slavery evil?" the result was unanimous: yes. But the second question—"Are those who own slaves evil?"—came back as a firm no. Over the following four decades, cognitive dissonance and other compensating mechanisms slowly reshaped southern Protestantism to regard slavery not as evil but as a positive good. God made no mistakes; therefore, some were called to be servants and some masters. Only God could emancipate a slave.

Slaveholders became psychological acrobats. If a master raped a twelve-year-old slave, it was because (he thought) she was a hypersexual Jezebel. Although slaveholding families lived in fear of being murdered in their sleep in a slave uprising, white southerners somehow convinced themselves that those same enslaved people would fight for the Confederacy. Being a white woman on a plantation required exceptional mental gymnastics.

William Faulkner wrote of the South, "The past is never dead. It's not even past." Kirkpatrick does not flinch from the implications of his argument that a nation that experienced this sort of collective psychosis wrought a deep wound that Americans carried into the present. The legacy of these "collectively shared characteristics," Kirkpatrick writes, "still lives in the hearts and behaviors of twenty-first-century Americans."

It would be naive to think that the psychopathology that enabled slavery did not shape the nation's economic, social, and political systems and replicate itself in those institutions over the century and a half that followed. Kirkpatrick writes in closing that he hopes that "people will begin to draw connecting lines from antebellum Southern racist slavery to twenty-first-century racism." The hard history of slavery, here unsparingly depicted, is baked deep into the American psyche.

—Glenda Elizabeth Gilmore
Peter V. and C. Vann Woodward
Professor of History Emerita
Yale University

Preface

Put every crime perpetrated among men into a moral crucible, and dissolve and combine them all, and the resulting amalgam is slaveholding.

— Illinois Congressman Owen Lovejoy, 1860

In 1965, an eighteen-year-old African American man named Jimmie Lee Kirkpatrick transferred to my almost all-white high school from his all-Black high school. Jimmie and I were both seniors. We never became friends in high school. We would see each other in the hallway. We had the same last name. We'd go, "Hey, Cuz."

We had grown up in the 1950s and 1960s in Charlotte, North Carolina, a segregated southern city. Jimmie was an outstanding football player. He figured that once a school redistricting plan was completed, he could transfer and would stand a better chance of getting noticed, maybe getting a football scholarship. It turned out to be true.

Now, Jimmie had what you call "game." He averaged twelve yards a carry. He scored nineteen touchdowns and our football team won the regional state championship our senior year. Our team had some highly gifted athletes, but Jimmie stood out. He was Jim Brown caliber.

Jimmie got a football scholarship to Purdue. As a freshman, he was returning kickoffs and punt returns in the 1967 Rose Bowl.

Each year, North and South Carolina pick the best high school seniors to play in an all-star football game called the Shrine Bowl. In the fall of 1965—our senior year—Jimmie was not chosen. In fact, no Black player had ever been chosen. I was upset by that, because it seemed to me this omission was just blatant racism. The color of his skin kept Jimmie off that all-star team.

Because of his temperament and personality, Jimmie graciously accepted, in the press, his not being selected, publicly praising his two teammates (both white) who were chosen. Jimmie kept his disappointment to himself.

One of the South's best civil rights attorneys, Julius Chambers, filed a class action lawsuit against the Shriners, challenging the obvious racial discrimination in the Shriners' annual all-star selection process. Although it was too late to affect the 1965 player choices, Chambers's lawsuit ultimately prevailed, and Black players were chosen for the Shrine game the following year and each subsequent year.

As the lawsuit made its way through the court, racist elements in our community violently voiced their objections to Chambers's efforts. Chambers's office and house were firebombed. In 1965. In my hometown. The Klan showed up. I was pretty upset by that.

As was true for many high school seniors, I was applying to college. My beloved brother, Robert Kirkpatrick, was completing his doctorate in English at Harvard, and he convinced me to make Harvard one of my college choices. His advice was simple and wise: "You've got to write an application essay that will capture the admission committee's attention."

So I wrote about Jimmie: a Black classmate I barely knew, who had the same last name as mine, who was incredibly talented and had been an obvious subject of racial discrimination.

That was about the extent of it. My brother's guidance and my essay about Jimmie got me an interview. The admissions officer and I talked about the situation in Charlotte, the firebombings, and the civil rights implications. I got into Harvard with a scholarship to boot. I would not see or hear about Jimmie Lee Kirkpatrick for the next forty-six years.

In 2012, Gary Schwab, a sports editor for the *Charlotte Observer*, stumbled onto Jimmie's story in the archives of the paper, and the *Observer* located Jimmie in Portland, Oregon, where he lives with his wife and children. Schwab and his coauthor, David Price, did a great three-part series on Jimmie and his football/civil rights story. I read those three articles—collectively called "Breaking Through"—with great interest, because I sometimes wondered what had happened to him after high school.

I sent an e-mail message through the editor of the *Observer* to Jimmie, expressing my desire to speak with him if he was willing. One afternoon soon after, my secretary handed me a message and said, "Your cousin from Oregon called." Then she added, "I didn't know you had a cousin in Oregon."

I chuckled. "That's funny. I do now." I returned Jimmie's call, and we talked for two hours.

Professionally, as a forensic psychologist, I used my initials—H. D.—as my signature. That was how the signature line read on the e-mail I sent to Jimmie.

As Jimmie and I were talking, he asked, "What's the 'H' stand for?"
"Hugh," I responded.

There was this pause, and then he said, "I know a lot about your family."
I said, "Really? What do you mean?"

Jimmie proceeded to tell me that he'd been doing genealogic research for about a decade, and with the help of another researcher, Jimmie had located the original baptism records from Sharon Presbyterian Church in Charlotte that showed his great-great-great-grandfather, Sam Kirkpatrick ([unknown]–1866), was enslaved by Hugh Kirkpatrick (1803–1883).[1]

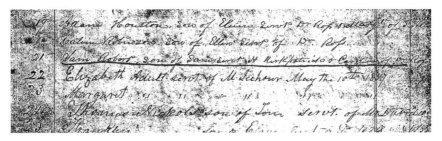

"Colored Infant Baptism" Record. *Sharon Presbyterian Church, Mecklenburg Co., NC*

The author's antebellum Kirkpatrick ancestor, circa 1855

This was more than a little shocking to me. Hugh was my great-great-grandfather.

Recovering from this news and gathering my wits about me, I responded, "Okay, turnabout is fair play." I then told Jimmie that I had written my college essay about him. And I said, "Your story about being discriminated against, got this white boy, who was the ancestor of the guy who held your ancestor in bondage, into the Ivy League."

He said, "Really? You're kidding me."

Subsequent to this life-changing telephone call, Schwab heard about our conversations and the time we began spending time together, and wrote another three-part series about Jimmie and me, about our family history. This second series was called "A Binding Truth." Both *Observer* series won the prestigious Green Eyeshade Award.

Jimmie's news about my paternal ancestors being slaveholders truly stunned me. The news Jimmie delivered to me and the conversations we have had and continue to have—now over the course of eight years—about our families and the peculiar institution of American slavery altered the course and direction of my life. This book is not a work of fiction. I consider the truth Jimmie gave to me to be a gift of immeasurable proportion.

Jimmie and I had deepening conversations in which I learned that, on the eve of the Civil War in 1860, Hugh Kirkpatrick enslaved thirty-two people, which put him in the "planter" class. Ten years earlier, the 1850 Federal Slave Schedule 2, taken in September 1850, shows he enslaved thirty-four people during that census (see figure on page xv).[2] As was the custom, Hugh's surname, Kirkpatrick, is the only one listed. His enslaved are identified by their age and gender only. He listed nineteen males, fifteen females. Fourteen of the male enslaved were fourteen years old or younger, the youngest being three, and nine of the female enslaved were fourteen years old or younger, the youngest being one year old.

I had grown up being told that my Kirkpatrick family—my father's folks—earned its living as dairy farmers, which was true in some generations. But when they first came to the colonies in the mid-eighteenth century, my Scots-Irish, Associate Reformed Presbyterian family established plantations and kept enslaved people. It is quite possible the white Kirkpatricks were dairy farmers from their colonial beginning, but if they were, they were using enslaved labor in the eighteenth and nineteenth centuries. Jimmie opened an ancestral door I did not know existed. In the months ahead, I learned that Hugh Kirkpatrick's grandfather John (my great-great-great-great-grandfather; 1741–1808) arrived in the colonies around 1762 from Ireland and settled in what that same year became Mecklenburg County, North Carolina. The 1790 federal census showed that John enslaved three people (see figure on page xvi). John's name is written five lines from the bottom of the left-hand column.

This book, *Marse: A Psychological Portrait of the Southern Slave Master and His Legacy of White Supremacy*, is a direct result of learning that I am a descendant of southern slaveholders, some of whom belonged to the so-called planter class because they owned thirty or more enslaved persons. I needed to try to understand Marse Hugh's psychology, although this book is not just an effort to understand my great-great-grandfather. It is a journey into the mind and behavior of the white male elite southern slave master who psychologically managed to justify enslaving another human being. The research and writing I have done over the past eight years have turned into the psychological exploration captured in this book. Jimmie has become my good friend, my cousin, my family, my brother, and my mentor. Marse became my examinee.

Listing of thirty-four enslaved people held by Hugh Kirkpatrick.
Schedule 2, 1850 Federal Slave Census

Listing of three enslaved people held by John Kirkpatrick, the author's great-great-great-great-grandfather. *1790 Federal Census*

One afternoon, while doing some reading, I called Jimmie at his home in Portland to share a concern I thought he should know about. I had been pondering where my post–Civil War ancestors may have carried and stored their racism after the war was lost. I said to Jimmie, "Don't be surprised if I find a Klan robe in the closet somewhere."

Jimmie paused for a moment, then chuckled. "Cutty, I'm not going to be surprised. After all, Kirkpatrick has 3 Ks in it."

Surprised by his response, I asked, "How long have you been thinking about that?"

And he said, "All—my—life."

This book has some autobiographical flavor comparable to the personal-historical narrative found in *The Making of a Racist* by the historian Charles B. Dew, a book that blew my doors off.[3] Dew's personal story was so parallel to my own. My work also found inspiration from Edward Ball's outstanding and courageous first book, *Slaves in the Family*.[4] Another book that continues to have a profound impact on me is Wendell Berry's *The Hidden Wound*.[5]

This book is not a genealogical exposition. The rationale for using the name "Marse" (a synonym for "Master") in this book's title is explained more fully in the introduction. This work is about trying to understand the psyche of *the* Marse, the southern white racist man who reached a bargain with himself and his beloved South that owning thirty or more human beings was perfectly acceptable. This book is not about one particular man; it is a psychological examination of a general historical class of southern, planter-class, slaveholding men.

The scheme of this work is psychohistorical, as seen through the lens and methodology of applied clinical and forensic psychology. These two fields were my professional specializations, in civil and criminal law, for more than forty-five years. My work here results in a psychological autopsy, utilizing psychological methods and an understanding of the history of those times.

In my work as an expert consultant and witness in forensic psychology, a typical criminal case would be one in which I was retained to try to help explain psychologically why an individual defendant acted in certain ways. I was usually asked to aid my client—either defense counsel or the court—in understanding likely or probable explanations for the defendant's actions, some of which seemed, at first blush, to make no sense. I learned early on that human beings can and will do some horrible things to other human beings. I forensically examined my professional cases using an applied multimethod, multihypothesis approach. My final analysis of a defendant's behavior might cause him or her to sink or swim within the relevant legal circumstances. My guiding principles for my professional work were objectivity and psychological truth.

Forensic psychology, by definition, is the application of psychological methods and procedures to a circumstance in which there is a legal context or question, the understanding or comprehension of which might be helped by an exploration of its psychological dimensions. The forensic expert is asked to address at least one central question—the "referral question"—usually put to the expert by the retaining attorney or the court. For example, in a homicide case, the defense counsel might ask the expert, "What was the defendant's likely state of mind at the time of the murder?"

I must clarify something important here. I am not answering whether or not Marse is a criminal. He was and he is. In today's light, he is guilty of serious crimes. He committed crimes against humanity. He enslaved other persons. In his own antebellum legal and sectional culture, he was not a criminal, at least not most of the time. That's the point, isn't it? Marse had to become comfortable with being engaged in horrible, criminal acts at the most basic human level. As I apply various hypotheses to attempt to explain Marse's psychology and behavior in certain areas, I will not be entertaining whether or not he engaged in criminal behavior. Such is my modern bias. Such is today's clear truth.

Since it's a given that Marse's psychosocial history is replete with heinous crimes, such as abducting, transporting his enslaved prisoners in inhumane and often deadly conditions, maiming, using physical and psychological violence, imprisoning, sexually assaulting, enslaving, abusing and neglecting children, committing family-ectomy, flogging, and committing terror lynchings, to name a few, there is a clear, affirmative answer to the question, "Did he do these things?" His crimes are defined now through many sources, including first-person narratives by former enslaved persons, unmarked graves of enslaved persons, plantation records, an extensive retrospective social judgment lens, and an ever-expanding motherlode of historical research, particularly demonstrating the extent to which Marse's powerful hands steered America's brand of enslaved-labor capitalism. Additionally, the horrible "truth" about slavery is being unearthed and memorialized in powerful ways, such as the National Museum of African American History and Culture in Washington, DC, and two places in Montgomery, Alabama: the Legacy Museum: From Enslavement to Mass Incarceration and the National Memorial for Peace and Justice (see figure on page xix). America is having an emphatic reckoning with its Black slavery history as never before.

I began writing this book well before the cultural and political seismic shift that occurred (and continues to occur) in large measure in America because of a series of murders of Black men and women by white police officers, not the least of which was the lynching of George Floyd in Minneapolis on May 25, 2020. The video of Floyd's murder allowed millions to

National Memorial for Peace and Justice by MASS Design Group, Montgomery, Alabama. *Photograph by the author*

see the truth of the underlying racism ravaging our country. If my book has any impact, my hope is that people will begin to draw connecting lines from antebellum Southern racist slavery to twenty-first-century racism.

This book is not aimed at an understanding of "why" Marse committed these acts against Black Africans. My goal here is to explore a deeper, core question: *How* did Marse become psychologically comfortable with owning, as property, another human being? My focus will be on the so-called elite southern white slaveholders who enslaved thirty or more people, with special attention to the top echelon of enslavers who held hundreds in bondage and a few Grandees with over a thousand. Our nation's first president, George Washington, was a slaveholder. As the historian Andrew Delbanco informed us, Washington, "as a child of eleven, had inherited ten slaves from his father. By 1770, he owned over a hundred."[6]

It's not enough to say the slaveholder enslaved people because he was a racist. It's not sufficient to explain the slave master's behavior in economic terms. The capacity to reach an emotional place in oneself that justifies owning another person seems insidiously complex. My great-great-grandfather, Marse Hugh, a man I was named after, reached this emotional place. So had his father and his father's father. Obviously, the same was true for George Washington and his father.

Marse Hugh Kirkpatrick had at least three sons who fought for the Confederacy. Marse Hugh's grandfather, a man I now consider Marse John Kirkpatrick (1741–1808), was my great-great-great-great-grandfather. A Scots-Irish Calvinist Presbyterian, he came to the colonies from the Ulster area of Ireland around 1762, apparently through the port of Charles Town, traveled north, and established a plantation just south of Charlotte, North Carolina. As noted above, he enslaved three people in 1790. He helped build Sardis Associate Reformed Presbyterian Church on his plantation land. These are my people. I initially undertook writing this book as a way of trying to make some sense out of my family history. I decided if I forensically investigated the mind of the white southern slave master, I might discover lots of things. My research and findings led me well beyond discoveries about my ancestors.

My client for the findings contained in this book is the court of public history. I have approached "Marse" here as the subject of a comprehensive forensic psychological examination. My findings about Marse's psychology are based on my review and analysis of multiple collateral resources. Many of these resources were naturally the research and analysis of many brilliant, gifted historians who have devoted their entire careers to the subject of slavery. My primary sources include narratives and autobiographies by formerly enslaved people and the diaries, plantation logs, and publications of slaveholders, as well as the sermons and proslavery defenses of slavery by southern clergymen. Many scholars have written insightfully about various psychological aspects of slaveholders. There is also the significant work of the social psychologist Phillip Zimbardo, who has taught us so much about the corrupting potential of power. I gleaned from these scholars their psychological insights into the minds and behaviors of the slaveholders as I developed a comprehensive psychological portrait of the American white southern elite slave master utilizing collateral sources and my own skills and training.

The portrait of Marse I present is my interpretation of his ethics and behavior. My goal has been to reach findings in my analysis that are helpful toward an understanding of Marse and go well beyond a "more likely than not" evidentiary standard (51 percent in psychological statistical parlance) and perhaps beyond the "clear, cogent, and convincing" evidentiary standard (75 percent), aiming for a "beyond a reasonable doubt" standard (98–99 percent). The court of public opinion and public history will have to decide whether or not I succeeded.

There is no way I could have kept myself from writing this book. I have now identified three generations of my paternal family as slaveholders. I have become best friends with a Black high school classmate, Jimmie Kirkpatrick, whose ancestors were enslaved by my ancestors. I have visited the graves of these Black and white Kirkpatricks. The latter have etched marble headstones.

In the same cemetery, the Black Kirkpatricks have rocks, and these were placed there only recently by a wonderful scout troop who took on this disgrace as a humanitarian project. I have attended a large Black Kirkpatrick family reunion in my hometown. Through wills and other public records, Jimmie and I have identified the names, genders, and ages of many of the enslaved people my ancestors owned. In 2018, I taught a course at the University of North Carolina at Charlotte titled "Up Close and Personal: the History of Slavery in Mecklenburg County."

When I learned the harsh truth about my ancestors' slaveholding history, I was working full-time as a forensic psychologist. I became conflicted. I had forensic cases that demanded my time and expertise, but what I felt compelled to do was dig more deeply into the world of slaveholding. A psychological path seemed to make sense. I retired from my private practice, dived into the history of American slavery, and began to swim in my southern pools of racist slavery. I framed my referral question, as I would do in any forensic psychological examination, as, "How does a man justify to himself that owning another human being as property is morally and ethically acceptable?", identified my client as the general public, and began analyzing the relevant records. As I studied and chewed on the data about southern chattel slavery, I realized how deeply wounded I was from my family's history. I became acutely conscious of how slavery is a significant emotional bridge from America's past to its present and future. I understand how slavery wounded us all in one way or another. The trauma of the wound of slavery is rocking America to its core right now. This book is a summary of the different paths I took, my findings, and the bases for those findings. It's also a book that is different than how I initially imagined it, because the time for staring down racist white supremacy in the face is right now.

I chose the word "Marse" for part of this book's title not only because it's a synonym for "Master," but also because it offers an ambiguity. It refers to a collective class title, the caste of the American southern slave master. It also refers to an individual: master. My great-great-grandfather may well have been called Marse Hugh.

There are four reasons why I think there is value in utilizing forensic psychological methods in an exploration of Southern elite slaveholding. First, the original definition of "forensic" derives from the Greek word that means "public forum." Under Roman law, the word meant "in a court of law." I am using its original meaning: an examination in a public forum. Second, forensic psychological methods, when applied comprehensively and competently, force the examiner to be fair and objective. A forensic examination of a human being demands an analysis of the good, the bad, and the ugly. A balanced approach guards against bias. I have a bias: Slaveholding was wrong and immoral. It was a crime against humanity. Does this conclusion bear out? Do the historic data support or negate such a conclusion? Is such a conclusion defensible in light of the historic data? Third, seeking a comprehensive evaluation of the subject requires an examination of as many relevant resources as possible. I do not claim to have exhausted all the many possible resources. A finding or a conclusive statement must stand on a minimum of two sources. In this way, a forensic psychological exam is akin to investigative journalism. A story based on two independent sources can likely stand up. A forensic finding based on a minimum of two independent sources can likely stand up. A fourth reason is that a forensic examination must rest on the examiner considering multiple and often rival hypotheses. For example, did slaveholding add to the character strengths of the slave master or diminish them? Did slaveholding produce only deleterious effects on the enslaved? Was there any validity to the slaveholder's claim that the enslaved benefitted from slavery?

As shocking as it was for me to learn about my family's slaveholding history, I feel deeply grateful for the truth Jimmie Kirkpatrick revealed to me about my family—no, *our* families. My primary goal in the writing of this book is to reveal some relevant and hopefully healing, psychological truth about antebellum southern racist slavery.

Introduction:
The Psychology of the Deceased

$\mathcal{M}$arse as an enslaver is dead. This book aims to explore, define, and conceptualize a psychological portrait of a dead man: a historically well known, both despised and revered, somewhat romanticized and idealized dead man. It is a psychohistorical autopsy of a man named "Marse," an outdated title synonymous with "Master," "Mars," "Mas," "Marster," "Mausta," "Mastah," or other variations of address commonly used by Black enslaved people and white freemen to acknowledge by title and position the American southern slave master. This book portrays characteristics or traits collectively shared by a particular class of slaveholders framed by thirty-one years in the antebellum South (1830–1861). They inserted themselves early into the list of key players who developed what would become the American colonies. The southern American Marse has had a long life. After an examination of the deceased's mind and behavior, the book explores an argument that Marse is really not dead. For most of my life, I thought he was. I was wrong. As I developed and wrote this book, I realized that the Marse of the past still lives in many of the hearts and behaviors of twenty-first-century Americans.

THE PSYCHOLOGICAL QUESTION IS, "HOW"?

At a general, almost legendary level, there remains little doubt about *why* the southern slave master did what he did. There may be a continuing debate about whether or not slavery was the single greatest cause of the Civil War, but Marse the slaveholding statesman stands in a clear light. As a racist white elitist, he held Black people in bondage. He saw Black Africans as inferior subhumans. History has had Marse in its crosshairs for a long time. As a white

American Southerner, Marse embraced and developed a bound labor system and an economy that were racist to their cores. This slavery-based system is commonly referred to as the South's "peculiar institution." The question that compels me here is *how* did he psychologically do what he did? Just how did a slave trader justify what it took to abduct, chain, imprison, sexually exploit, punish, transport, control, and murder captured people? How did Marse justify to himself that owning another human being was morally acceptable? It seems impossible to objectively look at American southern slavery—the South's peculiar institution—and not judge it as right or wrong.

While most historians well understand slavery in general and American slavery in particular, much more can be said about the psyche (the inner psychodynamics) of the slave master. When I began my research for this book, I quickly came upon the work of historians Elizabeth Fox-Genovese and Eugene Genovese, who have contributed brilliantly to understanding the mind of the slave master.[1] The work of historian James Roark is also instructive as he offered sharply identified insights into the mind of the slave master once the master had no slaves, and how Marse's mind reconstituted itself after "the impact of secession, war, defeat, emancipation, and Reconstruction."[2]

THE RELEVANCE OF THE TITLE "MARSE"

I have chosen "Marse" because it is an apt title for the subject of this work: the elite white American slaveholding Southerner. In his discussion of the book *Eneas Africanus* (an apparent proslavery racist parody) by American journalist and poet Harry Stillwell Edwards (1855–1938), the word "Marse" appears as Charles Dew relates the character Eneas's outcry to his "master's" question, "Eneas, you black rascal, where have you been?" Eneas responds, "Oh, Lord! Marse George! Glory be ter God! Out o' de wilderness!"[3]

I found additional support for calling this project "Marse" from a most unexpected source. With the help of one of General Robert E. Lee's officers, Major Robert Stiles (1836–1905), I offer a further explanation for my choice of the word. Although "Marse" was a title given to a white master by his Black enslaved people, it was far more than a Black dialectical form of "Master." In his book *Four Years under Marse Lee*, Major Stiles explained his use of the word "Marse" as not only a nickname given to General Lee by his men but a word with several explicit meanings.[4]

Beyond the word's use as a nickname, Stiles's second explanation is surprising: "In the first place, it is *military*. . . . This quaint title yet rings true upon the elemental basis of military life—unquestioning and unlimited obedience. It embodies the strongest possible expression of the short creed of the soldier:

'Theirs not to reason why
Theirs but to do and die.'"

Stiles informs us that it is a distinctively southern title, "applied in reverent affection, but also in defiant yet pathetic protest. It was, in some sense, an outcry of the social system of the South assailed and imperiled by the war and doomed to perish in the great convulsion."[5]

This dimension of the word is surprising because it puts the white Confederate soldier and the Black enslaved on an equitable power-dynamic playing field not often considered: "The title 'Marse Robert' fitted at once the life of the soldier and the life of the enslaved, because both were based on the principle of absolute obedience to absolute authority."[6] Stiles continued: The term "undoubtedly originated among our negroes, being an expression of their affectionate reverence for their masters, by metaphor transferred to the one great 'Lord and Master' of us all." By Stiles's report, southern white men in general and rebel soldiers especially often referred to God as the "Old Master."[7]

According to Stiles, the reverential application of "Marse" to Lee was also paying homage to the man's character and bearing. Character was a major focus among nineteenth-century people. Marse Robert was revered.

To put a fine point on the meaning of "Marse," Stiles wrote, "There is no way in which I can illustrate more vividly the almost worship with which Lee's soldiers regarded him than by saying that I once overheard a conversation beside a camp fire between two Calvinists in Confederate rags and tatters, shreds and patches, in which one simply and sincerely inquired of his fellow, who had just spoken of 'Old Marster,' whether he referred to the one up at headquarters or the One up yonder."[8]

Furthering his elucidation of the meaning of "Marse," Stiles reveals Lee's beliefs about Black slaves' relationship to authority. When Lee was asked his opinion about allowing armed slaves to join the Confederate cause, Stiles stated, Lee believed such an experiment would naturally work because "that

General Robert E. Lee, Photograph by L. C. Handy (May 1869). *Library of Congress*

unhesitatingly and unlimited obedience to authority—the first great lesson of a soldier—was ingrained, if not inborn, in the Southern slave." This opinion by Lee foreshadows one of the self-defeating traits of the American southern elite slaveholder to be discussed in the body of this book—the trait of self-deception. Just how much applied denial have Americans—myself included—used to pretend Marse is dead?

Chronology

17th C	Throughout most of this century, indentured servants filled the bulk of the colonies' labor needs.[6]
1619	First Black African slaves brought to Jamestown, Virginia, by English privateers who had seized the enslaved people from a Portuguese ship.
1640	War between Scots-Presbyterians and England.

By this year, there were forty thousand Scots in Ulster.
"Between 1640 and 1655, [the Caribbean islands] were transformed into sugar colonies . . . the English began their slave trade which lasted from 1651 to 1808, and which introduced an estimated 1,900,000 Africans to the Caribbean."[7]

1650	Battle at Nations Ford (Mecklenburg County, NC) between the Catawbas and Cherokees, resulted in one thousand dead in the Catawba tribe and eleven hundred in the Cherokee tribe.
1657	The first known permanent white settler in North Carolina, Nathaniel Batts, had a house at the western end of Albemarle Sound.
1663	March 24, 1663, King Charles II (formerly titled prince of Wales) granted a charter for the colony of Carolina that made eight proprietors the "true and absolute lords and proprietors of the province."[8] Among these eight men were: Sir John Colleton, a royalist, who was appointed to the Council of Foreign Plantations, a resident of Barbados; Sir William Berkeley (governor of Virginia); Sir Anthony Ashley Cooper (later earl of Shaftsbury), chancellor of the exchequer; Sir George Cartaret, vice chamberlain of the household and treasurer of the navy; Edward Hyde, earl of Clarendon and the king's first minister and lord high chancellor of England; William Craven, the earl of Craven; George Monck, duke of Albemarle, among other things, who (according to Powell, 54), had been a general in Cromwell's army but switched over to help the monarchy be reestablished; and finally John Lord Berkeley, a strong supporter of the crown.[9]

The duke of York, with a group of investors, launched the Company of Royal Adventurers Trading to Africa, later to become the Royal African Company. Four of these investors were among the Lords Proprietors who established North Carolina.

1665	Proprietors planned three counties in Carolina: Albemarle, Clarendon, and Craven.
1669	The Fundamental Constitutions of Carolina, "supposedly written by philosopher John Locke, Ashley Cooper's protégé, who served for a time as secretary to the Proprietors." William S. Powell, *North Carolina Through Four Centuries*, 1989, 57. This document carved Carolina into a feudal system run by nobility.
1680s	The shift from indentured servants to slave labor began to occur in the colonies.
1680	Virginia passed its first slave code.
1683	South Carolina passed its first "Act to Prevent Runaways."[10]
1691	A Virginia trader named Daniel Pugh kidnapped and sold several Tuscarora Indians "onto ships bound for Caribbean sugar plantations."[11]
1700	There were a million Scots in Ireland.

At least forty thousand and perhaps well over fifty thousand enslaved people were held in the colony of North Carolina.

1708	The governor of South Carolina estimated there were fourteen hundred Indian slaves in South Carolina among a total population of 12,580.[12]
1710	New Bern, North Carolina, was settled and founded.
1711	The Tuscarora War began in North Carolina, when the Tuscarora in September captured Christoph von Graffenreid, founder of New Bern, and John Lawson, an influential surveyor. "When talks with the captives broke down, Tuscarora, Coree, Neuse, Bear River, and other Indians who had gathered at Catechna (hereafter referred to as the Catechna Alliance) executed Lawson and launched a devastating surprise attack against settlements along the Pamlico, Neuse, and Trent Rivers and Core Sound."[13]
1712	Separation of North and South Carolina occurred, with the commissioning of Edward Hyde as the first governor of North Carolina.
1727	Another mass exodus of Scots-Irish took place from Ulster province, following a succession of three bad harvests in a row, the "great potato famine." Many of these came to America as indentured servants.
1729	King George II purchased seven of the eight proprietors' shares of Carolina. According to Kratt, the king may have done so because of the proprietors' mismanagement.[14]
1730	"As late as 1730, Quaker merchants in Philadelphia were importing and selling West Indian Negroes."[15]
1730–1745	Large migration of Highland Scots to North Carolina—including Flora Macdonald.
1731	The famous English preacher George Whitefield came to the colonies, his second of seven visits—his preaching up and down the eastern seaboard, sparking the "Great Awakening." Citing Drake, Erskine in *The Plantation Church* points out that "Negro spirituals" in part developed because of the "camp meetings" which began with the first Great Awakening in 1739.
	"The Great Awakening had the effect of highlighting the importance of religious instruction for enslaved persons which was seen by many within the church as a religious duty that would enhance the master-slave relationships and at the same time increase productivity on the plantations. It was a win-win situation for both the church and the master. The truth is, slavery emerged as a Christian institution." Pg. 76 in Erskine.
	Whitefied (sometimes spelled Whitfield) was a strong supporter of the legalization of slavery. It is said he had four thousand acres and fifty slaves. "Whitefield in Georgia advocated the introduction of slavery and rum for the economic development of the colony. He even owned slaves himself." Pg. 75 in Erskine, *The Plantation Church*.
1735–1770	Seventy thousand to seventy-five thousand enslaved people were brought into Georgia and North Carolina.
1749	Anson County, North Carolina, established. Mecklenburg County later was carved out of Anson County.
1750	Forty thousand enslaved people lived in the low country (South Carolina, Georgia) of the South, whereas 145,000 lived in Virginia and Maryland.
	By 1750, "each colony in the various regions of British North America had gone through comparable stages of development": 1. invasion and conquest of native Americans and their lands 2. the replacement of indigenous peoples by increasing numbers of European Americans, including significant indentured labor

	3. increasing numbers of enslaved African Americans

3. increasing numbers of enslaved African Americans
4. sufficient efforts by whites began a significant, viable export trade.[16]

1754–1755   A succession of North Carolina governors made a special effort to attract colonists from Ulster and Scotland.

1756   Enslaved people comprised some 16 percent of the population of both Newport, Rhode Island, and New York City. "Princeton's first nine presidents were all slaveholders at various points in their lives."[17]

1762   Mecklenburg County was named after the birthplace of the new bride of King George III of England—Queen Charlotte of Mecklenburg-Strelitz, Germany.[18]

1763   Kratt informs us that in this year, George August Selwyn's agent, Henry McCulloch, sent surveyors to the emerging Charlotte Town, to sell and execute deeds, for lands already settled by the Scots-Irish, who did not take kindly to Selwyn and McCulloch's efforts. These proud Scot-Irish "attacked the surveyors, breaking their instruments and measuring chains."[19]

1765   The so-called Sugar Creek War (aka the "Selwyn land riots") in Mecklenburg County, a fight over land ownership between Lord Selwyn's men, led by Henry McCulloh [McCulloch], and a local band, led by Thomas Polk. According to Morrill, quoting Bowers, Polk eventually had a personal land holding of "over 15,000 acres" and he and his relatives "owned 81 slaves."[20]

1768   Charlotte, North Carolina, was established on 360 acres of land purchased from George Augustus Selwyn.

The people of Mecklenburg County declared, "We shall ever be more ready to support the government under which we find the most liberty."[21]

1771   Queens College for men was established in Charlotte, but King George III refused to approve its charter. Its name was changed to Queens Museum, but still not approved by the king. Nevertheless, in defiance of the crown, it operated without a charter as the first college in North Carolina.

1774   Hezekiah Alexander built his house in Mecklenburg County. Morrill says the Alexander clan owned more than 160 slaves.[22]

1775   By this year, probably two hundred thousand Ulstermen immigrated to America, mostly all Presbyterians. Vann says between two and three hundred thousand Scots-Irish were living in America.

Leyburn estimated that one hundred thousand Scots-Irish came as indentured servants.[23]

1776   Thomas Jefferson, who held three hundred enslaved individuals in bondage, drafted the Declaration of Independence.

1777   North Carolina passed a law designed to curb emancipation; the law denounced "the evil and pernicious practice of freeing slaves in this state."[24]

1780–1784   Pennsylvania, Massachusetts, New Hampshire, Connecticut, and Rhode Island abolished slavery within their borders.

1783   Erskine informs us that, after the American Revolution, many American Blacks founded churches wherein Africa was a central and crucial part of their identity. Revivals in the South contributed significantly to the conversion of Blacks to Christianity: "In this emotionally charged atmosphere, enslaved people encountered a form of Protestant worship that resembled the religious celebration of their African homelands."[25]

1785	David Walker, an African American, was born in Wilmington, North Carolina; he would become the first African American to offer a written indictment of slavery. In the late 1820s he published *An Appeal to the Coloured People of the World*. He argued, among other things, that Egyptian slavery was nowhere near as racist as American slavery.[26]
1786	Between 1786 and 1788 Josiah Collins brought enslaved West Africans to dig the Somerset Canal (in North Carolina) between the Scuppernong River and Lake Phelps to establish Somerset Place Plantation, drain the pocosin wetlands, harvest timber, and develop agricultural cropland.
1787	The Constitutional Convention was held. In one of its decisions, it prevented Congress from outlawing slavery for twenty years. The effect was that between 1787 and 1807, more enslaved people were brought into the United States than during any two other decades in history.[27]
	The Fugitive Slave Clause was added to the Constitution.
	Quobnah Ottobah Cugoano wrote *Thoughts and Sentiments on the Evil and Wicked Traffic of the Slavery and Commerce of the Human Species*.
1790	February 24: The first Presbytery of the Associate Reformed Presbyterian Church in the South was organized in Long Cane, Abbeville, South Carolina, also known as the Presbytery of the Carolinas and Georgia. It was under the leadership of Dr. Thomas Clark. This is the date given for the founding of the Sardis ARP Church in Mecklenburg County, North Carolina.
	A thousand tons of cotton were being produced every year in the South.[28]
	"In 1790 the United States produced about 3,000 bales of cotton. The figure increased to 178,000 in 1810 and ballooned to more than 4 million bales on the eve of the Civil War."[29]
1790s	A massive slave revolt occurred in Haiti. In 1791 the population of Haiti included 450,000 enslaved people, 30,000 free persons of color, and only 40,000 whites.[30] "In 1791, the Blacks of Haiti rose up against both the whites and free persons of color and a 12-year armed struggle began that ended with the Proclamation of the Republic of Haiti in 1804."[31]
1792	In response to the revolt in Haiti, South Carolina introduced legislation to prohibit the importation of slaves.
1793	The invention of the cotton gin. According to Kolchin, this device allowed for the separation of the seeds from the short-staple cotton in a relatively efficient way. Short-staple cotton was easier to grow and could grow in more places than the long-staple variety of cotton. This allowed for a tremendous expansion of cotton production throughout the South.
	This invention "enabled farmers to ship about twelve times as much cotton to market than they could before, and the world price decreased by approximately one half. This meant that industrious individuals who owned substantial amounts of land and the requisite labor supply could increase their annual income by 600 per cent. Before the cotton gin, virtually no cotton was grown in the Piedmont."[32]
1798	John Kirkpatrick (the author's great-great-great-great-grandfather) owned more than seven hundred acres and four slaves. At the time of his death in 1808, he enslaved over fourteen people.

1800   "At the end of the eighteenth century, the average sugar plantation [in the Caribbean] was staffed with 180 enslaved individuals; in Virginia and Maryland the average plantation had less than 13 enslaved people."[33]

According to King, the Reformed Presbytery had passed an act that no slaveholder would be kept in the church. "The people heartily favored this position even though the bulk of the Reformed Presbyterian Church was located in the South. Since the Associate Reformed Church remained silent on this question, and more and more of Associate Reformed people purchased enslaved people, the Reformed Presbyterians found less and less in common with their Associate Reformed brothers. Instead of remaining in the South to testify against the evils of slavery, however, these Covenanters moved away from the problem."[34] King says many moved to the northwestern states.

1802   Salem Academy established by the Moravian community. *Recently, the college has been coming to some terms with its slaveholding history and issued an apology.*

1807   Southern Mecklenburg's several largest landowners now individually possessed between three and six enslaved people.

The British Parliament abolished the slave trade but not slavery itself.

1808   By a congressional ban, importation of enslaved people ceased. Sublette and Sublette emphasize the tremendous impact this date and this law had on changing the nature of slavery in the South. Slavery moved from the *importation* phase to the *breeding* phase. Interstate slave trading became big business.[35]

1810   The enslaved population of America was twice what it had been in 1770.

1819   By this time, Jefferson himself came to the defense of southern "rights" against those who would limit the spread of slavery into Missouri.

An economic depression occurred, e.g., South Carolina experienced an abrupt end to prosperity.

1820   The United States passed India as the world's largest cotton producer.

1822   The population of Charleston was 24,780, only 10,653 of whom were white.

1823   Richard Furman writes his Exposition of the Views of Baptists, the most important proslavery argument to come out of Charleston, South Carolina, in the 1820s. Furman's arguments were used to respond to the "religiously inspired Vesey plot." Furman argued that the Providence of God had saved Charleston from a slave revolt. He advocated that a master might hold an enslaved person "according to Christian principles" and that evil attached to slavery only through the "individual who abuses his authority."

1828   William Lee Jr. and his wife, Mary Ann McKnight, established their plantation off McAlpine Creek in Mecklenburg County.

John C. Calhoun argues that individual states have the constitutional right to "nullify" laws imposed by the federal government.[36]

The firm of Franklin and Armfield was organized. It became the largest slave-trading enterprise in the South, operating out of Alexandria, Virginia. Before they retired, each partner had accumulated fortunes in excess of a half million dollars.[37]

1830s	Brazil imported more than four hundred thousand enslaved people.[38]
	Between 1830 and 1860, Virginia exported more than three hundred thousand enslaved people; North Carolina, about one hundred thousand. Much of this exporting had to do with the western movement of the country to other "promised lands."
	The North Carolina General Assembly passed the Free Negro Code, which attempted to restrict free Blacks' contact with antislavery advocates and enslaved people.[39]
1831	William Lloyd Garrison published his newspaper *The Liberator* in Boston.
1832	John C. Calhoun resigned as Andrew Jackson's vice president and reentered the US Senate to fight a federal tariff that was benefitting only Northern manufacturers.
	South Carolina claims the right to nullify federal laws.
	Thomas R. Dew of William and Mary published "Professor Dew on Slavery," a description of the economic and moral necessity of slavery.
1835	Davidson College was established by the Concord Presbytery.
	The American Anti-Slavery Society declared an information war on the South. It began to deluge southern mailboxes with antislavery material.[40]
1836	Congress enacts the "gag rule," automatically tabling without debate all petitions on the subject of slavery.[41]
1838	Slavery abolished in Jamaica.
	Frederick Douglass escaped to New York City from slavery in Baltimore, Maryland.
1840s	Mecklenburg County instituted "slave patrols" whose outward purpose was "to prevent negroes from holding meetings at night and on Sundays."
1845	Even though the Synod of the South remained essentially silent on the issue of slavery—i.e., it never condemned slavery—it passed an act in 1845 "which in effect recognized that slaves had souls. Some slaveholders did not admit that their slaves had souls, and were, therefore, not entitled to hear the gospel and be educated in the tenets of the Christian religion. Some slaves showed no respect for the institution of marriage; neither did some masters respect the dignity of marriage among slaves. Often negro families would be split when husbands, wives or children would be sold."[42]
	The Baptist Church split over slavery. The Southern Baptists now saw their ministers free to promote slavery as a Bible institution.[43]
	Frederick Douglass's *Narrative of the Life of Frederick Douglass, an American Slave*, is published.
	Texas is admitted to the union as a slave state.
1847	Charles Colcock Jones of Georgia wrote a book entitled *Suggestions on the Religious Instruction of Negroes in the Southern States*, which was published by the Presbyterian Board of Publications.

1848	Calhoun held a caucus of southern senators and representatives in the Senate chamber and gave his "Address of the Southern delegates in Congress to the Constituents," advocating slavery as a state right and that forcing the emancipation of enslaved people was an act of aggression.[44]
	James Watt Kirkpatrick (the author's great-grandfather) was born in the Sharon Township. At age sixteen, he volunteered in the Confederate army.
	The California Gold Rush begins.
1849	Harriet Tubman escapes from slavery and soon begins the Underground Railroad.
1850	By the second quarter of the nineteenth century, the Sharon District's enslaved population outnumbered its white population. In a population of approximately 800 persons, 374 were white and 426 were Black.
	Dr. Joseph Ross of the Sharon Township (Mecklenburg County) had accumulated more than one thousand acres of land and twenty-four enslaved people. "He was ably prepared to discourage any local outbreaks of abolitionist sympathies."[45]
	Forty-four percent of the population of Mecklenburg County was enslaved.[46]
	Passage of the Fugitive Slave Law.
	Charlotte had approximately 456 slaves, constituting 44 percent of the town's population. Charlotte had 36 free Black inhabitants.[47]
	The slave trade officially ended in the United States.
1851	Harriet Beecher Stowe's *Uncle Tom's Cabin* is first serialized.
1852	Alabama's legal code codified the slave's dual character: (1) his status was as property (chattel); (2) the slave was a person to whom the master owed food, clothing, and care. The customary phrasing across the South was slaves were referred to as "chattels personal."
1854	The Republican Party is formally organized.
1856	Proslavery forces sack Lawrence, Kansas.
	The US Supreme Court ruled in its *Dred Scott* decision, wherein "Chief Justice Roger B. Taney had stated explicitly that Black people have 'no rights which the white man is bound to respect.'"[48] The Supreme Court of the US declared in its *Dred Scott* decision that the enslaved man Dred Scott could not sue for his freedom "because he was not a person, but property."[49] This decision meant that enslaved people were not citizens.
	Lincoln helps form the Republican Party in Illinois.
	Massachusetts Senator Charles Sumner is almost beaten to death by South Carolina representative Preston Brooks on the floor of the US Senate chamber.
1858	There was a reconciliation merger among the Synods of the West, Illinois, New York, and the Associate Synod to form the United Presbyterian Church of North America. The Synod of the South did not join, in part over the matter of slaveholding.
1859	John Brown leads a raid on the federal arsenal at Harpers Ferry, Virginia. Colonel Robert E. Lee stopped Brown's attempt at an enslaved uprising.

1860   Lincoln is nominated for president at the Republican National Convention and is elected on November 6.

The secessionist drumbeats began loudly in the Deep South: Mississippi, Alabama, South Carolina, and Georgia. These four states sent secessionist commissioners—the "Apostles of Disunion"[50]—into neighboring states to spread the secessionist message. "In all some fifty-two men served as secession commissioners in the critical weeks just before the Civil War."[51]

On December 20, South Carolina secedes from the Union.

"In 1860 more than 85 percent of the [North Carolina] state legislators were slaveholders, the highest percentage in the South."[52]

Several Black churches were founded near Sharon: Lloyd Church, Matthews-Murkland Presbyterian, and Smithfield Baptist.

By 1860, a million tons of cotton were being produced every year in the South. Kolchin says the South's production surpassed 4 million bales on the eve of the Civil War. "Cotton created a seemingly insatiable demand for slave labor."[53]

"Millions of enslaved people and their ancestors had built the enormous wealth of the United States; indeed, in 1860, 80 percent of the nation's gross national product was tied to slavery."[54]

"By the 1860s five hundred enslaved people could fetch close to half a million dollars in Cuba."[55]

"By 1860, the American South was producing two-thirds of all the commercially grown cotton in the world and about four-fifths of the cotton that Great Britain's mammoth textile industry consumed every year."[56]

The enslaved population in the South had grown from a half million in 1790 to 4 million by 1860.[57] "Slaves born in Africa comprised only 20 per cent of the Black population at the end of the American Revolution and by 1860 almost 100 per cent of the slaves in the United States were native born."[58]

"In 1860 the average sales price for a healthy, young bondsmen [sic] was equivalent to the price of an average house."[59]

"In 1860, there were in the South 385,000 owners of slaves distributed among 1,516,000 free families. Nearly three-fourths of all free Southerners had no connection with slavery through either family ties or direct ownership." In North Carolina, one-fourth (25 percent) of families owned slaves.[60]

By 1860, enslaved individuals constituted about one-third of the population of the South.[61] "At prices quoted on the markets of the day, those nearly four million human beings were worth something like $3 billon."[62]

By the time of the Civil War, there were nearly 4 million enslaved people in the United States.

By 1861, seven southern states seceded.

In July, Timothy Meaher bought a sailboat and tried to smuggle 110 enslaved people into Mobile (Alabama) Bay. They offloaded their enslaved captives and, fearing they were about to be caught, they burned and sank the boat *Clotilda*.

The typical master owned between four and six enslaved. The federal Census Bureau reserved the term "planter" for a master who owned at least twenty slaves. "Only one out of eight southern masters belonged to this group—some forty-six thousand in total. But as a group, they controlled more than half of all the South's slaves and an even larger share of its total agricultural group."[63] As is noted elsewhere in this book, the almost complete consensus among historians that, as determined by the federal census, twenty or more enslaved people held by an enslaver put him or her into the "planter class" According to my research, the federal census never defined the "planter class" as being determined by twenty or more enslaved people.

"In 1860, slaves composed approximately 40 per cent of the local population (6,800 of 17,000), making Mecklenburg County one of the highest in terms of the number of bondspeople in the North Carolina Piedmont."[64]

"The true planter aristocracy embraced ten thousand families that owned fifty or more slaves apiece." These were the people who had the right of way in business and politics.[65]

An interesting example is the Rev. Charles Colcock Jones, who spearheaded the campaign to bring a proslavery form of Christianity to southern bondspeople: he owned 129 enslaved people on three plantations in coastal Georgia's Liberty County.[66]

Hugh Kirkpatrick (the author's great-great-grandfather) owned thirty-two enslaved people in 1860, one of whom was Jimmie Lee Kirkpatrick's great-great-great-grandfather, Sam Kirkpatrick.

"At the very apex of the South's social pyramid stood about fifty southern planters, each of whom owned at least five hundred slaves. . . . The richest planter in NC was Thomas P. Devereux, the father of Catherine Devereux Edmondston. . . . He enslaved more than one thousand people."[67]

More than a third of the legislative seats in North Carolina, Alabama, and Mississippi belonged to full-fledged planters. In South Carolina, planters held more than half of the legislative seats.[68]

To understand the power and influence of slaveholders even more: in a Senate speech in 1858 by James Henry Hammond, he said, "We, the slaveholders of the South, took our country in her infancy, led it to independence, and have since then continued 'ruling her for sixty of the seventy years of her existence.'"[69] Since the American Revolution, nearly all of the occupants of the White House were slaveholders (Washington, Jefferson, Madison, Monroe, Jackson, Tyler, Polk, and Taylor).

The 1860 census estimated that one in ten enslaved people cultivated tobacco; another one in ten raised sugar, rice, or hemp; and more than half worked in cotton fields.

The population of Charlotte, North Carolina, was 2,265.

On November 30, the Mississippi legislature authorized Governor Pettus to appoint secessionist commissioners to every slave state, to inform these other states of Mississippi's forthcoming secessionist convention, and "to seek the support of those states for whatever measures would promote the 'common defense and safety' of the South."[70]

On December 20, two Alabama commissioners addressed a joint session of the North Carolina legislature calling for Southern unity. On this same day, South Carolina passed its ordinance of secession. The vote was unanimous (169–0).

On December 26, the South Carolina convention appointed seven commissioners to send to Georgia, Florida, Alabama, Mississippi, Louisiana, Arkansas, and Texas. Virginia and North Carolina were later added to the list.

1861   On January 9, South Carolina batteries opened fire on the *Star of the West*, an unarmed federal vessel trying to bring supplies to Fort Sumter.

On January 22, a public meeting at the Mecklenburg County courthouse chaired by Hugh Kirkpatrick (the author's great-great-grandfather and namesake) was reported in the *Western Democrat*. Kirkpatrick and the duly assembled called for immediate support of North Carolina's secession.

In his inaugural speech in March , Lincoln said, "I have no purpose directly or indirectly to interfere with the institution of slavery in the States where it exists: I believe I have no lawful right to do so and I have no inclination to do so."[71]

Harriet Jacobs, after escaping from slavery in North Carolina, published her *Incidents in the Life of a Slave Girl*.

1863   Lincoln signed the Emancipation Proclamation.

• *1* •

A Brief Psychological Portrait of the American Southern White Elite Planter Class

DEFINITION OF SLAVEHOLDER

If a person "owns" or "holds" another person as property; as chattel; as a forced, bound laborer, the identified owner is, by definition, a slaveholder, an enslaver. It ultimately does not matter if the number of enslaved held is one or one thousand. Enslavement of people by force has been part of human history for thousands of years. The antebellum southern slave master, however, was special. The South's enslavement industry was based on skin color and the ownership of humans as property. It was the South's peculiar institution. This book paints the psychological portrait of a special group of white slaveholders—the majority male—in the South, portrayed through a window of about thirty-one years, 1830 through 1861—a group who saw themselves as the South's ruling class. As historian James Oakes succinctly stated: "The slaveholders were a ruling class if ever there was one, but they justified their power by defining themselves as a superior race."[1]

So, there we begin. An elite group of southern white men and women who positioned themselves as *the* ruling class based on assumed racial (read: racist) superiority. As Oakes pointed out, slavery was their means of "upward mobility"; he added, "The ownership of slaves became for many immigrants the single most important symbol of their success in the New World, although few of them ever participated in the economy of the large plantation."[2] I will not go into much detail or analysis of the typical southern slaveholder, the small yeoman farmer or city dweller who enslaved but a few people. The important point is that owning an enslaved person became a status symbol for white folks. The status achieved by the slaveholder was far from simply being symbolic. The enslaved were *property*. They had a monetary value attached to them. As historian Bruce Levine put it: "Slaves were by far the most valuable properties one could own in the southern states."[3]

Although the term "slave master" is commonly used to describe slaveholders, the term "master" was not just reserved for slaveholders, for this appellation had a wider usage. As historian Stephanie McCurry pointed out, the term "master," in the realm of property rights in the low country of South Carolina, attached not only to planters, but adult freemen, who were masters of their households no matter the size of their landholdings. McCurry also emphasized that it was not uncommon for a slave-based plantation to be physically adjacent to a nonslaveholding gentleman farmer's legally owned property. Conflict between these elite planters and the white yeoman farmers sometimes would erupt when the yeoman would trade goods with the planter's enslaved people. Over time, the "politically pivotal" yeoman became the white majority, but not the region's majority, for that was Black.[4] In 1850, for example, the Black population of the low country in South Carolina was 70 percent of the total population.[5] This statistic stands out as being significant, because it means that the 30 percent of whites in the South Carolina low country somehow had to accommodate themselves to the psychological effects this Black/white ratio had on them. I make the argument in chapter 7 that whites would have to pretend they were comfortable being surrounded by so many enslaved people.

DESCRIPTIVE STATISTICS

Summarizing the research of a number of slavery historians, the following section offers a broad look at the "generic" American slaveholder. Oakes offered the following sketch of the slaveholder: "A statistical portrait of typicality can provide the basis for a fuller examination of the patterns of slaveholding in America. The average slaveholder was forty-four years old, most likely male, still more likely white. Whatever his ethnic heritage, by 1850 he was almost always native-born, and more than nine times out of ten he was born in the South."[6]

Let me be clear about these statistics. Although by 1850, Marse was most likely native born in the South, prior to 1850, from the beginning of our nation, there were many slaveholders keeping Africans in bondage in many other parts of the country, most particularly in the Northeast. By the late seventeenth century, enslaved individuals could be found in every American colony. American slavery specialist Peter Kolchin noted, "As late as 1790, about one household in five in New York City owned slaves."[7]

Oakes continued,

The average slaveholding was eight or nine [individuals], but the typical master owned fewer than that. The median value of the slaveholder's land was just under three thousand dollars. Eighty percent of the time his chief employment was in agriculture, either as a farmer, planter, or overseer. The only surprise in all of this is that the middle-aged white farmer with perhaps a handful of slaves quickly disappeared from the history books, replaced by a plantation legend that bears little resemblance to historical reality.[8]

Oakes, of course, bridged by reference to the elite "planter class" stereotype plantation owner. Although there is some risk in promoting a stereotypical image of the wealthy, white planter, he did exist. As we shall see, it was the number of enslaved people held by the enslaver that will fill in the portrait of the planter caste.

It is important to keep in perspective that most Southerners did not own slaves. As historian Kenneth Stampp pointed out, "In 1860, there were in the South 385,000 owners of slaves distributed among 1,516,000 free families. Nearly three-fourths of all free Southerners had no connection with slavery through either family ties or direct ownership. The 'typical' Southerner was not only a small farmer but also a nonslaveholder."[9] Bruce Levine added to the slaveholder portrait, "The typical master owned between four and six slaves." They were, however,

> considerably less wealthy than those masters who owned at least twenty enslaved people. Only one out of eight southern masters belonged to this group—some forty-six thousand in total. But as a group, they controlled more than half of all the South's enslaved population and an even larger share of its total agricultural wealth. Some planters were far richer than others. The true planter aristocracy embraced ten thousand families that enslaved fifty or more people apiece.[10]

Stampp concurred with Levine: "The planter aristocracy was limited to some ten thousand families who lived off the labor of more than fifty slaves. The extremely wealthy families who owned more than a hundred slaves numbered less than three thousand, a tiny fraction of the southern population."[11]

Historian James Roark offered slightly different numbers: "On the eve of the Civil War, the planter class numbered about forty-three thousand Southerners, more than 90 per cent of whom were male and almost all of whom were white."[12] These data would also suggest that the female elite planters—the "mistresses"—were approximately forty-three hundred in number (10 percent). In spite of these statistics, it is the legendary, archetypal image of Marse that we almost automatically see in our mind's eye when the term "slave master" is spoken. Granted, it's a stereotype; yet he lived.

CLASS STRUCTURE

Not surprisingly, the enslavers had their own intraclass structure or hierarchy. Historians placed planter-slaveholders into three distinct categories, descriptions that are based on multiple factors, including number of enslaved held, size and number of plantations, farms, or other bound labor-based endeavors, location, soil, products, cultural influences (including family and country of origin history), status of the slaveholder, net worth, and the sheer economics of the enslaver's enterprises.

At the bottom of the American southern slaveholding world were small-scale yeoman farmers who relied mostly on family labor (often including the enslaver himself) and indentured European servants (i.e., bound migrants). By definition, a yeoman was "a person who own[ed] and cultivate[d] a small farm; one belonging to a class of English freeholders below the gentry."[13] These farmers probably held five or fewer enslaved individuals. Many Europeans paid their way to the colonies by becoming indentured servants. After an indentured servant reached his or her term of service—as a general rule, a term of seven years—the small-scale southern farmer might purchase Black Africans as labor replacements. The ownership of an enslaved person or two was common among wealthier city or town dwellers. The enslaved individual owned by a city-dwelling lawyer, minister, or banker might be called by different labels—such as "servant," "waitingman," "right-hand man," "valet," or "personal body servant"—but the enslaved person was still "enslaved": namely, "a person held in servitude as the chattel of another."[14]

On the next upward rung on the slaveholder hierarchy was the so-called planter class. The word "planter" obviously derives from the same root as "plantation," but it would be an error to assume that all members of the planter class owned or lived on plantations. "Planter" is more accurately associated with the activity of planting an agriculture product of some type or engaged in some type of farming, such as a dairy farm. The word "planter" is generally agreed upon by historians to categorize slaveholders by the numbers of persons enslaved and the circumstances in which they lived. "Planter" also referred to a person who planted crops. It was a synonym for farmer. In the first book of the Old Testament, the book of Genesis, Noah is described as a "planter" (Gen 9:20). Noah's central role in forging the American white southern planter class is described in detail in chapter 6.

Technically, a yeoman farmer with two or three enslaved people who planted and grew crops could call himself a planter, but the historiography of southern slavery has established that admission to the planter *class* was awarded when a slaveholder acquired a minimum of twenty slaves. Oakes wrote, "To own twenty slaves in 1860 was to be among the wealthiest men in America, easily within the top five percent of southern white families. Barely one in twenty slaveholders owned that many bondsmen, and not one in a hundred southern white families was headed by such a man."[15] As an example, "[i]n the eighteenth century, the wealthiest Virginia planters usually owned several estates, their home plantations averaging three thousand acres and eighty slaves. The median value of their taxable property was nearly 25,000 pounds."[16]

Historian Chalmers Davidson used thirty slaves held as the cutoff for proper designation of a slaveholder into this "planter class,"[17] as does Peter Kolchin, although the latter argues for a more relaxed categorizing, saying that there probably was not much difference between a slaveholder with twelve slaves and one with twenty, he advocated for maintaining "the distinction between a 'farmer' (with few or no slaves) and a 'planter' (with many)."[18] Bruce Levine stated that the federal Census Bureau reserved the term "planter" for a master who owned at least twenty slaves.[19]

PLANTER REDEFINED

Although many slavery historians credit the federal Census Bureau as establishing that the term "planter" was to be reserved for slaveholders who owed twenty or more slaves, I was unable to confirm this. Thomas Cole, a colleague, reported that based on his reading of the US Index of Census Questions, the Census never defined "planter" as someone who owned at least twenty enslaved people. Describing the information gleaned from the instructions given to census takers, he summarized, "The population censuses from 1790 to 1860 asked for the number of slaves in a household and sometimes their ages. The slave schedules of the 1850 and 1860 census collected information about the name of the slave owner and the number, sex, age, and color of the persons he or she held as slaves. One can count the number of slaves belonging to an individual owner, but the Census did not record or use that number." Further, by analyzing how the term "planter" was used, Cole examined the 1850 census of a sample county—Barnwell County, South Carolina—which showed nine families listed on the first page of the census, and the heads of all [nine] of the households "identified as 'planter,'" even though the data recorded, Cole noted, "showed that two did not own slaves at all and that the others owned between 1 and 14 slaves." This suggested the term was used by farmers and the census taker to describe their profession, occupation, or trade, and did not relate the term to the *number* of slaves held. Ten years later (in 1860) these heads of these same families described themselves as "farmers." There does exist a non-census source where holding twenty enslaved people was significant: the Second Conscription Law, passed by the Confederate States of America in 1862, exempted one man from military service in a household for every twenty enslaved people the family held. Scholars since then have used the twenty-slave threshold to analyze the planter class.[20]

Historian Jane Turner Censer used the number seventy to refer to planters in her analysis of enslavers in southern states.[21] Censer's number appears to be an outlier. As stated above, even though the defining number of enslaved required to be a part of the planter class appears to vary, the majority of researchers and historians agree that the minimum number is between twenty and thirty. Twenty to thirty people held in bondage is but the floor; as we shall see, there developed in the South an elite class with slaveholding numbers that hit a very high ceiling.

At the top of the slave master pyramid was the "elite": This term is reserved for very wealthy, large-scale enslavers. Addressing this elite class of slaveholders, Levine stated, "The true planter aristocracy embraced ten thousand families that owned fifty or more slaves apiece."[22] Stampp stated that the truly wealthy slaveholding families—fewer than three thousand overall—enslaved more than a hundred people. Historian William Kauffman Scarborough identified a top-tier level of the slaveholding elite. Tabulating data from the 1850 and 1860 Federal Slave Schedules, he reported census data that said in 1850 there were twenty-six such families and in 1860 there were fifty families who comprised this elite class. The fact that the number of elite planters—the ruling race—doubled in a decade informs us about just how much profit the South's enslaved-based economy was generating in this ten-year period.

Scarborough described this top tier: "At the very apex of the South's social pyramid stood about fifty Southern planters, each of whom owned at least five hundred slaves."[23] This same author listed Joshua John Ward of South Carolina as the largest elite slaveholder in the entire South in 1860, with 1,146 slaves.[24] Typically, these "Grandees" were individuals who had multiple holdings (properties and enslaved people), frequently across county as well as state—and for a few, country—boundaries.[25]

Apparently putting aside humanitarian concerns, much of the American South and many other businessmen across the country and some European countries (notably Great Britain) developed a love affair with Marse and rewarded him with immense political and economic power: "The great planters of the antebellum South exerted immense influence within their region and profoundly affected the destiny of this nation."[26] The political and economic influence of the elite slaveholders was profound. In 1860, more than a third of the legislative seats in North Carolina, Alabama, and Mississippi belonged to full-fledged planters. In South Carolina, planters held more than half of the legislative seats.[27] When Marse began to make some serious money, he had many admirers and business associates beyond the South, not just in the North but worldwide.

The political power, dominance, and overall impact of the southern planter class were astounding, considering what a minority they were: "Of the fifty delegates who eventually assembled in Montgomery [to consider the South's secession from the Union], forty-nine owned slaves, and twenty-one were full-scale planters."[28] To restate this: Forty-nine out of fifty delegates who gathered to decide if the South would rebel against the federal government were slaveholders, and half of these men held at least twenty enslaved people, more likely hundreds. Only one nonslaveholder took part in this calamitous decision. This objective fact—that the convention membership that decided on southern secession was composed almost exclusively of slaveholders—seems to be the strongest argument for pinning slavery as the principal cause of the war. While I know it's not that simple, or even accurate, it is quite extraordinary just how much power and influence Marse and his brethren racist slaveholders had over this question. Then, of course, there was the other compelling factor driving the decision to go to war. There was a lot of capital at stake. Follow the money.

As James Oakes pointed out, "What slaveholding did to the economic pyramid of white society was to expand its highest stratum. In 1860, the twelve wealthiest counties in the United States were below the Mason and Dixon line."[29] Historian Edward E. Baptist noted that in 1860, total US wealth was $16,160 million, (which is $16.16 billion); the enslaved population in the United States was 3,953,760 and the value of the enslaved population was $3,059 million ($3.059 billion).[30] Oakes offered a similar figure for the valuation of the enslaved in 1860: "At prices quoted on the markets of the day, those nearly four million human beings were worth something like $3 billion—an immense sum, especially at that time, a sum that exceeded the value of all the farmland in the South, a sum fully three times as great as the construction costs of all the railroads that then ran throughout all of the United States."[31]

PERSONALITY AND CHARACTER TRAITS

As I began thinking about the logical and plausible features of the elite slaveholder's personality, what jumped out at me was what was missing. An argument can be made that the primary deficit in a slaveholder's personality was the suspension or eradication of empathy, which led many outsiders to comment about what they saw as missing in the enslavers they met. Historian Bertram Wyatt-Brown quoted Matthew Wheelock, a British critic of slavery in the American colonies, who opined in 1770 that "slaveholding gave the Virginia and Maryland gentry 'a certain haughtiness.'"[32] Quoting the Reverend Andrew Burnaby (after several years of Burnaby's travels in the American colonies), Wyatt-Brown wrote, "'Their authority over their slaves . . . renders [Virginians] vain and imperious, and intire [*sic*] strangers to the elegance of sentiment, which is so peculiarly characteristic of refined and polished nations.'"[33] A missing personality feature: the "elegance of sentiment."

No two historians have added more to our understanding of the psychology of the southern slaveholders than the historians Elizabeth Fox-Genovese and Eugene Genovese. They identify a number of "Southern" characteristics. Some of the more salient ones include: (a) a people apart from others; (b) a reputation built on honor and duty; (c) a people of courage; (d) a people prone to frankness; (e) immensely proud people; (f) people noted for their vanity; (g) a people who exhibited an excessive loyalty to friends; (g) a people who were dignified; (h) a people who denied any concerns about public approval, as if they lived in moral isolation; (i) a people who were unyielding and immovable on matters of principle; (j) to the degree these enslavers exalted their own being, they became vulnerable to usurping the place of God.[34]

Marse was a member of a special class. What made members of this class "special"? Genovese explained: "[The] history of [American slavery] was essentially determined by particular relationships of class power in racial form."[35] As he pointed out, slaveholders in the South "grew to be a particular type of men and women."[36] Weaving together observations made by others, Genovese added to the list of personality features the following characteristics of the southern slaveholder: He was intelligent and well versed in a range of subjects; exhibited firmness, forbearance, and kindness; and demonstrated a "reckless and cruel pride which made even angels fall."[37] Genovese explained the fall of these angels by quoting W. E. B. Du Bois: "The psychological effect of slavery upon [the white master] was fatal. The mere fact that a man could be, under the law, the actual master of the mind and body of human beings had to have disastrous effects. . . . Their 'honor' became a vast and awful thing, requiring wide and insistent deference. Such of them as were inherently weak and inefficient were all the more easily angered, jealous, and resentful; while the few who were superior, physically or mentally, conceived of no bounds to their power and personal prestige."[38] Marse's image of himself, at times, included being something akin to a medieval knight or king dedicated to medieval chivalry. In this reverie, the enslaved were his "serfs." His overseer, if he had one, was "the king's hand." Minimally speaking, Marse was a proud, arrogant patrician.

Scarborough added further to our construction of the slaveholder's personality portrait: "Well-bred, cosmopolitan in background and outlook, intellectually curious, broadly educated, articulate, trained for leadership, and gifted with exceptional entrepreneurial skills, they constituted one of the most significant groups in American history."[39]

Combining traits and features of the slaveholder from flattering self-portraits and from sources of harsh criticism, Genovese poetically summarized the personality picture of the southern slave masters:

> They were tough, proud, and arrogant; liberal-spirited in all that did not touch their honor; gracious and courteous; generous and kind; quick to anger and extraordinarily cruel; attentive to duty and careless of any time and effort that did not control their direct interests. They had been molded by their slaves as much as their slaves had been molded by them. They were not men to be taken lightly, not men frivolously to be made enemies of. And they wallowed in those deformities, which their slaves had thrust upon them in the revenge of historical silence—deformities which would lead them to destruction as a class. The Chinese have a proverb: "A hero may risk his whole world but will never surrender his concubine or his horse." The slaveholders were heroes.[40]

Quoting William Henry Holcombe's southern diary entry in 1855, wherein Holcombe of Natchez described Southerners in comparison to Northerners, Genovese added: "Southerners—Individually brave to rashness—collectively cautious and wise. Individually excitable—collectively possessed and dignified. Individually resorting to violence—collectively to suasion [sic]. Individually sensitive to the point of honor—collectively less so, singularly calm and forbearing and forgiving."[41]

Notably absent so far from this summary of personality features is the southern slaveholder's adherence to his Protestant Christian faith. Historian John Patrick Daly described as "the antebellum truism" advanced by Southerners: "the [antebellum] American mind thus far is cast in a religious mold." Daly argued, "The mold referred to was the evangelical idea of individual moral autonomy and accountability."[42] Racist enslavement it seemed stood on two assumed ideological pillars: (1) that Black Africans were inferior and subhuman and (2) that the "Good Book" totally sanctioned slavery. As Fox-Genovese and Genovese pointed out, things might have been very different if slaveholders had abandoned their churches to keep their personal property, but that, as we know, was not the outcome: "But Southern evangelicals, having cited chapter and verse, successfully enlisted the Bible to unify the overwhelming majority of slaveholders and nonslaveholders in defense of slavery as ordained by God. The antislavery spokesman [sic] failed to demonstrate that the Bible repudiated slavery; primarily, they appealed to the ideals of the Enlightenment and the Declaration of Independence."[43]

In the run-up to secession and the War, the abolitionists' intellectual arguments against slavery were crushed, muted, or silenced by the South's religious defense of slavery. For an analysis of how the abolitionists lost this intellectual and spiritual war, see chapters 4 and 5. Historian Harry S. Stout persuasively argued that both the North and the South saw themselves headed to a "just war, a holy war." The thousands upon thousands of soldiers who were to fall in battle were viewed as "martyrs."[44]

Another aspect of the slaveholder's personality was his view of himself as being engaged in—called upon by—a second revolution. The southern secessionists "portrayed themselves as the new American revolutionaries who, like their ancestors, wished to declare their independence and throw off the shackles of tyranny."[45] The Southerner, whose blood boiled in the face of tyranny, by becoming an enslaver, became a tyrant. This fact is extremely important psychologically, for Marse had to internalize a tyrant—a racist authoritarian—as part of his being, and at the same time build an impregnable "wall"—perhaps composed largely of vanity and honor—if you will, around this feature of his psyche. The full-blown tyrant lurked in the dark recesses of his unconscious mind, always ready to erupt when needed, but with its existence essentially hidden and denied. The psychological effort it took for the slaveholder to deny the full existence of his tyrant was lethal to him.

It is this element of the southern mind—the devout foe of tyranny—that is probably what would have made me fight for the South if I had been in my teens in the 1860s. All rebel children—especially boys—were taught that the Yankees were the aggressors. Fighting the Union was like fighting the British crown. Fighting for freedom was good fighting. The battle cry in the streets of some contemporary American communities by those who reject a mask-wearing imperative in the midst of the COVID-19 pandemic is, "Liberty!" It is a very selfish plea for personal freedom. When the dust settles and we have controlled COVID-19, I think we'll find that a great many Americans, especially men, who aggressively defied mandates from authorities to wear masks will turn out to be Southerners or certainly sympathetic to the South. I think we can assume that all of the Confederate flags displayed across America are not being waved just by Southerners.

Daly further addressed another important feature of the southern personality: The Southerner developed a sense of the importance of the "force of character," which "became a Southern evangelical and American obsession."[46] As we shall see in chapter 6, one of the powerful, and consistent over time, criticisms aimed at Ham, Noah's son, was Ham's alleged loss of character in the story of Noah in Genesis 9:18–27. Marse believed a "[f]orce of will would produce a conquering moral wholeness."[47] He believed he could, by force of will, make himself into a grand, enlightened character. This self-view is one of the vital taproots of pathological narcissism and its companion pathology—narcissistic immunity.

With all the freedom and power racist slavery gifted to Marse, he was proud as a peacock, and he looked haughty to many others. Scarborough contributed further to the slaveholder portrait: The "elite" slaveholders "shared certain common social and cultural characteristics. Among these were large families; a relatively high infant mortality rate; an extraordinary degree of intermarriage, extending not infrequently to first cousin unions;[48] a cosmopolitan life-style and outlook; surprisingly close social, economic, and cultural ties with the Northeast; an emphasis upon quality education for both males and females; a catholicity of intellectual interests; and—not least—a confident belief in God as the omnipotent regulator of human affairs."[49] Understanding this last characteristic is vital. Marse believed in his heart of hearts that slavery, ultimately, was managed through God's plan. The fact that slaveholders and Christian divines got racial slavery insinuated into God's plan in such a convincing manner is one of the world's best long cons, and it still has twenty-first-century legs!

All Southerners—no matter their skin color—have had some "Southernist" experience—that is, being perceived as not so intelligent because of where we were from or how we talked. "He's just a dumb Southerner" was the trope in the air, expressed out loud or not. In the book he edited—*All Clever Men, Who Make Their Way: Critical Discourse in the Old South*, Michael O'Brien challenged some of the biases about American Old South intellectual competence. He strongly disagreed with the common bias as expressed here:

> Very few are disposed to grant any vitality to the mind of the Old South. That it was superficial, unintellectual, obsessed with race and slavery, enfeebled by polemic is a ruling assumption of American scholarship. . . . The planter class, which dominated the region, withdrew from its previous cosmopolitanism, grew out of touch with modern intellectual developments when it once had led them, became frantic with worry or guilt over the place of slavery in the Union, was isolated on remote and supine plantations far from the invigoration of urban life. Skepticism became displaced by the emotionalism of evangelical religion. Thought had become prejudice.[50]

O'Brien pointed out that most planters lived in cities and small towns, not on remote, isolated plantations. Their writing and scholarship were most often delivered in speeches and sermons or printed in pamphlets, periodicals, and newspapers. Writing or publishing a book would have been rare. Periodicals such as the *Southern Quarterly*, *De Bow's Review*, or the *Southern Literary Messenger* were commonly used for slaveholders to express themselves publicly. O'Brien made the point that antebellum Southerners thought about subjects other than slavery and he made the telling point: "Very few writers were planters . . . But most Southern intellectuals had as little to do with planting cotton as the *New York Times* book reviewer has to do with the sweatshops of Wall Street."[51] He emphasized that, although concerns about slavery certainly were central to the planter class, these concerns were not a "debilitating obsession" with Southerners as a whole.

To illustrate this point, O'Brien pointed out that even when arguments about secession were reaching their crescendo circa 1851, these arguments only reached 35 percent among the articles published in the *Southern Quarterly Review*. He went on to say that because *De Bow's Review* "was peculiarly dedicated [in apparent frequency] to the study of economic and political matters and hence slavery," this popular antebellum journal, as a primary source, has figured disproportionately in historians' bias about the Southerner's obsession with matters of slavery.[52] O'Brien also challenged the view that the Southern planter was debilitated by the machinations of an anti-intellectual, fundamentalist evangelicalism, asserting that this was only a "half-truth." As the reader will see in chapters 4 and 5, the evangelical influence on the elite Southern planter was much more than a half-truth.

The southern evangelical argument that emphasized character development and economic success elevated this argument to include regional character development: "The proslavery focus on the proving and building of regional character, therefore, demanded recognition of Southerners' providential right to political and economic power, as well as their right to hold slaves. The evangelical ideal of character connected all of these positions."[53] That amalgam constitutes an endorphin-laced euphoria fired straight into Marse's belief system: a self-image of a man of high character, southern pride, given by grace and God to command a right to political and economic power, with a capital labor force of enslaved people. Fox-Genovese and Genovese captured the hypocrisy of this southern pursuit: "They searched the past for a template for which it meant to be human: nobility, honor, courage, piety, loyalty, faithfulness, generosity, and a capacity to survive both victory and defeat with grace whether in public matters or private. And they took for granted that these qualities were compatible with power over others."[54]

As these same historians pointed out, many proslavery spokesmen proclaimed that slavery had wonderful effects on the personalities of the masters, thus creating men of great character.[55] A sure path to grandiosity: slaveholding will strengthen my character. An imagined scene: as Marse's personal enslaved manservant adjusted the knot on Marse's tie, standing behind his master in front of the full-length mirror, Marse could satisfactorily size up his own reflected image and think to himself, "I am a better man for helping these negroes."

ADEPT AT IMPRESSION MANAGEMENT

In time, in the run-up to the Civil War, the slave master had to contend with being vilified and rejected by many people in the world, especially if the enslaver was engaged in slave trading (as the elite planters almost by definition had to be, because of their debt load and insatiable need for more and more forced labor). A truly conscious enslaver might have harbored a suspicion that the rest of the world might be right. This was a disturbing thought, one that had to be buried, denied, transformed, emotionally vaporized.

Marse developed a trait familiar to Southerners: Slaveholders of the Upper South managed to create a public impression of antislavery sentiment, or at least raise public questions about the institution, while profiting from the slave trade by sending their vast numbers of their enslaved to the Lower South (e.g., the Mississippi Valley). Making so much money helped ease the pain of public criticism. Marse had to work hard psychologically to maintain a clear conscience. Often, this state of mind was achieved through his religious beliefs, combined with his view of himself as benevolently paternalistic. A syntonic state of mind could be more or less maintained by convincing oneself, "I'm doing God's work."

Even if he wanted to walk away from slaveholding, Marse could control any antislavery impulses or intrusive fears he might have about emancipation through his belief that he was "called" to do God's work related to slavery, combined with his deeply held fear of the wrath of God, which, as a major tenet of evangelical Christian belief, befell anyone who did not follow God's commands. As an evangelical Christian, Marse had to get right with the tyranny of the Lord: "Slaveholders lived on a high wire. They had to balance a public stake in the decent treatment of slaves; a compelling need to support their authority at almost any cost; and a psychological as well as ideological need for reassurance that they were kind as well as stern."[56]

To achieve his balance on this high wire, Marse became adept at impression management, the social and diplomatic skills needed to manipulate how the world outside saw him (leaving no appearance of impropriety) and how his enslaved people—Marse's private, inside world—knew without a doubt how much psychological and physical violence he or his enforcer would use to maintain control and power over them. Historian Walter Johnson evaluated the slaveholders' skill at impression management as *performance*. In an earlier work, *Soul by Soul: Life Inside the Antebellum Slave Market*, from his study of slaveholders' written correspondence, Johnson noted that, frequently between and among family members, slaveholders managed the impression of themselves rendered to their own kin and peers: "These letters, then, can be read as remote performances of the self, self-consciously produced representations

that antebellum slaveholders offered to one another as versions of themselves
. . . of striving sons, masterful patriarchs, anxious brides, and dutiful wives,
all of the recognizable social identities available to antebellum whites as they
tried to make themselves make sense to someone else."[57] Johnson's analysis
of enslavers' letters showed that slave masters often represented themselves to
one another (i.e., slaveholder to slaveholder communication) by reference to
their enslaved.[58]

One of the most powerful control methods used over the enslaved was
the very real threat of family separation. Marse arrogantly and contemptuously
determined that Black Africans did not have family or relationship loyalties
and loving attachments like white folk, and thus really weren't negatively
affected or harmed when loved ones were ripped away in a trade deal.[59] Slave
trading, or Negro speculation, as it was known, included family-ectomies.
Imagine the mind of a man who looked at a mother holding her infant child
and thought, "She will suffer no offense if I sell her baby."

If this were nothing more than a cruel thought and it ended there, with
no action taken, so be it. But if Marse concluded it was okay for him to sell the
child and he did so, he thus, despite his self-image of being a Christian steward
of his enslaved, became inhumane, cruel, and sadistic. The splitting of Black
families as punishment or for profit was attempted murder of the soul for the
enslaved and a self-inflicted murder of the slaveholder's soul.

The extent to which slaveholders engaged in the separation of families
has been a subject of much scholarship. Johnson pointed out that in the antebellum South, as the need for slave labor in the southwestern United States
increased dramatically in the 1850s, causing "unfathomable suffering among
the enslaved (50 percent of slave sales during the antebellum period involved
the breakup of a family)."[60] Enslavers and their families, to a great degree, convinced themselves that their enslaved people were part of their family, so it just
would not do to admit that part of the slavery business—a really ugly part—
meant that sometimes, usually for economic reasons, a master sold a member
of one of his enslaved families "down the river." This crisis is a central part of
the story in Harriet Beecher Stowe's *Uncle Tom's Cabin*.[61] In his book *Slaves in
the Family,* Edward Ball described a conversation between himself and a Ball
relative, where she opined that there was not much, if any, selling or separating families in the Ball slavery business, but the author knew better from his
analysis of Ball family plantation records: "In the archives of the state of South
Carolina, in the city of Columbia, there were receipts for slave purchases made
by the Balls, but there were also receipts for slaves sold by the family."[62]

Documentary historian Willie Lee Rose reprinted the story of the sale of
an enslaved mother's son. She captured the plaintive sorrow of Maria Perkins,
a Virginia enslaved woman whose letter to her husband, Richard Perkins

(enslaved elsewhere) informed him not only about the sale of her son, but her own and another child's impending sale to yet another slave trader.

> Charlottesville, Oct. 8th, 1852
>
> Dear Husband I write you a letter to let you know my distress my master sold albert to a trader on Monday court day and myself and other child is for sale also and I want you to let [me] hear from you soon before next cort [*sic*] if you can . . . a man name brady bought albert and is gone I don't know where . . . I am and ever will be your kind wife.[63]

A RIGHTEOUS SHIELD OF PSYCHOPATHIC PROVIDENCE

An enslaver might somehow manage to internalize the following central assumption: Enslaved people were in a far happier condition than they would be if they were liberated:[64] "In short, Southern whites constructed ideas about the emotional nature of the slave that precluded the possibility of their suffering."[65] Psychologically, this is an extraordinary state of mind to reach. Such a state of being resided in the dark realm of psychopathy, where the absence of a conscience was a defining feature. Empathy—a human's capacity to connect with the interior, emotional life of another human—is the heart and soul of human consciousness, and it is therefore absent in the mind of the psychopath. Although the lack of a conscience is principally the most troublesome feature of the psychopath, there are other contributing deficits. Writing about the psychopath, psychologists Paul Babiak and Robert D. Hare informed us: "Psychopathy is a personality disorder. . . . [P]sychopaths are without conscience and incapable of empathy, guilt, or loyalty to anyone but themselves."[66]

Here my analysis of Marse's mind is possibly insulting to some readers, for the enslaver's mythic belief that "slavery was freedom" for the enslaved rested on Marse's assurance that he was doing God's work. His evidence was the power of the evangelical inerrant word on the subject of slavery and Marse's obvious financial and material success. This southern evangelical embrace and providential justification for racist slavery was ethically and morally rotten.

Our brand of enslavement, the elite slaveholders mused, was just another unique variation of all the master-slave relationships since human time began. To support these myths, "Ante-bellum Southerners attached considerable significance to, and found considerable solace in, the fact that they had not invented human bondage."[67] "By 1860, history for Southerners had become world history, and they took special pleasure in evidence of the ubiquity of slavery."[68]

WHITE PRIVILEGE AND SUPREMACY

How important was skin color to Marse? John F. Townsend of South Carolina offers a fitting racist response to this question. Townsend was a state senator, a member of the South Carolina House of Representatives, and was one of the signers of the South Carolina Ordinance of Secession. He wrote an antebellum pamphlet called "The Doom of Slavery in the Union." In this proslavery tract, Townsend appealed for support for slavery from nonslaveholders:

> "In no country of the world," he argued, "does the poor white man, whether slaveholder or non-slaveholder, occupy so enviable a position as in the slaveholding States of the South. His color here admits him to social and civil privileges which the white man enjoys nowhere else." In the slave states, continued Townsend, "the status and *color of the black race* [italics in the original] become the badge of inferiority, and the poorest nonslaveholder may rejoice with the richest of his brethren of the white race, in the distinction of his color."[69]

There's a statement that sounds like straight up "I'm White and I'm Proud." "Whiteness" defined the white Southerner's identity, whether he was an enslaver or not. The class hierarchy that existed in the South among slaveholders was founded on a firm belief in a racist hierarchy, regardless of a slaveholder's class status. It was not just a racial hierarchy; it was a racist hierarchy. If we were able somehow to magically ask the attendees of the 1860 secession convention in Alabama, they would all agree they were on the top tier. They were the system's nobility—the so-called Grandees.

PRIDE

The elite southern white planter lost his humanity in the bargain he made with racist slavery. His capacity for being fully human became stunted and withered. Daly leveled quite an indictment of the elite southern slave master: The slaveholder in the "planter class" had a narcissistic strain of pride flowing through his veins and deep in his DNA; "in its encouragement of pride, of mastery, of aggression and control, the Old South did little to imbue its planter class with human skills."[70]

Writing about his own ancestors, Ball perfectly described the planter narcissistic pride and the longevity of entitlement:

My father's people, the Ball family of South Carolina, belonged to America's first elite, the planter class, a group long defunct in economic fact but not necessarily in its idea of itself. In some places in the South, the descendants of slaveholders comprise a distinct society with its own folkways, memories, and pride. Families such as mine know who they are, in part because if your people once owned vast tracts of land, gorged themselves on exquisite things, and were followed through life by clouds of workers and servants, many of whom called you "master," the memory of these experiences is not allowed to fade. Instead, it is preserved and honored. Such a memory might give you, generations later, in the present, a feeling of belonging and a sense of tradition—but also a sense of what it means to be entitled, an invisible psychological support and a feeling that one might deserve whatever is on offer from the world.[71]

The South Carolina Ball clan owned twenty-five different rice plantations for two hundred years along the Cooper River. It was a slaveholding dynasty of the first order.

The elite slave masters had a self-image founded on a great deal of pride: "The Civil War was the critical moment in the planters' history, and their responses to events provide valuable insight into the mind and character of the South's antebellum aristocracy." For example, the "Confederacy paid dearly for the pride of the many brave officers and soldiers who lacked the discipline and submission to military and political authority that war requires. Pride easily passed into recklessness, and Southerners, especially slaveholders, could forget the words of the Good Book: 'Pride goeth before destruction, and a haughty spirit before a fall' (Proverbs 16:18)."[72] Many soldiers were brutally shredded, pridefully running pell-mell into withering fire, lined up in formations of honor, riding, striding, running into a slaughter. Pride led Rebels to challenge authority, desert to return home to attend to their small farms, and grow increasingly resentful of the Confederate government's favorable treatment of planters and the institution of a mandatory draft. Marse didn't have to serve if he owned twenty or more slaves: straight up planter policy. Twenty or more forever enslaved was a deferment and kept the planter class from going to war or becoming Confederate soldiers.

HONOR

Honor commanded a distinctive place in the elite slaveholder's personality. Wyatt-Brown suggested an understanding of the principal role of honor in the slaveholder's mindset that may hold a significant key toward understanding the elite planter class: "Above all else, white Southerners adhered to a moral code that may be summarized as the rule of honor."[73] Wyatt-Brown opined that it was the South's perceived threat to its honor that, no less than slavery, led to the secession from the Union.[74] The white elite slave master saw himself as an honorable man, and he was, in many ways, but he nevertheless managed to ignore the hypocritical paradox of treating Blacks as inferior and squaring this self-appraisal with building his world on the backs of forever enslaved people. As historian Stephanie McCurry rightly declared, "Paradox, irony, and guilt have been three words used by historians to describe white Southern life before the Civil War. They are popular terms because it is hard for us to believe that Southerners ever meant what they said of themselves. How could they so glibly reconcile slaveholding with pretensions of virtue?"

Marse's honor was sacred. It was a character trait stretching back for centuries, to the British Isles and Western Europe. Wyatt-Brown explained the components of honor:

> Honor has three basic components, none of which may exist wholly independent of the other. Honor is first the inner conviction of self-worth. Seemingly, that sense of personal completeness would comply with modern notions of individuality: all men are created equal. . . . The second aspect of honor is the claim of that self-assessment before the public. . . . The third element is the assessment of the claim by the public, a judgment based upon the behavior of the claimant. In other words, honor is reputation. Honor resides in the individual as his understanding of who he is and where he belongs in the ordered ranks of society.[75]

What this tripartite definition means, at bottom, is that the southern community, the southern culture, had to agree and reinforce Marse's self-image as being a man of honorable character. This precipice of honor was thus founded on the psychosocial acceptance by the southern general public of Marse's ethics and his behavior. This acceptance by most of the southern population is evidence of the complicitous contract Southerners—slaveholders or not—had with enslavers and slavery itself.

Although there were many likely motives, I think it was a defense of the South's intellectual honor that drove a distinguished group of five of the South's preeminent intellectuals to draft the South's principal proslavery argument. It was written for the South, not for an antislavery audience. Historian Drew Gilpin Faust described the intellectual influence of these five southern slaveholding elites. These men stood tall as proslavery, political fire-eaters:

In the proslavery argument, [James Henry] Hammond, [George Frederick] Holmes, [Edmund] Ruffin, [Nathaniel Beverly] Tucker, and [William Gilmore] Simms made their most concerted attempt to reconcile transcendent with practical aims, spiritual conviction with mundane ambition. To the twentieth century, such application of intellect in the service of human exploitation may appear incomprehensible, even unforgiveable. Yet the five Southerners found in the defense of slavery a logical—and in some ways necessary—culmination of their endeavors to institutionalize moral stewardship and thus establish a recognizable place for mind in their society. Ironically, they were to invoke timeless intellectual values and nationally shared evangelical commitments to justify the South's peculiar institution.[76]

Law professor and historian Paul Finkelman noted that "Edmund Ruffin (1794–1865) was one of the most fanatic proslavery theorists of the late antebellum period . . . this long-time advocate for secession was given the honor of igniting a fuse to fire the first shot on Fort Sumter. When the war ended with the Confederacy in ashes, Ruffin shot himself in the head with a pistol, preferring death to the prospect of living in a reconstructed Union where slavery was illegal."[77]

In a treatise he wrote in 1853, Ruffin offered a sample of his racist thoughts. Here, he was commenting on "free negroes": "Still to this day, and with but few individual exceptions, the free negroes in every State of this Confederacy, are noted for ignorance, indolence, improvidence, and poverty—and very generally, also, for vicious habits, and numerous violations of the criminal laws."[78]

Historian Larry E. Tise gave us a proslavery sample by another of these notable men. Focused on the words and actions of William Gilmore Simms, Tise wrote,

> Following the lead of conservatives and anti-abolitionists, Simms rejected the words of the Declaration of Independence for those of "a greater philosopher than Thomas Jefferson." Finding in the writings of William Shakespeare support for the growing emphasis on order, stability, and harmony, Simms wrote, "Democracy is not leveling—it is, properly defined, the harmony of the moral world. It insists upon inequalities, as its law declares, that all men should hold the place to which they are properly entitled."[79]

This self-generated (and self-congratulatory) view of slavery's moral and historic importance led the South to play out a tragedy of epic proportions. This type of rationalization transformed slaveholders into tragic figures. As Genovese and Fox-Genovese eloquently stated: "Indeed, their desperate need to deceive themselves propelled Americans, Black and white, into our greatest national tragedy."[80]

POLITICAL AND ECONOMIC POWER

As early as 1786, James Madison predicted that the United States would become a major cotton-producing country.[81] Standing solidly on the backs and necks of Black African enslaved people and with the eradication or displacement of the United States' native population, "the entry of the United States into the empire of cotton was so forceful that cotton cultivation in the American South quickly began to reshape the global cotton market. . . . [I]n 1820 the United States produced 167.5 million pounds. Exports to Great Britain increased by a factor of ninety-three between 1791 and 1800, only to multiply another seven times by 1820. . . . What distinguished the United States from virtually every other cotton-growing area in the world was planters' command of nearly unlimited supplies of land, labor, and capital, and their unparalleled political power."[82]

Marse stood tall on the world stage because between 1800 and 1850, he and his fellow politicians had expanded enormously the cotton-friendly lands of the United States. By 1850, "67 percent of U.S. cotton grew on land that had not been part of the United States half a century earlier. The fledging U.S. government had inaugurated the military-cotton complex."[83] Even though small farmers or small-time planters grew cotton, it was the exports from the larger plantations that fed the global market. "85 percent of all cotton picked in the South in 1860 was grown on units larger than a hundred acres; the planters who owned those farms owned 91.2 percent of all slaves."[84] Hold that picture in your mind: 85 percent of all southern grown cotton was cultivated on tracts of land no less than one hundred acres and the vast majority of the enslaved labor force for this effort was owned by a small group of elite slaveholders. It is these men I hold in my mind's eye as the subject of this book: the members of the board of directors and chief executive officers of the military-cotton complex.

In a relatively short span of thirty-four years, America saw just how prescient Madison was about the country's reliance on cotton production. As historian Andrew Delbanco informed us,

> As early as 1820, the United States overtook India as the world's greatest cotton producer. At the time of the founding, cotton accounted for barely 7 percent of the nation's exports; by the eve of the Civil War, that figure had risen to more than 60 percent. In 1844, as estimated by one antislavery newspaper, "twelve hundred million dollars worth of human beings" was held by two hundred thousand slaveholders. . . . By the 1850s, according to historian Eric Foner, the economic value of enslaved "men, women, and children when considered as property exceeded the combined worth of all the banks, factories and railroads in the United States."[85]

A major goal based on the Southern elite's expected outcome of the Civil War was the creation of a separate nation that would hold its own on the world stage. Cotton, to the delight of many American and European businesses, made the United States a world power. Pointing to the research of a fellow historian, Delbanco stated, "The historian Matthew Karp, in documenting the outsize influence of antebellum southerners over American foreign policy (ten of the first sixteen secretaries of state were from slave states), writes of 'the paradox of the 1850s,' by which he means 'slaveholders growing more confident abroad but becoming more beleaguered at home.'"[86]

Cotton needed land and labor. Marse became quite adept at land speculation and slave trading as means of diversifying and increasing his wealth. The practice of trading in enslaved people was something most slaveholders and nonslaveholders viewed with distaste, if not contempt. I would surmise that for the enslavers, it was but a feigned contempt, for the acquisition of unlimited forced labor was central to feeding the slavery system with fresh Black bodies. It could be called a shadow operation, but it was rampant among elite slaveholders, whether or not they participated directly or through agents. As Oakes pointed out, "After land speculation, slave trading was one of the planters' most profitable and widely practiced enterprises."[87] Speculation of enslaved people was a dirty, lucrative business.

As historian Michael Tadman underscored, slave trafficking was a profession in the American colonies as early as the 1780s.[88] Slave trading, by definition and in actual practice, included enslaved family separations, a consequence most slaveholders wanted to deny. Baptist comments on trading of the enslaved:

> As early as the mid-1820s, people who visited the Mississippi Valley had been noticing this new breed of entrepreneurs. They were young men who were getting rich fast by specializing in one commodity—humans. Buying masses of enslaved people for low prices in Virginia and Maryland, these young men "thrust them into the prison-house for safe-keeping," drove their enslaved purchases "handcuffed through the country like cattle," and boated them down the rivers and around the cape of Florida to New Orleans or elsewhere to the southwest.[89]

And, as will be shown, this minority of white slave masters controlled an inordinate amount of America's political and economic power. Historian Ira Berlin offered a sweeping view:

> Armed with the power of the state and unprecedented agglomerations of capital, planters chased small [land]holders from the countryside and monopolized the best land. To work their estates, they impressed or enslaved indigenous peoples, or, in the absence of native populations,

"Enslaved Coffle" Statuary Group, National Memorial for Peace and Justice, Montgomery, Alabama; entitled "Nkyinkyim Installation" by sculptor Kwame Akoto-Bamfo.
Photograph by the author

imported large numbers of servants or slaves. . . . In theory, the planters' rule was complete. The Great House, nestled among factories, shops,
barns, sheds, and various other out-buildings, which were called, with a
nice sense of the plantation's social hierarchy, "dependencies," dominated
the landscape, the physical and architectural embodiment of the planters'
hegemony. But the masters' authority radiated from the great estates to the
statehouses, courtrooms, countinghouses, churches, colleges, taverns, race-
tracks, private clubs, and the like. In each of these venues, planters practiced the art of domination, making laws, meting out justice, and silently
asserting—by their fine clothes, swift carriages, and sweeping gestures,
their natural right to rule. Although the grandees never achieved the total
domination they desired, it was not for want of trying.[90]

America was quite enamored with the American southern white elite
slaveholder from our nation's beginnings. Thirteen white southern men
occupied the White House from our nation's inception to the beginning
of the Civil War. Enslavers dominated our nation's diplomacy. The white
Southern slaveholder controlled a disproportionate share of America's

governance: "The ideological confidence and worldly sophistication of American slaveholders cannot be separated from the control of the American state power. . . . In the two decades before the Civil War, proslavery elites and their largely compliant northern allies maintained a vise-like grip on the executive branch of the U.S. national government."[91] Roark addressed the link between planter profits and slaveholding power:

> The large profits returned by cotton, rice, and sugar in the 1850s were reflected in the growing cultural and political power of the slaveholders. The voice of the South was never entirely the voice of its elite, but influence was heavily concentrated in planters' hands. . . . The South's white population accepted slavery, the planters for their own reasons and the nonslaveholding white majority because it insured white supremacy and white democracy, and offered the promise of white equality.[92]

Slave masters managed to ignore the fallacy that if all men are naturally endowed with such inalienable rights as life, liberty, and the pursuit of happiness, these principles did not hold for enslaved people, other people of color, or women. This position was intellectually dishonest, contradictory, and hypocritical. Slavery proceeded directly from the white slaveholder's belief that Blacks were inferior and were certainly not entitled to any inalienable rights.

While American history is replete with glorious deeds of many of these men of great character, who, as statesmen, held many of the highest political and military offices of our country, what was the emotional cost? Author Wendell Berry has written a powerful answer to that question. In his book *The Hidden Wound*, Berry makes a compelling argument that the "white man" carries significant trauma, a "hidden wound," from the toxic effects of racial slavery. This wound remains significantly untreated by most of us and insidiously supports and feeds the racial divisiveness today.[93] I address in more detail the contemporary nature of this hidden wound in the concluding chapter of this book.

As astutely observed by Genovese, "molded by their slaves as much as their slaves had been molded by them" illustrated the significant psychopathological, relational component of racist slavery.[94] Enslaved people had a powerful, emotionally eroding effect on their masters, an effect that was not much noticed or admitted by the slaveholder. I chose "erosion" here because it speaks to the slow, but inevitable toxic effect slaveholding had on the enslavers' mind and behavior, and on the South as a region. Over time, as the slaveholder had to employ multiple psychological defenses to dampen any positive feelings he held for his chattel property or to fend off any regret or remorse for the horrors racist slavery perpetrated in his life, this dynamic murdered Marse's conscience. Slaveholding, in effect, was to be the cause of Marse's psychic death.

Although southern enslavers rationalized that they were simply carrying on a pattern that had existed since civilization began—one group of dominant people always held others as enslaved people—the South's brand of slavery became a peculiar institution not because it was quaint, but because it was racist and based on skin color. Being Black and being enslaved became synonymous in the antebellum South. White supremacy was created out of whole racist cloth.

The white racist slaveholder saw himself and the southern region as being founded on honor and pride, two characteristics that were vitally important to southern identity and at the same time became self-destructive. Marse convinced himself that racist slaveholding was not only righteous but honorable. The slave master paid scant attention to the deleterious effects of slaveholding on the slave master himself, with slavery eroding his basic humanity. As a racist institution, slavery molded the slaveholder—albeit in significantly different ways—as much as slavery molded the enslaved.

• 2 •

The Elite Enslavers' Core Assumptions and Beliefs about Black Africans

HELPLESS HEATHENS ALL

An assumption is anything taken for granted, a presumption. A person's beliefs are founded on his or her assumptions. The world is flat; I will fall off if I sail to its edge. It would be an error to think that a person's beliefs always drive his or her behavior. They do not. A person's behavior is what that individual *says* or *does* and is not necessarily driven by his or her beliefs.

To fully understand the enslaver's psychological relationship with his enslaved captives, we must understand his basic assumptions about Black Africans. As stated in chapter 1, the slaveholder principally stood on two basic assumptions: Black Africans were subhuman and the Protestant Christian Bible totally sanctioned slavery. Because Blacks were judged as naturally inferior, whiteness was superior to blackness, an assumption that was centuries old. It was a purer color on the spectrum of colors; in fact, it was the purest, the zenith of colors, the essence of supremacy. The enslaver decided Black Africans were inferior not just because of their color, but because of their so-called primitive existence. All whites, slaveholders or not, viewed themselves as superior. As historian Ibram X. Kendi pointed out, we can find an American colonial taproot for this assumption of Blacks' inferiority in Puritan Cotton Mather's plea: "The Puritan colonists are 'the English Israel'—a chosen people. People must religiously instruct all slaves and children, the 'inferiors,' . . . But masters were not doing their job of looking after African souls, 'which are as white and good as those of other Nations, but are Destroyed for lack of Knowledge.'"[1] Kendi's point here is that Mather was declaring the color of souls to be white. Mather was also saying that while slaves may have white souls, they are damaged souls, destroyed by ignorance.

Quoting Brown University historian Karl Jacoby, Professor David Livingstone Smith of the University of New England wrote: "Slavery was an institution that treated humans like domestic animals. . . . Yet clearly humans and livestock were not the same—or were they? The easiest solution . . . was to invent a lesser category of humans that supposedly differed little from brute beasts" and "Slave owners and merchants had a vested interest in the subhuman status of Africans, for if Africans were lower animals, then it was right and proper to treat them as such."[2]

To strengthen their anchorage on the backs of Black Africans, some proslavery advocates assumed that because they were animals, they had no souls. The question of whether or not Black Africans had souls was deliberated for decades among white folks, especially among the white evangelical clergy. As historian Walter Johnson illustrated, this racist assumption remained strong among whites in the early twentieth century, moving W. E. B. Du Bois in April 1903 to publish his book *The Souls of Black Folk*, in which he eloquently decreed "in profoundly antiracist fashion that Blacks were not soulless beasts. Black folks were fully human, and Du Bois made Americans 'listen to the strivings of Black folk.'"[3]

As Johnson pointed out, the states in which slavery existed are often referred to as "slaveholding states," even though the majority of the whites who lived in those states did not own slaves "and even though nearly half the people in those states were, in fact, slaves."[4] Nevertheless, white supremacy bonded racist slaveholders and nonslaveholders. Nonslaveholders were able tangentially to join the club called the "ruling race." This faux membership to the ruling racist club was the Southern elite slave master's long confidence game, adroitly played on his fellow (lower-class) whites. Johnson persuasively argued, "As long as they did not go so far as to diminish the value held by actual slaveholders, nonslaveholding white men were baited by a hope that they might one day accede to a full share of slavery—that they might one day be men in full."[5] There's the implicit promise: slaveholding men in full. Once the idea of enslaving a servant pricked a person's consciousness, a nonslaveholding white man or woman who became seduced by the criteria of what was considered to be a successful person never felt complete until he or she owned a slave, yet the white man's reaffirmed psychological, moral, and ethical safety net was his skin color. Even if he didn't own a slave, or even if he was an abolitionist, his whiteness gave him a leg up. Always.

Sociologist and psychiatrist Jonathan Metzl brilliantly described the long-term mortal effects of this arrogant view of whiteness. Whites form a view of their whiteness that they bet their life on: "A central political script then emerges in ways that, in its worse moments, defines the boundaries of white America in relation to real or imagined others who want to take what it has or be what it is."[6] Even though Metzl focused his analysis on a more contemporary perspective, the deification of whiteness and the fear of nonwhiteness were the central elements composing the structural foundation of pride on which the white enslaver posed.

Traversing the ethically diseased path that judged an entire people as subhuman presumed a solid, morally clear direction. The white southern elite enslaver anchored his views of African slavery on a corrupt morality. The core of Marse's immorality was his imagined, abstract, reality-distorting, racist belief that Black Africans were essentially incompetent, subhuman heathens. *Everything else about southern racial (read: racist) slavery turns on this assumption and belief.* Let me be clear: His belief was founded on the enslaver's bedrock assumption. The Black African was not human. The Black African was certainly not of the lineage from Adam and Eve.

After quoting the most famous thirty-five words penned by Thomas Jefferson in the Declaration of Independence—"We hold these truths to be self-evident, that all men are created equal, that they are endowed by their Creator with certain unalienable Rights, that among these are Life, Liberty and the Pursuit of Happiness"—Smith pointed out that despite the reverential ring these words carry for many Americans, the question hanging in the air was *who* was meant by the terms "all men" or "they"? Jefferson, himself a substantial enslaver, did not really mean "all" men or, for that matter, *any* woman. The group of men known as "the Founding Fathers" left out "from this circle of united interest drawn by the Declaration of Independence: Indians, Black slaves, women."[7] It seems strange to me that this question—Who was Jefferson referring to in his use of the word "men"?—frequently gets asked within historiography. There is no reason to ask it, unless someone is trying to foster a false hope that one of our preeminent founders might have meant more. Jefferson and his colleagues meant white male beings. As Smith pointed out,

> The uneasy relationship between the economic attractions of slavery and the Enlightenment vision of human dignity was a long-standing one, and for those torn between the demands of conscience and the seductions of self-interest, there was a way out of the dilemma. They could deny that African slaves were human, and in this way they could square the moral circle. By dint of a sleight of mind, the very men who insisted on the God-given right of all humankind to liberty could, in good faith, countenance and participate in the brutal and degrading institution of slavery. Many of the great thinkers of the Enlightenment, who had championed the concept of individual rights and defined the philosophical underpinnings of the great American experiment, routinely excluded nonwhites from the category of the human.[8]

As a student of religious history and an avid reader of religious publications, the educated, elite slaveholder knew well the origins of the relationship between slavery and God's law. By the end of the sixteenth century, "European thinkers had added African people to the list of species descended from a different Adam" (as had been the Native American people), who, according to Kendi, were "a people unmentioned in the Bible."[9]

In his seventeenth-century treatise, *A Christian Directory*, British minister Richard Baxter "urged slaveholders across the ocean [in the colonies] to follow God's law in making slaves into Christians," urging enslavers to make it their chief goal to buy and use slaves, to win them to Christ, and to save their souls. According to Baxter, Kendi informed us, the slave master's prime directive was to "let their Salvation be far more valued by you than their Service." This wish or prayer for slaveholders was nothing more than a pipe dream. According to Kendi, Baxter preached of the possibility of "some kind of benevolent slavery" that would be helpful to the African people.[10]

White slave masters convinced themselves that Blacks, because of their inferior status, inherently were missing key human elements: "Subhumans, it was believed, are beings that lack that special something that makes us human. Because of this deficit, they don't command the respect that *we*, the truly human beings, are obliged to grant one another. They can be enslaved, tortured, or even exterminated—treated in ways in which we could not bring ourselves to treat those whom we regard as members of our own kind. This phenomenon is called *dehumanization*."[11] Smith defined this term in a simple, clear manner: "the act of conceiving of people as subhuman creatures rather than as human beings. . . . When we dehumanize people we don't just think of them in terms of what they lack, we also think of them as creatures that are less than human."[12]

With the exception of his appreciation of some enslaved laborers' advanced skills—such as rice planting—Marse was generally clueless about his enslaved people's intelligence. He wrongly interpreted his enslaved workers' submission as docility and lack of will.[13] A powerful example—maybe the best example—is explored in chapter 6, where the effects of the story of Noah in Genesis 9:18–27 are discussed. Marse was not the least bit interested in the objective history of Africa and its advanced civilizations and kingdoms. Despite his view of himself as bright and knowledgeable about the world and its history, all a slave master needed to know about Africa was it was populated by the God-cursed family of Black Ham and Canaan.

THE CHOSEN

The primary source for these racist beliefs derived from the master's spiritual identity—for the most part, a Protestant Christian identity, which included a powerful strain of immutable religious beliefs. Consider, for example, John Knox's interpretation of Calvin. In the sixteenth century, Knox established Calvinist theology in Scotland within Presbyterian doctrine:

> Calvinism . . . to which the Scottish and Irish Presbyterians had ascribed, was an Old World notion that certain people, called the "Elect," were chosen by God to be saved and everyone else was damned. No amount of personal effort or pious living could change this outcome. However, it held that work was the will of God, and while men were not to lust after wealth, they were to reinvest the profits of their labor into further ventures. Using profits to help others rise from a lesser level of subsistence violated God's will, since they weren't earning through their own labor.[14] It was impossible to know who was a member of the Elect—but it was assumed that vagabonds and lazy people were damned, but hardworking, successful people were most likely among the chosen. This work ethic, that infused hard work with divine dignity, became fundamental to Protestant thinking and the American work ethic.[15]

Through hard work and divine dignity, the elite became the Elect. To these self-appointed elite, Black Africans and American born Blacks were lazy, subhuman, indolent, and thus damned.

When the economics of slavery are titrated through a Calvinist belief system, a bedrock of Reformed Presbyterian beliefs was that God chose an elite group (of men only) composed of previously saved individuals—the "Elect"—to succeed and diversify their profits in further ventures. There was a strict limitation based on a strict belief. Charity work and donations to the less fortunate violated God's will, because people living at a lesser level of subsistence—that is, lazy people—were where they were in life because they were not working hard enough. Being poor is self-inflicted. It's not difficult to discern here the thread of racism that holds that Black people should remain poor.

As Marse practiced his particular Christian denomination's tenets and principles about slavery, historian Eugene Genovese pointed out that "the master-slave relationship rested, psychologically as well as ideologically, on the transformation of the will of the slave into an extension of the will of the master."[16] These efforts to ensure that the enslaved people's will was Marse's will created an enormous, cancerous blind spot in Marse's psyche:

Thus, no matter how obedient—how Uncle Tomish—Christianity made an enslaved person, it also drove deeply into the bondsman's soul an awareness of the moral limits of submission, for it placed a master above his own master [i.e., God] and thereby dissolved the moral and ideological ground on which the very principle of absolute human lordship must rest. It was much more than malice that drove so many Southern masters to whip their Black prisoners for praying to God for this and that and to demand they address all grievances and wishes to their earthly masters.[17]

Here the master became the tyrant when he perceived that his enslaved were attempting to have their own relationship with the will of God.

An enslaved individual's keen observation that Marse thought he was God created an important imperfection in Marse's chains of domination. The enslaved that endured Marse's deification of himself knew the master was not God, no matter what the master said or did. The ultimate irony is that the slave master became enslaved to the slave industry. The enslaved person was capable of discerning, in his or her own psyche, that the Marse was not his or her God, that Marse was weakened in the eyes of the enslaved because of his attempts to be God. At this important juncture between the lives of the master and the enslaved, once Marse assumed the role of God, he lost his integrity in the eyes of enslaved people. His humanity power was then bankrupt. This slave master stance was extremely grandiose and profoundly self-destructive.

For the record, my ancestors—Scots-Irish Associate Reformed Presbyterians who settled in North and South Carolina in the midseventeenth century—on the question of slavery, stayed firmly attached to the Synod of the South, which "as far as is known, never made an official statement which condemned slavery."[18] One could infer that my people stayed silent on the problems with slavery but embraced a faith that supported it, and, more pointedly, owned and used enslaved labor. According to religious historian R. A. King, in 1845, the South Synod passed an act recognizing the slaves had souls. In addition to this arrogant conclusion, this same act did offer some positive guidance, stressing the sanctity of marriage and an instruction to masters to try to keep Black captive families intact. The South Synod apparently stayed silent on the laws in the South that supported and protected slavery.[19] King says that the South Synod lost its "moderate spirit" after 1850, suggesting that it became more racist.

WE ARE FAMILY

Marse convinced himself that his plantation and all its inhabitants were "family." As historian James Oakes informed us, "To a large extent, slaveholders who spoke of their Black 'family' were employing colloquial speech patterns that were common throughout antebellum America, for theirs was an age obsessed with the family."[20] The slave master saw himself as the benevolent father, and his enslaved were "his people." By the eighteenth century, "the reality of the plantation as a household induced a sensibility expressed in the language of 'family.'"[21] The idea that a family existed among perpetually enslaved people and the slaveholder's kinsmen is a warped reality. For example, a slave master could not and would not sell or trade one of his own family members for profit or punishment.

Taking this a step further, the slave master saw his enslaved people—all of them, adults and children—as children. Consequently, enslaved children might witness their own father or mother whipped, beaten, or separated and sold. Enslaved parents would be witness to their own children being beaten, whipped, or sold by the slave master, or perhaps even seduced or sexually assaulted. The slave masters claimed to use their power not only to improve the enslavers' own lives, but also the lives of their dependents.

Historian Michael Tadman made a highly convincing argument that this notion of "family" was created by a composite of several aspects of the slave master's personality: This portrayal of Blacks and whites being part of the family was in part self-deception and public relations. A slave master might have a close relationship with "key slaves," such as house slaves, mistresses, or drivers, but by and large, the slaveholders viewed African slaves with contempt. Marse saw himself as a benevolent patriarch, in control of and in charge of his "children."[22]

Historians Eugene Genovese and Elizabeth Fox-Genovese, citing slaveholder Hugh Davis of Alabama, noted that "plantation management [was] the province of the master, who must govern by a patriarchal 'code of love.'"[23] The king's grace. This arrogant stance solidified Marse's belief that he was basically omniscient and omnipotent in the affairs of the enslaved. These same historians, quoting Samuel Galloway of Georgia, wrote: "Each family is a unit in the mart. The family is the reservoir into which commodities flow, and from which each member receives continuous supplies. The patriarch gathers around him a circle of dependents."[24]

If a slave master convinced himself that he didn't like tyrannical monarchs, he deceived himself that he was a kind patriarch, a benevolent king who ran his household as his castle. Ironically, many elite planters' ancestral family histories derived from a long, bloody history of fighting monarchy.

Large group of enslaved people on Smith's Plantation, Beaufort, South Carolina.
Library of Congress

In the heat of passion, was a slaveholder able to draw a line between how he disciplined his slaves and how he disciplined his own children? Historian John Patrick Daly offered a view: "Providentialism reflected the prevalent theory that God not only had created the universe but sustained it moment to moment. Nothing occurred by chance. God handed out success and spankings in perfect accordance with the individual's moral choices. God's scheme of rewards and punishments, Providence, almost *was* God to antebellum evangelicals."[25]

A way of thinking about the quotidian effects Providentialism must have had on the mind and behavior of the slave master was that he could explain or excuse his actions, no matter how base, impulsive, or extreme, as God's will, because God has his hand in every event at every moment: "The Lord giveth and the Lord taketh away" (Job 1:21).

SEXUAL PROPERTY

In this complicated realm of sexual relationships, carnal entitlement for many enslavers was the core belief. In 1660 and 1661, the Virginia legislature passed a law that conferred the legal status of any child born between an English-man and a slave to the child's mother. This law opened the door for white enslavers to reap financial reward from relations "upon a negro woman."[26] The potential for financial gain led to the potential for slave breeding, a topic discussed more thoroughly in chapter 8. To cover their bases, by the end of the seventeenth century, both Maryland and Virginia legislated severe penal-ties for white women who had relations with nonwhite men.

The psychological trope driving white privilege and freedom to be sexu-ally aggressive with Black females was based on a massive projection: White slaveholders imagined enslaved women as being exceptionally sexually aggres-sive toward them. This projection moved the site of the sexual desire to the women. It was psychopathologically brilliant. This projection allowed the slaveholder to simultaneously deny his own sexual desires and yet allow him to be tantalized by the obvious desires of the slave girl. Rapes of Black women by white men, were rarely reported: "Black women were thought aggressively to pursue white men sexually; and Black men were thought to aggressively pursue white women sexually. Neither could help it, the racist myth posited. They naturally craved superior whiteness."[27] See chapter 4 for a discussion of the psychological dynamics driving this predatory sexual projection. Sexual assaults and rapes of enslaved girls and women by enslavers, by their family members, and by their employees, such as an overseer or driver, were com-monplace. "Historians have been acutely aware that masters and their male kin represented the greatest sexual threat to their female slaves."[28] It took a great deal of creative denial and minimization by the white women of the house-hold to endure the realities and consequences of these violent emotional and physical assaults. "Mistresses and overseers' wives shared some suffering and humiliation notably from their husbands' philandering in the slave quarters."[29]

The history of one of the South's most prominent Grandees and a dis-ciple of John C. Calhoun, James Henry Hammond (1807–1864)—South Carolina state representative, US senator, and state governor—illustrates how the entitled view of slaves as sexual property can merge with other psychopa-thology. As historian Andrew Delbanco framed it: "Hammond was incalcula-bly smug and vulgar by comparison to his mentor. He was a sexual predator whose abuse of young girls, despite his avid preference for the white race in all other matters, did not stop at the color line. Preying not only on his own teenage nieces but on at least one of his female slaves as well as her twelve-year-old daughter, he was shameless."[30] There were no child abuse statutes

For Sale,
A NEGRO GIRL,
Nearly 19 years of age. She is well versed in all kinds of house work, and is a very
good spinster. It is believed she will particularly suit a farmer. She is a slave. For
terms enquire of *John N. Simpson,* Esq. New
Brunswick—*Samuel Leake,* Esq Trenton—or
of the subscriber in Princeton.
ELIJAH SLACK.,
July 18.   3tp

Advertisement for sale of a "Negro girl." *Joseph Yanelli, "Princeton Fugitive Slaves,"*
Princeton Slavery Project, http://slavery.princeton.edu/stories/runaways

aimed at protecting children from abuse and neglect in America until the early
1970s.[31] There were certainly no sexual assault statutes protecting enslaved
children. These women and children were seen as property and bodies to be
used and exploited.

This subject, the sexual exploitation of children, takes us into a complicated realm of the slaveholder's psyche. Age and assumed maturity of children
have been looked at vastly differently throughout human history. Imagine if
you will, a forty-two-year-old white slave master sexually desiring to have
intercourse with *his* enslaved charges. In the case of a female enslaved, she is
his legal property. Does her age matter? Do twenty-first-century values have
any relevance to such an assault? He had the power and authority to sexually
exploit and rape her (or him) at his will.

Throughout history, men have married girls, a phenomenon that still
occurs in some parts of the world. The decision or obligation to marry is
obviously different from a sexual assault. The latter is forcible rape, although
history has also shown us forcible marriages. A slave child (or his or her parents) could not give consent for the slave master to rape the child. The slave
master had no boundaries on his sexual proclivities. His predatory business was
his business, unless he did something so egregious as to bring attention to his

behavior. If a master preferred preadolescent or very young adolescent girls as his sexual partners, virtually nothing could stop him; the same can be said if he were sexually attracted to young boys: "[T]he rape of a slave child posed no similar social and economic burden to a white slaveholder, unless the rape was accompanied by significant violence. In fact, in older slave girls, rapes could result in pregnancies that would actually benefit the master. . . . In all probability, when made aware of sexual assault of slave girls, masters took matters into their own hands, if they acted at all."[32]

Sexual intimacy between whites and their enslaved people was common. A white woman who had sexual contact with a Black man might irretrievably lose the respect of society, but white men paid no such price. Male lust and the acting out this lust were a fact of life. Marse felt quite entitled to a few sexual indiscretions, exploitation, assaults, and rape. The king was untouchable. He had narcissistic immunity. It seems inaccurate, or an experiment in fanciful denial, to think of Marse's sexual relationships with his slaves as consensual. The average age difference (forty-two for the white male and eighteen, or likely younger, for the Black female) made any sexual encounter an assault. The power differential made it so. A slave could not say no to the master or to anyone who had the master's surrogate power. Consider the range of possibilities in the ways a planter might respond if sexually rejected by an enslaved servant. As historian Bertram Wyatt-Brown clearly stated, "Miscegenation between a white male and a Black female posed almost no ethical problems for the antebellum Southern community, so long as the rules, which were fairly easy to follow, were discreetly observed."[33] These rules were: (a) the relationship, even if long-standing, had to have the appearance of being casual, and the distinction between rank and race had to be quite clear; (b) the Black sexual partner had to be sexually attractive in white men's eyes (light skin and comely features were a plus); and (c) the sexual pairing could not be part of the slaveholder's dysfunction, such as alcoholism or dereliction of duty. These rules appear to suggest an understanding of Thomas Jefferson's complicated relationship with Sally Hemings.

As a young man, Marse saw it as a point of honor to end his virginity and be a man. The easiest path was an enslaved girl or woman: "If the initial effort were clumsy or brutal no one would object, in view of the woman's race and status. Moreover, Black girls were infinitely more accessible and experienced than the white daughters of vigilant, wealthy families. . . . Overseers who took liberties in the quarters were a constant cause of complaint."[34] Marse's wife was generally too closely supervised to have much opportunity for a sexual dalliance or infidelity, but it did happen on occasion, though mainly among the middle and lower orders of the white South, "not the wealthy, churchgoing matrons of Charleston and Richmond."[35]

If a white woman was discovered to have had sex with a Black man, her ace-in-the-hole, honor-saving defense was an allegation of rape. Sexual assault allegations—genuine or false—were the basis of many court-ordered hangings and many horrible extrajudicial lynchings: "From the perspective of the slaves and to our own cold eye, the protection offered by the slaveholders' internalization of Christian and chivalric values did not add up to much."[36]

FREEDOM'S BLOCKADE

In yet another bending of reality, the slave master believed that Black people could not handle freedom. Black Africans and African Americans, Marse determined, were not constitutionally fit to survive the rigors of self-sufficiency. By 1800, beginning with South Carolina, one after another, the southern state legislatures began to restrict enslaved individuals' access to freedom.[37] White southern slave masters who ran the South's political machines began to concretize the legal structures to keep Blacks in a perpetual state of powerlessness, with no personal or legal control. Many of these oppressive legislative actions and policies still find significant racist traction in the twenty-first century, such as ongoing systemic efforts at voter suppression and vote eradication.

Marse found it desirable to show favor to some enslaved people over others; for example, an individual might become a "servant" or "favored sexual partner" and become alienated from the other slaves because of his or her special status. This hierarchy led to a "slave elite." One of the most common divisions, of course, was between the "house slave" and the "field slave." These were the "key slaves," which Tadman defined as "drivers (assistants to white overseers or planters), drivers' wives, and certain senior domestics . . . rank-and-file slaves are almost invisible."[38] These "elite" slaves paid a terrible psychological price: "To enjoy the bounty of a paternalistic master, a slave had to give up all claims to respect as a responsible adult, all pretensions of independence."[39]

SLAVERY WAS A WAY OF LIFE

Imagine developing a worldview that almost anywhere one looked, there was contentment. Enslavers employed multiple rationalizations to defend themselves against too much concern about their slaves. Chief among these was that slavery was touted as less a business than a way of life. Among the slaveholding elite, this was the southern racist slavery-based life. Slave masters convinced themselves that their enslaved people were content with their servitude. Imagine the mental gymnastics it took to convince yourself, and portray to others, that your business concerns, standing on the backs of forced labor, were but a mere secondary concern to an overall enlightened way of life. Additionally, management of his slavery business often required Marse to travel a great deal. Marse would have to convince his wife and family of this "fact" to justify his many business trips: "Missy, all this is for you, honey, and the children. I have to support our way of life. It's God's wish."

The psychology of the slave master and his belief that he held a superior, divine duty combined to create a smoke-and-mirrors self-deception. Objectively, in the affairs of religion and eternity, all men, including the enslaved, stood on the same ground. In his heart of hearts, the master did not truly believe this, because to believe this type of spiritual equality meant giving up a lot of ground, most particularly that Black slaves were inferior beings: "[T]he meanest Slave is as immortal as his Master."[40] If that were true, then it made sense to split the slave's soul from his or her body: "Since it was the immortal soul, and not one's place in the temporal [physical] order, that gave 'importance to a being,' it was the duty of Christian masters to strive to convert their enslaved prisoners. This 'solemn and important trust' was as sacred as that of parents to their children, and to neglect it was nothing short of an 'inhuman cruelty.'"[41] Most masters agreed that a personal provision by the master of religious instruction to his slaves was best, at least within the proper limits. Most masters quickly determined that it was not good practice to teach one's bondservants how to read and write. Reading skills might lead the enslaved into dangerous waters, such as other passages of the Bible or the meaning of handbills and posters.

Marse was shrewd in his twisted, self-serving logic. The master believed in his heart that "freedom is not possible without slavery." Ponder that for a moment. The master's freedom was dependent on the enslavement of Blacks. The interconnection between freedom and slavery is a significant piece of the slaveholder's psychological worldview: "Slaveholders believed that men of good will should desire to extend freedom as far as possible, while recognizing that many people lacked the capacity to live free; that the freest societies in world history were based on slavery; and that freedom could be sustained only through the subjugation of all laboring classes. Thus, they resolved to sustain a Southern slave society even in a hostile world."[42] This became a profound rationalization: The southern slave masters' personal and cultural freedom became dependent on the enslavement of Blacks; the South's way of life, by God. "Slavery provides freedom" was a comforting thought: psychotic, but comforting. Why psychotic? Marse's reality-distorting sense of his being free in the world derived from his being part of a racist, totalitarian, cruel, and oppressive system of slavery that was a blatant crime against humanity.

A SECOND REVOLUTION

Nevertheless, racist enslavers had a divine mission. Really, if Marse was honest in his relation with his Protestant Christian God, he had no choice. White racist southern masters believed slavery was their divine duty. Secession from the Union was perceived as a revolutionary act; to many Southerners, it was a second American revolution—albeit a regional one—necessary to maintain their freedom and culture: "In the 1850s, efforts to portray the American Revolution as a Southern-led conservative movement increased in volume and intensity."[43]

Slaveholders deceived themselves:

> Southerners brave enough to face history as a story of horrors had somehow to account for the horror of the slaveholding regime that commanded their firm allegiance. They ended by convincing themselves that slavery, on balance, offered a measure of mitigation on the ground that it provided all the enslaved with masters who protected them against a much worse fate. As self-deception, their dialectical gyration remains intriguing. As apologetics well short of their best efforts, it did them no honor.[44]

At bottom, the slave master believed he was protecting Blacks, who, if set free, would be unable to survive in the world on their own. It was dominant, profoundly arrogant benevolence. Enslaved people were taught that eternal salvation for their soul or spirit would be their reward for faithful service.

A PSYCHOTIC REACTION

Sometimes, as noted previously, the enslavers' beliefs became floridly psychotic. A psychosis, by definition, is an obvious distortion of reality. The psychosis takes control of the person's behavior in varying degrees. Individuals experiencing psychosis evaluate their thoughts incorrectly; they make incorrect inferences from reality.[45] For example, when an individual hears and believes commands that he terrorize and shoot as many innocent elementary school children as he can, his thoughts and subsequent actions are psychotic. The slave master's reality, at times, was frankly psychotic. In the run-up to the Civil War, proslavery advocates claimed that "in all respects slavery makes no difference between the slave and any other man."[46] On this point, as Daly noted, proslavery advocates were attempting to convince the world—particularly the North and its abolitionists—that there was no difference between slavery and free labor: "One key social fact, slaveholding, became a sacred badge of success as a result of the evangelicals' saturating the South in their religion and moral outlook on success and power."[47]

Psychologically, the "Southern mind," as it pertains to slavery, had two relatively dominant threads: order and honor. Religious historian Stephen R. Haynes provided a good argument for and summary of the scholarship that highlights the "Old South's attachment to slavery as a function of its commitment to a strict timocratic code."[48] A timocracy is a government founded on the love of honor as its primary motive.

By 1860, "chattel slavery had become in literal truth, a *peculiar* institution, and Southerners knew it. . . . The one supremely relevant fact was that Southerners were among slavery's last apologists—that theirs was a 'Lost Cause' even before they took up arms to defend it. Being culturally isolated, living in an unfriendly world, was a frightening experience which made many of them angry and aggressive."[49] As I argue in chapter 4, these elite slave masters had to employ multiple conscious and unconscious defense mechanisms to contain their fears and the stress of managing a racist slavery-industrial complex.

In the mind of the typical white Southerner, slaveholding or not, slavery was freedom. This is the heart of the tragedy. Most "Rebels" were not fighting to keep their slaves, for the majority didn't own any in the first place. They were convinced (and manipulated) by the elite members of the military-slavery complex into believing that their personal and regional freedom was tied to the existence and maintenance of the institution of slavery. Most of the poor whites who comprised the bulk of the Confederate army, simply put, hated the Black enslaved—or, more accurately, people of color in general—or at a minimum saw Blacks as inferior. Most Confederate whites viewed Blacks with contempt.

The South's proslavery clergy wove together a mantle of a divine bound-labor economy intertwined with individual free will. As Daly stressed,

> Evangelical ministers categorically stated, of course, that the divine economy would never serve a secular end, especially one that undermined individual agency. Still, their faith that God would never vindicate selfishness allowed them to come very close to legitimizing an ethic of pure self-interest.[50] The distinction between "virtue is power" and outcomes of power are virtuous was never drawn carefully prior to the Civil War. A sacralization, not a mere defense, of slaveholding was implicit in the moral discourse that promoted this confusion.[51]

The Southern evangelical divines preached that there was no reason to worry because they convinced themselves and their white flock that their Christian God would never allow psychopathological narcissism to exist.

As further evidence of psychotic thinking, the slaveholder viewed slavery as a reciprocal accommodation. Slaveholders convinced themselves that, because their enslaved people needed protection and support, bondspeople actually preferred slavery to freedom. Oakes explained how self-deceptive this stance was: However, "[a]s an involuntary labor system, slavery was exploitative by its very nature, based ultimately on force, and so functioned in a way that made it all but impossible for either slaves or masters to fulfill their reciprocal obligations."[52] Slaveholders saw themselves as a natural aristocracy, a view that manifested in pretentiousness. Ponder this for a moment: owning a Black person could purchase you an aristocratic position. In the 1830s to the 1860s, a powerful measure of success for a white man in America was the owning of an enslaved human being—or hundreds.

UNSPOKEN TRUTHS

It was emotionally dangerous for the elite enslaver to look too deeply into the bottomless well of racist slavery: "Southerners chose not to dwell on the dark side of slaveholding,"[53] that is, the fact that they could lawfully severely punish a runaway or sell a slave away from his or her family. These options cannot be minimized. In the eighteenth century, a slave who was caught stealing (a capital offense) would most likely be hanged.[54] The enslaved people knew that their masters could kill them with little to no consequence. Although slaves knew they could be murdered, Marse also held the power to separate families. This devastating intervention was much easier and less messy than lynching a slave. The reality of this possibility was a palpable deterrent against a slave family's rebellious impulses. The Fugitive Slave Act of 1850, passed by the US Congress and signed into law by President Millard Fillmore, required that all runaway enslaved people, once captured, even if in a nonslaveholding state, by law had to be returned to their masters.

The perceptual distortion by the master was so great about the true nature of the master-enslaved relationship, rebellious bondspeople genuinely perplexed the master. Slave rebellions were attributed to outsiders, such as abolitionists: "In South Carolina during the 1830s, Senator William Smith and representative William Drayton proudly proclaimed that, if war came, Southern slaves would fight shoulder to shoulder with their masters."[55] This proud stance was undercut by three realities: Once the South initiated the draft, many planters paid a fee to keep themselves or their sons out of the war; most Confederate leaders were adamantly opposed to arming Blacks to join the fight, despite the fact that Blacks had well served the United States as soldiers during the Revolution and the War of 1812; and, perhaps most importantly, enslaved persons generally did not want to fight for the South.

Slaveholders became convinced of their own superiority, while simultaneously convincing their enslaved people of their inferiority. Slaveholders and slave traders used nonhuman terms to refer to Black human beings: *property, slave, chattel, stock, head.*[56] The chained lines in which slaves were forced to walk were called "coffles." The man with the whip was the "driver."

According to South Carolina historian Walter Edgar, plantation owners often preferred the slave driver to be Black.[57] Imagine for a moment what it would take for a Black man, enslaved himself, to psychologically adapt to the role of a "driver," armed with surrogate

"The Slave Driver." *National Museum of African American History and Culture, Washington, DC. Photograph by the author*

power and a whip. It most certainly would lessen the risk of being in the line of fire, but it would also alienate him from his own humanity.

The minority of Southerners who were slaveholders hoped to convince all whites within the South that Blacks were their mortal enemies.[58] Witness the ferocity and hatred that drove the Confederate soldiers, commanded by Bedford Forrest, to massacre three hundred Black soldiers at Fort Pillow in Tennessee on April 12, 1864. This effort drove some of the carnage of the Civil War, but it took root and fueled considerable terrorist activities after the defeat of the South. Forrest was the first leader of the initial version of the Ku Klux Klan.

The leadership of the Confederacy became self-destructive: It refused to seriously consider arming its slaves to defend the South, even though slaves represented about 40 percent of its population.[59] However, we do know from Major Robert Stiles's account that "Marse Robert" E. Lee apparently gave the notion of arming slaves some racist-based consideration. There was a "racial ideology" deeply embedded into Southern whites' psyches that Blacks were inferior, and thus serving alongside them would be demeaning.[60]

The contradiction here must be clear: If the slave was so content with his servitude, why did the slave master and the slave system exert so much tyrannical and cruel control? What did it take for a slave master to deny how much fear he had to create to achieve this "contentment"? Or, stated differently, how much time, money, and effort went into creating the inhumane domination and control measures to ensure this false view of contentment? And, of course, there was the ongoing problem of runaways; why would a contented enslaved individual try to escape?

Slavery, by its very nature, could never be a relationship between equals. This is the fundamental truth that belies any effort by any slavery apologist to talk about the love or family-inclusiveness slaveholders held for their slaves: "In structure and practice, slavery allowed only limited room for the intrusion of personal feelings into the master-slave relationship, and such feelings were not invariably benevolent."[61]

As historian James L. Roark informed us, planters had never been moral citizens: "A rural class, intensely individual and local in outlook, jealous of any intrusion into plantation affairs, planters always tended to think of themselves as individual sovereigns who happened to give sustenance to the state."[62]

• 3 •

The Surprising Sketch of the White Southern Female Elite Slaveholder

AN INFLUENTIAL MINORITY

Men are the focus of this book because the male gender comprised the majority of the southern planter class of slaveholders. While men may have controlled American statecraft, however, they were not the only slaveholders. Historians Elizabeth Fox-Genovese and Eugene Genovese quoted David Ruggles, a free Black abolitionist in New York, who wrote: "'Nothing is more easily demonstrable than the fact that slavery owes its continuance in the United States chiefly to the women.' Ruggles scorned the 'slaveholding ladies of the South' who occupied the highest ranks of southern society and 'notoriously' drove their slaves ferociously, proving themselves 'inexcusably criminal.'"[1]

Although the primary purpose of this book is to portray a psychological portrait of the American southern elite white male enslaver in the time frame of 1830 to 1861, it would be an error to discount or overlook the substantial contribution white southern female slaveholders—particularly through their significant defense of slavery—made to the southern chattel slavery industry. As historian William Kauffman Scarborough pointed out, even though there were "occasional expressions of resentment by planter women against specific abuses and inconveniences that they encountered in their male-dominated world, these rarely extended to a complete 'rejection of the system that established their sense of personal identity.'"[2]

When viewed in the context of a slaveholding household or plantation family, antebellum slaveholding white women were commonly referred to as "mistress," a term that was the semantic equivalent of "master." My goal here is not to paint any substantive psychological portrait of these mistresses, although I do offer some hypotheses about various psychological issues, including the degree of their cruelty toward their enslaved.

As enslavers themselves, these women were distinct from the women and girls who worked alongside the yeoman farmers of the low country South. Historian Stephanie McCurry highlighted this distinction: "Women's work in the fields, although customary, was customarily ignored and even denied. A collusive silence surrounded one of the labor practices that most clearly distinguished yeoman farms from plantations, that set yeoman wives and daughters apart from their planter counterparts, that dangerously eroded the social distinctions between free women and slaves, and that cut deeply into the pride of men raised in a culture of honor."[3] The implicit message here is that manual agricultural labor was a task best suited for bound laborers. Marse and his mistress wife viewed yeomen females toiling in their fields with either benign neglect or contempt. Those white women working those fields were not quite white. As Fox-Genovese informed us, "There is almost no evidence to suggest that slaveholding women envisioned themselves as the 'sisters' of yeoman women, although there may have been some blurring at the margins when kin relations crossed class lines. . . . In general, but for women in particular, class relations in southern society remained essentially hierarchical."[4]

As historian Peter Kolchin noted, even though only one-quarter of all southern whites owned slaves in 1860 and there was a boundary between white slaveholders and white nonslaveholders, "ambitious yeoman farmers scrimped and saved in order to mark their status by purchasing slaves of their own: doing so, although far more dreamed of acquiring slaves than ever succeeded in doing so, there was considerable movement (in both directions) across the slave-owning line."[5]

WHO WERE THESE WOMEN?

As to these southern slaveholding women, historian James Oakes offered the following data: "Women comprised another ten percent of the slaveholding class, and in significant ways they differed from male masters."[6] These differences were: (1) these female slaveholders almost always inherited their enslaved Black Africans from their deceased husbands; (2) their average age was fifty (seven years older than the average for male masters); (3) 90 percent were listed in the US censuses as having no occupation; (4) illiteracy was four times more common among slaveholding women compared to male slaveholders; and (5) "more than one of five female masters could not read or write."[7]

What kind of personal power did these mistresses find for themselves in their patriarchal world, grounded in the organizing principle of the southern slaveholding household? That's the central question addressed by two historians—Catherine Clinton and Elizabeth Fox-Genovese—who expanded on the work of historian Anne Firor Scott in portraying the antebellum white female slaveholder.[8] Clinton argued that the slaveholder mistresses were "slaves of slaves": "The plantation mistress found herself trapped within a system over which she had no control, one from which she had no means of escape. Cotton was King, white men ruled, and both white women and slaves served the same master."[9] Clinton viewed the white slaveholding mistresses as victims but interestingly contradicts herself at the end of her book with a call for further scholarship on this question. Writing more than three decades ago, Clinton ended her book with the keen observation that southern plantation mistresses were not victims and added a warning to us not to engage in self-deceit about slavery:

> American slavery bred many strong and sturdy monsters. Racism, class oppression, and sexual exploitation remain indestructible among us; they have outgrown their parent and prowl with few restraints. . . . Modern society is riddled with such deception. We flatter ourselves that we have slain the dragons, conquered the devils, defeated the dead relics of our past. Yet we are haunted by the rattling of the chains. Despite our projections, all our debates, our countless investigations, we still have to transcend the legacy of slavery. We continue enthralled, surrounded by monsters and masks, condemned perhaps not to repeat history, but certainly to rewrite it.[10]

Several historians challenged Clinton's opinion that these women were oppressed.[11] Historian Bertram Wyatt-Brown, for example, stated that Clinton's central slave-female analogy used to unify her work was deeply flawed: "But like the men they lived with and for, southern women enjoyed the benefits of slavery in full measure . . . for all the whimperings of discontent that [Clinton] has found in antebellum correspondence, plantation women largely accepted the world that provided them with the good things of life."[12]

In her data regarding these white slaveholding mistresses, Clinton referenced the unpublished manuscript of Elizabeth Craven, who surveyed the nineteenth- and twentieth-century slave interviews conducted by the Works Progress Administration interviewers.[13] According to Clinton, Craven found that 75 percent of the nineteenth-century slave narratives discuss the mistress, whereas only 40 percent of the twentieth-century interviews mention the plantation mistress. According to Craven's analysis, "Overall, 55 percent of the references to the mistress were positive, 35 percent were unfavorable, and 10 percent were decidedly mixed. . . . In general, slaves and former slaves saw the master as the source of authority on plantations; over 80 percent reported that plantation mistresses had little or no authority. Influence was all the power they could exercise."[14]

Clinton's summary of Craven's research revealed a contradiction of sorts, because within these narratives, many of these formerly enslaved people described the mistress as being the source of discipline for household slaves: "Thirty percent of the nineteenth-century slave narratives reported physical punishment ordered by the mistress. Most of these complaints were from house servants and children; punishments ranged from spanking to whipping. Of the minority of slaves who alleged cruel treatment, only 10 percent claimed that the mistress herself had whipped or beaten them."[15] Although Clinton concluded that only a small percentage of mistresses were accountable for punishment, she wisely stated that the "nature and extent of their role in the physical abuse of slaves remains to be revealed."[16]

Returning to Craven's unpublished work about the slave narratives, Clinton wrote,

> Craven finds that many of the incidents demonstrating a mistresses [*sic*] cruelty involved a female slave allegedly intimate with the master. When slave owners sexually harassed or exploited female slaves, mistresses sometimes directed their anger, not at their unfaithful husbands, but towards the helpless slaves. This was irrational, irresponsible, reprehensible behavior, and yet totally understandable. The mistress could not hurt the master, but she could hurt the slaves.[17]

Fox-Genovese argued that these women were not oppressed slaves to the system. These were women who "benefitted from their membership in the ruling class."[18] Fox-Genovese took strong issue with Clinton's view that these women resembled enslaved women "in being the victim of the double burden of patriarchy and slavery."[19] Other reviewers of Fox-Genovese's book, *Within the Plantation Household*, addressed several perceived weaknesses in her analysis. Historian Kathleen C. Berkeley, for example, pointed out that Fox-Genovese omitted any analysis of the effects miscegenation had on the intimate relationships between Black and white women in the household, a likely robust and volatile source of interpersonal and emotional conflict.[20]

Scarborough agreed with Fox-Genovese's main thesis: Slaveholding mistresses did not see themselves as oppressed by slavery, "nor did they challenge or oppose the slave system."[21] These women did not sympathize with the conditions of the enslaved, but exercised "a virulent form of racism that was 'generally uglier and more meanly expressed than that of men.'" Scarborough concluded: "Slaves in the antebellum South were oppressed; the wives and daughters who owned them were not."[22]

Quoting Fox-Genovese, historian Stephanie E. Jones-Rogers wrote:

> Yet Fox-Genovese admitted that "as slaves would have been the first to insist, and as both male and female slaveholders well knew, mistresses could very well be the devil. A mean mistress stood second to no master in her

cruelty, although her strength was less." This was particularly characteristic of white women's relationships with enslaved women in the household, for on the grounds of physical strength they were less likely than men to kill them.[23]

Scarborough declared that there was one arena—an intimate one—in which planter women were oppressed: "frequent and often unexpected pregnancies . . . . [T]he birthing of large numbers of children within a relatively short span of time had a profoundly debilitating effect, both mentally and physically, on those who were obliged to undergo this traumatic experience. . . . Population census returns confirm the assertion of Elizabeth Fox-Genovese that most slaveholding women bore a child 'every year or two during their adult lives.'"[24] Scarborough cited the example of Gertrude Thomas, the daughter of Georgia cotton planter Turner C. Clanton, who "gave birth to ten children and suffered several miscarriages during a period of twenty-two years."[25]

A LIMITED GOVERNANCE ROLE

These slaveholding mistresses, as was true for all women in the nineteenth century, had their assigned place. On the world stage, men almost exclusively administered the industry of slaveholding: "By the middle of the [nineteenth] century southern masters ruled over the wealthiest and most dynamic slave society the world had ever known. If slave labor had an international future, they would certainly command it."[26] As the title of Matthew Karp's book—*This Vast Southern Empire: Slaveholders at the Helm of American Foreign Policy*—indicates, these elite slave masters commanded the American ship of state, and their goal was to advance the international cause of slavery: "The founding of the Confederate States of America was but one of their bold foreign policy efforts. . . . The ideological confidence and worldly sophistication of American slaveholders cannot be separated from their control of American state power."[27]

White female slaveholders did not play a direct role in American statecraft, although they were very interested in politics, particularly during the secession crisis, voicing their opinions to their husbands, fathers, and brothers as well as among themselves. A small subset of these women voiced their defenses of slavery in widely circulated contemporary publications such as the *Southern Quarterly Review*, *Southern Literary Messenger*, and *De Bow's Review*, or in their published essays and unpublished diaries.[28]

For the most part, southern women accepted that their position was secondary to the dominance of paternalism. These white mistresses appeared to grant paternalism its dominance in their lives. "Southern women, more so than northern, accepted exclusion from voting and political office as natural and proper and [scorned] those who tested the boundaries of good taste. A lady expressed political opinions, but of course she deferred to the opinions of father, brother, or husband. . . . A gentleman did not refuse to hear her opinions, much less presume to question her Christian principles and loyalty to the South."[29] It's difficult not to infer that the posture many of these mistresses took towards the "superior" male gender was but feigned. "Women bore, largely in silence, their assignment to an inferior place in society and even within the household, but few tolerated the contempt that sometimes accompanied it from men who were not gentlemen."[30]

THE HOUSEHOLD MARKET

Elite planter slaveholding women expanded the meaning of the slave market. As noted by history documentarian Willie Lee Rose, Fredrika Bremer of Finland observed only male slave buyers and sellers during her visits to various New Orleans slavery markets in December 1850.[31] While it is possible there were no women present that particular trip, it may be that she did not "see" them because she did not expect to find them there.

In her recently published work, Jones-Rogers offered a compelling analysis of the contribution to the southern institution of slavery by these white female slaveholders.[32] Her study challenged fellow historian Wyatt-Brown's notion that these women had "no prescriptive right." When describing their political and financial strengths in the slaveholding world, at times her words imply some admiration for their power in the middle of a patriarchal world; at other times, and this is the heart of her analysis, she describes these women in a cold, calculating, often brutal light. The cohort of women she addressed are not defined by their numbers—except that they enslaved ten or more people—but by their actions as enslavers.

Jones-Rogers challenged historian Walter Johnson's assertion that "by purchasing slaves for their wives and children, male slaveholders—for it was only men who went to the slave market—gave both a form and a function to their patriarchal authority";[33] "the slave market was a site of perceived sexual and social disorder, not a place for a white lady to be."[34] Jones-Rogers argued that when the definition of slave market is expanded beyond the architectural boundaries of the commercial spaces associated with the slave market, white southern women, as young girls, were exposed—in their own homes and communities—to a broad and deep view of slave trading. It also seems plausible that the psychology of the girls and boys who lived in slave-trading communities, such as Charleston and New Orleans, would be affected—positively or negatively—by the public displays of slavery in the open markets. Further, it was not uncommon for a planter's child to be given an enslaved individual as a gift on a special occasion, such as a birthday.

Jones-Rogers expanded the definition of the slave market to include the plantation household:

> The slaveholding household was a place of coerced production and reproduction, racial and sexual exploitation, and physical and psychological violence. It was a place where white southern women grew accustomed to the violence of slavery, contemplated the sale and purchase of slaves, and used the bodies of the enslaved people they owned in ways that reinforced their pecuniary value. The household became an extension of the slave market, and white women capitalized upon their access to both.[35]

As Jones-Rogers pointed out, white females were common fixtures in many slave markets. More significantly, these women often became savvy entrepreneurs in the African slave trade itself: "White slave-owning women frequently did not need to go to the slave market because the slave market came to them."[36]

Historian James L. Roark offered the following observation: "Women planters were, of course, not new to the South, having been on the scene since the earliest Southern settlement. On the eve of the war, thousands of women legally owned plantations, and scores actually managed them. But for most women, total responsibility for a plantation was 'a new strange business.'"[37] According to Roark, circumstances for totally running a plantation fell to the planter's wife when the men departed for the war; beyond his statement that plantations "were owned by thousands of women" and managed by "scores," he offered no data on the extent of white female slaveholders, who most often became slaveholders through dowries and inheritances.

Although Jones-Rogers also did not offer any descriptive statistics (other than that they owned ten or more slaves) about the numbers of these female slaveholders, she offered powerful evidence that these women, the "mistresses of the market," exhibited a forceful independence and contribution, without assistance from their husbands or men in general, in almost the full spectrum of slaveholding. Historian Edward E. Baptist underscored the emerging power of the white female slaveholder in the 1840s: "Planter women's active support for proslavery positions increased dramatically during the 1840s, in both private letters and public writings."[38] Baptist emphasized that these women seized upon the personal economic benefits of slaveholding. Slave ownership gave these women wealth, power, and station, amounting to a clear motivation to maintain and push the slavery system.

Jones-Rogers's work dispelled the stereotype image of the vulnerable southern belle, most commonly thought of as isolated and fearful in the Big House, herself a victim, dependent on the largesse and whims of Marse, her husband, and seeking an alliance at times with the Black Mammy, who was significant in helping to raise the mistress's children. To the contrary, these women were not cowed by fears of slave rebellions nor dominated by a sadistic overseer:

> For them, slavery was their freedom. They created freedom for themselves by actively engaging and investing in the economy of slavery and keeping African Americans in captivity. Their decisions to invest in the economy of slavery, and the actions that followed those decisions, were not part of a grand scheme to secure women's rights or gender equality. Nevertheless, slave ownership allowed southern women to mitigate some of the harshest elements of the common law regime as it operated in their daily lives.[39]

ARDENT SLAVEHOLDING DEFENSE

Despite the male majority among southern slaveholders, there is compelling historical evidence that this group of white southern females was a significant force in the maintenance and fierce defense of southern chattel slavery: "Of course, everyone knew forceful women, stern in rectitude, commanding in personality, but by no means were such formidable matrons recognized as part of a formal matriarchy. They held power by virtue of willfulness, not prescriptive right."[40] These women teamed up with the proslavery divines from their churches and temples and helped to orchestrate a most formidable argument that southern slavery was God-blessed freedom. Unless a successful argument can be made that the white slaveholding mistress was under some kind of spell or suffering from some type of persecution syndrome—such as the Stockholm Syndrome—then why would these women defend, encourage, and promote a system that enslaved and oppressed them?[41]

Louisa McCord (1810–1879), born Louisa Susanna Cheves in Charleston, South Carolina, was perhaps the most formidable southern female proslavery defender. As Karp described McCord, "Born and married into the highest grade of South Carolina planter aristocracy, McCord distinguished herself as a poet, playwright, and essayist.[42] In the 1850s she emerged as perhaps the most aggressive defender of slavery in the South."[43] Between 1849 and 1856, she published articles on "political economy, women's rights, and slavery in the

Southern Quarterly Review, De Bow's Review, and *Southern Literary Messenger;* also fugitive poems in the *Southern Literary Gazette.*"[44] Here is a sample of her voice (written in 1851 and reviewed in *De Bow's Review* in 1852) in a chapter entitled "Negro-mania":

> If the negro be an inferior man, the struggle against God's will, which aims at putting him upon the same footing as the superior, is not only impious work in so far as it is a blind and foolish one . . . we find vicious malevolence and ignorance combining their power to raise some higher law than any which God has sanctioned; and because the Black man cannot reach the level of the white, they would even drag down and degrade the white to *his* capacities.[45]

ANCHORING THEIR RIGHTS

An argument can be made that many of these women initiated or were the recipients of legal actions that were precursors to American family law policies. Because enslaved people were recognized as valuable property, these women often successfully established legal protections for their sole ownership of their enslaved property, with the help of their families, legal counsel, churches—the courts of Jesus Christ—and the courts. These white mistresses may not have been at the helm of the ship of state, but they clearly did "their own bossing" when it came to protecting their property rights, by utilizing prenuptial and postnuptial agreements, wills, codicils, deeds, mortgages, insurance policies, judgments from their congregations, and contracts: "Laws dating back to the colonial period routinely recognized that mistresses owned enslaved people in their own right, and these same laws acknowledged the fact that these women were capable of exercising mastery over the enslaved people they owned."[46]

Jones-Rogers described slaveholding mistresses as a group of relatively liberated women who were not dismayed or stymied by the commonly understood male-dominated patriarchy of the antebellum South. Although they may not have felt dismayed or stymied, they undoubtedly developed a huge reservoir of emotions about their role as second-class citizens. As girls, they were raised in the care of enslaved people, usually female, whom they often owned. As young women, they learned the slavery business through their families. Their fathers often instructed their daughters on how to discipline their enslaved people, sometimes brutally.

Mothers and their daughters sometimes punished an enslaved person together. This kind of family-based ethic most certainly laid the groundwork for psychopathological bonding between white slaveholding parents and their white children: "They came to understand that there was no inherent chasm between violence and ladyhood in everyday life, even in the eyes of white patriarchs. They also learned that the intimacies that might have been forged between a white slaveholding child and her Black enslaved companion over the years made no difference to the power that their society accorded to this young white girl over her racial 'inferiors.'"[47] Historian William L. Andrews cited the 1862 narrative of John Andrew Jackson (c. 1825–1896), a fugitive slave from South Carolina:

> [Jackson] remembered what his plantation mistress did to keep her domestic slaves in a state of perpetual fear. "She would tie the female slaves, who did the domestic work, to trees or bedposts, whichever was handiest, and whip them severely with a dogwood or hickory switch, for the slightest offence, and often for nothing at all apparently, but merely for the purpose of keeping up her practice. She would also make her daughters whip them, and thus she brought up her children in the way they should go, and in consequence, when they were old enough they did not depart from it."[48]

These young white female slaveholders quickly learned that slavery brought them financial power and independence. Owning humans at an early age—through gifts or inheritance—gave them a unique autonomy. When they married, which they usually did, they did not have to live under the protective cover of their spouse, because these women owned Black people outright. Some of these white women saw the value in breeding the enslaved. Jones-Rogers wrote about the story of the enslaved family of F. H. Brown, whose enslaved grandmother "bore twenty-six children during her lifetime."[49] As Andrews noted, "Female slaves were also advertised and sold as articles for 'the fancy trade' (to cater the purchaser's sexual agenda) or as 'breeders,' women whose fertility could increase their asking price irrespective of the kind of work they could do."[50]

In its final analysis, Jones-Rogers's portrait of white female slaveholders was not pretty. These women were keen on making money from slavery, they "conducted transactions with slave traders, who bought slaves and sold slaves to them as they lounged comfortably within the confines of their own homes."[51] These women often brought their own personal and legal ownership of slaves to a marriage and worked smartly and successfully to protect their enslaved property.

Jones-Rogers argued that the WPA interviews provide a picture of just how much these "mistresses" impacted their enslaved people's lives.[52] For example, a former slave named W. L. Bost, who was interviewed at age eighty-eight in 1937, had this to say about the protection she and other enslaved people received from her plantation mistress:

My mother and grandmother both belonged to the Bost family. My ole Massa had two large plantations [near Newton, North Carolina]. It took a lot of niggers to keep the work goin' on them both. . . . Old Missus she was a good woman. She never allowed the Massa to buy or sell slaves. There never was an overseer on the whole plantation. The oldest colored man always looked after the niggers. We niggers lived better than the niggers on the other plantations.[53]

A CERTAIN CRUELTY

The Bost interview transcript does not mention any punishment, so it is inconclusive from his account as to whether the slaves on the Bost plantations were flogged or not. We do not know if the interviewer asked any questions about punishments. Fox-Genovese informed us of the omnipresent necessity of the slaveholder's whip: "Mistresses, even the kindest, commonly resorted to the whip to maintain order among people who were always supposed to be on call; among people who inevitably disappointed expectations; among people whose constant presence not merely as servants but as individuals with wills and passions of their own provided constant irritation along with constant, if indifferent, service."[54]

Curiously, Oakes's descriptive statistics (described above) about these mistresses did not address this seemingly unusual but apparently prevalent behavior—the comparatively brutal treatment of their slaves—that appears to have been normative among this group and seems also to differentiate these female slaveholders from the men. Although Oakes pointed out that these women constituted 10 percent of the slaveholding class, he did not mention them as perpetrators of punishment of their enslaved people.[55] Numerous other historians do state that white slaveholding women frequently exhibited a degree of cruelty that often exceeded their male slaveholding counterparts.[56] Jones-Rogers wrote, "Henry Watson proclaimed of his mistress, 'She seemed to take delight in torturing—in fact, she made it a pastime; she inspired everyone with her terror.'"[57]

Commenting on the general circumstances of southern women in the early nineteenth century, John Chester Miller noted:

Permitted little share in the amusements and no share whatever in politics of males, and surrounded by a small circle of household slaves, women tended to become indolent, self-indulgent, frustrated, and unhappy—and quite tyrannical to their slaves as were their husbands, brothers, and fathers. The slowdown and the "playing dumb" resorted to by some slaves as a form of passive resistance to slavery exasperated the wife of William Byrd

II to such a degree that she lashed the slaves herself and had to be restrained by her husband from doing them serious physical harm.[58]

Andrews related the experiences of former slave "Box" Brown, who in his 1851 narrative, reported that his wife was abused by her Richmond master's wife, "because the mistress found displeasure in her servant's manners 'as too refined for a slave.'" The mistress's displeasure eventually reached a point that she directed her husband to sell Box's wife.[59]

Frederick Douglass described the brutal murder of his wife's cousin, a young girl between fifteen and sixteen, by the wife of Giles Hicks, "mangling her person in the most horrible manner, breaking her nose and breastbone with a stick, so that the poor girl expired a few hours afterward."[60] The coroner determined the girl died from this severe beating. Her offense? Falling asleep and not hearing Mrs. Hicks's baby crying. All three—the slave girl, Mrs. Hicks, and the baby—were in the same room, but Mrs. Hicks became enraged at the enslaved girl for being so slow to respond. Noted Douglass, "There was a warrant issued for her arrest, but it was never served."[61]

Douglass related another circumstance in which a female slaveholder was cruel to two female slaves, Henrietta, aged twenty-two, and Mary, about fourteen,

> and of all the mangled and emaciated creatures I ever looked upon, these two were the most so. [The master's] heart must be harder than stone, that could look upon these unmoved. The head, neck, and shoulders of Mary were literally cut to pieces. I have frequently felt her head, and found it nearly covered with festering sores, caused by the lash of her cruel mistress. I do not know that her master ever whipped her, but I have been an eyewitness to the cruelty of Mrs. Hamilton.[62]

Historian Jane Turner Censer related a story about "Sarah Alston, a great [North Carolina] planter's widow, [who] wrote her grandson about the carriage her carpenter had built for him and indicated she was not adverse to seeing it drawn by slave youngsters: '[the carpenter] put two seats in your carriage, so little brother might ride with you, I reckon it will take all your little waiting men to pull it, unless you *hitch the old grey*.'"[63]

Historian Theodore Weld described the 1839 testimony of a former slaveholder, Dr. David Nelson, a family physician: "I was one day dressing a blister, and the mistress of the house sent a little Black girl into the kitchen to bring me some warm water. She probably mistook her message, for she returned with a bowl full of boiling water; which her mistress no sooner perceived, than she thrust her hand into it, and held it there until it was half-cooked." Weld cited another example, from the testimony of Mr. John

Clarke, a New York resident and member of the Presbyterian church, speaking in reference to Mistress Turner, wife of the Honorable Fielding S. Turner, Judge of the Criminal Court in New Orleans: "I repeatedly heard while in Lexington, Kentucky, during the winter of 1836–7, of the wonton cruelty practised by this woman upon her slaves, and that she has caused several to be *whipped to death*. . . . I was repeatedly told while I was there, that she drove a colored boy from the second story window, a distance of 15 to 18 feet, on to the pavement, which make [*sic*] him a cripple for a time."[64]

Harriet Jacobs, formerly enslaved, described another horrible cruelty exhibited by these white mistresses: "Southern women often marry a man knowing that he is the father of many little slaves. They do not trouble themselves about it. They regard such children as property, as marketable as the pigs on the plantation; and it is seldom that they do not make them aware of this by passing them into the slave trader's hands as soon as possible, and thus getting them out of their sight."[65]

Although it was Marse who understandably gets identified as the sexual predator in the historiography of racist slavery, Jones-Rogers points to an additional type of dehumanizing abuse—sexual exploitation—of female slaves perpetrated by white slave owning women: the slave-based brothel.

> Slave-owning women who set enslaved women to work in the "negro brothels" also benefited from their engagement in slave-market activities, and their livelihoods brought the markets in slaves and sex together. . . . Acting as brothel keepers, white women initiated the sexual violence against enslaved women, and acting as mistresses of the household they personally orchestrated acts of sexual violence against enslaved women and men in hopes that the women would produce children who would augment their wealth.[66]

How can it be explained psychologically that white female slaveholders were often more abusive, perhaps more prone to being cruel, than their male counterparts? *Merriam-Webster's* notes that cruelty is derived from the word "cruel," which it defines as "disposed to inflict pain or suffering: devoid of humane feelings."[67] The philosopher David Livingstone Smith says we best understand what cruelty means when we see it as a deliberate act to cause harm.[68] Any hypothesis addressing this question must be based on understanding that these women were mistresses—quasi rulers—of "the Big House," or household, no matter its particular configuration. When the male planter—the patriarch—was an absentee master, with or without an overseer, these women were most often the plantation home's chief operating officer or "junior partner." The plantation household (not the field or crop work) was their dominion, and the house staff was composed most often of more female slaves

"Ladies Whipping Girls." *Photograph of woodcut from* Pictures of Slavery in the United States of America, *1834, p. 109, Library of Congress*

than male slaves. If we think of their cruel punishments as manifestations of psychological and behavioral defense mechanisms, then it is clear that their frequently extreme behaviors toward their enslaved people were seriously maladaptive, if not psychotic.

A sadistic female slaveholder who herself felt victimized, regardless of whether or not she was a victim of someone or something, might be prompted by an impulse to exercise her uncompromising power as a means of compensating for her subjective experience of feeling victimized. Objectively, there were certainly slaveholding women who were victims of domestic violence within their marriages. It could be argued that a female enslaver who was herself a domestic violence victim was striking out at her own denied, but painful, subservient self. Severe punishment of Black people—especially enslaved females—in this instance was but cathartic rage. This overwhelming rage could override the customary reluctance of most slaveholders to personally administer severe punishment: "By delegating brutal forms of mastery to subordinates, slave-owning men and women cleansed themselves of the dark taint that subsequently stained the men who carried out their orders."[69]

In her powerful book *Killers of the Dream*, author Lillian Smith offered another perspective explaining the white female slaveholder's vengeful rage. Smith's narrative was somewhat in accordance with Clinton's view of these mistresses as victims. Smith painted these mistresses as women experiencing a unique type of slavery-generated domestic victimization. Many of these white women bore the pain and humiliation, as Smith wrote, "that her child preferred Mammy to her and that was fine, wasn't it, for it gave her so much more time to attend to all she had to do? . . . This giving up of one's men and one's childhood to colored women—for the girl-child was shaped as subtly as little boys by the nurse-mother relationship—took on the unreal, shadowy quality of a dream; a recurring dream that southern white women could not rid themselves of. "[70] It is not hard to imagine that a white female slaveholder, stuck inside this "shadowy dream," might develop some deliberate fantasies of cruelty. Smith described the white mother's mental condition as a shameful sore, as a wound that could not be acknowledged. One can imagine that a female house slave's transgression—a minor household accident perhaps—could be perceived as something more serious or threatening by the white mistress. Perhaps this mistress became tormented by her own identity confusion: Who really ran this house? One can imagine that she developed a strong paranoid streak in her character. Her trust dissolved. Resentment pathologized into rage. Her rage could erupt without warning, or her rage could slowly coalesce, coiling into a deliberate act of cruelty. Again, quoting from Smith's analysis of these mistresses' world:

> We cannot forget that their culture had stripped these white mothers of profound biological rights, had ripped off their inherent dignity and made them silly statues and psychic children, stunting their capacity for understanding and enjoyment of husbands and family. It is not strange that they became vigilant guardians of a southern tradition which in guarding they often, unbeknownst to their own minds, avenged themselves on with a Medea-like hatred.[71]

A white slaveholding mistress could impulsively kill her Mammy or one of Mammy's children or one of Mammy's extended family, or sell Mammy's husband, with almost no negative consequence and certainly with no expected, accurate explanation. If the mistress wanted to be exquisitely cruel and maximize harm, she could demonstrate her authority and sell her Mammy's child down the river, ripping Mammy's family apart. The mistress thus might convince herself that, for a time, she had settled the score.

EXTRAMARITAL PREDATION

The plantation held even darker secrets, which could and did generate homicidal rage or at least cruel fantasies of intentional harm. In addition to losing their children to the tender nurturance and mercies of the Mammy, they lost their husbands, brothers, sons, and other male kin or potential suitors to the Black seductress, these slave women whose children became lighter and lighter in skin tone. Marse, "succumbing to desire, . . . mated with these dark women and fathered children who, according to [the masters'] race philosophy, were 'without souls'—a strange exotic new kind of creature, whom they made slaves of and sometimes sold on the auction block."[72] Chattel slavery did not bring only freedom and leisure to the Big House, although there were times when the gaiety was real. It brought a companion shadow: marital misery, deceit, heightened immorality, treachery, and so-called mulatto children. Fantasy displaced truth. What was really going on was swept out the back door.

Marse might have told himself that his wife took no notice when he purchased an attractive fifteen-year-old enslaved girl—"a fancy"—at the market and gave her a special place in *his* household. The abandonment rage his wife must have felt by his unilateral, cruel, narcissistic, and predatory action was likely palpable. His mistress-wife was faced with the daily presence and special status of her husband's sexual mistress. Johnson called the question:

> Whether they were buying these high-priced women to be their companions or simply their toys, these slaveholders showed that they had the power to purchase what was forbidden and the audacity to show it off. . . . As Mary Chestnut put it, sex between slaveholding white men and their female slaves was "the thing we can't name . . . Every lady tells you who is the father of all the mulatto children in everybody's household, but those in her own she seems to think dropped from the clouds or pretends so to think."[73]

The reaction Chestnut described—the mistress ignoring or denying the presence of a light-skinned child with her husband's eyes and hair color being right in front of her—is known in psychology as an autistic fantasy, which is defined as "excessive daydreaming as a substitute for human relationships or more direct and effective action in dealing with conflicts or stressors."[74]

In her biography of Louisa S. McCord, author Leigh Fought gave us a stark example of the denial used by some plantation mistresses—in this case, her subject the outspoken McCord, a plantation owner in her own right—in the face of "the violent behavior of masters towards their slaves. This violence took many forms, of which the most common and visible were rape and beating."[75] According to Fought, within the body of McCord's relatively extensive analysis of the subject of slavery, she does not mention miscegenation: "Despite her dread of racial amalgamation, she failed to observe the existing amalgamation from masters' sexual abuse of their female slaves. The subject of miscegenation lay somewhere between a taboo and a source of rage for most southern women."[76]

In one of his three autobiographical narratives, Douglass described male slaveholders who often had a "double relation of master and father" to their female slaves. He went on to write that this double relationship was "a constant offense to their mistress. She is ever disposed to find fault with them, they can seldom do anything to please her; she is never better pleased than when she sees them under the lash, especially when she suspects her husband of showing his mulatto children favors which he withholds from his Black slaves."[77] Douglass went much further, pointing out that this growing population of mixed-race children ironically became a broadside against the racist Curse of Ham myth culled from Genesis 9:18–25: "Every year brings with it multitudes of this class of slaves [fathered by white men]."

Portrait of Frederick Douglass. *National Museum of African American History and Culture, Washington, DC. Photograph by the author*

Douglass deftly untied the scriptural knot between racist scripture and African slavery:

It was doubtless in consequence of a knowledge of this fact, that one great statesman of the south predicted the downfall of slavery by the inevitable laws of population. Whether this prophecy is ever fulfilled or not, it is nevertheless plain that a very different-looking class of people are springing up in the south, and are now held in slavery, from those originally brought to this country from Africa; and if their increase will do no other good, it

will do away the force of the argument, that God cursed Ham, and therefore American slavery is right. If the lineal descendants of Ham are alone
to be scripturally enslaved, it is certain that slavery in the south must soon
become unscriptural; for thousands are ushered into the world, annually,
who like myself, owe their existence to white fathers, and those fathers
most frequently their own masters.[78]

A rejected white slaveholding mistress probably would not risk torturing or killing her husband's "fancy," but she plausibly would easily become
enraged at one of her own female slaves as a type of object substitution. She
might suspect or make up out of whole cloth that this other woman sometime
in the past had been with her husband too. She could suddenly become a fem-
inine tyrant—a veritable Medea—and frame in her mind this bound woman
as nothing but a subhuman beast. Her husband might have to intervene in her
atrocious actions, but his entitlement, narcissism, or possible autistic fantasy
would not allow him to ponder the depth or source of his wife's rage.

Douglass described another of his experiences while enslaved in Baltimore in approximately 1827, when he was about eight or nine years old. His
master's wife, Sophia Auld, was long a kind mistress who had begun teaching
him to read and write. "[H]er face was made of heavenly smiles," Douglass
wrote, "and her voice of tranquil music." But that changed after she was
severely admonished by her husband for that kindness—and became a different, cruel person.

As Douglass wrote,

> Slavery soon proved its ability to divest her of these heavenly qualities.
> Under its influence, the tender heart became stone, and the lamb-like
> disposition gave way to one of tiger-like fierceness. The first step in her
> downward course was in her ceasing to instruct me. She now commenced
> to practice her husband's precepts. She finally became even more violent
> in her opposition than her husband himself. She was not satisfied with
> simply doing as well as he had commanded; she seemed anxious to do
> better. Nothing seemed to make her more angry than to see me with a
> newspaper.[79]

This cohort of white southern female slaveholders was a force. They
were a powerful minority. Not only did they achieve independence and financial gain from the enterprise of slavery, some of these women were chattel
slavery's greatest proponents. As historian Jones-Rogers emphasized,

> Scores of formerly enslaved people provided a different understanding of
> the institution of slavery, their female owners' knowledge of its workings,
> the part these women had played in their continued subjugation, and the

reasons many white southern women were so adamantly opposed to its abolition. And the white women's economic investments in slavery lay at the heart of such accounts. . . . Time and time again, with their slaves not far from hearing, white slave-owning women articulated their wish to remain invested in slavery and pass their financial legacies on to their children.[80]

This sketch of the white southern female slaveholder addresses some of the complicated issues she dealt with and suggests various hypotheses as to why psychologically she directed or engaged in extreme cruelty toward her enslaved people. The ultimate question of how she could justify owning another human being and her crime against humanity must be addressed in the reader's mind in the same context as these questions are analyzed and explained pertaining to the white male elite slave masters in other chapters of this book. She was a product of the same sectional, political, social, economic, and familial fabric and, while her role was most often different from the male's role, she developed adaptive and maladaptive defense mechanisms of her own.

I have made no effort here to dive deeply into the collective lives of these white mistresses. Nevertheless, I came away with some observations and opinions that may have some merit. I don't think Clinton's thesis of these women as victims can be totally dismissed, but I do think she is wrong in suggesting that all these mistresses were victims, "slaves of slaves." My argument is that, while there were undoubtedly some white female slave owners who were victimized and brutalized—particularly if they had the misfortune of marrying a pathologically prideful, tyrannical patriarch prone to excessive alcohol consumption and violence—there existed a group who were relatively independent and did not feel victimized.

Nevertheless, these slaveholding mistresses, when compared with non-slaveholding mistresses, led complicated lives, circumscribed by the racist slavery industry. All of their relationships were affected—often negatively—by slavery, and they had few levers of control. They also had little education. After their husbands' deaths and after inheritance issues or estate settlements were completed, most of these women continued their lives as if they were male masters. All they knew was to keep going, and their unhappiness, as it sprang forth from time to time, was 100 percent focused on the enslaved.

Fox-Genovese and Jones-Rogers independently made a compelling argument that the majority of white female slave owners were a strong force that enjoyed the benefits of slavery, defended it, and advocated for the institution. Based on my research of the female slaveholders' male counterparts, I agree. These plantation mistresses were invested in slavery's economic power and its personal and sectional generation of wealth. This personal and sectional investment came with a heavy price.

It seems self-evident that in order to understand these white slave-owning mistresses, we must make judgments about their words and behaviors as human beings in their own right and how they acted with and toward people they enslaved and held prisoners for life. At bottom, there was no kindness in slavery. No matter how kind a slaveholder might act toward her enslaved people, the relationship was a fraudulent one. Owning another person was a crime against humanity. There was clearly a continuum of behavior toward the enslaved that might run from kind and Christian on one end to brutal and sadistic on the other end. It is still a continuum of owning human beings for forced labor. A slaveholder, whether male or female, is someone who justified and defended owning other human beings.

• 4 •

Common and Idiosyncratic Enslaver
Psychological Defense Mechanisms

A NATURAL HUMAN DEFENSE

Over the course of more than thirty-five years as a clinical and forensic psychologist, I concluded that human behavior is best defined as "what people say and do." Furthermore, it is most often true that how people act is more valid than what they say. Human behavior provides external factors from which we can infer internal thoughts and emotions. Humans naturally and instinctively employ numerous psychological and behavioral methods, including defense mechanisms, to survive and attempt to control and negotiate the world. A defense mechanism essentially is an "automatic psychological process that protects the individual against anxiety and from awareness of internal or external stressors or dangers."[1]

In 1994 and 2000, the American Psychiatric Association identified thirty-one psychological defense mechanisms used by human beings to negotiate their way through the world and grouped these mechanisms into two types.[2] Type one is composed of eight adaptive defense mechanisms that help relatively healthy individuals deal with other people and society in effective ways. These eight are:

- Anticipation
- Affiliation
- Altruism
- Humor
- Self-assertion
- Self-observation
- Sublimation
- Suppression

A detailed description of these adaptive defenses is contained in appendix A.

Type two defense mechanisms are twenty-three defenses that are all, in one way or another, maladaptive. (These are listed in appendix A.) These maladaptive psychological mechanisms hinder or block the individual from interacting with others and society in healthy ways. These defenses range in degrees of severity along a continuum of functioning. For example, on the least severe end of the spectrum, a person may overly rely on intellectualization in his daily life, dealing with perceived threats to his well-being by excessively using abstract thinking. This individual tends to overgeneralize about people or events. On the severe end of the continuum, for example, an individual fails to suitably interact with others due to a gross distortion of reality. This individual denies objective experiences and perceives people and events through a psychotic distortion. A detailed description of these maladaptive defenses is also contained in appendix A.

Psychological defense mechanisms serve as connections to the human collective. All humans have them, and because of this fact, we can make plausible inferences and accurate generalizations about people from identifying and analyzing the natural defenses expected to be employed in response to known or reasonably inferred "internal or external stressors or dangers."[3]

Because they are timeless, universally available to all human beings, and inherently part of what allows humans to function, defense mechanisms provide a model that can be appropriately applied toward a retrospective understanding of the psychology of the American southern white male elite slaveholder. If we take a situation that we know is common to a planter-class enslaver in the antebellum South, we can make some assumptions about how he would react. The slaveholder's mind becomes accessible to us.

When I began my research and analysis of the mind and behavior of the southern slaveholder, I realized just how unique becoming and being a racist slaveholder really was, a uniqueness that developed over time from America's precolonial period through the South's antebellum period. The South's brand of racist slaveholding had its peculiarities. I determined that using a cookie-cutter approach toward an understanding of these southern slaveholders, by simply applying all thirty-one twentieth- and twenty-first-century defense mechanisms to nineteenth-century racist slave masters, would not be accurate because such an approach would overlook or fail to capture specific maladaptive defenses that racist slaveholding, by its very nature and in that time, demanded of the enslaver.

Once I determined that racist slaveholding made peculiar, special demands on the slaveholder—demands intrinsic to racist slaveholding—I realized I needed to apply some poetic license to my psychological autopsy of the slaveholders' defenses. *Merriam-Webster's* defines poetic license as "a deviation from fact, form, or rule by an artist or writer for the sake of the effect gained."[4] Thus, as the reader will see, I have taken some liberties with the creation of some uncommon and unique descriptors of some of the maladaptive defenses manifested by southern slaveholders, while omitting the application of some conventional maladaptive defense mechanisms.

Despite the planter's wish to live in a peaceful place where bound labor toiled for his happiness and profits were high, the institution of slavery had a threatening underbelly. In the quotidian rhythms of plantation life, there were constant circumstances that challenged the master and mistress. To make my point, I ask the reader to consider the following scenario while becoming aware of the defensive coping responses you might feel if you were in the scenario.

Imagine a white southern elite enslaver and his family, living on a large, remote cotton planation in the low country coastal area of South Carolina in 1830. For purposes of generating his lucrative crop, the master imprisons seven hundred enslaved African Americans (mostly male) and houses them in wooden shacks—more like barracks—along the edges of the swamp that parallels the river. He and several white employees operate a slave labor camp. The working conditions for the enslaved are brutal, the punishment is harsh, and the environment is highly toxic due to mosquito-borne malaria.

Most days, of control necessity, the planter or his overseer must punish a slave perceived to be making some kind of trouble, such as being too slow to respond to a command or being too light on his quota of cotton. When the white planter and his family go to bed at night, each white person has to utilize various defense mechanisms to cope with the reality of his or her circumstance. If his children sometimes feel afraid or sad from watching one of their favorite enslaved companions thrashed, how do they cope? And if the planter sometimes finds it difficult to calm his children's fears or anger, or if the planter himself frets about a slave rebellion, what psychological defenses does the planter call upon or are brought to him unconsciously by his psyche?

The life of prominent South Carolina statesman, governor, US Senator, and elite slaveholder James Henry Hammond provides some significant examples. Circumstances at his 10,800-acre plantation, Silver Bluff, housing 147 slaves, most assuredly evoked internal anxieties in response to very real external events. As historian Drew Gilpin Faust informed us, Hammond and his slaves generally worked compromises between them to keep harmony,

> but for some Silver Bluff residents there could be no such compromise. Instead of seeking to avoid the domination inherent in slavery, these individuals overtly challenged it, turning to arson and escape as expressions

of open rebellion. Throughout the period of his management [of Silver Bluff], Hammond referred to mysterious fires that would break out in the ginhouse on one occasion, the millhouse or plantation hospital on the next. . . . Between 1831 and 1855, when he turned most record-keeping over to his sons, Hammond noted fifty-three escape attempts by his slaves.[5]

As Faust noted, according to Hammond's records, none of these escape attempts were successful. Most remained at large an average of forty-nine days. Hammond and his drivers forced the runaways to come back because Hammond disciplined the rest of the enslaved force—those who remained on the plantation: "On at least one occasion he determined to stop the meat allowance for the entire plantation until the runaways came in. In another instance, he severely flogged four slaves harboring two runaways."[6]

What can be inferred about Hammond's psychological defenses in light of his actions? By punishing his remaining slaves, he adaptively anticipates his solutions, and is clever and strategic, because he knows the enslaved community will inform the runaways what the consequences are to others. Punishing others is also a maladaptive defense, because he displaces his feelings about the runaways onto other, less threatening people.

Hammond was a meticulous man, illustrated by the detailed content of his manual of plantation management rules, "designed for use on a large estate in the 1840s and 1850s."[7] Hammond considered himself to be a kind man. In Hammond's own words, written primarily for his overseers' instruction, here's what he said about punishment of his enslaved labor: "The highest punishment must not exceed 100 lashes in one day & to that extent only in extreme cases. The whip lash must be one inch in width or a strap of one thickness of leather 1½ inches in width, & never severely administered. In general 15 to 20 lashes will be sufficient flogging. The hands in every case must be secured by cord. Punishment must always be given calmly & deliberately & never when angry or excited."[8]

Let's look at Hammond a bit further, in a different context. When Hammond discovered one of his slaves committed infidelity, thus causing trouble within the plantation's enslaved population, he acted as judge "and meted out whippings," noted in his 1840 diary entries.[9] Hammond, however, was a hypocrite. Hammond fathered two children with two different enslaved women, who "confronted not only the sexual and emotional demands of both their master and his son [Harry] and the implicit, if not explicit, threat of physical coercion but also the bitter resentment of Hammond's wife, who discovered his liaison and attempted to end it by demanding the sale or effective banishment of his slave mistresses."[10] In this example, a slaveholder was punishing enslaved individuals for their infidelity while at the same time sexually assaulting and impregnating two Black females, deceiving his wife and adding his own offspring to his enslaved population. If we assume Hammond was disturbed by his hypocrisy, he undoubtedly had to suppress these thoughts or feelings. He acted in an omnipotent way, both as a family judge with his enslaved people and as an entitled master. He probably worked hard to deny that his own sexual exploitation would cause his marriage any trouble.

These natural psychological defenses are necessary. As defined by the American Psychiatric Association, "defense mechanisms mediate the individual's reaction to emotional conflicts and to external stressors. Some defense mechanisms (e.g., projection, splitting, acting out) are almost always maladaptive. Others (e.g., suppression, denial) may be either maladaptive or adaptive, depending on their severity, their inflexibility, and the context in which they occur."[11]

This chapter examines the principal defense mechanisms American southern planter-class white male slaveholders most likely employed to negotiate the slavery-industrial complex in the midnineteenth-century antebellum South. My research identifies not only the most common adaptive and maladaptive defenses, but also posits eleven idiosyncratic (peculiar) defense mechanisms that I argue were developed by slaveholders because of the specific dynamics of slaveholding. I contend that these defensive mechanisms were specific to chattel slavery. By its very nature, acknowledged or not by individual slave masters, slavery created chronic stress for the enslaved and the enslavers. Marse's defense mechanisms allowed him, in his own interior being, to psychologically justify owning and controlling another person as property. In spite of the profits, the slavery-industrial complex was chronically stressful for the majority of slaveholders, stress they worked very hard to deny, conceal, and overcome when they could. Historian David Brion Davis observed, "Masters also uneasily sensed that circumstances might transform a truly loyal and devoted slave into a vengeful enemy. . . . To the outside world, Southerners presented a brave façade of self-confidence."[12]

Slaveholding caused the master to cross a moral barrier. At a fundamental level, slaveholding was stressful for both master and slave, but in highly different and unequal ways. The beginning point—the initial step—for a slaveholder was acquiring (usually through abduction, purchase, trade, or inheritance) a human, against that person's will, whom he now claimed as a capital asset. The master-enslaved relationship, such as it was, was based on coercive control and punishment. This initial step was a stressor that demanded that the white planter cross a moral threshold in order to own another human being. Marse not only had to control his enslaved chattel, but also had to manage his personal stress that immediately surfaced upon acquiring bound labor ownership.

SLAVEHOLDERS' ADAPTIVE AND MALADAPTIVE
PSYCHOLOGICAL DEFENSES

Most slave masters employed some reasonably predictable, contextually normative, and expected defense mechanisms upon which to ground their self-concepts as slaveholders. For example, Marse was well known for his affiliating good nature, his Christian altruism, his assertive prowess as a businessman, and as a man who could tell a humorous yarn. The southern planter was concerned about his image, engaged in successful impression management, and would most certainly have adaptively thought through his future business engagements. The slaveholding elites were intellectually sophisticated and cosmopolitan in their outlook.[13]

Slave masters developed a sharp eye and keen business sense about the slavery industry, local and worldwide. Historian Matthew Karp observed, "Southern elites kept the international politics of slavery under constant surveillance, tracking threats to slave property across the hemisphere and monitoring oscillations in global attitudes toward emancipation. . . . [S]laveholding leaders sought to keep pace with the constant strivings of the mid-nineteenth-century world—the expansion of commerce, the march of empire, the advance of science, and the reshaping of state power."[14] American slavery scholar Eugene Genovese noted that "the slaveholders were a well-educated class by the standards of nineteenth-century America and by those of much of Europe as well. Their religious, political, and social leaders were intellectually impressive and stood up well in comparison with their northern counterparts."[15] Historian Michael O'Brien agreed: "There were a great many men, and a very few women, who were interested in ideas. . . . They were lawyers, politicians, clergymen, planters, diplomats, teachers, newspaper editors: Sometimes several of these simultaneously. Most lived in cities and small towns, rather than on plantations."[16]

Regardless of their profession or station in life, the slaveholding elite developed effective business skills, a determination to run their own affairs, and a fondness for making money. Slavery became a cash-generating machine. As O'Brien summarized this southern slave master character trait: "The South had inherited from its founding statesmen a deep engagement with the management of money."[17]

Psychological defenses are woven into the human brain. Although the nomenclature and operational dynamics for defense mechanisms have evolved along with the modern fields of mental health and mental illness, their existence and interplay between humans and their emotional world are timeless and existed in the minds and behaviors of slaveholders. The gestalt of racist slavery generated various kinds of stressors between the enslaver and the enslaved. This chapter identifies and discusses the slaveholders' handling of these stressors through the lens of nineteenth-, twentieth-, and twenty-first-century psychological and psychiatric clinical experience and research, and infers the existence of the coping defense mechanisms, which were undoubtedly part of the slaveholder psyche.

For the white elite southern slaveholder, money and power were slavery's dark heart. As historian David Brion Davis pointed out, "In 1860, out of a white population of some eight million, roughly ten thousand families belonged to the planter 'aristocracy.' Fewer than three thousand families could be counted as owners of over one hundred slaves. Only one out of four white southerners owned a slave or belonged to a family that did."[18] Even though most southerners did not own slaves, many had an emotional investment in slavery, for many white men and women saw the potential of owning slaves as a means of increasing their status and worth.[19] "By the start of the Civil War, 6,000,000 enslaved people—men, women, and children—were held in bondage, the largest number in the history of the Western Hemisphere."[20]

These statistics might suggest that the numbers of large enslavers were so small as to be insignificant, but nothing could be further from the truth: "By the middle of the [nineteenth] century, Southern masters ruled over the wealthiest and most dynamic slave society the world had ever known. If slave labor had an international future, they would certainly command it."[21] These select, elite white slaveholders effectively used their defense mechanisms to keep their eyes on the prize: making money.

The white slaveholding elite—the slave master aristocrats—dominated the money, the land, poorer white farmers, most of the enslaved, and the power. Historian Stephanie McCurry, writing about the inequality of power and authority among white masters in the low country of antebellum South Carolina, argued,

> By any calculation, the planter elite in the Low Country controlled a greater proportion of wealth than its counterparts elsewhere in the South. In 1850, when the richest tenth of propertyholders in the plantation districts of the South Carolina Upcountry owned about 55 percent of the real wealth, their lowcountry counterparts owned a staggering 70 percent. Taken together, the top quarter of low country propertyholders claimed about 90 percent of the wealth, while the entire bottom half, in whose ranks the yeomanry were squarely placed, claimed less than 5 percent. . . . In 1850 the wealthiest planters in St. Peter's Parish (those who owned more than 500 acres and 100 slaves) controlled fully half of the improved acreage and owned almost half of the slaves, despite the fact that they constituted a mere 13 percent of farm operators.[22]

Historian Caitlin Rosenthal observed that "in 1860, more millionaires lived in the slave South than in the rest of the United States. The wealthiest plantation districts boasted concentrations of fortunes to match the wealthiest northern neighborhoods. . . . Planters earned these fortunes not despite slavery but because of it."[23] In order for the slavery-industrial complex to succeed, the elite slaveholders, out of necessity and will, made their psychological defenses work effectively, but as we know, these defenses led to tragedy.

SLAVEHOLDING GENERATED A MIXTURE OF DEFENSES

From my analysis, the elite slaveholder manifested most of the positive defenses that facilitate an individual's relatively successful interactions with others and society—and four primary maladaptive psychological defenses to defend and cope with chattel slavery: denial, projection, delusional projection, and rationalization. In addition, they manifested eleven uncommon, idiosyncratic psychological defenses that were slavery specific. The general horror and crime against humanity perpetrated by the slaveholders necessitated some unique psychological efforts to bind the self-inflicted, traumatic wounds of slaveholding. After an examination of the most common defenses employed by slaveholders, I will analyze the peculiar slavery-specific defenses.

FOUR COMMON, FREQUENTLY USED MALADAPTIVE DEFENSES

Denial

Denial is probably the most frequently used human defense mechanism. When an individual, consciously or unconsciously, employs denial, he or she engages denial as a central coping mechanism.[24] The most significant target of denial for the slave master was the peculiar institution of slavery itself. Slaveholders denied the objective reality of the negative effects of coercion, control, and domination that was at the heart of slavery. Slavery did not function out of loyalty; it worked because of fear, punishment, and coercion.

Whites' distorted perceptions of Blacks allowed them to deny their own brutality and the physical and sexual exploitation of Blacks. For the planter or mistress who took a direct role in the punishment of his or her enslaved people, such as whipping an enslaved person, this role of punishing to obtain behavioral compliance most assuredly took an emotional toll on the punisher. Denial allowed whites to maintain their self-image of religious piety and righteous, honorable moral character and to ignore or minimize any pain and suffering of the punished.

Projection

Projection consists of attributing to others those feelings and experiences that we personally *deny* having ourselves and that we usually repress by dismissing them from our awareness. Projection is well served by denial as a potent companion defense mechanism. Fear of slave rebellion was always in the back of the white slaveholder's mind. An enslaver who felt threatened by his slaves and used violence against them might adopt a Christian persona and bearing and project potential explosiveness and threats onto his slaves. Think of the preacher who sees and decries sin everywhere but denies having a sinful impulse himself. Although slave insurrections did happen across the Caribbean and the South, the slave master minimized or denied his own violence by projecting its potential source onto the enslaved.

Through projection, Marse deceived himself by mistakenly and conveniently imagining that his enslaved females directed lustful fantasies toward him. "People who deny or repress their own sexual impulses project them on others and rate others as more lustful than in fact they are," argued psychologists Martin E. P. Seligman and David L. Rosenhan in their textbook *Abnormality*.[25] "She wants me," a master might think before raping an enslaved woman. Through the unconscious use of projection, Marse could dismiss his sexually assaultive behaviors as nothing more than responding to a enslaved girl's sexual aggressiveness or seductiveness. I am not saying projection was the sole basis for excusing or explaining the sexual abuse of the enslaved; it was simply one psychological tool available. Such projection contributed to the mythology of the Black woman as Jezebel.

By casting the enslaved girl or woman into the role of Jezebel, Marse could righteously judge himself to be the seduced victim. In Christian scripture, Jezebel was "a woman of Thyatria who called herself a prophetess, and seduced some members of the Christian Church there to commit fornication and eat things sacrificed to idols."[26] Marse used maladaptive projection to distort a helpless, powerless enslaved girl or woman into a formidable seductress and to intellectually and emotionally distance himself from his own aggressive actions and any undesired consequences. If he coupled his projection with the aid of seriously maladaptive denial, he might be able to feign surprise upon the birth of his light-skinned baby by his enslaved child-concubine. By employing maladaptive denial, he might be able to successfully distance himself from any emotional pain his assaultive actions surely would have caused his wife, his family, and the enslaved woman and her people.

Distorted perceptions of Blacks allowed whites to deny their own brutality and physical and sexual exploitation of enslaved people. These distortions allowed whites to maintain their self-image of religious piety and righteous, honorable moral character. As history professor John Patrick Daly asserted, "Projection of the categories of saved and damned, good Christians and heathens, onto racial differences assured white believers they had achieved a proper measure of moral and spiritual elevation over the general run of God's creatures."[27] In the case of a sexual assault on an enslaved girl, Marse could conceal his true sexual predatory motives from himself, his wife, and his family by developing an elaborate, false, maladaptive projection coated in a rationalized explanation.

Delusional Projection

From the beginning of slavery and the slave trade in the American colonies, the masters' distorted view of Black Africans was shaped by a delusional projection, a psychological means by which the individual deceives himself by projecting false beliefs onto others.[28] Dynamically, the traits the slaveholders inaccurately saw—projected—in the enslaved were justified by delusional false beliefs. Delusional projection involves making incorrect inferences about external reality that run counter to the individual's beliefs. The earliest European slave traders saw the people of sub-Saharan Africa and the Native Americans as "incomparably primitive."[29] "Primitive" is the lowest rung on the alleged ladder of human hierarchy. This delusional projection allowed Europeans to dismiss or misunderstand many of the advanced civilizations of southern Africa. Seeing Black Africans as inferior, more animal-like than human-like, allowed Europeans to assure themselves of their superiority.

The perceived "savage" or "heathen" aspect of Blacks provided a complex psychological mechanism for the white slave master. As psychologist Philip Zimbardo observed, "We fear evil, but are fascinated by it. We create myths of evil conspiracies and come to believe them enough to mobilize forces against them. We reject the 'Other' as different and dangerous because it's unknown, yet we are thrilled by contemplating sexual excess and violations of moral codes by those who are not our kind."[30] Quoting religion scholar David Frankfurter on the social construction of the evil other, Zimbardo clarified how this delusional projection of the "other" works:

> [T]he construction of the *social* Other as cannibal-savage, demon, sorcerer, vampire, or an amalgam of them all, draws upon a consistent repertoire of symbols of inversion. The stories we tell about people out on the periphery play with their savagery, libertine customs, and monstrosity. At the same time, the combined horror and pleasure we derive from contemplating this

Otherness—sentiments that influenced the brutality of colonists, missionaries, and armies entering the lands of those Others—certainly affect us at the level of individual fantasy as well.[31]

The fantasy-driven beliefs that white men and women held about Black male Africans were a slightly different twist on the mechanism of delusional projection. For example, within their delusional projection, they imagined Black males' alleged excessive, insatiable sex drive and predilection for raping white women. The master's delusional projection fed his imagination while simultaneously protecting him from acknowledging his own sexual predations. It was a repetitive psychological tool used to drive white men to brutal, sadistic treatment of Black males. The testicles were often the target or physical site of sadistic abuse and murder of Black males who were lynched. Targeting of Black male genitalia symbolized domination for the slaveholder and utter humiliation and defeat of the enslaved man. Historian Walter Johnson described the horrors of sexual predation in the world of some slaveholders: "Behind closed doors, in outbuildings, or in the woods at the margins of the fields, the choreography of service, surveillance, and space defined a landscape of sexual violence. . . . In *Humphreys v. Utz*, the Supreme Court of Louisiana [in 1853] quietly determined the guilt of a slaveholder who had nailed an enslaved man's penis to the bedpost in the owner's room."[32]

The choices of the type and severity of punitive measures inflicted on the enslaved often were stimulated by the slaveholder's delusional projection. Addressing the dynamics of punishment of the enslaved in the seventeenth century, historian Peter Kolchin informed us that "slaves who transgressed could look forward to a wide range of gruesome punishments—most imposed informally by owners and overseers but some officially meted out upon sentence by special slave courts that existed in all Southern colonies—including branding, nose splitting, amputation of ears, toes, and fingers (and less often of hands and feet), castration, and burning at the stake."[33] Over time, slaveholders decreased their use of severe forms of punishment, although they did not disappear entirely, as the Louisiana case above illustrates. By the second half of the eighteenth century, extreme punishments "not only were far less common than they had been but also met with widespread public disapproval; it became unfashionable to boast of cruelty to one's slaves. Instead, many slave owners began to talk about how much they cared for them."[34] And just because they stopped boasting about their cruel punishments, did not mean these cruelties ceased altogether.

As societal pressures began to condemn overt cruelty and torture of slaves, the planter enslaver developed the delusional projection that slavery would expand because it was the most benign way to manage labor. The masters strengthened their psychological defense by imagining that the enslaved were part of their family. As historian Kenneth M. Stampp noted, "By the 1830's the fateful decision had been made. Slavery, now an integral part of the southern way of life, was to be preserved, not as a transitory evil, an unfortunate legacy of the past, but as a permanent institution—a *positive good*. To think of abolition was an idle dream. Now even native Southerners criticized the peculiar institution at their peril."[35]

Marse developed a delusional belief that slavery, as the best capitalist system in the world, would come to dominate the world's markets. This distortion was partially responsible for convincing Marse that France and England would support the South should war come. Karp made a keen point about southern slaveholders' world economic vision:

> Unlike London financiers or New York railway executives, the leading men of the South could not envision a global future without the fundamental institution of African slavery. Their continents were to be civilized with the enforced toil of dark-skinned workers, and their oceans were to be opened as highways to the rich produce of bound labor. . . . For the southern masters who celebrated it, slavery could claim a distinguished history, a flourishing present, and a glorious future. In both the American world they made and the global order they craved, southern elites understood the growth of slavery as no more and no less than "the true progress of civilization."[36]

This projected delusional view of racist slavery's unassailable supremacy would eventually drag Marse's mind into a psychotic distortion.

Rationalization

On a grander, collective scale, a powerful minority group of elite enslavers perfected the coldest and most calculated rationalization: Slavery was just business. This was a rationale held by many of America's founders, North and South. Slavery as business became the perfect engine of the Southern political economy. Slaveholding "united the interests of capital and labor," proclaimed John C. Calhoun in an 1838 speech to Congress.[37] Southern planters validly perceived that the number of Northern men and many international entrepreneurs in other parts of the world—particularly England—were complicit in reaping the profits that flowed from slave labor.

Southern slaveholders glossed enslavement with a false, noble veneer and disavowed any notions of meaningful harm to their enslaved people. As historian Edward E. Baptist captured it:

> Yet the massive and cruel engineering required to rip a million people from their homes, brutally drive them to new, disease-ridden places, and

make them live in terror and hunger as they continually built and re-built a commodity-generating empire—this vanished in the story of a slavery that was supposedly focused primarily not on producing profit but on maintaining its status as a quasi-feudal elite, or producing modern ideas about race in order to maintain white unity and elite power.[38]

Some historians saw secession as protection of the South's economic system, "in which people were money."[39] Certainly not all, but most, elite slaveholders were morally corrupt capitalists. The elite Marse allowed profit to trump all else.

Slave masters lived on a rationalized platform that viewed Black bound labor as subhuman. They psychologically understood them to be property and legally codified them as property. These were not simply labor laws governing the bondsmen as workers. White slave masters publicly and proudly declared that Blacks were, by virtue of their being Black, slaves for life, and that their status was that of laborers held as property.[40] Southern state legislatures made it essentially impossible for any slaveholder, no matter his degree of slaveholding or social status, to emancipate slaves. All slaveholders had to abide by these laws. In this respect, slavery laws controlled whites too.

Southern theologian James Henley Thornwell delivered a sermon on May 26, 1850, in Charleston, South Carolina, that provided a brilliantly articulated, rationalized defense of slavery: "Explicitly written as a defense of the religious instruction of slaves, [his] sermon was in essence a philosophical vindication of slavery and a carefully reasoned demonstration of the Christian duties of masters. . . . The heart of Thornwell's sermon dealt with the question of the definition of slavery."[41] Departing from the commonly held belief that slaves were subhuman, Thornwell rationalized that slaves were human because they had a conscience, which could not be owned by another. What the master owned was the slave's labor. Slaves were obligated, said Thornwell, "to labour for another, determined by the Providence of God, independently of the provisions of a contract. . . . The right which the master has is a right, not to the *man*, but to his labour, the duty which the slave owes is the service which, in conformity with this right, the master exacts."[42]

Masters took out slave deeds, mortgages, and insurance policies on their enslaved persons, and commonly left them as property bequests in their wills or gave some enslaved as gifts to the masters' children. Historian Bonnie Martin described the use of purchase money mortgages and equity mortgages by slaveholders with slaves as the collateral: "During the eighteenth century residents [of St. Landry Parish] generated much more cash and credit using equity mortgages. More than two-thirds of the capital raised by these equity loans used slaves as all or part of the security."[43] Equating them with other nonhuman property allowed the slave master to dehumanize the slaves.

Historian Charles B. Dew explored the cadre of war-mongering commissioners—the "Apostles of Disunion"—who traveled the prewar South beating war drums. They embodied the southern elite's rationalization for secession and war by painting a convincing nightmare for the South if it remained with the Union.[44] The run-up to the war created considerable anxiety and ambivalence for many Southerners and for the nation as a whole. The move toward secession was an emotional crisis of epic proportions.

Many southern slaveholding elites were excited about leaving the Union. Faust captured the emotional reaction of Hammond, noting that Hammond was delighted and embraced secession: "'I went into it with all my Soul.' Once the first step had been taken, he insisted that no compromise should halt progress toward the southern confederacy that he still regarded as 'the cherished dream and hope of my life.' . . . Belittling the likelihood of war with the North, he confidently expected diplomatic recognition from England and France within forty days."[45] Hammond defiantly challenged the antislavery forces: "No, you dare not make war on cotton. No power on earth dares to make war upon it. Cotton is king."[46]

ELEVEN IDIOSYNCRATIC, SLAVERY-SPECIFIC PSYCHOLOGICAL DEFENSE MECHANISMS

The institution of racist chattel slavery created within the minds and actions of the white male elite southern slaveholders specific defense mechanisms necessary to cope with the realities of racist slavery's inhuman elements. These eleven defenses developed to protect the slaveholder from the many horrible realities of slaveholding. I have created the names of six defense mechanisms—listed first—that are unique to racist slaveholding. These descriptors will not be recognizable as common defense mechanisms in contemporary psychological or psychiatric terms, but they appear apt to understanding Marse's psychology. These racist, enslavement-centric terms are:

- A profound lack of self-criticism
- Psychopathy
- Christian comfort
- Psychologically syntonic slaveholding
- Paternalism
- Alienation

The remaining five—Black stereotypes, self-deception, splitting, psychopathological entitlement, and psychotic reality—have some of their historical roots in common psychiatric terminology.

BLACK STEREOTYPES

I begin with Black stereotypes because the application by antebellum whites of these characterizations of Blacks was so prevalent. Over time, four to five Black stereotypes of slaves developed among southern planters: "Sambo," "Nat," "Buck," "Mammy," and "Jezebel" characters. "Nat" and "Buck" were the same stereotype. Historian John Blassingame's research revealed another Black male figure, "Jack," the enslaved, who worked cooperatively as long as he was well treated.[47] These distinctive types became perfect objects upon which the planter could project all of his conscious and unconscious thoughts and feelings about slaves. Sambo and Nat became binary subtypes of the Black male African inferior heathen. Mammy and Jezebel thus too became conventional views of inferior Black females. As historian George Fredrickson pointed out, "What was truly universal about the Black stereotype was its inherently dichotomous or contradictory nature."[48] Quoting Phillip Curtin's description of planter ambivalence in Jamaica, Fredrickson wrote: "'The attitude of the master toward the slave was a combination of fear on the one hand, leading to the picture of the slave as the lazy savage and murdering brute, and a desire to justify the institution on the other, leading to the picture of the happy Negro, harmless but fitted only for his life of hard work.'"[49] The Sambo character became the most frequent and popular figure described by Southerners, an effort that gained considerable momentum beginning in the 1830s.[50] Sambo most frequently was the servant who met guests and visitors at the Big House.

Sambo (also known as "Uncle Remus," "Jim Crow," "Uncle Tom") was docile, passive, yes-suh, compliant, faithful, superstitious, and clownish. Nat (e.g., Nat Turner or Denmark Vesey) was untrustworthy, dangerous, sexual, rebellious, savage, and revengeful. Historian Stephen R. Haynes underscored this point: "Nat was the incorrigible runaway, the poisoner of white men, the ravager of white women who defied the rules of plantation society. [He was] subdued and punished only when overcome by superior numbers or firepower."[51]

In *Uncle Tom's Cabin*, Harriet Beecher Stowe portrays Sambo, a Black male slave, as a brutal, sadistic slave driver. Historian David Stefan Dodding-ton explains these seemingly contradictory images of Sambo: "Stowe painted Sambo as a leering and sadistic figure, but emphasized how such behavior only made sense in the context of his wider degradation: Simon Legree had trained his drivers 'in savageness and brutality as systematically as he had his bull dogs.'"[52] Mammy became the competent, wise Black woman who birthed the white and Black babies and healed the sick. Many white Southerners—adults and children—developed close relations to Mammy. This image was so central to the southern psyche that "the Daughters of the Confederacy suggested in

1923 that Congress set aside a site in Washington for a suitable memorial to the antebellum plantation Mammy."[53] Alison M. Parker noted that "the Senate passed it, but the bill stalled in the House after fierce opposition from Black women, including Mary Church Terrell and Hallie Quinn Brown, members of the National Association of Colored Women."[54]

The master made great efforts to repress the Nat character, but it remained quite alive in his consciousness, frequently stoking Marse's fear of being poisoned or having his throat cut. Real slave insurrections fed the content of the slaveholders' stereotypes. On August 21, 1831, Nat Turner, an enslaved Virginian, along with five of his "disciples," had mounted a violent and bloody revolt—a crusade, as they saw it—believing they had been given a task by God. Over a two-day period, Turner and "about seventy freed men" killed "at least fifty-seven enslavers across a twenty-mile path of destruction" before their rebellion was put down.[55] By late 1831, Nat became a demon in the elite slave master's mind.

SELF-DECEPTION

This particular defense had self-destructive effects on Marse. Self-deception is the psychological means by which an individual tricks or fools himself about something of significance. It is a process by which the person adheres to a belief, assumption, or action that seems self-protective but in reality is self-defeating. Self-deception is not the same as denial, which is the refusal by a person to accept something as real. Self-deception is more complicated, for the individual builds an inner narrative about the subject or issue in question and grounds the narrative on a foundation that will likely, over time, collapse and bring defeat to the individual. Enslavers viewed slaves as exhibiting friendship and loyalty, especially as the South moved toward secession. Genovese and Fox-Genovese identified a poignant example of this mental process: "Slaveholders grasped at every expression of slaves' goodwill as genuine. . . . Nothing pleased masters and mistresses more than to receive cheerful greetings from slaves."[56] Slave master Matthew Estes characterized the master-enslaved relationship this way in 1846: "One result of Southern Slavery should be mentioned . . . I allude to the nearness and kind sympathy which the relation engenders. This, on the part of the master, is heightened from a knowledge of the fact that the slave can never be his rival in any of the pursuits of life; consequently, there cannot exist the feeling of hostility and jealousy which rivalry often creates."[57] The objective reality white slaveholders missed is captured "in a song sung by generations of Negroes:

'Got one mind for white folks to see,
'Nother for what I know is me;
He don't know, he don't know my mind.'"[58]

The enormous self-deception the slave master had to employ to shield his senses and what conscience he had from the pain and rage of his slaves—over time—generated a palpable psychosis. This self-deception, in part, accounts for the widespread surprise among slaveholders when, at the end of the war, many of their slaves ran away. White church congregants were shocked that the slaves they had baptized and Christianized, who for generations had lived with their family, wished to leave the white churches and establish their own houses of worship.

Slaveholders convinced themselves that slavery elevated Black Africans above the degradations and barbarism of their original culture. Writing in his autobiography about the white man's enslavement of the Black man, Malcolm X addressed the self-inflicted damage whites had done to themselves. He was being critical of the effects of the white superiority complex on the white race: "But I want to tell you something. This pattern, this 'system' that the white man created, of teaching Negroes to hide the truth from him behind a façade of grinning, 'yessir-bossing,' and head-scratching—that system has done the American white male more harm than an invading army would do to him."[59]

Such a psychological sleight of hand was essential to keep the slave master unconscious of the emotional truth of his slaves and of slaveholding in general. A tear of despair in a slave's eye would be seen, out of self-deceptive, self-protective necessity, as a joyful tear. Despair and depression would be viewed as laziness and sloth. A slave suicide, killing him- or herself out of hopelessness, would be seen and ruled as an unfortunate accident or viewed simply as a financial loss. Exhibitions of anger by slaves were viewed as insolence and would not be tolerated. African slaves had no reason to be angry. The master, by God's grace, had reason to be angry when disobeyed. The master expected appreciation and loyalty. Punishment and anger were often fused in Marse's psyche.

Historian Willie Lee Rose observed that "Frederick Douglass once wrote that he had never heard a slave, while *still* a slave say that he had a bad master. White visitors were sometimes baffled by this phenomenon, but Ethan Allen Andrews [writing in 1836] . . . understood that a slave could not safely express himself on this matter, and concluded that slave-owners—all protests of slave loyalty aside—actually slept 'upon the verge of the volcano' of insurrection."[60] The defense of denial—in concert with self-deception—worked overtime to keep at bay possible paranoia about slaves breaking out of the slave labor camp.

Enslavers further deceived themselves with their view of slaves exhibiting friendship and loyalty—especially as the South moved toward secession.

Part of the self-deception was the masters' and mistresses' overreliance on the Sambo stereotype in defending themselves and the institution of slavery. Historian Stephanie E. Jones-Rogers illustrated the concern about image that some slaveholders, in this case a slaveholding mistress, exhibited: "According to Emmanuel [an enslaved individual], after parading all the enslaved children she owned in front of her plantation guests, her mistress would turn to her guests and ask, 'Ain't I got a pretty crop of little niggers coming on?'"[61] Stampp addressed the slaveholders' self-deceptive, immensely self-congratulatory view of their slaves' supposed contentment: "It may be a little presumptuous of one who has never been a slave to pretend to know how slaves felt; yet defenders of slavery did not hesitate to assert that most of them were quite content with servitude. Bondsmen generally were cheerful and acquiescent—so the argument went—because they were treated with kindness and relieved of all responsibilities; having known no other condition, they unthinkingly accepted bondage as their natural state."[62] South Carolinian slaveholder T. W. Hoit wrote in 1860, "If the African is entitled to his freedom, he is also entitled to the privilege of remaining in servitude; a privilege which nine tenths of the Negroes in this country are well known to crave. . . . His right to remain a slave is not his own, but the right of civilization."[63]

In another example of self-defeating self-deception, slaveholders convinced themselves they were genetically intellectually superior to African Americans. Philosopher David Livingstone Smith noted that proslavery advocates solved the dilemma created by founder and slaveholder Thomas Jefferson's words "all men were created equal" by rationalizing that enslaved Africans were not human: "By dint of a sleight of mind, the very men who insisted on the God-given right of all humankind to liberty could, in good faith, countenance and participate in the brutal and degrading institution of slavery."[64] Mary Boykin Chestnut wrote in her diary in 1861 as she listened to a white contemporary teaching Sunday school to enslaved children: "I sat there listening more than an hour. I know how hard it is to teach them, for I have tried it . . . I determined to wait until they developed more brains."[65]

Moreover, enslavers deceived themselves by creating romantic historical myths. For example, they contended that African Americans and Native Americans fought loyally side by side with whites in South Carolina's backcountry during the Revolutionary War. While there may have been some collaboration like this, historian James Oakes reminded us that Native Americans were being pushed out of their native lands and were also acquiring Black slaves: "As Southerners, [Native Americans] found their progress judged by their white neighbors according to the strength of their devotion to Black slavery. The prevailing test of successful colonization was the number of Native Americans who became slaveholders."[66]

Perhaps most insidiously, southern enslavers psychologically worked hard to convince themselves that a successful revolt by the enslaved was impossible. Almost every slave management method and procedure, including frequently applied violence as well as draconian laws and public policies, were designed to control Black people and ensure the dominance and safety of whites. Marse expended enormous psychic resources convincing himself and others that, despite a few rebellions among the enslaved, slavery would not only endure but also command the world stage. For the white Christian slaveholder, given that racist slavery was God given, it would be only God that would take it away.

Insurrections among some of the enslaved did occur, keeping white slaveholders on edge. The state of Georgia went so far as to try to keep its residents from bringing enslaved laborers into the state. Oakes pointed out that fears of slave insurrections were significant enough that as early as 1741, "a Georgia inquiry commission reaffirmed the colony's ban on slaves, 'for those

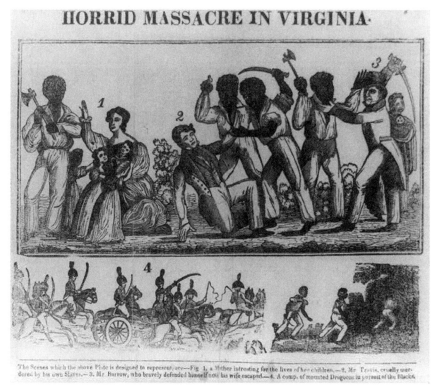

"Horrid Massacre in Virginia." *Composite scenes of Nat Turner's Rebellion. Photograph of woodcut, 1831. Library of Congress*

are all secret enemies.'"[67] In 1850, slaveholders put in place a fugitive slave law, and white communities established patrols, militias, and armories and major arms depots at the ready.[68] The Slave Rebellion web site asserts that between 1526 and 1864, there were 313 documented slave insurrections.[69]

Despite their fears of slave insurrections, some southern enslavers even assumed that Black slaves as a group would fight for the Confederacy when the time came, an assumption that became a grand delusion, adding to the morass of enslaver self-deception.[70] After an intense debate about using enslaved people in the Confederate army, the "Confederate government finally authorized the use of Black troops, but only reluctantly. In March 1865 [one month before the war ended], it passed a weak Black enlistment bill."[71] Using twisted, racist logic, the Confederacy gave slaves the freedom to fight for the Rebel cause but did not guarantee the slaves their emancipation if they did. Black troops never materialized. Those who did serve in the army were servants and menial laborers, and later were teamsters and cooks.

McCurry commented on the Confederacy's ambivalence about deploying Black troops: "Confederate politicians had begun the war boasting of slavery as an element of strength and admitting no concern about slaves' allegiance or potential opposition." However, McCurry points out that "by late 1863 some in high military circles were already acknowledging slavery as 'one of our chief sources of military weakness,' and slaves as the enemy within." She identifies "a wave of insurrectionary activity on the plantations that weakened their owners' nationalist commitment, thwarted every government effort to make their labor count militarily for the cause, and, in a dangerous, highly risky mass movement of people across the lines, transferred their military labor and service to the enemy."[72]

After initially suffering from the delusion that enslaved people would fight for them while remaining enslaved, slaveholders ultimately concluded and rationalized that Blacks were too cowardly to fight and would make inferior soldiers, despite significant, objective, historical data about Blacks as fighters to the contrary. Genovese addressed this racist criticism: "But Black soldiers had fought bravely for their country during the Revolution and especially during the War of 1812, when they won a ringing proclamation from Andrew Jackson for their bravery at the Battle of New Orleans."[73] Certainly, the North welcomed the mobilization of Black soldiers, although there was racial tension between Black and white Union soldiers. As historian Harry S. Stout noted, "Forty-two thousand Black men from the border states served in the army and 2,400 more in the navy. . . . In all, 180,000 to 200,000 Black soldiers fought for the North, with killed or wounded totaling 68,178, or more than one-third of the total engaged."[74]

SPLITTING

Splitting helped slaveholders emotionally and cognitively defend themselves by oversimplifying an industry of horrors. Splitting is a primitive defense mechanism with which the individual distorts and reduces his self-image, complex events, circumstances, or other people into simple categories, such as "good" or "bad," "good" or "evil."[75] Psychologically splitting an object—including a person—or situation or idea into simple, unrealistic terms is done without the benefit of reason or self-criticism. It is a mental process "consisting of the active dissociation of mutually contradictory feelings, perceptions, and ideas into 'all good' and 'all bad.'"[76] Splitting is an emotional oversimplification. Nowhere was the application of splitting more destructive to the southern elite slave master's mind than in the Christian Southerner's relationship to his or her God. The South, particularly its Presbyterian divines, split Christianity's God into two—a southern God and a northern God. Making God's allegiance simple offered a soothing defense of Southerners' prewar anxieties. Historian Mitchell Snay illustrated the proclaimed true religion position of the South:

> In accord with the interpretation of secession as an act consistent with American political values, southern clergymen claimed that the South was the true heir to the American tradition of civil religion. They took these two central expressions of this tradition, the idea of America as God's Redeemer Nation and the image of the United States as the New Israel, and reshaped them to apply exclusively to the South. . . . The South had become the Redeemer Nation and the New Israel.[77]

The North was psychically excised out of the spiritual picture. That's splitting at its worst.

Benjamin Morgan Palmer of New Orleans (1818–1902), one of the South's most prominent and powerful Presbyterian clergymen and proslavery advocates, gave a sermon on Thanksgiving Day 1860 in front of two thousand congregants. He was one of the founders of the *Southern Presbyterian Review* and was influential in establishing the Southwestern Presbyterian University in Memphis (now Rhodes College).[78] Snay quoted from Palmer's sermon: "In this great struggle, *we defend the cause of God and religion.*" To Palmer, said Snay, abolitionism was "undeniably atheistic."[79] Palmer's position that the atheist North was attacking the South's providential duty to administer slavery was a clear example of "splitting."

A PROFOUND LACK OF SELF-CRITICISM

Enslavers became psychopathologically blind to their own troublesome, self-defeating beliefs and behavior. Power, money, and bound labor caused Marse to lose his capacity for self-criticism or objective self-observation. Profit and greed sabotaged the slaveholder's ability to evaluate his own beliefs and actions. O'Brien pointed to the discipline of "political economy" that gripped the psyche of southern intellectuals and politicians, which allowed them to fend off antislavery broadsides.[80] As McCord, a southern woman, wrote in *De Bow's Review* in 1856, "Science cannot be swayed by prejudice and outcry. . . . All that is now needed for the defence of United States negro slavery and its entire exoneration, is a thorough investigation of fact, fact! fact! fact! . . . and Political Economy . . . will and must be our judge."[81] Historian James Hervey Smith defined economy "as the art of increasing the amount of human comfort and enjoyment, and diminishing the sum of human suffering and want, by the agency of wealth. Domestic economy is this principle applied to the cares of a family; political economy, the same system directed to national concerns."[82] In Marse's mind, a Black slavery-based domestic and political economy was best for the nation, and most assuredly for the Confederate nation.

John Caldwell Calhoun, eminent South Carolinian, US Senator, vice president, and slaveholder, was arguably one of the most eloquent and influential defenders of southern slavery. In two speeches given by Calhoun in 1836 and 1838, we can hear the self-defeating lack of self-criticism:

> "As for ourselves," he observed in 1836 when debating the abolitionist petitions, "I feel no apprehension . . . [A]s great as is the danger, we have nothing to fear if we are true to ourselves. We have many and great resources; a numerous, intelligent, and brave population; great and valuable staples; ample fiscal means; unity and feeling of interest, and an entire exemption from those dangers originating in a conflict between labor and capital. . . . With these impressions, I ask neither sympathy nor compassion for the slaveholding states. We can take care of ourselves."[83]

The South eventually chose a self-destructive path along the lines of Calhoun's persuasive, grandiose delusion.

PSYCHOPATHY

Some southern slaveholders developed psychopathy as a defense mechanism. A true psychopath is a person—generally a man—who for many reasons fails

to develop a conscience. He is not affected by his feelings. Guilt is not an emotional state that troubles the psychopath: "Psychopaths are without conscience
and incapable of empathy, guilt, or loyalty to anyone but themselves."[84]
Historian Matthew Talbert argued that the descriptor "morally blind agents"
is a synonym for psychopaths.[85] Many slaveholders demonstrated numerous
behaviors that would be consistent with the psychopathic individual identified
by Hervey Cleckley in his 1976 book *The Mask of Sanity*.[86] As the title implies,
these individuals portray a mask of sanity

> in which pervasive emotional deficits are hidden behind a veneer of
> overtly normal cognitive and linguistic behavior. The psychopath presents
> as normal on first impression but upon closer inspection is found to be
> profoundly lacking in the ability to connect or to empathize with other
> people. In this regard, Cleckley's classic criteria for psychopathy included
> absence of nervousness, lack of remorse or shame, egocentricity, incapacity
> for love, and general poverty in major affective reactions, as well as reckless
> and irresponsible behavior.[87]

I am not suggesting here that all slaveholders were psychopaths or that
they were incapable of empathy for everyone. They could be kind, loving,
and empathetic to members of their family and people within their social or
business circles. Their psychopathy emerged in relationship to Black people.
They could appear to empathize with their enslaved laborers, but that was but
a part of Marse's mask of sanity.

There were, of course, some slaveholders troubled by slavery, and they
had some empathy for the enslaved, but their empathetic feelings became very
inconvenient and put them at odds with their slaveholding peers and slavery
laws. For example, a slaveholder might appear to have a relatively harmonious
relationship with some of his slaves, particularly house slaves such as Mammy,
and at the same time have no hesitation to sell or trade one of these slaves
when the slaveholder decided it was economically advisable or prudent as a
demonstration of power. Most enslaved people knew full well that any emotional tie the enslaver had with them was tenuous at best and could change
for the worst in a heartbeat.

What drives this cruel, irresponsible behavior? Quoting from Gary
Watson's article "The Trouble with Psychopaths," historian Dana Kay Nelkin wrote, "That psychopaths are in this way 'into' or 'behind' the mischief
and pain is what constitutes their malice . . . they can set themselves directly
against others' aims as such. Part of their intent in cruelty is to subordinate
others' agency to theirs, in a way that seeks the others' recognition of their
ability to do just this, like a child hurtfully teasing a dog or sitting on her little
brother."[88]

A sound psychological argument can be made that individuals with psychopathic tendencies would be attracted to, if not mesmerized by, many aspects of the slavery-industrial complex. There were elements of racist slavery that were compatible with the dark traits of the psychopath. For example, the autocratic system, moving forward on the backs of bound labor, proved extremely profitable for a small, powerful group of slaveholding aristocrats. In its earliest manifestations, southern racist slavery necessitated regular, guilt-free, sadistic punishment of others. Given that psychopaths enjoy bullying, they were attracted to a system in which bullying was a rampant method of control. Clever, sophisticated manipulation was admired by one's slaveholding white peers, as it was highly useful, and being charming, as is often true of psychopaths, was a plus.

It may seem harsh to suggest that an examination of the mind of the southern slaveholder should consider that some psychopaths were attracted to becoming clergymen. As Genovese and Fox-Genovese pointed out, "Proslavery theologians believed that slavery encouraged moral evil to a lesser extent than did the North's free-labor system."[89] It was delusional for the chattel slavery–driven South to claim the North's free-labor economic system was truly evil, which led to the South's rejection of the abolitionist stance that slavery was wrong. As Snay informed us, clergymen such as Presbyterian pastor Robert Lewis Dabney of Virginia clarified the South's position on slavery. Writing a series of articles about the slavery controversy in the Richmond *Enquirer* in 1851, Dabney asserted that "this question of *moral right* [italics in the original] is at the bottom of the whole matter." Dabney argued that the Bible could successfully challenge the abolitionist stance: "Because the Bible defended slavery, pressing the sectional controversy on the Word of God would push the abolitionists 'to unveil their true infidel tendencies.' They would be forced to array themselves against the Bible, which would alienate true believers in the North."[90] Genovese and Fox-Genovese pointed out that the Reverend George D. Armstrong of Virginia, in his *Christian Doctrine of Slavery* in 1857, "projected slavery as the solution to the class war in free labor countries."[91]

If slaveholding men or women were persuaded by their guilty feelings about enslaving another human being, they could have freed, albeit with some legal risk, their enslaved people, declared themselves nonslaveholders, perhaps become abolitionists, moved out of the slaveholding South (as many did), or at least tried to stop enslaving people. A psychopathic enslaver would have to reach a state of mind devoid of guilt to allow her- or himself to find slavery acceptable. The absence of guilt adds a psychopathic strain to the master's personality. Not all slaveholders were full-blown psychopaths, but all racist enslavers suffered, to varying degrees, from a deterioration of conscience.

One final comment on the nature of psychopathy: It is common for many people to think of the psychopath and the antisocial personality as the same thing. In terms of its personality structure, the psychopath is closely aligned with the antisocial personality, but it is not the same. Antisocial types—formerly called sociopaths in earlier psychiatric formulations—and psychopaths differ in many respects. Antisocial types have chronic conflicts with authority and society. Psychologists Hugues Herve and John C. Yuille reported empirical research about children and adolescents which showed that "adults with psychopathy constitute a subgroup of individuals within a larger population of persons who all display persistent antisocial behavior across the life span." The subgroup of children and adolescents who manifest psychopathy not only display persistent antisocial behavior but show "callous-unemotional traits."[92] Herve addressed the history of psychopathy as both a condition and a personality: "Descriptions of psychopaths, instrumentally impulsive individuals with poor behavior controls who callously and remorselessly bleed others for purely selfish reasons via manipulation, intimidation, and violence, are found across time and cultures."[93] Early precursor descriptors of the psychopath were: a person exhibiting "madness without delirium," someone who is "morally deranged," or an individual who is "morally insane" or "morally defective."[94]

In the late twentieth century, based primarily on the work of Cleckley and Robert Hare, psychopathy became a well-defined and accepted clinical syndrome.[95] A psychopath is glib, superficial, and charming. Affectively, he shows little to no remorse or guilt. His affect is shallow. He enjoys stimulation, while at the same time he has poor behavior controls, which were probably exhibited early in his life. He can be very impulsive. His opinion of himself is grandiose. He lies with great ease and exhibits almost no empathy for anyone. He can be very irresponsible. He is a con man, self-centeredly manipulating others. When confronted, he takes no responsibility for his own actions, easily blaming others. His basic posture toward other people is parasitic. He may seek unrealistic goals, and he may engage in various, versatile criminal behaviors. In addition to the telltale absence of a conscience as a central defining characteristic, he brazenly displays the ability to ignore the common laws and behavioral expectations generally observed by the vast majority of humans. He is immune to normative behavior.

Based on the substantive evidence that has come to light about Thomas Jefferson and Sally Hemings, an argument can be made that Jefferson's complicated, renowned life, and his sexually assaultive relationship with Hemings, make him at a minimum a great statesman, slaveholder, hypocrite, and a man with some psychopathic traits who was guilty of child sexual exploitation and rape. Jefferson was a complex man. Publicly, he almost seemed to regret the "necessity" of slavery (he was not antislavery), for he enslaved hundreds of individuals on multiple plantations. He was a proponent of returning enslaved people to Africa rather than allowing them to assimilate into America. Ironically, he expressed the fear that "if the slaves were freed, the sexual ardor of Black freemen would be turned against white women."[96]

Despite his position, he sexually assaulted one of his young slave girls, Sally Hemings, who bore him numerous children. A protégé of Jefferson's, James Callender, angered by the president's refusal to grant him patronage, revealed in the press in 1802 the secret of Jefferson's relationship with his enslaved girl: "By this wench Sally, our president has had several children."[97] According to historian Ibram X. Kendi, Jefferson survived this assault politically, but it stained his character. Historian John Chester Miller noted that Jefferson saw himself as "a 'good' master; kindly, compassionate and considerate of his servitors' well-being."[98] Jefferson had to manage an objectively defined, personal set of actions he took that included his being a perpetrator of the sexual exploitation and rape of an enslaved Black girl. To see himself as "compassionate and considerate to his servitors' well-being" demanded he utilize massive denial and self-deception about some significant aspects of his life.

Historian Annette Gordon-Reed described her own visceral reaction to reading the entries of Jefferson's *Farm Book*, a journal in which "he recorded the names, births, family configurations, rations, and work assignments of all the people enslaved on his plantations. . . . Still it was wrenching to hold the original and to know that Jefferson's actual hand had dipped into the inkwell and touched these pages to create what was to me a record of human oppression."[99]

Not all slave masters were psychopaths, but there is no question that the white elite masters who established the ten thousand aristocratic slaveholding families controlling most of the southern slave industry, built this country on the backs of enslaved people, and drove this country to war had significant psychopathic characteristics. It was Marse's psychopathy that kept him from being a moral person with enslaved Black African and American-born enslaved people. His psychopathic character traits psychologically defended him against his humanity and, at the same time, facilitated his capacity to commit crimes against humanity. He fits literature scholar Stephen Greenblatt's definition of an "aspiring tyrant," characterized by

> the limitless self-regard, the law-breaking, the pleasure in inflicting pain, the compulsive need to dominate. He is pathologically narcissistic and supremely arrogant. He has a grotesque sense of entitlement, never doubting that he can do whatever he chooses. He loves to bark orders and to watch underlings scurry to carry them out. He expects absolute loyalty, but he is incapable of gratitude. He has no natural grace, no sense of shared humanity, no decency.[100]

CHRISTIAN COMFORT

With the descriptor Christian comfort, I am guilty of taking the most liberty. The term is meant to convey the spiritual comfort and psychological relief the slaveholder derived from his Protestant Christian religion. The majority of elite southern enslavers belonged to the Episcopal Church. Marse felt in his bones that the North was hell-bent on thwarting God's will. Although I discuss in chapter 5 the significance of Christianity as a major political and spiritual defense of slavery, here I emphasize that, as a source of *psychological* comfort, evangelical Protestant Christianity became a defense mechanism for the slaveholder. Woven from threads of self-deception and splitting was the Southerner's assumption and belief that his Christian God was on the South's side. This faith-based belief was a bedrock for much of the Confederacy. This Christian comfort was perhaps the best argument the slaveholder had in support of slavery, because it could let the slaveholder off any morality hook. The psychological formula was simple: Aided by the processes of splitting and self-deception, slavery was for the positive good and abolitionism was for the negative bad.

Christianity became a bedrock for southern slaveholding and lucrative for many preachers. As the influence of religion swept over the South in the 1830s and 1840s, some spiritually minded folks began to realize that there was money in religion. As O'Brien observed, "Religion became a boom business. In 1860, an urban Southern minister might expect to earn quadruple the average income for a free, adult, white American."[101]

Daly, quoting Joseph Wilson, a proslavery minister and the father of President Woodrow Wilson, noted that "Christianity made everything the best of its kind."[102] If war came, Marse was 100 percent certain God would fight for the South. Quoting Tennessee Presbyterian William H. Vernor, Daly gave us another example of the southern clergy's confidence about God and slavery: "The institution of slavery according to the Bible is right. Therefore in the contest between North and South, He will espouse the cause of the South and make it His own."[103]

This comforting belief became the South's grand delusion: God was on the South's side. God gave the South—actually gave to a small group of privileged white people—a seemingly limitless supply of bound labor and cotton. As O'Brien informed us, slaveholder elite James Henry Hammond saw morality as irrelevant to mere humans; morality was God's business: "Men dealt with the world 'as it is' and ideality was irrelevant. The only pertinent question was, how fared the Southern world? Rich, powerful, and successful was Hammond's answer, for cotton was king. What else did anyone need to know?"[104]

SLAVEHOLDING BECAME PSYCHOLOGICALLY SYNTONIC

The slave master had to become psychologically harmonized with enslavement. He developed a positive sense of self by becoming comfortable with
being on top of the presumed human hierarchy. In the theoretical language
of ego psychology, when a belief or attitude squares comfortably, is in tune
with and harmonized with an individual's self-view, this relatively comfortable
fit between a person's sense of self and his belief can be described as *syntonic*.
Sometimes, considerable mental gymnastics are required to achieve psychological harmony. The American slaveholder had to create a place in his psyche
where owning Black people was syntonic with his sense of self. He could
utilize this psychological balance and square it with how he acted as a slave
master. Ultimately, to master a syntonic state of mind, the slave master had
to find ways to deceive himself. As Genovese and Fox-Genovese explained,
southern slavery came to rest on a fatal self-deception: "Lewis Clarke, having
experienced enslavement firsthand, uttered a last thought that encompassed
everything necessary: 'There is nobody deceived quite so bad as the masters
down South; for the slaves deceive them, and they deceive themselves.'"[105]
    Slaveholders turned to natural law as the cornerstone of their syntonic
sense of self in relation to slavery. As James Warley Miles, a proslavery Episcopalian minister in Charleston, wrote in 1861, "it is much more forcible, and
to the purpose, to affirm that the relations of the white and Black races result
from Natural Law, just as much do the effect of the Law of gravitation."[106]
From the vantage point of Southerners who embraced the natural law argument, natural law endowed Blacks with inferiority, dependency on whites,
and inequality with whites: "A conception of society as naturally hierarchical,
ordered by a series of ranks and subordination, flowed from this assumption
of human inequality."[107]

PATERNALISM

Paternalism is certainly not automatically thought of as a psychological defense
mechanism. Paternalism is ordinarily defined as "a system under which an
authority undertakes to supply needs or regulate conduct of those under its
control in matters affecting them as individuals as well as in their relations to
authority and to each other."[108] An argument can be made, from a psychological perspective, that paternalism can be viewed and defined as a male defense
mechanism. The roots of paternalism stretch back to the history of human
development when the male species assumed its dominant role.

Merriam-Webster's indicates that the root of paternalism derives from the Latin *pater*, meaning father, and it further defines paternalism as "a policy or practice based on or characteristic of paternalism." Paternalism is closely related to the word "patrician," which *Merriam-Webster's* defines as "a member of one of the original citizen families of ancient Rome; a person of high birth; a person of breeding and cultivation."[109]

Southern antebellum paternalism as a social construct is difficult to define. It seems Hydra-headed, with many sources and causes. There is its root in the Roman *patron*, asserting the right and privilege of male dominance. It has its biblical origins. God was male; Jesus was male: "A benevolent Deity served as the supreme model for the 'munificent' earthly father, and the patriarchal family in turn furnished the example for all social relations."[110] It grew from the notion that there is a human hierarchy, and white men were at the top. Slaveholders—especially the white male elite—saw themselves at the top of the hierarchy of all white men as well, and dominant of all women regardless of their race or color.

Paternalism is woven into Christianity and replicated its English roots in the American colonies: "The belief that a highly structured social order was natural—in fact, divinely inspired—had arrived in the New World with the earliest Englishmen and eventually became the basis of the paternalistic defense of bondage."[111]

Southern slaveholders demonstrated the application of paternalism as a psychological defense against acknowledging the objective reality of the master-enslaved relationship. Consider, for example, Henry Watson Jr., who wrote from his Alabama plantation to a northern friend in 1861:

> Most people here feel an attachment to their servants similar, in some respects, to that we feel for our children. . . . We feed them, clothe them, nurse them when sick and in all things provide for them. How can we do this and not love them. They too feel an affection for their master, his wife and children, and they are proud of his and their successes. There seems to be a charm in the name of "master"—they look upon and to their master with the same feeling that a child looks to his father. It is a lovely trait in them. This being the case, how can we fear them?[112]

Religion shored up paternalism by placing white men above all things on God's green earth. Paternalism bequeathed a position from which southern men "espoused a world view that celebrated the positive virtues of many forms of inequality. . . . Their peculiar combination of hierarchically sanctioned male dominance in the household and bourgeois egalitarianism among men in the public sphere can best be described as paternalism. For paternalism invokes a specific metaphor of legitimate domination: the protective domination of the father over his family."[113] As the single occupant of the pinnacle of the hierarchy of humanity, Marse's paternalism caused him to look down arrogantly on other people.

One of the most important efforts slaveholders made toward synchronizing themselves with slaveholding was to make racist slaveholding not just familial, but fraternal. The enslaved became "friends." One of the most profound aspects of the slave master's self-deception and his bid for some harmonized psychic balance was his belief that he, the master, was the best friend the slave ever had. The emotional source for this belief was the centuries old bedrock of white paternalism. "As the slaves' self-anointed friend, the master offered protection, for the enslaved people, against the slaves' incompetence and emotional fragility. Privately as well as publicly, Southerners insisted that the slave recognized his master as his 'best and most faithful friend,'" argued Genovese and Fox-Genovese.[114] From his paternalistic perspective, Marse saw his enslaved people as inferiors who needed care.

Slaveowners thought of their bound laborers as "my people." Stowe detonated this paternalistic fraud in her 1852 antislavery novel *Uncle Tom's Cabin*. Stowe's novel vividly portrayed the horrors of paternalistic slavery, showing its emphasis on greed, exploitation, the falsehood of white slaveholders actually caring about their slaves, and the violence perpetrated by the white slaveholders and their minions.

Writing about Stowe's book, Stout noted that "more than three hundred thousand copies were sold in 1852, its first year in print. The two-million plus copies sold over the next decade made it the bestselling novel in American history in proportion to population."[115] Stowe challenged the dynamics of the Fugitive Slave Act, which was sending Blacks—fugitive and free—back to enslavement. As Kendi observed,

> For the cosmic shift to antislavery, Stowe did not ask Americans to change their deep-seated beliefs. Stowe met Americans where they were: in the concreteness of racist ideas. She accepted the nationally accepted premise of the enslaver. . . . Stowe offered Christian salvation to White America through antislavery. In order to become better Christians, White people must constrain their domineering temperament and end the evil outgrowth of that temperament: slavery.[116]

ALIENATION

Although alienation is not normally considered a defense mechanism, it is a clinical term describing a psychiatric condition. Alienation is a means by which the individual divorces himself mentally from important painful or troublesome aspects of selfhood. This mental condition was recognized among some unfortunate nineteenth-century patients, and the medical doctor who specialized in rendering expert forensic opinions about these mentally alienated patients was called the "alienist." As a concept frequently used in modern day marriage and family psychology, alienation is the development of a set of beliefs and behaviors by a person to explain and justify the rejection of another person, such as the rejection of a parent by a child. Alienation may be thought of as a creation of a false reality.[117] As whites came to assume that Black Africans were not only children but also subhuman and racially inferior, proslavery advocates perceived Blacks through the distortions of alienation. Viewing an adult human being as a child is a glaring example of alienation.

The concept of "moral alienation" can be seen as a subtype of alienation and helps explain one of the "costs" of slave ownership on the master.[118] As generally used, "moral alienation" means the corruption of an inherent moral faculty through a conscious and willful choice of evil, but the slave master went further and explicitly rejected any argument that slavery was evil. Racist slaveholding was obedience to God's law. By adhering to an unassailable paradigm that God made Black Africans to serve whites in perpetuity, the slave master developed a narcissistic immunity from any external condemnation. This denial of the evils of slavery nevertheless exacted a profound moral alienation within the psyche of the slave master. The master became alienated from his humanity, which is the dark heart of the wound from the effects of racist slavery on many white Americans.[119]

Marse did not practice alienation willfully or consciously. Alienation worked on and wormed into him because he needed to simplify and minimize the enormity of the slavery industrial complex. Once he convinced himself that morality is God's territory and the slave master gets a pass on personal moral concerns, the master committed moral suicide. It was a soul death that could and did last for generations. This "moral alienation" became a significant portion of the white southerner's Black slavery-based historic traumatic wound.

Historian Andrew Delbanco described another poignant type of alienation, a painful, antebellum condition generated by "the inconsistencies and paradoxes of the fugitive slave problem. . . . Men and women from all walks of life were pulled into a maelstrom of contradiction as they tried to come to terms with it. It not only alienated neighbor from neighbor, friend from friend, but divided people within themselves." Delbanco described a few examples of the alienating tugs and pulls among people in the North and South as they struggled with the fugitive slave law: "Some who had been slave owners came to abhor their former way of life. Ministers in the North who preached against slavery told their parishioners that sending slaves back to the South was a civic duty. Judges who deplored slavery as a godless injustice nevertheless felt bound to enforce the law."[120]

Cultural amnesia is another aspect of alienation. By becoming a slave-holder and thus implicitly a tyrant, it appears that Marse developed cultural amnesia about his own ancestral and personal history. This was especially true if his ancestors were Christian Protestants who hailed from the British Isles and Western Europe. He had to purge from his memory his own struggles—personal and ancestral—with the hatred of tyranny. America began as a victory over tyranny. Insurgents established America.

Hammond's writings, speeches, and behavior, continue to offer rich targets for our understanding of cultural amnesia. Faust told the story of Hammond's desire to "consolidate the traditional accouterments of dynastic rule."[121] Denying his "undistinguished" roots, he commissioned a British genealogist to develop a Hammond family chart back to English nobility. When the genealogist, who apparently had some ethics, reported in writing that Hammond's family only came from "good honest yeomen," Hammond threw the letter into the fire and refused to pay the researcher's bill.[122] Hammond had to convince himself that he was born to rule others.

PSYCHOPATHOLOGICAL ENTITLEMENT

Not all entitlement is maladaptive or psychopathological. For example, a child is entitled to care that promotes the child's protection and well-being. A public official is entitled to certain agreed-upon privileges befitting his or her rank or official status. As applied to slaveholding and the trading in enslaved people, psychopathological entitlement began when one man or one man's marauding party abducted, captured, traded, or paid for another human being and held him or her as a hostage in perpetuity by force, intimidation, and punishment. The mantra of the entitled slaveholder is, "I want that," "I deserve that," or "That's mine." From a racist perspective, the mantra is, "That's mine by right—because I am white and thus superior and the enslaved person is Black and thus inferior." In combination with other defense mechanisms, such as self-deception and paternalism, white male slaveholders became infused with a self-destructive view—albeit mostly unconscious—of themselves as entitled to subjugate and dominate Black Africans and African Americans.

Given that much of the South in the second half of the eighteenth century saw itself as the new Israel and many believed that God had given African slavery to the enslavers for the region's benefit, psychopathological entitlement flowed from the slaveholders' unassailable belief that the white slaveholding people of the South were the chosen. Entitlement is the glue that binds the enslaved to the enslaver's ownership. The southern cause was an entitled and thus just cause. The slaveholding South felt entitled to secede from the Union and drag the country into a disastrous war.

A PSYCHOTIC REALITY

As stated earlier, a psychosis, by definition, is an exhibition by the psychotic person of an obvious distortion of reality. The slaveholder who deceived himself into believing that some of his slaves regarded him as their best friend, while holding the power of life or death over these enslaved people, was engaged in a psychotic rationalization. The master inferred an interpersonal reality between himself and his slaves that was grossly distorted. Ponder this hypothetical for a moment from the paternalistic slave master's perspective: His favored enslaved female, whom he named Cleopatra after his favorite queen, who now is his best and most faithful friend, is also a person he kidnapped, inherited, traded for, or bought and paid for; is inferior to him; is like a child to him; is almost totally dependent on him. She is someone who will never be equal to him, whom he cannot trust, who he does not love in the same way he loves his legitimate children, who he might sexually assault or exploit at his pleasure, who he might sell for a profit when she becomes fourteen, who will inherit nothing from him, and who he must control by whatever means necessary, sometimes using harsh methods. She is his property that he can lash or kill or order killed if the reason is justified. Yet the slaveholder convinces himself that his best friend/slave is content. That is psychotic thinking. That psychotic rationalization was the air the racist, paternalistic slaveholder breathed.

According to Daly, in the years immediately preceding the Civil War, proslavery advocates claimed that "in all respects slavery makes no difference between the slave and any other man."[123] If planter slaveholders could have displayed bumper stickers, a popular one might have read, "Slavery Is Freedom." Some proslavery scientists in the 1850s "abandoned the biblical timeline and the unity of races to argue that Blacks were the product of a separate creation, and an inferior species rightly enslaved."[124] This latter example illustrates an even more florid psychosis, exacerbated by grandiosity.

MARSE'S FATAL PSYCHOLOGICAL DEFENSE SYSTEM

Southern white male elite slaveholders constructed a complex psychological defense system to manage their slavery-industrial complex. Relative to his emotional defenses, Marse's autopsy shows he had at least eight adaptive defenses he could employ: anticipation, affiliation, altruism, humor, self-assertiveness, self-observation, sublimation, and suppression (for a more detailed description of these adaptive defenses, please see appendix A).[125] As detailed above, the elite slave master also applied common and slavery-specific defenses that were detrimental to his mental health and thus were maladaptive. By its very nature, racist slaveholding bred other, more insidious psychological defenses in the slaveholders' emotional and behavioral repertoire. Racist slaveholding contained brutality, harshness, and traumatic events that the slaveholder had to protect himself from knowing, feeling, or comprehending deep within himself. Racist slavery was emotionally costly to the slaveholder. The wound runs deep and wide.

The reckless idea of secession and white Southerners' subsequent belief that God favored them to win the ensuing Civil War becomes understandable when one considers the formidable psychological defense mechanisms that structured southern slaveholders' daily lives. These gifted and privileged men, many of whom were great statesmen, lawyers, physicians, clergymen, business titans, and presidents, mixed their adaptive and relatively common maladaptive defenses with other highly pathological defenses that grew out of the evil essence of racist slaveholding itself. They regularly deceived themselves, became grandiose about their limitless power, and ran a system of oppression that systematically humiliated, dehumanized, and traumatized millions of Black people. White Southerners went into battle armed not only with weapons, but also with a psychological defense system that convinced them that they would triumph. Within that psychopathology bloomed the seeds of their defeat.

Karp offered a chilling, clear analysis of the consequences wrought by the profound stranglehold the South's planter elite had on the United States: "Southern secession, of course, was not a pure product of anxiety and weakness. Slaveholders may have been pushed out of the Union by political defeat, but they were also pulled into the Confederacy by their ravenous ambition."[126]

Karp concluded that it was not simply the slaveholder's "ravenous ambition" that led to the formation of the Confederate States of America, but the South's self-defeating, grandiose certainty that the Confederacy, firmly grounded on a slavery-based economy, would dominate the world stage:

> If southern elites had been concerned only about the physical security of slavery as a regional institution or the maintenance of their political standing in a local context, then a risky and potentially violent separation from the Union could never have received their support. . . . In the Confederate spring of 1861 southern leaders were confident that their enterprise could thrive on the world stage. The South's institution of African slavery, they

believed, had helped establish the safest, strongest, and most successful republican government in history.[127]

It was to be a new slave-based nation, founded on liberty and justice for all white people. Marse's adaptive and maladaptive defense mechanisms served him well for a time and made him enormous wealth. Ultimately, however, his defenses failed him, blinded him, wounded him, and overwhelmed him, bringing disaster in the form of the Civil War.

· 5 ·

Unassailable Divine Defense
of Racist Chattel Slavery

SPIRITUAL PROGENITOR

A psychological portrait of Marse would not be complete without a thorough discussion of how organized Protestant Christianity in the antebellum South dictated that if you believed in God, you must believe that God ordained southern racist slaveholding and all that implied about the slaveholding south-ern caste system. This chapter offers that discussion and takes a detailed look at the biblical justification for slavery, a justification that laid the groundwork for secession and the inevitable religious war known as the Civil War.

When the history of southern racist slavery is brought into the sunshine for some additional examination, one clear fact leaps up: The primary progeni-tor of racist slavery was Christianity. As historian Hector Avalos stated,

> Despite the thoroughly modern manner in which biblical ethics are often represented, the Bible endorses horrific ideas and practices. One of these horrific practices is slavery, one of the most tragic and vicious institutions ever devised by humanity. For about 1900 of the last 2000 years of Chris-tian history, it was self-described Christians who kept slavery, in some form or another, a viable institution. Yet, many modern historians and biblical scholars still claim that the Bible was a main factor in abolition.[1]

The main point of Avalos's book, quoted here, "is that reliance on biblical authority was instrumental in promoting and maintaining slavery far longer than might be the case if we had followed many pre-Christian notions of freedom and anti-slavery sentiments."[2] As historian Paul Harvey informed us,

White supremacist racial [read: racist] thought emerged early in the modern world. It fatally shaped interactions between Europeans and Africans from the 15th century forward. Religious divisions drawn by Europeans between those of Christ and those in the heathen world became part of defining what race meant. "European" or "English" meant "Christian," and in future centuries that also came to mean "white." "African" meant "heathen." Thus, from early in southern history, religion created race, and race thereafter shaped religion.[3]

HISTORICAL JUSTIFICATION

In the early sixteenth century, Rome had a hand in the trading of enslaved people. Permission was given by papal decree in 1503 to capture and buy and sell Black, heathen Africans "because if the Christians bring them to these lands and make use of their services they will be more easily converted to our faith."[4] Although the papacy may have been focused on converting the heathen Africans to Catholicism, the notion of Christianizing Black Africans was mostly a ruse to acquire free slave labor. Initially, throughout most of the seventeenth century, the major labor force in the colonies was indentured servants, many of whom emigrated from Ireland. These Irish men and women were a mixture of Irish Catholics and Scots-Irish, the latter being primarily Presbyterians from Ulster, who had emigrated mostly from the Scottish lowlands.[5]

In the 1680s, a shift from indentured labor to slave labor began to occur in the colonies. There were no plans by anyone in the slavery trade or enslavement business to give any equality to enslaved people, even if they were baptized as Christians. In 1664, the colonial assembly in Maryland declared that baptizing a slave as a Christian did not make the slave free; enslaved people remained bondsmen for life. White supremacists solved the problem of equality by declaring that Black Africans were subhuman.

With the numbers of Black slaves growing exponentially in the colonies, southern states began to react. Virginia passed its first slave code in 1680 and passed its first Act to Prevent Runaways in 1683. In 1669, a document entitled The Fundamental Constitutions of Carolina (which at the time included both North and South Carolina) declared that church membership by Blacks gave them no special status, and that every (white) freeman of Carolina "shall have absolute power and authority over his negro slaves." By 1700, there were between forty and fifty thousand enslaved humans in the colony of North Carolina.

By 1717, the once powerful spiritual doctrine regarding the concept of the Elect faded into history as the thousands of European immigrants flooded the colonies and began to transform the American wilderness. Rather than these newcomers seeing themselves as a special group chosen by God to conquer the New World, the American character developed out of individual effort, self-reliance, personal responsibility, proclaimed white supremacy, and entitlement. All across America, religious authorities decreed that Black enslavement was a gift from God, and the evidence for that gift was found strongly and repetitively in the Protestant Christian Bible. As will be discussed in chapter 6, finding biblical support for racial slavery took some creative exegesis, because slavery, in its many forms since the beginning of world history, had never been about enslavement based on the color of the enslaved's skin. Euro-Americans sought a biblical justification for having the white race enslave the Black race, that would at the same time create a God-given racial hierarchy. By the 1730s, white Christian interest in converting Black enslaved people to their religion began to fade away. Slaveholders foresaw trouble in teaching Black enslaved humans to read, especially the Bible and later, abolitionist handbills and pamphlets.

In an 1861 lecture, Henry Ward Beecher said, "The South claims that the United States government is bound to make slavery as good as liberty for all the purposes of national life. That is the root of their philosophy. . . . They don't any longer talk of the evil of slavery. It is virtue, a religion. It is justice and divine economy!"[6]

Historian John Patrick Daly added: "A theologically minded Presbyterian or an ambitious plantation lord (though often one and the same person, or aspiring to be) could easily share the same providential language. Between 1831 and 1861 southerners solidified a culture that accomplished just that end—fuzzy moral ideology that brought regional unity and confidence."[7]

Historian Lacy K. Ford pointed out that the Episcopal pastor Frederick Dalcho, based in Charleston, South Carolina, "echoed Furman in advancing that slavery and Christianity could coexist in southern society [circa the 1830s]."[8] Ford informed us, "The ownership of slaves violated no moral precepts of Christianity as long as masters provided sufficiently for the slaves' physical and spiritual needs. Nor did Christian treatment of slaves or teaching slaves to read undermine the discipline necessary to maintain the institution, as long as masters modulated their kindness with firmness and the teaching of scripture done under appropriate white supervision."[9]

Marse believed in his heart that "freedom is not possible without slavery." The interconnection between personal and sectional freedom and slavery is a significant piece of the southern slaveholder's psychological worldview: "Slaveholders believed that men of good will should desire to extend freedom as far as possible, while recognizing that many peoples lacked the capacity to live free; that the freest societies in world history were based on slavery; and that freedom could be sustained only through the subjugation of all laboring classes. Thus, they resolved to sustain a Southern slave society even in a hostile world."[10] This became a profound rationalization: The masters' personal and cultural freedom was dependent on the enslavement of Blacks. Personal freedom for the African slave was out of the question. The acceptance of digging one's heels in on the proslavery side, even if it meant hostility from the rest of the world, was a self-inflicted wound to the average Southerner. In honor of Elizabeth Fox-Genovese and Eugene Genovese's contribution on the subject of the slaveholder's mind, we might call it the fatal self-deceptive wound.

RELIGIOUS JUSTIFICATION

As law professor Paul Finkelman declared, "The largest single body of proslavery literature is based on religious defenses of slavery. Such defenses appealed to the overwhelmingly Protestant, often evangelical, Southern population."[11] Although there are many complex aspects to comprehending the mind of the slave master, it is his identity as a Christian that, to my mind, is key to understanding how one person can justify owning another. While I acknowledge there were slaveholders who were not followers of the Christian faith, it is fair to say the majority in the South called themselves Christians. It was Marse's identity as a Christian that became the bedrock of his slaveholding validation. Although from the beginning, America defined itself as a Christian nation, over time, the South co-opted Protestant Christianity through its evangelicalism and a rabid defense of slavery and created what Southerners in their minds and hearts saw as the one true God-blessed religion. God was on the South's side. As we shall see, the war for the South, at bottom, was a holy war.

With his Protestant shield, Marse could align his individual morality, his personal freedom, and his profit-making endeavors (slaveholding, slave trading, and the massive product profits derived from enslaved labor) with God. Marse recognized that personal freedom was not to do as one chose, but the ability to choose what Providence intended. This fundamentally means being in tune with the mind of the Lord. Marse based his "character," that all-important essence of being in the nineteenth-century American mind, on the "rewards" he received from being a good Christian. A flourishing slaveholding business was economic and divine proof that he was right with the Lord. As Daly explained, "Evangelicals held that the real purpose of individual effort was the assignment not of wealth but of moral merit. . . . This providential mind-set let evangelicals see themselves as moral agents engaged solely in acts of will that built character."[12] This mindset also allowed Marse to see his slaveholding as having no taint of evil, thus creating a huge moral, relatively unconscious blind spot, like the dark side of the moon.

Mainly in response to the Vesey plot of 1822, Southern Baptist preacher Richard Furman wrote his *Exposition of the Views of Baptists*, the most important proslavery argument to come out of Charleston, South Carolina, in the 1820s. Furman argued that the Providence of God had saved Charleston from Vesey's slave revolt. He advocated that a master might hold a slave "according to Christian principles" and that evil attached to slavery only through the "individual who abuses his authority."[13]

Not only did the North and South divide the nation, the Protestant Christian citizens split their Christian God in half. In his book *When Slavery Was Called Freedom*, Daly wrote a compelling analysis of southern religion and slavery. As we may infer from its title, his insights about the South's linkage of enslavement with Christian religion appears disturbingly accurate about how and why southern evangelicals and slaveholders used some brilliantly constructed "fuzzy logic" to defend slavery. According to Daly, the heart of the South's defense of slavery emanated out of a southern evangelical moralism: "Southern morality was an amalgam of Protestant traditions and blunt materialism, because evangelical ministers tended to sacralize the American institutions under which their denominations expanded."[14]

God's plan was defined in large measure by sectional economics, which in turn created sectional delusions. A belief in God's plan seemed to dominate the American psyche in both the North and the South. The North became convinced that a free-labor economy was God's plan, while the South became convinced its slaveholding was *really* God's plan: "A religiously inspired delusion operated at the heart of both evangelical proslavery dreams and northern free-labor moralism."[15] As Daly pointed out, once the United States elected an administration and Congress from a new party that promised no more new slave territories, there were "[n]o more rewards from God for the South."[16] Southern evangelicals saw this position as the North and the Republican Party as interfering with God's plan, particularly as it applied to the development of the new western US territories.

Historian Mitchell Snay, in his book *Gospel of Disunion*, provided a helpful road map for understanding the extent to which the gospel of religion commanded the spiritual and political march to separation and disunion for the South. As he pointed out, there "are three compelling reasons to turn to religion in order to understand the origins and nature of Southern separatism":

(1) the centrality of religion to culture and society in the antebellum South; (2) the centrality of religion (in the North and South) in the conflict over where slavery could and could not exist; and (3) the tracing back of the roots of the bond between religion and nationalism to early America. On this last point, "[s]ecular and religious motifs were woven into the belief that America had a unique role in bringing the Kingdom of God to this world. . . . The relationship between religion and Southern separatism can be most efficiently and reliably traced through the thoughts and actions of the Southern clergy."[17] Snay referred to the historian E. Brooks Holifield, who named these clergy the "Gentlemen Theologians"—the elite of the Southern clergy.[18]

Here is a sample of six prominent proslavery Southern theological elites linked with one of their sermons:

1. George D. Armstrong, *"The good hand of our God upon us." A Thanksgiving sermon preached on the occasion of the South's victory at Manassas* (1861)
2. William Barnwell, *The Divine Government. A Sermon for the Day of Thanksgiving, Humiliation and Prayer* (1856)
3. Iveson Brookes, *A Defense of Southern Slavery against the Attacks of Henry Clay and Alexander Campbell by a Southern Clergyman* (1851)
4. Samuel Dunwoody, *A Sermon upon the Subject of Slavery* (1837)
5. Robert Hayne, *Defence of the South. General Hayne, in Reply to Mr. Webster of Massachusetts* (1830)
6. Leonidas Polk, *A Letter to the Right Reverend Bishops of Tennessee, Georgia, Alabama, Arkansas, Texas, Mississippi, Florida, South Carolina and North Carolina. From the Bishop of Louisiana* (1856)

These men and their peers spread their influence through sermons, lectures, writings, and newspapers, and helped build churches, colleges, and universities.

During the American colonial period, many Christian ministers, especially of the Presbyterian and Episcopal faiths, stepped past any concerns they may have had about controlling or emancipating enslaved people and, in an act of sublimation, instead became focused on Christianizing slaves. As historian James L. Roark informed us about colonial clergy, "Moreover, churchmen themselves rarely had doubts about the essential justice of slavery, only about its practice. They were probably among the most ardent supporters of the Southern cause."[19] In a 1757 sermon, Presbyterian Samuel Davies, sermonizing on the duties of slave masters, framed the racist hierarchy of slavery for his white congregants when he stated that "Christianity establishes and regulates [masters and slaves], and enjoins every man to conduct himself according to the [providential distinctions between those who rule and those who are to be ruled]."[20]

As early as 1797, the Presbyterian General Assembly took a vote on whether or not slavery was evil. This austere assembly weighed in on the issue of slavery and piety: To the question, "Is slavery evil?" they voted yes. To the question, "Are all who hold slaves of moral evil?" they voted no.[21] *Slavery is evil, but owning a slave is not morally evil*—here is the evangelical sleight of hand in plain view. The institution of slavery is viewed as evil, but its practitioners are let off the hook.

Decades before the Civil War, a nationwide political and moral war about American slavery was waged on multiple fronts. In the South, the primary religious denominations used their clergies' voices to advance the cause of slavery. On the other hand, in 1834, the Baptists called for "a speedy emancipation . . . this antislavery sentiment seemed limited to the upper South, especially North Carolina and Virginia."[22] Some denominations continued to try to advance the effort of Christianizing slaves. Methodism, for example, used traveling preachers to reach the rural areas, and Methodists became the leading missionaries to the enslaved. Additionally, both politically and spiritually, the notion of sending freed slaves back to Africa (the colonization movement) gained momentum from 1818 into the 1820s.

Finkelman's book *Defending Slavery* offered a brilliant exposition of proslavery thought in the South, providing a selection of original documents from law, politics, medicine, and religion. This concise volume included proslavery writings, speeches, and sermons from notable proslavery advocates.[23] For example, in 1851, the Georgia Baptist preacher Reverend A. T. Holmes wrote an essay—*The Duties of Christian Masters*—that was not only written for masters about the religious care of their slaves but was also a strong argument for the legitimacy of slavery. Here are some of its highlights: "*man is master*"; the relationship between master and servant is by divine appointment; the duties of the master

are all of Divine requirement. Every duty is a command, and God must be regarded as commanding the master to perform those duties to his servants, which the relations he bears to them involves and imposes. . . . We infer, lastly, that the master should be the *teacher* [italics in original] of his servant. Ignorance, in a peculiar sense, attaches to the negro, and ignorance . . . is one principal cause of the want of virtue, and of the immoralities which abound in the world.[24]

Finkelman summarized the South's religious defense of slavery as follows: Most biblical patriarchs, including Abraham, owned slaves; God took Job's slaves away from him during his testing of Job; the book of Leviticus details elaborate laws for governing slaves; fundamentally, the law of the Old Testament assumed the existence of slavery and offered ways it should be regulated, but did not condemn it. The New Testament also assumes the existence of slaves: "The Corinthian letters proclaimed that slaves should be satisfied with their lot: 'For he that is called in the Lord, *being* a servant, is the Lord's freeman; likewise he that was called *being* free, is Christ's servant.'"[25]

If Southern slavery was to work, Marse had to relinquish his own ethics and moral reasoning to a higher authority (the Bible and his religious leaders) and accept the decrees of that authority without question. A sensitive slaveholder might feel some pain for having to punish his slaves, but the slavery system depended on the enslaver maintaining unwavering domination and control over his enslaved people. Examples of physical violence against the enslaved were easily found in the Christian Bible. Hebrew law stated that insubordination was punishable by death: "The punishments recognized by the Mosaic Law were death, chiefly by stoning, and in extreme cases the burning or hanging of the body; chastisement, the stripes not to exceed 40 (Deut. 25:3)."[26]

There were men who obviously needed no justification for racist slavery other than the almighty dollar. Slavery brought a minority of Southerners some handsome profits. In the seventeenth and eighteenth centuries, slavery was extremely important as an economic driver not just to the United States but to the British crown as well.

Sometimes the southern clergy found it important to sort the wheat from the chaff. Although most Methodists were against slavery and from the late eighteenth century were engaged in educational efforts for enslaved people, Methodist parson William G. Brownlow (1805–1877) articulated a forgiving attitude toward slavery: "Bad men abuse negroes, good men do not and in all cases, the abuse arises from the character and disposition of the master; and not from the system."[27] Brownlow's message was clear: Don't criticize our system. It works well. Any troublesome aspects of our slavery system emanate from individuals, not the institution. It stands firmly on the Divine Rock, the "Rock of Ages." Another highly influential defender of slavery was Professor Thomas R. Dew (1802–1846), who was to become president of the College of William and Mary. As Daly noted, Dew offered a rock-solid theological defense: "Dew put theological and moral glosses on his laissez-faire doctrines, suggesting that the barriers to antislavery and the laws of necessity were laws of God."[28] The psychological workings of the slave master's mind became infused with his belief that he held a superior, divine duty, a trust between himself and his God. The only thing higher in this hierarchical creation was Jehovah himself.

Frederick Douglass offered no sympathy and expressed a strong condemnation of Southern religious masters:

> I assert most unhesitatingly, that the religion of the south is a mere covering for the most horrid crimes,—a justifier of the most appalling barbarity,—a sanctifier of the most hateful frauds,—and a dark shelter under which the darkest, foulest, grossest, and most infernal deeds of slaveholders find the strongest protection. Were I to be again reduced to the chains of slavery, next to that enslavement, I should regard being the slave of a religious master the greatest calamity that could befall me. For of all slaveholders with whom I have ever met, religious slaveholders are the worst. I have ever found them the meanest and basest, the most cruel and cowardly, of all others.[29]

While there is no question that money, power, and greed were at the heart of the development of slavery and the eventual stranglehold that the slavery economy had on the South (and on the nation as a whole), its primary justification clearly derived from Protestant Christian clergy. The perception and belief that God and the Bible sanctioned slavery were the main ingredients of the glue that made Marse a voluntary hostage to slavery. How a good, kind-hearted individual soul can come to accept the practice of slavery is what so much of psychologist Phillip Zimbardo's work has to teach us.[30] To paraphrase Marx, it seems clear, from a twenty-first-century perspective, that religion was the opiate of the slaveholder. From Zimbardo: "I argue that while most people are good most of the time, they can readily be seduced into engaging in what would normally qualify as ego-alien deeds, as antisocial, as destructive of others."[31] He named this dynamic the Lucifer Effect. Please don't think for a moment that I am letting Marse off the hook because he was seduced. He was. But there were multiple Sirens pulling his slavery ship toward the rocks.

The masters claimed to be paternalistic Christian masters. Christians saw the Muslim Moors as infidels and felt justified in taking them as enslaved people: "Moors captured in North Africa and in the Spanish peninsula were held in bondage in Italy, Spain, Portugal, and France."[32] Many educated American slave masters used these historical precedents to justify the bondage of all Africans.

In what appears to be a work self-published in 1859 by the Presbyterian minister Reverend Fred A. Ross (1796–1883), entitled *Slavery Ordained by God*, the author highlighted some of the strongest proslavery arguments in the marketplace on the eve of the Civil War.[33] Ross rained scripture, logic, and humor down on his readers. He hammered the abolitionists and the North into pieces. He proclaimed and thundered God's support for slavery: "This

harmony and union can be preserved only by the view presented in this volume, i.e., that *slavery is of God,* and to continue for the good of the slave, the
good of the master, the good of the whole American family, until another and
better destiny may be unfolded."[34]

The central themes of Ross's exposition were: (1) God never said slavery
is a sin and (2) the Golden Rule and slavery can and do coexist. He argued
that slavery was only evil in certain circumstances; that equality was only the
highest form of social life; that the subjection to authority, even slavery, was
at times better "for a time" than freedom; that slavery, like all evils, had its
corresponding and greater good; that the Southern slave, "*though degraded compared with his master, is elevated and ennobled compared with his brethren in Africa*";
and that all Southerners must accept that God never intended the relation of
master and slave to be perpetual. Understanding this last point is crucial to
grasping Ross's argument: Leave the South alone and, with God's guidance, it
will sort out the issues of slavery as God's wisdom dictates. Many Southerners
internalized this belief: An external attack on Southern slavery was an attack
on God himself.

This divine belief was what might be called Marse's bottom line. It's
what made Marse's position on slavery unassailable. God and the South would
sort out slavery. No one, no other authority, no other government, had any
provenance in the matter. The enslavement of Black Africans was God's will
and his gift to Marse. Any and all antislavery efforts were Satan's work. The
enslavement of Black Africans and African Americans was a covenant between
the southern enslavers and God.

Ross built his proslavery arguments on some cleverly placed rocks: that
the subjugation of the Black African was God's command, thus it was not
sinful, and that the harmony of the Union depended on the North and the
South accepting that slavery, although a degraded condition that had become
an evil, a curse on the South, brought blessings for a time to the South and
to the Union.

Ross also railed against the obvious hypocrisy in the slavery system and
pointed out in an 1857 speech that the General Assembly of the Presbyterian
Church, which had been standing *against* the system of slavery, was at the same
time allowing justifications in support of slavery.[35] He confronted the hypocrisy of certain southern synods where slaveholders were affiliated with their
churches; he challenged the Assembly to appoint committees to go and count
the number of slaves owned by these men; and to determine "the extent to
which slaves are held from an unavoidable necessity imposed by the laws of
the States, the obligations of guardianship, and the demands of humanity."[36]
He challenged northern synods to establish investigative committees and
report back on such enterprises as Northerners engaged in slave ship building

and outfitting, the slave trade between states, the money made by Northerners who benefit economically in commerce with slave traders, the orders sent to New Orleans and other Southern cities for slaves to be bought and sold, the number of northern churchgoers who buy food and cotton raised by slave labor, the number of northern church members who have intermarried with *slaveholders*, and thus become slaveholders themselves, or "enjoy the wealth made by the blood of the slave."[37]

Ross challenged these churches to identify the numbers of northern church members who were descendants of men who kidnapped Black Africans and brought them to Virginia and New England,[38] and further, to tally the aggregate and individual wealth of such men and identify "what action is best to compel them to disgorge this blood-stained gold, or to compel them to give dollar for dollar in equalizing the loss of the South by emancipation."[39]

Ross knew much of his challenge was tongue-in-cheek, but he ratcheted it up: He called for these northern churches to identify church members, ministers especially, who advocated *murder* in resistance to the laws of the land, who owned stock in underground railroads for fugitive slaves, and who owned stock in Sabbath-breaking railroads and canals. He called for a tally of northern church members who were either cruel husbands or hen-pecked husbands. Ross fired a broadside at Stowe's *Uncle Tom's Cabin*, asserting that the "*impression made by this book is a falsehood.*"[40]

The following quote may or may not be the vilest and most extreme racist statements Ross ever made, but in support of the southern slave master's God-ordained duty to hold slaves, he wrote:

[The Southern master's] obligation is high, and great, and glorious. It is the same obligation, in kind, he is under to his wife and children, and in some respects immensely higher, by reason of the number and the tremendous interests involved for time and eternity in connection with this great country, Africa, and the world. Yes, sir, *I know*, whether Southern masters fully know it or not, that *they hold from God*, individually and collectively, *the highest and noblest responsibility ever given by Him to individual private men on all the face of the earth.* For God has intrusted [*sic*] to them to train millions of the most degraded in form and intellect, but, at the same time, the most gentle, the most amiable, the most affectionate, the most imitative, the most susceptible of social and religious love, of all the races of mankind,—to train them, and to give them civilization, and the light and the life of the gospel of Jesus Christ. And I thank God he has given this great work to that type of the noble family of Japheth best qualified to do it,—to the Cavalier stock,—the gentlemen and ladies of England and France, born to command, and softened and refined under our Southern sky. May they know and feel and fulfil [*sic*] their destiny! Oh, may they "know that they also have a Master in heaven."[41]

Ross articulated a favorite rejoinder to antislavery and emancipation sentiments: If God is the master, and if God ordained slavery, then he, and only he, can decide if and when emancipation is to be allowed: God Almighty, not the government, not the president. An evangelical proslavery advocate could quickly see that Abraham Lincoln would come to play God. God made slavery. Speaking as God's servant, Ross stated in 1856, "God has a great deal to do before he is ready for emancipation."[42]

Ross returned to one of his favorite themes: the North's hypocrisy about slavery because of how much money was being made by lots of powerful people, North and South, and worldwide.[43] There was a lot of accuracy in this criticism.

He also took on the briar patch of the will of God versus man's own will. Ross laid out a simple way out of that conundrum: "*Shall man submit to the revealed will of God, or to his own?*" Citing no sources, Ross preached:

God, in making all things, saw that, in the relations he would constitute between himself and intelligent creatures, and among ourselves, NATURAL GOOD AND EVIL, would come to pass. In his benevolent wisdom, he then *willed* LAW to control this *good* and *evil*. And he thereby made *conformity* to the law to be *right*, and *non-conformity* to be *wrong*.

The Christian path was clear: Being right and doing right meant conforming. Being wrong and doing wrong meant not conforming. Setting aside for the moment the quandary about who or what revealed God's will, violating God's will became a sin, which in turn evoked punishment. In this model, wisdom came from a correct reading of God's revealed will. The Bible was the primary source for God's commands: the inerrant word. A Christian who fixed his obligation to God stood on the ground of revelation. If you fixed your obligation elsewhere, you abandoned the revelation ground and you abandoned the will of God and his word and put your definition of what's right into the self of the heart, a path Ross argued will take the individual down a path of making God's will subordinate to the individual's heart.

English Anglican cleric George Whitfield won his fame as one of the principal preachers—and arguably the most popular—of the First Great Awakening, a religious revivalist movement of the 1730s and 1740s that spawned many "New Lights" Baptists, who were to withdraw from old, established churches and become known as "Separate Baptists."[44] Whitfield's open-air revivals may have inspired many Baptists, but he identified himself as a Calvinist Methodist. Whitfield was a strong supporter of the legalization of slavery. It is said he had four thousand acres and fifty slaves: "Whitefield [*sic*] in Georgia advocated the introduction of slavery and rum for the economic development of the colony. He even owned slaves himself."[45] As Fox-Genovese and Genovese stated, Whitfield "won the heart of planters by denying the sinfulness of slavery and supporting the demand to introduce slaves into the colony. No serious challenge to slavery thereafter developed anywhere in the Lower South."[46]

THE IMPORTANCE OF THE BIBLE

The Bible, as God's word, was the source for settling all questions of right and wrong. Writing in 1855, Presbyterian theologian Albert Barnes stated,

> There are few writers on morals, and probably none of reputation, who would undertake to defend a position that was plainly *against* the teachings of the Bible. It may be safely affirmed that there is not a legislative body that would take the ground of openly legislating against the Bible; there is not a judge on any bench who would pronounce a decision that would clearly be contrary to a principle laid down in the Sacred Scripture; there is not a department of government that would not admit that if the Bible has settled a question, it is final.[47]

Southerners found a solid defense—indeed, heaven-derived support—for slavery in the Christian Bible: From the great eighteenth-century evangelist George Whitfield onward, defenders of slavery pointed to Genesis 15:14, in which the great patriarch Abraham prepared for war with his "armed and trained servants, born in his own house, three hundred and eighteen."[48] This scriptural citation is possibly an error, for it is Genesis 14:14 that reads: "And when Abram [*sic*] heard that his brother was taken captive, he armed his trained servants, born in his own house, three hundred and eighteen, and pursued them unto Dan."

In 1840 the proslavery clergyman Reverend Mr. Crowder of Virginia said, "In its moral aspect, slavery was not countenanced, permitted, and regulated by the Bible, but it was positively instituted by God Himself—he had, in so many words, enjoined it."[49] Here, the good Reverend Crowder opined that God had commanded or ordered slavery. Crowder expressed a belief that became central to many Protestant Christian clergy and slave masters. Even if a Christian slave master developed misgivings or pangs of conscience about slavery, these stirrings put him at odds with the Almighty, Mosaic Law, and the teachings of Jesus.

If God commanded that slavery be implemented, as Crowder's use of the word "enjoined" indicates, if a slave master had pangs of conscience about slavery, he would be forced to assess his view of God. That's some powerful insulation against confronting oneself, as it would mean confronting one's perceptions and understanding of God's own morals and ethics.

If Marse needed a perfect way to assuage his conscience and justify his enslavement of human beings, the Bible was the answer. To Marse, slavery was part of God's divine order. To the Protestant Christian God-fearing slave master, God blessed the slave industry, in all its aspects. In the Bible, the slaveholders and their divines found that God authorized racist inequality.

As has been noted elsewhere, teaching the enslaved to read was controversial in the South. Ford pointed out that Edward Laurens, a South Carolina congressman representing Charleston, objected and declared that teaching slaves to read would lead to a slave becoming "dissatisfied with his lot and thus invite insubordination."[50] In November 1834, the South Carolina legislature passed a bill further restricting enslaved activities, including making it illegal to teach slaves to read or write. As Ford stated, this ban only applied to slaves and not freedmen, but if any slave or freedman was found guilty of teaching slaves to read or write, he could be subject to fifty lashes.[51]

THE OLD TESTAMENT

Grounded in biblical references, proslavery advocates had a strong historical argument that Israelites held slaves as well as indentured servants. The Old Testament justified the perpetual enslavement of the enemies of Israel—the Canaanites, for example.[52] An indentured servant, say, a Hebrew debtor, had to be set free after seven years. According to Genovese and Fox-Genovese, "The historical scholarship of the early nineteenth century had said as much, and by the 1850s A.A. Porter, De Bow, and T.W. MacMahon confidently declared the scriptural argument settled in favor of the South."[53] The southern slave master did not have to consider for one minute that he had to let an enslaved person go after seven years, for the Black children of Ham and Canaan were enslaved forever (see chapter 6).

In the Old Testament book of Leviticus 25, God spoke to Moses on Mount Sinai, and gave various prescriptions for Moses to convey to the children of Israel, whom God had brought out of Egypt as God's servants.[54] In verses 44–46, Christian proslavery advocates found unequivocal support of perpetual slavery from God:

Both thy bondmen, and thy bondmaids, which thou shalt have, *shall be* of the heathen that are round about you; of them shall ye buy bondmen and bondmaids. Moreover, of the children of the strangers that do sojourn among you, of them shall ye buy, and of their families that are with you, which they begat in your land: and they shall be your possession. And ye shall take them as an inheritance for your children after you, to inherit *them for* a possession; they shall be bondmen forever.[55]

It seems clear from these verses that God allowed his servants, the children of Israel, to buy slaves from people around them perceived to be "heathens" and these bondmen and bondmaids became possessions (chattel) "forever" and could be passed as inheritance from generation to generation. As Ross summarized these verses, "Sir, I do not see how God could tell us more plainly that he did command his people to buy slaves from the heathen about them, and from the stranger, and from their families sojourning among them."[56] Abolitionists would find this a difficult scriptural argument to overcome.

THE NEW TESTAMENT AND JESUS'S POSITION ON SLAVERY

Once colonial legislatures determined that a slave's conversion to Christianity did not make him "free," most masters initially encouraged baptism among the enslaved, a practice they abandoned later. These colonial baptisms were not the baptism ritual described by the apostle Peter in Galatians 3:25–29, which recognized that all people, "neither Jew or Greek, there is neither bond nor free, there is neither male or female: for ye are all one in Christ Jesus."[57] This was legislative paternalism, codifying a racist, conditional, hierarchical baptism. One could argue it was baptizing the enslaved into an eternal childlike, albeit Christian, dependent state.

What do we learn about Jesus's position on slavery when we consult the Bible? Jesus saw slavery as it was practiced by the Romans, whose enslaved population was made up of people conquered and imprisoned as part of Rome's march to world domination. Was Jesus neutral on it? Did he condemn it? Did he support it? Did he preach against it? If slavery were a sin, the proslavery clergy argued, Jesus would say so. Historian Jennifer A. Glancy, who derived a great deal of her analysis of Jesus's parables from the Gospel of Matthew, stated that "the most prominent and consistent aspect of the parabolic construction of slavery in Matthew is an emphasis on the vulnerability of the enslaved body to violence, notably to brutal disciplinary practices. . . . They reinscribe the slaveholding ideology of that world. Like other literary productions of that era, the Matthean parables represent slaves as bodies inscribed by the whip."[58] Avalos offered his own analysis: "Jesus certainly has no problem with slavery, and never spoke of it as being sinful or ethically abhorrent."[59] Marse certainly heard nothing in his home, church, or school that would make him question whether God or even Jesus thought that slavery was sinful or unethical.

Glancy offered a compelling analysis of the figure—the trope—of the slave in the parables of Jesus.[60] As she pointed out, Jesus used many familiar elements of Mediterranean life in his teachings, and these elements included slaves and their disciplinarians. According to Glancy, "Allusions to slaves and masters are common in the parables of Jesus."[61] The customs and practices of slavery in the first century were well known to Jesus: "In the parables of Jesus, the bodies of slaves are vulnerable to abuse."[62] Slavery scholar Keith Bradley noted, "The fact remains, however, that slavery caused no one in antiquity a crisis of conscience or an agony of the soul as it did abolitionists in later history, and as it still does some modern historians today. For a thousand years and more slavery was not a problem in classical culture."[63] The true American southern gentleman of the planter class saw himself as a classicist, and, even better, as a Renaissance man. Marse was very comfortable with a classical view of slavery. He sometimes gave his slaves names from antiquity, like Cicero, Caesar, and Brutus. Marse may well have considered this a clever inside joke.

Glancy pointed out that, while slave figures were not central in Jesus's teachings in the Gospel of Mark, they were ubiquitous in Luke and Matthew. For example, Matthew's representations of slaves in six different parables (13:24–30, 18:23–35, 21:33–41, 22:1–10, 24:45–51, and 25:14–30) offered descriptions of the slave body, in five of these parables, as the site of abuse and discipline. In chapter 18: 23–35, Matthew related a teaching parable of Jesus in which Jesus described a lord's servant, to whom the lord had shown leniency and mercy about an unpaid debt to the lord, in a similar situation with his own servant; the servant grabbed his servant by the throat, refused to listen to the man's pleas for patience, and threw him into prison. The parable continued. When the lord learned that the servant to whom he had shown mercy had not done the same to his own servant, the lord "was wroth, and delivered him to the tormentors, till he should pay all that was due unto him." Here is a clear example, sanctioned by Jesus, that torture of a servant was permissible.

The slave master and southern evangelicals easily found biblical justification for slavery and the northern abolitionists found no effective counterarguments in the teachings of Jesus. But the Good Book offered not only justification, but also multiple examples underscoring that slaves' bodies were legitimately subject to violence. Notably, Jesus did not preach against the use of violence on slaves.

THE RISE OF THE ABOLITIONISTS

As Snay pointed out, there was a "call and response" between the North and South about the slavery controversy. In the North, a rising storm of abolitionism gathered strength. Historian Andrew Delbanco described an example of the southern response: "By the 1830s, many southern states had passed laws banning publication and distribution of any kind of antislavery writing."[64] Powerful antislavery, personal narratives, written by prominent former enslaved men such as Charles Ball, Frederick Douglass, and Henry Bibb, "appeared in growing numbers in the 1830s and 1840s."[65] These narratives spelled out the horrors of southern slavery. All this set the stage for an organized abolitionist educative effort on the evils of slavery aimed directly at the whole American population, although largely targeting the South. Snay wrote, "The role of religion in the development of Southern separatism began in earnest in the summer of 1835 when a political maelstrom came sweeping down from the North, striking with fearful accuracy at the heart of Southern slavery."[66] This effort, led by the American Anti-Slavery Society, was experienced as an attack on the South's states' rights, on its honor, and on its integrity. Looking for a plausible scapegoat, wrote Snay, Southerners came to "blame the British for the existence of slavery in the colonies, cited their own inalienable rights of property, and suggested that Blacks were really not part of humanity."[67] These were weak proslavery arguments. Evangelical religion would come to offer slavery a greater defense.

Avalos gave us an example of a resolution against abolitionism passed by the Hopewell Presbytery of South Carolina in 1836:

1. Slavery has existed in the church of God from the time of Abraham to this day. Members of the church of God have held slaves bought with their money and born in their houses; and this relation is not only recognized, but its duties are defined clearly, both in the Old and New Testaments.
2. Emancipation is not mentioned among the duties of the master to his slaves, while obedience, "even to the forward [*sic*] master" is enjoined upon the slave.
3. No instance can be produced of an otherwise orderly Christian being reproved much less excommunicated from the church, for the single act of holding domestic slaves, from the days of Abraham down to the date of the modern abolitionists.[68]

Proslavery advocates found centuries old, solid ground in the Bible: "Biblical authority was employed perhaps more often than any other single argument in the proslavery arsenal. The debate over the morality of the slavery that pitted Southern clergymen against Northern abolitionists centered on the Bible."[69] Arguing that the external support for chattel slavery became unassailable is not erroneous or hyperbolic. The Christian Bible, as the word of God, was the ultimate authority, perceived to be unerring. A solid steel scriptural wall protected the peculiar institution of Southern slavery. The abolitionists declared that slavery was a sin, but racist slaveholders and their divines successfully argued that the Bible did not support such an antislavery position. Christian abolitionists who believed in the inerrancy of the Bible, accepting that it was the word of God, were stymied because they could not mount a solid counterargument against slavery without somehow attacking the word of God.

Religious scholar David M. Goldenberg pointed out that Gayraud S. Wilmore, an African American theologian, said that racism, to be defined properly, required elements of "domination and exploitation."[70] The Israelites' history provided a solid model protocol for American southern white Christian domination and exploitation of enslaved people. Southern politicians and clergy believed that the South was aligned with Israel and associated the enemies of Israel with the North, which was populated, they declared, with infidels. As Fox-Genovese and Genovese stated, most abolitionists pointed out that the Israelites practiced some form of indentured servitude, and that ancient Israel had two types of servitude: (1) enslavement for foreigners and (2) indentured labor for Israelites.[71] The abolitionists emphasized that the Israelites did not enslave people based on race or the color of their skin. This argument had little effect on proslavery advocates.

Religious historian Avalos criticized the abolitionists' antislavery efforts. He maintained that abolitionists actually whitewashed biblical and Christian slavery, quoting G. E. M. de Ste. Croix: "It is often said that Christianity introduced an entirely new and better attitude toward slavery. Nothing could be more false."[72] Antiabolitionist southern scholars found support for slavery in the Bible because it's there: "If anything, pro-slavery advocates had an upper hand in any scriptural debate with abolitionists."[73] Avalos made a profound point: In the intellectual battles between slavery advocates and abolitionists on the question of slavery, the proslavery forces won. Returning to the Old Testament, proslavery advocates found further biblical support not only for enslavement but also for systematic violence: "That God commanded, not merely allowed, the Israelites to hold slaves (Deuteronomy, 20:10–16) became a proslavery staple."[74] This is a powerful passage, for it says, in brief, that if the Israelites came upon an adversary's city, they were to offer peace, and if the proffered peace was accepted by the inhabitants, the Israelites could take its citizens "as tributaries unto thee, and they shall serve thee." But if there was resistance, the Israelites were to lay siege to that city, and once it was conquered, "thou shalt smite every male thereof with the edge of the sword." These verses explicitly paired enslavement of captured people with male-exterminating violence.

New Testament scholar J. Albert Harrill declared:

> In the late 19th century conflict over the Bible and slavery, American abolitionists, many of whom were Christian evangelicals, ransacked Scripture for texts condemning slavery, but found few. As a consequence, they developed new hermeneutical strategies to read the Bible to counter the "plain sense" (literalist) reading of proslavery theology. . . . Most embarrassing for today's reader of the Bible, the proslavery clergymen were holding the more defensible position from the perspective of historical criticism. The passages in the Bible about slavery signal the acceptance of an ancient model of civilization for which patriarchy and subjugation were not merely desirable but essential.[75]

Avalos argued that the abolitionists used three primary hermeneutical strategies in their efforts to counter the biblical defense of slavery: one, *representativism*, which essentially was a cherry-picking of scripture that supported an antislavery ethical view (and ignored scripture that supported the horrors of slavery, such as slavery itself and genocide); two, *trajectorialism*, an interpretive approach to scripture that "grants that certain undesirable biblical practices exist, but they are nonetheless a step in the right direction or represent advances"; and three, *reinterpretation*, which is an exegesis model that allows the original meaning of a text "to be erased or changed to fit a later or modern context."[76] Needless to say, Avalos argued, these strategies were largely ineffective.

To state the obvious: the run-up to the Civil War rang loudly with the rancorous debate between proslavery advocates and abolitionists. For simplicity's sake, I make that debate as between the North and the South. By 1860, the South won, no contest. Within the Bible, slaveholders found solid, God-based justification of slaveholding. The southern Protestant Christian clergy became a united voice for secession; "the result was that by fighting the intellectual debate over slavery with biblical arguments, the South was in fact fighting the antislavery forces on their strongest ground."[77] By employing the strategy of "the best defense is a great offense," the proslavery forces rode a muscular spiritual charger into the Holy War with the abolitionists. The southern elite slave master became convinced that the abolitionists, by challenging slavery, were actually challenging God's word. The true God was on the South's side and would lead it to triumph over the North and establish a new, God-blessed southern nation.

It is vitally important that both the recorded history of humankind *and* the Bible countenanced slavery as being a fact of life. Neither God Almighty, the Prophets, Jesus, nor his disciples condemned slavery. This is not something the proslavery divines and politicians had to make up out of whole cloth. As Avalos said, the abolitionists "whitewashed" biblical slavery. In this intellectual and spiritual fight, the proslavery advocates triumphed—to a point.

SLAVE TRADE CONFLICT

Over time, practical as well as moral issues naturally arose about the acquisition of enslaved people. There were political and moral skirmishes about slave trading—especially the African slavery trade, which the US government had abolished in 1808, having stamped slavery as "immoral." Slave trading was naturally divided into two broad categories: the abduction, sale, and purchase of humans brought from Africa and the West Indies; and the abduction, sale, and purchase of enslaved people born in the United States. Then, on January 1, 1808, a new federal law went into effect banning the importation of slaves into the United States, in both the North and the South. From that point on, the slave trade was limited by law—in theory, but often not in practice—to the purchase and sale of enslaved people born in the United States. The trade of homegrown enslaved people not only continued, it thrived. Thus, after 1808, the external trade of bringing enslaved people from other countries to "Christian America" lessened considerably or went further underground, and the practice of internal, domestic buying and selling became the norm. Any non-US-born captives had to be smuggled into the states.

Prior to 1808, Christian slave traders saw themselves as agents of the "true" religion and thus agents of the "true" civilization. One of the first acts by slave traders, once they brought their human cargo to "civilization," was to baptize these African heathens, thus making them Christians. Roughly, the sequence was that the slave trader would acquire these human beings, by whatever means necessary, from their native lands; pack them in horrible conditions—shipped or in chained forced marches; transport them to a holding area, such as a slave prison in Cuba; have them baptized by a priest or minister and give them a "Christian" name; then chain and imprison them until they could be shipped to their market destination to be enslaved forever. The documentary *Traces of the Trade: A Story from the Deep North* offers a powerful, retrospective view of these practices.[78]

Historian Michael Tadman's research on the subject of slave trading debunked a number of myths about the southern slave master, at the same time providing a relatively clear picture of who Marse really was as revealed by the business of slave trading.[79] The central picture Tadman painted is that, on average, despite masters' efforts to portray themselves as benevolent paternalists toward their enslaved, they were actually narcissistically engaged in the constant separation of slave families, viewing slaves as less than human, as dependent children, and were quite comfortable with slave trading, so-called negro speculation. Slave trading was an integral part of the business of slavery. To control his enslaved people, the slave master maintained the threat of separating enslaved families over the heads of his bondsmen like the sword of Damocles. Nevertheless, when making a profit was possible or when addressing an economic problem, Marse did not hesitate to break up a slave family.

Despite the fact that Southern clergy preached and admonished the masters to treat their slaves with kindness, and despite the fact that some states had laws pertaining to the management of slaves, in reality there was little to no enforcement. Slaveholders did what they needed to do to maintain power and control. Selling members of enslaved families was just business.

Daly described the dilemma created by many Christians' blind acceptance of God's hand in material success: "Had so many Christians not been uncritically convinced that God's hand routinely dispensed material rewards, a more realistic analysis of the practical steps to overcome moral, economic, and political dilemmas might have been possible before the Civil War."[80]

United States Slave Trade 1830. *Library of Congress*

The South established a Christian conservatism that not only defended and justified slavery, but also insulated (some would say isolated) the South from the rest of the world. According to Fox-Genovese and Genovese, "Those who upheld and those who denied the divine sanction of slavery disagreed on the essentials of Christian doctrine and on the nature of conscience and moral standards. In consequence, they had incompatible visions of the social relations necessary to sustain Christianity in a sinful world."[81] America moved toward a Holy War.

The South was crushed by the Civil War. Many Southerners saw the war as holy and were certain that God was on the side of the South. In January 1861, South Carolina minister James Henley Thornwell addressed the question of secession with the following conclusion: "We prefer peace—but if war must come, we are prepared to meet it with unshaken confidence in the God of battles."[82] Snay expressed the idea that religion served as one of the South's unifying forces: "It helped forge a moral consensus around slavery, a consensus capable of encompassing differing political views and uniting a diverse and disharmonious South behind the banner of disunion. . . . The sanctification of slavery was perhaps the most important element in this moral consensus."[83] Daly added to this picture: "Religious proslavery ideas unified southern identity and morale with a seamless set of causes and motivations for combat."[84]

What did southern Christians have to say after the South's defeat? To conclude this chapter, I offer one perhaps fitting perspective. As historian Mark A. Noll wrote, John Adger, editor of the *Southern Presbyterian Review*, "writing immediately after the war [March 1866] about the manifest course

View of Richmond, Virginia, at the close of the rebellion. *Library of Congress*

of God's providence," had this to say: "After insisting on 'the justice of the Southern cause,' Adger also conceded that 'there was one error . . . into which we acknowledge that some Southern ministers sometimes fell.'" As Noll further stated, "Adger wrote that the mistake made by some Southern theologians was to believe 'that God must surely bless the right.' Adger added that what Southerners had forgotten was the lesson of history that God often let 'the righteous . . . be overthrown.'[85] Adger acknowledged that even though many ministers 'prayed fervently for the Success of the Confederacy, . . . the result was with God alone. . . . We accept the failure of secession, as manifestly providential. The overthrow of that just cause made evident not so much the prowess of its foes, not even their prodigiously superior resources, as it did the direct hand of the Almighty.' And so to Adger the only possible conclusion was that God was chastening his people for their own good. 'Yes! The hand of God, gracious though heavy, is upon the South for her discipline.'"[86]

· *6* ·

Scriptural Confabulation

The Story of Noah in Genesis 9:18–27

AFTER THE FLOOD

Although the antebellum Southern clergy used many biblical verses to justify chattel slavery, the spiritual heart of their argument lies within the first book of the Old Testament. In the words of historian David Brion Davis, "No other passage in the Bible has had such a disastrous influence through human history as Genesis 9:18–27."[1]

But when one first reads these verses, one might wonder why:

> And the sons of Noah, that went forth of the ark, were Shem, and Ham, and Japheth: and Ham *is* the father of Canaan. These *are* the three sons of Noah: and of them was the whole earth overspread. And Noah began *to be* a husbandman, and he planted a vineyard: And he drank of the wine, and was drunken: and he was uncovered within his tent. And Ham, the father of Canaan, saw the nakedness of his father, and told his two brethren without. And Shem and Japheth took a garment, laid it upon both of their shoulders, and went backward, and covered the nakedness of their father; and their faces *were* backward, and they saw not their father's nakedness. And Noah awoke from his wine, and knew what his younger son had done unto him. And he said Cursed *be* Canaan; a servant of servants shall he be unto his brethren. And he said, Blessed *be* the Lord God of Shem; and Canaan shall be his servant. God shall enlarge Japheth, and he shall dwell in the tents of Shem; and Canaan shall be his servant.

There is nothing in these verses about Blackness or skin color or slavery. While it is clear that Noah woke up and cursed his grandson Canaan (who is not present) to be "a servant of servants," how did these verses have such a powerful, disastrous influence throughout human history?

Southern divines, evangelicals, and slave masters cannot be entirely blamed for the transmogrification of these verses in Genesis 9—the story of Noah after the flood. They did not originate it; that was the evolution of interpretations over many centuries. But they refined it and honed it to a new intensity.

WHAT'S IN A NAME?

Genesis 9:18–27, this so-called curse, as momentous and important as it is, remains an intensely dramatic puzzle. For example, there is no consensus among biblical and historical scholars as to whether chapter 9:18–27 is most accurately called "Noah's Curse," "Ham's Curse," or the "Curse of Canaan." And, to complicate matters even more, these verses have gone by another descriptor: "The Drunkenness of Noah," as Genesis 9:18–27 was commonly called in Renaissance art history books, is the title of Michelangelo's interpretation of these verses as rendered on the ceiling of the Sistine Chapel.[2]

The Sistine Chapel ceiling depicts the book of Genesis including chapter 9. Michelangelo began this work in 1508 under the patronage of Pope Julius II.[3] Michelangelo's interpretation of the postflood story of Noah and his family in verses 18–27 was called "The Drunkenness of Noah," not "The Curse of Noah" or the "Curse of Ham."[4] The "Drunkenness of Noah," according to art historian Linda Murray, was "symbolic of man in his lost state wholly unconscious of God."[5]

Drunkenness of Noah by Michelangelo (1508–1510), Sistine Chapel ceiling, Rome. *Courtesy of Michelangelo.org*

A detail of the *Drunkenness of Noah* section of the Sistine ceiling over an entrance used by the laity shows five white men (not four).[6] (See figure on page 124.) Four of the men, Noah and his three sons, are in the right foreground engaged in animated talk. Noah is naked, laying on the ground with a wine pitcher near his side; two of the men are partially clothed and the fourth man is also naked. This fourth person has his head turned away from Noah and is presumably putting some garment over his father. I surmise that the man pointing at Noah is Ham, and either Japheth or Shem is holding Ham around the left side of his chest, listening to Ham while encouraging his other brother, with a gesture of his hand, to continue covering Noah.

The fifth man, a much smaller figure on the left, is intentionally in the background, both figuratively and literally. He is fully clothed and digging the soil with a shovel. Although he is not identified and is not at all part of these verses, as a figure he captures what is known about Noah, in this case, as a much younger man, before he got drunk and became unconscious: He "began to be a husbandman and he planted a vineyard" (Gen 9:20). This fifth figure is the artist's clever method to tell a larger historical background narrative about Noah, not contained within the verses at hand about the curse.

Significantly, perhaps, in an examination of Michelangelo's painting, we see that not only is Noah naked, but for the most part, his three sons are also. Only one son appears to be averting his eyes from Noah. What should be made of this? Is Michelangelo guilty of misinterpreting the Old Testament? There is evidence that Michelangelo read the Old Testament closely and repeatedly—as his biographer Ascanio Condivi (1525–1574) informed us.[7] Michelangelo probably wasn't reading the Latin/Vulgate version but an Italian translation of 1471. Many art historians assume that the iconographic program for the Sistine Chapel was shaped by a learned figure. Marco Vigerio della Rovere, a cousin of Pope Julius II, is a "prime candidate."[8] If Pope Julius II's cousin was "supervising" Michelangelo's work, are we to assume that the pope's cousin was allowed to misinterpret the text of Genesis 9?

A contemporary of Michelangelo, Giovanni Bellini, also executed a painting entitled "The Drunkenness of Noah," and his interpretation shows the figure of Ham laughing at his father's situation. (See figure on page 126.) Given the centrality of the figure of Ham, Ham's laughing or mocking clearly is a principal theme of Bellini's rendition. This tells us that the scriptural interpretation of Noah being mocked by Ham was part of sixteenth-century biblical scholarship or artistic license, despite the fact that the literal verses of Genesis 9 offer no evidence of Ham mocking or laughing at his father.

Michelangelo was painting for posterity a ceiling in one of the most revered Christian cathedrals in the world. The scenes he painted would have been approved by Pope Julius II, a man who, according to Murray, was "of

Drunkenness of Noah by Giovanni Bellini (1515). *Museum of Fine Arts and Archeology, Besancon, France*

strict piety and rigid decorum,"[9] which is a conundrum. If Genesis 9:18–27 was interpreted as "The Drunkenness of Noah," symbolizing man becoming wholly unconscious of God, how did these verses come to capture irrefutable, unassailable scriptural evidence that God, through Noah, put a spell on Ham and his son, Canaan, turned them into Black Africans, and made them racist enslaved people forever? How did the emphasis shift from Noah's inebriated state to his curse of Canaan (overlooking for the moment there is no mention in the verses of either God or Noah cursing Ham)? There is also no indication in the verses that Ham "mocked" Noah, a commonly used element of modern interpretations of Genesis 9:18–27. It seems obvious that when a drama of such importance has had, over centuries, four different titles, as well as added details such as the mocking allegation, there was and remains an unresolved debate about who and what the drama was about.

This biblical story of "the curse of Noah," which became a "world defining myth" for proslavery southern intellectuals and religious divines, also became a collective bending of reality. The interpretation of Genesis 9 as the basis for a biblical justification of Black slavery has been around for centuries. Biblical scholar and theologian David M. Goldenberg shed some light on the history of "the curse of Ham." Although many more biblical scriptures were used to justify slavery, "this biblical story has been the single greatest justification for Black Slavery for more than a thousand years."[10]

Religious historian Stephen Haynes summarized the scholarship of efforts to explain how Genesis 9:18–27 somehow managed to connect Ham with slavery and blackness. In his book *Noah's Curse*, Haynes described the evolution of the so-called curse of Ham as a biblical justification for racial slavery. He traced it to conditions in the tenth century BCE when the Israelite monarchy enslaved and debased the "Canaanites." He pointed out that in the third and fourth centuries CE, Genesis 9 began to be read as meaning a perennial curse on the "Hamites."[11] Haynes added that Black servitude was foreshadowed by Origen's (ca. 185–254) interpretation of Genesis 9, referring to Ham's "discolored posterity imitate the ignobility of the race," and St. Augustine (354–430) "saw the origins of slavery in Ham's transgressions."[12] According to Haynes, a biblical scholar named Ephrem of Nisbis (d. 373) supposedly paraphrased Noah's curse "with the words, 'accursed by Canaan, and may God make his face Black.'"[13] Haynes appeared to come down on the side of the debate that these varied interpretations remain controversial and research exists that questions the Christian connection of sexuality, Ham, and blackness.[14]

Historically, Haynes informed us that "long before modern writers attacked Noah's curse in an effort to sever the nerve that animated the Christian defense of slavery, early Bible readers resisted the textual logic of Genesis 9:20–27 and the momentum of the interpretive tradition."[15] These early Bible readers found fault with Noah's drunkenness and found fault with "the rabbinic tendency to temper Noah's reputation for righteousness" by glossing over his drunkenness. . . . "In contrast to the rabbis, the church fathers tended to downplay or excuse Noah's drunkenness."[16] If Noah's piety was to remain elevated, his getting drunk and falling naked in a stupor had to be effectively dismissed as inconsequential. According to Haynes, Augustine framed Noah's insobriety as his "suffering."[17] The famous evangelical divine John Calvin (1509–1564) did not view Noah's drunkenness lightly at all: "Calvin regarded the story as 'a lesson in temperance for all ages.' Because Moses did not indicate that Noah's drunkenness occurred the first time he tasted wine, Calvin concluded that the story teaches 'what a filthy and detestable crime drunkenness is . . . [causing the holy patriarch] to become a laughing stock to all.'"[18] Calvin's conclusion was another interpretation that projects a condition of shame that evoked being laughed at or "mocked," even though, as has been said, there is nothing in Genesis 9:18–27 that implied or conveyed Noah being laughed at. It seems reasonable to infer that the "mocking" interpretive theme associated with this story (and hung on Ham's character) was just that: an interpretation that helped move the disgrace and blame off Noah the patriarch planter onto Ham. In this example, Calvin (in the early sixteenth century) used Noah's drunkenness as a moral teaching story, while at the same time helped to raise or perhaps reinforce the already existing "laughingstock" motif.

According to Haynes, recognizing the significance of the proslavery argument resting on Noah's curse, the abolitionists attacked "the assumption that Negro slavery was a fulfillment of the curse of Canaan."[19] Notable among these antislavery writers was Samuel Sewall, who "observed that deriving a curse on Ham from Genesis 9 violated the natural meaning of the text."[20]

As stated in chapter 5, the proslavery intellectuals, plantation Grandees, and divines won the debate about the scriptural support for slavery, due in large part because there were Christians in both the North and the South who agreed on the consistency and infallibility of the scriptures. As Haynes pointed out, "For all their vitriol and social radicalism, American abolitionists did not contribute a great deal to the history of biblical interpretation. While aggressively attacking the biblical rationale for slavery, they failed to read against the textual grain in which Noah's curse was inscribed."[21] In other words, the abolitionists read the scripture in an orthodox manner, rarely disputing Noah's righteousness, or whether or not Ham or Canaan sinned against Noah. Except for Sewall, the abolitionists largely failed to apply the interrogative methods of an investigator against the actual text.

It is also important to remember that in the book of Genesis, God apportioned the world: From the ancestors of Shem and Japheth issued the Jews, all the nations of Europe and America, and a great part of Asia; and from the descendants of Ham and Canaan, the Canaanites (or Africans). Over time, as the word "slave" came to be synonymous with Black Africans, the word Ham (incorrectly it would seem) came to mean "Black" or "dark," and Noah's drunkenness became Noah's curse, which was transformed into a racist, airtight, scripturally based narrative in which Noah, with God's power and support, made Ham and his ancestors the founders of Black Africa, whose people, in turn, naturally and divinely became enslaved humans for the rest of the world to exploit and dominate. Black slaves became known as the "sons of Ham."

Davis informed us that in approximately 1500, the great Jewish philosopher and statesman Isaac ben Abravenel, having seen so many Black slaves in his native Portugal and in Spain, merged Aristotle's theory of natural slaves with the belief that the biblical Noah had cursed and condemned to slavery both his son Ham and his young grandson Canaan. According to Davis, Abravanel concluded that the servitude of animalistic Black Africans should be perpetual. And while it would be absurd to blame Aristotle for all the uses to which his writings have been put, his work provided the conceptual basis for much nineteenth-century southern proslavery ideology and scientific theories of racial inferiority.[22]

I will leave the decision of whether or not Abravenel should get the credit for this interpretive sleight of hand to biblical scholars. Abravenel concluded that these Black Africans are the natural slaves identified by Aristotle and are the product of God's curse, through Noah, who sent Ham and Canaan to populate Africa. It was a simple, logical connection. Or was it?

The timing of these views—Abravanel's interpretation of the story of Noah (approximately 1500) and Michelangelo's and Bellini's depictions of the same (1508 and 1515, respectively) suggest that the interpretation of Genesis 9 was very much in flux, at least in the early sixteenth century. Haynes referred to this phenomenon as an "emerging reality of racial slavery as effect rather than cause."[23] The faiths behind the interpretations contributed to the various and differing interpretations.

Davis made an important point. As the numbers of Black African slaves increased in the world, the two concepts of enslaved people and Blackness became conceptually fused: "Thus as we shall find, it was not an originally racist biblical script that led to the enslavement of 'Ham's Black descendants,' but rather the increasing enslavement of Blacks that transformed biblical interpretation"[24]—an astonishing and intellectually dishonest transformation. Christian Protestant proslavery evangelicals would most certainly have dismissed a Catholic (papal) interpretation of Genesis 9, such as Michelangelo's paintings on the Sistine ceiling: "Anti-Catholicism was in the marrow of the cultural tradition that Britain had bequeathed to the United States and its South."[25]

It was the biblical interpretation of the story of Noah and his sons in the book of Genesis that sealed the fate of Black Africans. Southern divines seized on this distorted interpretation with a vengeance. Not only did this twisted interpretation indict Blacks for dishonoring God, but Ham, his son, Canaan, and all their subsequent generations were transformed into Black Africans whose fate was eternal servitude in the newly established postflood order.

Goldenberg's research examined how the racist interpretations of these verses developed. In his most recent work, he explained the etiological origins of the Hamic myth as "showing how a myth explaining the origin of Black skin morphed into the exegetical justification for Black slavery."[26] He explains that, even though the Bible says nothing about skin color, Black skin gets woven into the biblical text. More accurately, Black skin gets projected into the story, because on the face of it, it is not there.

Summarizing his work, Goldenberg explained that Noah's curse was ostensibly about slavery—"servants" being the operant synonym—but over time the curse of slavery became fused with skin color. The obvious question is how did Ham (who was not the recipient of Noah's curse) become identified with the Black African? Goldenberg explained that there are several reasons, spanning centuries of interpretations, ultimately landing in the biblical exegesis of proslavery southern clergy.

First, one of Ham's sons was Kush, a name long associated with an area of Africa south of Egypt. Secondly, a Greek translation of the Hebrew Bible defined Kush as Ethiopia. Thirdly, the word "Ham" in Hebrew was translated as meaning "Black." This interpretation turns out to be incorrect, but it lodged itself as accurate for centuries. As Goldenberg pointed out, James Baldwin in his powerful work *The Fire Next Time* put the deleterious effects of the "curse of Noah" in a contemporaneous context when he wrote, "I knew that, according to many Christians, I was a descendant of Ham, who had been cursed, and that I was therefore predestined to be a slave."[27]

A fourth reason, explained Goldenberg, had to do with "the Syriac Christian work known as the *Cave of Treasures* . . . originally going back to the 3rd or 4th century. . . . [T]he work explains that Canaan's 'descendants were reduced to slavery, and they are the Egyptians, the Mysiens (*musaye*), the Kusshites, the Indians, and the abominable ones (*musraye*).' The ones cursed with slavery are dark skinned peoples, a point made clear in the Arabic version (around 750 CE) of the work, which expanded Canaan's descendants to include all Blacks: [Noah] was angry with Ham and said, 'Let Canaan be cursed, and let him be a slave to his brothers. . . . [Noah] increased in his curse of Canaan. Therefore his sons became slaves. They are the Copts, the Kushites, the Indians, the Musin (*musin*), and all the other Blacks (*sudan*).'"[28]

Advocates developed the theory in the Middle Ages that descendants of Ham were Black, and this theory was further developed in the sixteenth century. Goldenberg elaborated, "By the sixteenth century some Christian theologians were taking racial ground, and toward the end of the century racial interpretation swept England. In later centuries application of the Noahic curse to Blacks had special import in Germany, which emerged as the center of theological and philosophical speculation."[29] Over time, by the eighteenth and nineteenth centuries, Blacks were referred to as "the sons of Ham." This interpretation was not simply *racial*; it was *racist*. The Baptists of Arkansas illustrated the power of this racist interpretation of the "curse of Ham." Exhibiting a fantastic mix of religion and politics, "in 1859 the Arkansas Baptist Convention reasserted [Noah's] curse as racially specific."[30] Over time, the Ham myth became a bedrock belief in the Christian South upon which *racist* slavery was founded.

To illustrate some of the varieties of interpretations, I recite some of H. Hirsch Cohen's scholarship, in which he summarized some of the early interpretations of Genesis 9:18–27.[31] One theory was that Satan showed up and tricked Noah into getting drunk; another theory, found in the *Zohar*, "the medieval source book of Jewish mysticism," was that Noah was "driven into a drunken stupor by his idealism"; a third interpretation, depicted on the ceiling of the Sistine Chapel, was "the drunkenness of Noah as the tragic confrontation between youth and old age." Haynes (quoting Old Testament scholar John F. A. Sawyer), wrote that "what people believe a text means has often been far more interesting and important, theologically, politically, morally, and aesthetically . . . than what it originally meant."[32]

Cohen's own interpretation of Genesis 9:18–27 put the blame on the wine and linked it with sexuality. Cohen's rabbinical thesis was that Noah was feeling pressure from God to procreate (at six hundred years of age) and drank himself into a state of "helpless intoxication."[33]

Cohen contributed to the confusion about what Genesis 9:18–27 actually says. Does the specific verse say when Noah woke, he knew what his *youngest* son had done, or what his *younger* son had done?[34] Cohen said it was "youngest." *The Westminster Dictionary of the Bible* states that Ham was Noah's *youngest* son.[35] Cohen also asserted that "the narrator" omitted many lurid details of what happened in the tent between Noah and Ham.[36] Cohen did not clarify nor offered evidence to corroborate this claim. The narrator was not identified. What Cohen did say is that the "paucity of information as to what occurred in the tent stimulated the ancient Jewish commentators to enlarge upon the story with the lurid details allegedly omitted by the narrator."[37] This is most curious. Although the narrator is not identified, are we not to assume it was Moses, based on the fact that Genesis is the first book of Moses?

THE DRUNKENNESS OF NOAH—THE GREAT DRAMA OF HAM

As a sterling example of a Christian antebellum evangelical who likely helped shape Marse's religious beliefs, consider the sermons of the Reverend Fred A. Ross, discussed in chapter 5. Reportedly written as a counter to Harriet Beecher Stowe's 1850 book *Uncle Tom's Cabin*, Ross's proslavery arguments were compiled in a self-published book entitled *Slavery Ordained by God*.[38]

In the Holy Bible, Ross found scriptural support for African slavery time and time again, but he put considerable weight on Genesis 9, a source he referred to "as the great drama of Ham." A sample:

> When Ham, in his antediluvian recklessness, laughed at his father, God took occasions to give the world the rule of the superior over the inferior. *He cursed him. He cursed him because he left him unblessed.* The withholding of the father's blessing, in the Bible, was curse [*sic*]. . . . Ham was cursed to render service, forever, to Shem and Japheth. . . . Shem was blessed to rule over Ham. Japheth was blessed to rule over both. God sent Ham to Africa, Shem to Asia, Japheth to Europe.[39]

This was Ross's interpretive description, but it was a persuasive one. His position on this was commonly held among antebellum Christian evangelicals and slave masters. It also had its narcissistic attraction: The Anglo-Saxon and western European descendants of Europe were to be lords over the populations of Asia and Africa. The hierarchy of the world was established by God's Judeo-Christian covenant.

Take stock for a moment. If a revered evangelical preacher said Ham laughed at his father, you might want to know how he knew that, because it's not part of the scriptural drama of Noah. An incident or moment of laughter expressed by Ham is not in the verses. There's no mocking or laughing there. What's the preacher's source? We don't know. The "mocking" allegation apparently has been part of this scriptural narrative for centuries, but it is not in the verses. It has to come from an interpretation that includes false allegations of some kind.

Within the distorted narrative of Noah's curse, Ham (and his son, Canaan) became perpetrators of dishonor against God, Noah, and his family, and, as Ham and his ancestors became transmogrified into Black folks, Black slaves were viewed as inherently dishonorable heathens, prone to disorderly behavior. Honor was a steadfast principle of the southern self-image in the nineteenth century. Determining that Ham had dishonored God gave further reason to proslavery advocates to intensify their resentment and disdain of Black slaves.

The historians Elizabeth Fox-Genovese and Eugene Genovese pointed out that even though Genesis 9 was the "weakest link" scripturally for Southerners (i.e., there were other scriptural sources that were potentially much stronger), southern divines used Genesis 9:18–27 "to maximum political effect."[40] For example, Southerners could have used—and sometimes did find justification, indeed, heaven-derived support, for slavery in—other sections of the Bible: "From the great eighteenth-century evangelist George Whitfield onward, defenders of slavery pointed to Genesis, 15:14 [sic], in which the great patriarch Abraham prepared for war with his 'armed and trained servants, born in his own house, three hundred and eighteen.'"[41]

Haynes noted that

by the early colonial period a racialized [read: racist] version of Noah's curse had arrived in America . . . as white servitude declined and racial slavery came under attack, the curse's role in the American defense of slavery was increasingly formalized. By the 1830s—when the American antislavery movement became organized, vocal and aggressive—the scriptural defense of slavery had evolved into the "most elaborate and systematic statement" of proslavery theory, Noah's curse had become a stock weapon in the arsenal of slavery's apologists, and references to Genesis 9 appeared prominently in their publications.[42]

As Haynes pointed out, over time, readers of Genesis chapters 9–11 found justification for the themes of *"dispersion* and *differentiation,"* that is, the three-sons three continent model of the world,[43] and "[t]his prophecy of Noah is the *vade mecum*[44] of slaveholders, and they never venture abroad without it."[45]

THE SACRED PLANTER

After the flood, Noah, in effect, became the "first planter patriarch."[46] Over time, in the antebellum South, Noah became essentially the patron saint of the white elite planters. How comforting such an emphasis as that must have been to the minds and hearts of proslavery planter-class men seeking solid, spiritually authoritative justifications for racist slavery. After God destroyed all living things with the flood of forty days and nights and cleansed the earth's population, he established Noah as a second Adam. Noah was an elite planter who had elite status, not because he was a slaveholder (for he was not), but because of his esteemed biblical status. If he imbibed alcohol, Marse could easily forgive Noah for getting drunk, because Noah—the second Adam—was just like him, a planter. He was just like Noah. What a perfect fit! Marse could proudly see much of himself in Noah. He was a man like no other, a chosen white planter.

The acceptance and belief that Black people were the children of Ham weakened and eroded antislavery attacks: "Antebellum abolitionists as well as proslavery Southerners accepted that Blacks were the 'children of Ham,'" which was derived from an interpretation of Genesis 9.[47] Ham and his children had brought this curse on themselves because of a failure of character. For abolitionists who interpreted the Bible literally, there was little way of avoiding that Black people were Ham's children. For proslavery evangelicals and planters, Ham's curse supported their character-based racism.

A PROVIDENTIAL SAFETY NET

Psychologically and behaviorally, the slave masters and the South's Protestant Christian proslavery evangelical divines could always fall back to the Providential bottom line. God Almighty himself banished Black people, through the actions of Noah, to eternal servitude because of a failure of character. This point cannot be overemphasized. God was speaking through Noah. Noah's curse and banishment of Ham and his children to be Black, to be eternal servants, and to populate Africa—these were the words of God. God was working through Noah. As a spiritual and ethical position, this belief had profound implications, one of the most significant being that racist slavery was based on (read: faith in) God's morality and God's ethics. In the antebellum South, "churchmen themselves rarely had doubts about the essential justice of slavery, only about its practice. They were probably among the most ardent supporters of the Southern cause."[48]

Frederick Douglass made a keen observation about the fallacy of "Ham's curse." He pointed out that the annual births of thousands of so-called mulatto people—children of white men and Black slaves—objectively and empirically proved that the origins and consequences of southern slavery were not scripturally bound.[49] The primary response to Douglass's biting observation was silence and collective denial.

Protestant Christian slavery clerics developed consistent, loud biblical declarations supporting slavery. Proslavery Virginia Baptist Thornton Stringfellow contributed an essay (first published in 1841) entitled "The Bible Argument: Or, Slavery in the Light of Divine Revelation," to E. N. Elliott's 1869 book *Cotton Is King*, in which Stringfellow offered support for slavery from his examination of the Bible.[50] Stringfellow argued that if slavery is sinful, then all Christians who are involved with slavery should "wash their hands of it." He proclaimed that antislavery advocates did not know the Bible well, because if they did, they would find that the institution of slavery has received "the sanction of the Almighty in the Patriarchal age; that it was incorporated into the only National Constitution which ever emanated from God; that its legality was recognized, and its duties regulated, by Jesus Christ in his kingdom; and that it is full of mercy."[51]

Stringfellow posited that in Genesis, in the story of Noah's curse, "May it not be said in truth, that God decreed this institution [of slavery] before it existed; and has he not connected its *existence* with prophetic tokens of special favor, to those who should be slave owners or masters?"[52] Stringfellow asserted that God's decree of slavery, as given in Genesis, showed us the "moral character" of God. Stringfellow correctly points out that Jesus did not preach against slavery or make any effort to abolish it.

The bottom line for southern evangelicals and divines is that Noah, as God's agent, was the second Adam. After surviving the flood, Noah and his family repopulated the earth. Noah as the master, waking up from a wine-induced sleep, uttered a curse in response to Ham's sin that carried the full weight of God, relegating Ham's offspring to being the lowest of servants. As Ham and Canaan eventually came to be seen as Black-skinned, Blacks became synonymous with enslaved people. All Black people were designed by God to be enslaved, to serve their white masters. God ordained racial slavery. It was the natural order of things. Noah's drunkenness became Noah's curse. Southern evangelicals used a spiritual alchemy to turn Ham and Canaan Black, while simultaneously making one "brother" (and his progeny) inferior and subservient. Three brothers—Ham, Japheth, and Shem—were given sections of the world to populate. Ham and his progeny got Africa and the racist deal was done.

A GROSS SCRIPTURAL INTERPRETATION

Here in the twenty-first century, more than 150 years after the Civil War, it's clear that Genesis 9 has been grossly distorted and intellectually abused. But the book of Genesis remains a cornerstone of Christian thought. For much of humanity, it is considered the law. As Cohen said, "The real purpose of the Book of Genesis, like that of the rest of the Bible, is not to teach us scientific facts, but to tell us how God wants men to live in the world."[53] If the purpose of Genesis is to teach us how to live, then it cannot be denied that God's law informed humans that some men were masters and some were enslaved servants. What it did not say, until it got hijacked, was that God decreed—through Noah—that the descendants of Ham and Canaan were Black Africans condemned to be enslaved forever and ever.

What this meant for Marse psychologically was that, burdened by the realities and complexities of being an elite southern slaveholder and managing a dominating, bound labor system, he was carrying a lot of emotional baggage. Reassured by his preachers that God, through Noah, the second Adam, gave Black African slaves to Marse in perpetuity was simply joy beyond joy. Endorsed by scripture, the morality of the whole enterprise of slavery was Marse's shield as he charged into secession and a disastrous war. The anchor for the proslavery interpretation of Genesis 9:18–27 to justify racist slavery of Black Africans was that Noah's curse allegedly had God's approval. Southern slave masters and evangelical divines convinced themselves that God rewarded them, as descendants of Shem and Japheth, with "this cheap, humiliating, and involuntary labor,"[54] Black enslaved who allegedly were descendants of Ham. Marse felt honored, because God had given him Black slaves.

A TWENTY-FIRST-CENTURY FORENSIC
PSYCHOLOGICAL VIEW

"Noah's curse," from Genesis 9:18–27, is a story that, over time and through various interpretations, came to be freighted with serious allegations of sadistic sexual and emotional abuse. The interpretation of this story is not about an adult possibly perpetrating abuse on a child, but one of an adult-child, a son, allegedly perpetrating both emotional and sexual abuse on his aged father. In the context of twenty-first-century language, it is perhaps a story of sadistic incest, which would be a rare, almost unheard-of type of incest, if it were true that an adult son sexually assaulted his aged father. At a minimum, the story of the "curse of Noah" is about Ham, Noah's son, allegedly emotionally abusing his father to such a degree that his father inflicted a curse on Ham's progeny that lasts in perpetuity.

As it stands now, after centuries of investigations and interpretive conclusions, we have an unassailable case of a son (Ham) humiliating his father (Noah) by pointing out his father's nakedness to Ham's two other brothers. We have an understandably enraged father who inexplicably curses his grandson, who for reasons unknown is not present as this biblical drama unfolds. The curse, for reasons that are not clear, bypasses Ham and finds its target in Ham's son, Canaan, Noah's grandson.

The primary material for any and all conclusions drawn about "Noah's curse" is Genesis 9:18–27. Although there are variations in the wording depending on the source, the story elements have remained the same. If twenty-first-century empirical methodology used for the analysis of child abuse cases is applied to the "curse of Noah," what do we have? First of all, we note that the text contains no references to Black people, blackness, skin color, or Africans. Secondly, there is no clear evidence as to why Noah cursed Canaan, who was not physically present.

Historian Robert Alter suggested that the original intent of this passage was to justify the subjugation of the Canaanites, the descendants of Ham, by the Israelites, the descendants of Shem.[55] Noah got drunk from wine he made from his own vineyard, somehow became naked, and passed out, presumably in his tent. The possible reasons for his nakedness have been a great source of debate. Genesis 9:18–27 tells us nothing about how and why Noah's clothes came off. It seems reasonable to consider either Noah took them off or someone else removed them or helped Noah get naked. At the time of the flood, he was reportedly six hundred years old.

To a modern analyst, the initial obvious transgression in this story is Noah's overindulgence, which caused him to lose consciousness, followed by his excessive, indirect anger at his son Ham by wishing eternal servitude to befall Ham's son, Canaan, Noah's own grandson. We might also blame Noah for being naked, although, again, we don't know why. There is no hint in the text about why Ham entered his father's tent. Finding his father passed out and naked is certainly not, on the face of the available evidence, Ham's fault. The text offers no evidence that Ham, for any reason, plied his father with wine. Any untoward reasons had to be made up or concocted—*and, as we shall see, they were.*

Ham's reaction was to go tell his two other brothers. This seems natural enough, especially if Noah's condition was unusual and not a chronic or frequent event. Over the centuries, many scholars described Ham as "mocking" or "laughing" at his father. There is no hint of any such behavior in the text. This alleged "mocking" behavior on Ham's part is a part of later interpretations and shows up in some artistic depictions of the story, included in Bellini's rendition. (See figure on page 126.)

The other two brothers—Japheth and Shem—see fit to find a garment, avert their eyes, and cover their father's nakedness. Either Ham went with them to help with this task or he stayed outside. We have no way of knowing. Michelangelo's visual interpretation puts all three brothers, mostly naked themselves, inside and near Noah. (See figure on page 124.) Noah apparently woke up, maybe groggy, hung over, and angry. Somehow he learned, presumably from his sons, that Ham saw him passed out and naked, and that Shem and Japheth had covered him up. For reasons not explained at all, Noah put a *perpetual* curse of servitude on Ham's son, Canaan, who had absolutely nothing to do with this event within the confines of Genesis 9:18–27. There is an implicit allegation that Ham perhaps committed some transgression, but that transgression is unexplained. The curse is laid on Canaan. This is the first time Canaan is mentioned. According to Goldenberg, "Why Canaan was cursed if it was Ham who sinned is a question that has been debated for well over the past two thousand years."[56] That's a long time for a question of this magnitude to remain unsettled. But the text offers no clues.

Noah yells, "Cursed by Canaan; a servant of servants he shall be unto his brethren." If we interpret "brethren" to mean Canaan's actual kin, then this could mean that Noah was wishing some derogatory harm to befall Ham's son and subsequent generations.

With no clear explanation in the text, many scholars have interpreted Ham's "sin" or "crime" as the act of viewing his father's genitals. Culturally, such an act, accidental or not, according to Cohen, was considered a sin.[57] Presumably the biblical justification of this judgment derives from the story of Adam and Eve, who recognized their nakedness after they ate the forbidden fruit. Why would someone be considered a sinner if he accidentally saw another person's genitals—especially if Noah's nakedness was something he brought on himself because he was drunk and his thinking was impaired? Noah's nudity was either of his own doing or his clothes were taken off by someone else other than Ham (with or without Noah's consent). There is absolutely no indication in the text that Ham removed his father's clothes. On the face of it, Ham did nothing wrong, except to inform his brothers of their father's circumstance. If we assume Ham knew if anyone found out he had "sinned" by witnessing his father's nakedness, what then made him so careless or self-defeating as to admit his actions to his brothers, who in turn, he must have known, would tattle on him? Are we to assume that Ham knew that it was a major crime to see another person naked and that he immediately confessed his sin and threw himself on the mercy of his brothers and father? If so, this might suggest he had some integrity. What Noah expected Ham to have done otherwise is not obvious. If Ham found his father was drunk, passed out, and wearing no clothes, the responsibility for Noah's condition lies with Noah. There is no obvious crime by Ham to fit the punishment. Based on these verses, whatever "crime" Ham committed was vague at best.

How Noah felt about drinking too much, getting drunk, and passing out in a naked state is without commentary. An argument could be made that Noah, carrying the weighty mantle as the second Adam and now chosen by God to repopulate the earth after the flood, proud of his successful wine making, succumbed to the stress and strain of his tasks, drank far too much wine, and passed out in a naked state. Because he is to blame for this, an honorable man would have sought out his sons, apologized, assured them he was all right, and then reflected on what happened. It is possible to make an argument that Noah was embarrassed and ashamed and became defensively angry, lashing out, to the point of cursing someone (Canaan) who was not even there (or perhaps not even born yet).

In the earliest interpretations of Genesis 9, Noah's personal shame was the primary intent of the story. Noah's state was of his own doing, and yet over the course of centuries, the identity of the "actor" who was problematic shifted from Noah to Ham and Ham's ancestors. Over time, the theme of Noah getting drunk was minimized and then apparently totally denied, and various scholarly arguments were made to shift the blame to Ham. Noah was not held accountable by many scholars for any transgression. His biblical status as the second Adam allowed scholars and interpreters to deflect any blame away from Noah and to pass it along for eternity to some of his grandchildren, who somewhere over many generations became Black-skinned Africans. How many millions of enslaved Black Africans and Black African Americans suffered because of this racist interpretation of scripture?

These questions, inconsistencies, and questionable inferences have to be examined and answered. For example, can the contention that Ham mocked his father be corroborated? It's a nasty allegation and, if true, puts Ham in a terrible, dishonorable light. It seems reasonable that the proslavery hijackers of Genesis 9:18–27 considered various ways to denigrate Ham. Describing him as mocking his father—when there is no such description or intimation of such in the actual verses—is one such example. There is considerable biblical scholarship that describes Ham as mocking Noah, but there's not the slightest bit of corroboration in the original story.

Before I leave this examination of Noah's contribution to racist slave-holding, I am compelled to examine a reasonably contemporary and distinctive interpretation of the inebriated drama of Noah and his sons. In his work *The Drunkenness of Noah*, Cohen offered a psychoanalytically influenced twentieth-century interpretation (written in the early 1970s) of the book of Genesis. I include it here because it illustrates how broadly biblical scripture can be interpreted and because his analysis does not include any linkage between Noah's drunken state and Ham and his offspring becoming Black Africans doomed to eternal slavery. He stated that his analysis was highly influenced by Gaston Bachelard's book *The Psychoanalysis of Fire*.[58] Cohen's book is a scholarly interpretation of Genesis—specifically, Cohen attempted to explain "why a man worthy enough to be saved from the waters of the Flood should be portrayed later as lying naked in a drunken stupor."[59] In his preface, Cohen asserted that he wrote this book because "I had stumbled upon the one clue that eventually would lead to an explanation of Noah's drunkenness."[60] I think Cohen's overall view falls under the "You Can't Make this Stuff Up" category.

Here are Cohen's salient points:

1. The book of Genesis is "a single, unified composition, created according to plan from a multiplicity of traditions extant in ancient Israel."[61]
2. Michelangelo's rendition of the drunkenness of Noah for the Sistine ceiling "depicted the drunkenness of Noah as the tragic confrontation between youth and old age."[62]
3. Noah's drunkenness from wine should be understood symbolically.
4. Wine is understood to be associated with fire (sexuality).
5. Noah's task was to repopulate the world and his drinking was to enhance his virility and ability to procreate.
6. Noah is to be excused for getting drunk because his "determination to maintain his procreative ability at full strength resulted in drinking himself into a state of helpless intoxication."[63]
7. The Bible itself, Cohen asserted, gives us another example of drunkenness for the greater good. He pointed out, in the story of Lot and his two daughters, how they plied Lot with wine to help procreate (Gen 19:31–32).
8. Cohen concluded his analysis of Noah's drunkenness with "Noah deserves not censure but acclaim for having played so well the role of God's devoted servant."[64]

As to what happened inside the tent, after which Noah wakes up and "knew what his youngest [*sic*] son had done to him" (Gen 9: 24), Cohen offered an interpretation: More than Ham's voyeurism was involved. According to

Cohen, "The rabbinic sages of the Midrash and Talmud generally agreed that Noah was castrated in the tent."[65] The (unnamed, unidentified) ancient Jewish editors of Genesis were so horrified by what Ham had done, that they left out the details of the castration. One theory is that Noah's statement (the so-called curse) referred not to Noah's own youngest son, but to Ham's youngest son, Canaan. Cohen does not believe Noah was castrated; Ham's only sin (crime) was breaking a taboo by seeing his father naked. "Looking was not the simple act for biblical man that it is today," Cohen observed. Looking, or gazing, was considered to be "perilous" because "looking implies identification."[66] To the ancients, looking meant acquiring the characteristics of the object of one's gaze: "In short, looking became an act of acquisition."[67] Identification is a psychoanalytic term describing the process by which one person assimilates the characteristics of another person. As psychiatrist Robert Jean Campbell informed us, "In psychodynamics [identification is] a primitive intrapsychic defense mechanism in which the subject's self-representation is altered by taking on some aspects of another object and making them his or her own."[68]

According to Cohen, Ham's act of seeing his father naked was his making a claim to his father's potency: Ham "was telling his brothers that by looking upon his nude father, he thereby had acquired his father's potency!"[69] Although the text makes no mention of Noah's wife being with Noah, Cohen theorizes that Ham either saw Noah in the act of intercourse or saw him after Noah had intercourse or while he intended to have it: "Noah, the master of the earth, was the first to plant a vineyard" (Gen 9:20). Noah wasn't naked because he was drunk; he was naked because his actions were "preliminary to sexual intercourse."[70] Cohen further postulated that Ham secretly watched his father having sex, "peering from his hiding place to assimilate thereby his father's strength in his gloating stare," thus securing his place as the most powerful of the sons.[71] Ham's sin was thus an attempted power grab.

This act of assimilation is why Ham then had to go tell his brothers what he'd seen. Telling them forced them to acknowledge and legitimate his claim to the mantle of Noah's leadership. The "garment" that Shem and Japheth carried back into the tent, Cohen asserts, was Noah's garment, that Ham had brought out of the tent as evidence of what he had seen and where he had been: "Reconstructing the scene, Ham must have skirted the sleeping, naked Noah, picked up his father's garment that had been cast aside, and stepped outside to show 'the garment' to his brothers."[72] Shem and Japheth showed their father the respect he deserved by taking his clothing back to Noah, but walked in backward so they would not see their father's nakedness, and thus avoided committing the sin of Ham.

Somehow, Noah immediately knew what had happened to him. Noah could perceive—almost intuit—"Ham exuded his evil design, permeating the atmosphere and penetrating Noah's orifices."[73] Noah knew immediately what his youngest son had done. Cohen offered the following explanation of why Noah cursed Ham's son, Canaan, and not Ham: Noah was prevented from retaliating against Ham because Ham now held Noah's regenerative power. Canaan, on the other hand, did not, and thus was vulnerable to Noah's curse: "Cursed be Canaan: The lowest of slaves shall he be to his brothers" (Gen 9:24). Cohen concluded his theory: "Far from acting out of vengeance, Noah seemingly degraded the future generations of Canaan to frustrate Ham's design of transferring his newly acquired special strength and power to Canaan and his progeny."[74] Noah was countering Ham's power play.

Proslavery masters and evangelical clergymen could find an abundance of God's sanction of slavery in the Bible. The Bible did not make Ham a Black man. God did not make Ham Black. God, through centuries of interpretations of Genesis 9:18–27, made Ham indirectly and his progeny, particularly Canaan, servants to Ham's brothers, Shem and Japheth. The intellectual problem is that God also made Noah's progeny Shem and Japheth's "servants." The slave master, the proslavery preacher, the slave trader, and any thinking southern Protestant Christian had to find, of necessity, a biblical way to define the differences between being a "servant" to God, such as the master himself, or making the interpretation of "servant" to mean "Black slave." In this way, Black slaves became servants of the white masters.

Over time, the generic "slave" became a Black of African origin, the part of the world given by God through Noah to Ham, Canaan, and their progeny, who were to be slaves to Shem and Japheth. The words "Black" and "slave" became synonymous. Blackness was linked to being inferior. It would be impossible for me to link all the negative words, concepts, ideas, beliefs, myths, and lies that have been attached to the color black. As historian Hector Avalos pointed out, Goldenberg in *The Curse of Ham* "makes a compelling argument that, linguistically, the word Ham is not related to the word for 'Black.'"[75] Citing examples from the thirteenth century, Avalos points out "that color consciousness was there by the Middle Ages when evaluating slaves."[76]

Proslavery scholars and evangelicals traced the roots of racial slavery in the Bible to respond to the abolitionist's efforts to find condemnation of slavery in the Bible. Proslavery advocates and racist slavery defenders wanted not only to highlight and educate the nonbelieving, heathen abolitionists as to what the masters already knew—that God created slavery and was in the South's corner—but to justify their claimed superiority through the more comfortable padding of being the sons and daughters of Japheth, the founder of Europe. God had willed a hierarchy: Europe was number one, Asia number two, and Africa number three. Proslavery advocates founded their entitlement to be dominating of people they perceived to be inferior by maintaining and sometimes fabricating their European lineage back to the beginning of (European) time. They made "Noah's curse" become God's curse *through* Noah's mouth, but *out* of the mouth of God. Proslavery antebellum evangelicals, divines, and Southern proslavery scholars tinkered with and chopped Genesis 9:18–27 into a case of reconstructed identity. Ham, Canaan, all their progeny, and all the residents of Africa, were related by their Blackness and were the enslaved God had ordained: "If there is a 'representative' position in the Bible, it is one that accepts, endorses, or promotes slavery as a justified part of the human condition."[77] If there is a single abstract idea that became the poison that sealed the fates of many masters and millions of slaves, it was the scriptural sleight of hand that gave the master possession of his slaves' bodies, but not their souls.

· 7 ·

The Psychological Dynamics
of the Slaveholders' Fears

PALPABLE WHITE FEAR

What is fear? In contemporary terms, fear is anxiety, which psychiatrist Robert Jean Campbell defined as "an affect that differs from other affects in its specific unpleasurable characteristics."[1] Campbell offered Zygmunt A. Piotrowski's specific descriptions as a way of defining these "unpleasurable characteristics":

> [Anxiety is] a specific conscious inner attitude and a peculiar feeling state characterized by (1) a physically as well as mentally painful awareness of being powerless to do anything about a personal matter; (2) by presentment of an impending and almost inevitable danger; (3) by a tense and physically exhausting alertness as if facing an emergency; (4) by an apprehensive self-absorption which interferes with an effective and advantageous solution of reality-problems; and (5) by an irresolvable doubt concerning the nature of the threatening evil, concerning the probability of the actual appearance of the threat, concerning the best objective means of reducing or removing the evil, and concerning one's subjective capacity for making use of those means if and when the emergency arises.[2]

The reader will notice that Piotrowski connected the subjective experience of anxiety with "evil" as the threat. Fear is the expectation of danger. Undefined danger can become evil. Setting aside for the moment whether or not the slaveholder showed his anxiety or allowed anyone to know about it, what dangers or evil potentially or actually threatened Marse? Logically and objectively, there were many sources of anxiety for the white racist enslaver. Some fears were common and simply grew out of time and place, such as disease and natural disasters. Historian Andrew Delbanco wrote, "Whites, too, lived in fear—periodic, manageable, often based on next to nothing—but enervating nevertheless."[3] As a psychologist, I agree with Delbanco's analysis that slaveholders' fears were enervating, meaning weakening or robbing of vitality, but I would argue that, in addition to the fear-inducing events that came naturally with where and how they lived, slaveholders' fears were much more numerous and emotionally consuming, and they developed multiple defense mechanisms (as discussed in chapter 4) to cope with all that their slaveholding world put upon them. Slaveholding was a devil's bargain, and the slaveholder's contract with slavery brought many threats. Slave revolts—both real and imagined—may have been at the top of the slaveholder's anxiety list, but there were many more anxieties. Just below the persona of confidence laid profound fears and doubts that few white enslavers ever admitted to or discussed. Historian Bruce Levine, quoting William Howard Russell, an Irish-born journalist who was visiting the newly formed Confederacy in the spring of 1861, noted that there was "something suspicious in the constant never ending statement that 'we are not afraid of our slaves.'"[4]

Here, with the keen eye of a journalist, Russell doubted the veracity of the slaveholders' denial that they were afraid of their enslaved people. In the context of what it took for the slaveholder to set up the control and punishment system to force enslaved people to meet the master's demands, a slaveholder's protestations that he was not afraid of his slaves had as much credibility as a prison guard's boast in a modern-day prison that he had no fear of the inmates. In her discussion of North Carolina white slaveholders' attitudes—including indifference and condescension—toward their slaves, historian Jane Turner Censer wrote, "Blacks, however, could not always be ignored, and slaveholders feared that a more frightening aspect of their slaves' personalities existed. Insurrection and murder were subjects that planter families preferred to avoid but could not completely dismiss."[5]

Curiously, historian Bertram Wyatt-Brown offered a somewhat contradictory view, stating that his research shows that most southern plantation dwellers did not live in fear of their slaves. He emphasized that the fear of slave insurrections resided in the Southerner's mind as "an abstract, awesome danger" and gave these threats more significance than they warranted: "Southern plantation dwellers did not live in fear of robbery, rape, or massacre. They left doors unlatched, windows open, gates ajar. Slaves freely roamed in and out of the 'Big House' day and night, much to the wonderment of visiting Yankees and foreigners."[6] I disagree with Wyatt-Brown on this point and argue that any elite white planter whose slaveholdings might number in the hundreds, most with whom the master had no relationship, was in massive denial if he pretended to himself and his family that he felt safe. Psychologically, if a slave master truly felt safe, there would then be no need for all the control and punishment measures directed at the enslaved. The actual emotional atmosphere of the plantation would psychologically relate directly to the type and frequency of whatever power and control methods the master and his overseer used to keep order. If, for example, the surrounding community near a plantation had an active, effective slave patrol, then the planter and his family might have more reason to feel safe.

Slave masters were well versed in dispensing fear. The slaveholder knew how to create fear. The psychological foundation of the racist slavery system was the cultivation and growth of dominating fear—omnipresent, palpable fear. The slave master and mistress and their minions trafficked in fear. What these racist white folks did not allow themselves to feel too deeply were their own fears, their own anxieties that flowed from both an enslavement system based on dominating and dehumanizing other human beings and from a dangerous environment.

GENERALIZED FEAR OF SLAVES

First and foremost, the slaveholders had a generalized fear of slaves, as evidenced by all the steps they took to control and dominate their slaves. Slave masters might proclaim a bond between themselves and a few "trusted" slaves, but this trust was fraudulent. There was no equality in this so-called bond. It made plain sense that there existed in the minds of slaveholders a generalized fear of slaves, something one historian called "negrophobia."[7] Despite the enslavers' denial of any fear, the enslaved knew the master was afraid of them, and the enslaved knew they could not trust their master. Slave masters uttered a fiction to themselves and anyone else within earshot that their slaves were content with their inferior, natural station in life. Levine stated, "But even as they tirelessly repeated these stock phrases—and at one level believed them too—slave owners also worried that their slaves longed for freedom and would seize it if given the chance. . . . Frederick Douglass summarized the masters' problem more completely. The slaves' human intelligence combined with their equally human striving for freedom endangered the masters' power."[8] Levine further described the planters' fears: "But beneath that confident façade there had always lain profound fears and doubts. The same 'Africans' who normally appeared to be mild and docile as household pets, could under certain circumstances reveal a savage and violent side."[9] To emphasize his point, Levine described the diary entry of Georgia planter mistress Gertrude Thomas, who "could thus congratulate herself one day on her slaves' devotion to her and worry on another day 'that we are like the inhabitants at the foot of Vesuvius, remaining perfectly contented' while actually living 'among so many dangers.'"[10] Thomas's image is a powerful one, for it captures the potential, unpredictable volcanic aspect of the master-slave relationship.

As Delbanco informed us, Frederick Douglass encouraged the slaves' application of the slaveholders' fear: "Frederick Douglass urged America's slaves and their allies to 'reach the slaveholder's conscience through his fear of personal danger. We must make him feel that there is death in the air about him, that there is death in the pot before him, that there is death all around him.'"[11]

Slaveholders went to great lengths to act as if or boast that they were not afraid of their enslaved or a slave insurrection. Despite this posturing, imagine the anxious dreams of a white slaveholding woman whose husband was abroad on business, alone on a plantation literally surrounded by scores of enslaved individuals, a population of so-called Sambos and Nats. Historians Elizabeth Fox-Genovese and Eugene Genovese noted, "On the eve of secession, President James Buchanan told Congress, 'Many a matron throughout the South retires at night in dread of what might befall herself and her children before the morning.'"[12] In South Carolina, where the number of slaves outnumbered whites, "the expanding plantation economy of the lowcountry . . . helped to provoke white fears and set off an escalating cycle of oppression and resistance."[13] Oppression is a manifestation of fear, the type of fear that causes a person to see things in black and white, as good or bad. In the antebellum South, for many white elite slaveholders, the Black enslaved were an evil threat if they ever got loose.

Slaveholders recognized early in America's slavery history that they needed to put physical and emotional distance between themselves and their slaves. Historian Ira Berlin gave us an eighteenth-century example of a type of fortification from slaves and disease. In the mid-1740s,

> [as] the plantation system took shape, the [Carolinas] lowcountry grandees retreated to the region's cities, marking the social and cultural distance between them and their slaves. The streets of Charles Town—and, later, of Beaufort, Georgetown, Savannah, Darien, and Wilmington—sprouted great new mansions, as lowcountry planters, the wealthiest people on the North American mainland, fled the malarial lowlands and its Black majority.[14]

South Carolina historian Walter Edgar pointed out that a few white South Carolinians expressed their fears: "Often isolated on their plantations, amid a large number of Black slaves, South Carolina whites sometimes found life in the big house a bit unsettling."[15]

What other fears coursed through the master's mind? According to Delbanco, an unidentified fellow southern exile who departed the South with the famous Southerner-turned-abolitionist Angelina Grimke remarked to Grimke,

"'Two terrors were constantly before the minds of Southern families—fire and poison . . . the two weapons that slaves had in their hands.' By rumor, report, or family lore, most if not all white people had heard of slaves using one or the other."[16] Fear of being poisoned by a favored Black housekeeper or being burned to death in the middle of the night made for an uneasy sleep. Censer related the story of the sister of North Carolina planter Duncan Cameron, who "became almost hysterical over what she believed to be attempts to murder their father through arson and poison."[17]

Delbanco gave us a poignant example of the homicidal fears of a famous South Carolina slaveholder mistress, Floride Calhoun, the wife of John C. Calhoun. She "was convinced that slaves on her childhood plantation had tried to poison her father (not that he had any intention of freeing them), and for the rest of her life she lived in fear of being burned or stabbed in the night."[18]

Slavery generated capital, the cotton boom, and land speculation that flowed from the Upper South to the Lower South, bringing with this economic thriving some associated terror. Writing about the Mississippi Valley in the 1830s, historian Walter Johnson stated,

> An institution [slavery] that had been in decline throughout the eighteenth century in the Upper South was revivified in the Lower South at terrible cost; by 1860 there were more millionaires per capita in the Mississippi Valley than anywhere else in the United States. White privilege on an unprecedented scale was wrung from the lands of the Choctaw, the Creek, and the Chickasaw and from the bodies of the enslaved people brought in to replace them. The bright-white tide of slavery as progress, however, was shadowed by a host of boomtime terrors. Slaveholders feared that the slaves upon whom the Cotton Kingdom depended, as well as the nonslavehold- ing whites whom it shunted to the margins of a history they had thought to be their own, might rise up and even unite in support of its overthrow.[19]

Vigilance became the watchword for southern whites. Psychologically, it makes sense that the anxiety, increasing fear, and vigilance naturally morphed into hypervigilance and paranoia over time. As Levine noted, "Beginning with the lead-up to the 1860 election, southern masters and state and local officials worked to strengthen restrictions on southern Blacks, free as well as slave. This escalation of vigilance and discipline continued into the months of secession and the onset of war."[20]

Emotionally, it is exhausting for an individual's autonomic nervous sys- tem to be constantly on high alert. With little conscious awareness of his own fears, which he could not admit even to himself, Marse shared the human phenomenon of fear with the enslaved. Each was highly fearful of the other.

In order to survive and appear in charge of his life and enterprises, Marse had to develop a type of coping anxiety: not too much, not too little. If the slave master got too fearful or anxious, he could lash, torture, maim, sell, or murder a slave with few, if any repercussions for the master, although this ethic began to change. Marse worked hard to repress his fears, but he knew the white man's fear of Black Africans was real. He vaguely sensed his own anxiety lying just below the surface of his existence. It was like a black cat prowling around in the basement. He knew how easily it could be activated and jacked up. Excessive, brutal whippings and lynchings were vicious products of this fear. Enslaved Black laborers had their own Vesuvius, centered in the unpredictability of enslaver punishment, to accommodate.

SLAVE REVOLTS

The primary fear that appeared to be emphasized in the historiography of southern antebellum slavery was slave rebellion. Enslaved people sometimes began to revolt or flee as soon as they were captured. Emotionally, there were two dimensions of the fear of slave rebellion: One dimension was the real, objective fear that emanated from actual slave rebellion events. The other dimension was the imagined, subjective threat: the threat of revolts by enslaved people that often began with a vague rumor, misinterpretation of an event, or small conflict between a slave and a white person that mushroomed into a panic. In other words, there was the real threat of slave revolts that were actual events and there was the imagined world of slave revolts, events that happened only in the enslavers' minds.

Writing his 1899 brief history of slavery in North Carolina, John Spencer Bassett succinctly described the problem with white fear of slave rebellions: "The possibility of slave insurrections was a source of the greatest solicitude to the Southern whites."[21] In the late nineteenth century, "solicitude" meant "the state of being concerned and anxious."[22]

Since the beginning of Black African enslavement in the Americas, revolts by the enslaved population had happened and thus were part of the white slaveholder's knowledge or perhaps personal or regional experience, either by direct knowledge of reports (written or eyewitness) or by the legacy of fear that accompanied a white man's pursuit of the dream of becoming a slaveholder. As Delbanco pointed out, "Although slave rebellions were rare, quickly suppressed, and punished severely, fear of rebellion was common and constant."[23]

Slave revolts may have been relatively rare, but the reality of them kept the white slave master on edge, because revolts did occur. There was a lengthy history of slave insurrections, and not just in mainland America. Delbanco called the massive slave revolt in Haiti in 1791 the "terrifying precedent."[24] At that time, the population of Haiti included 450,000 enslaved humans, 30,000 free persons of color, and only 40,000 whites.[25] According to historian Noel Leo Erskine, "In 1791, the Blacks of Haiti rose up against both the whites and free persons of color and a 12-year armed struggle began that ended with the Proclamation of the Republic of Haiti in 1804."[26] Delbanco noted that "between 1791 and 1804, the island had been periodically convulsed by Black-against-white violence, including torture, rape, and murder of thousands of slave masters and their families—sometimes systematic, sometimes anarchic."[27] This well-known and successful Haitian slave rebellion was always a nightmare in the back of Marse's mind.

There were other revolts in mainland America. In the Upper South, Gabriel Prosser led a rebellion in Richmond, Virginia in 1800. Historian Kenneth M. Stampp informed us that there were "at least a thousand slaves . . . implicated."[28] With the help of other enslaved men, including Jack Bowler and George Smith, Gabriel devised a plan to seize control of Richmond by killing all of the whites (except the Methodists, Quakers, and Frenchmen) and then establishing a Kingdom of Virginia with himself as monarch.[29]

A BOLD STROKE FOR FREEDOM.

A Bold Stroke for Freedom. *Photograph from Woodcut. Library of Congress*

Gabriel's revolt, according to the research by historian Willie Lee Rose,

was the most sophisticated in political intention of all the slave plots uncovered. Gabriel's plan was frustrated by what the whites of Henrico County came to regard as the intervention of God. A vital footbridge by which the insurgents were to have approached Richmond was washed out by a torrential downpour of rain. The plot was revealed to the Richmond authorities by slave informers before Gabriel's plan could be revised.[30]

Approximately twenty-six slaves associated with the plot were executed, including Gabriel.

According to Bassett, in the extreme northeastern part of North Carolina in 1802, there were reports (read: rumors) of a slave revolt that threw the whites of this region "into paroxysms of terror." Although these rumors turned out to be false and no slave revolt was planned or occurred, based on false confessions extracted from the so-called leaders of the revolts—who confessed to the conspiracy after much whipping—"eighteen negroes were reported to have been executed and a large number to have been arrested."[31] The alleged "facts" coerced out of the enslaved in this case were largely preposterous, probably created by leading questions and aggressive, coercive interrogations, for example, on a particular night, the revolting slaves were to burn all the whites' houses, kill all white males over six, kill the women, Black and white, except the young white women who would be taken for wives of the slaves and the attractive Black women who would be kept as mistresses. According to Bassett, this insurrection was ultimately to take place across the entire nation.[32]

The increasing numbers of enslaved people in the US mainland had an impact on Marse's state of mind. By 1810, the slave population of America was twice what it had been in 1770.[33] According to Stampp, "By 1810 the southern slave population had grown to more than a million."[34] The growth of bound labor in the South increased exponentially Marse's fear of slave revolts.

On January 8, 1811, a slave insurrection erupted in the sugar-producing region of Louisiana called the German Coast, in which more than two hundred slaves revolted. Genovese stated that this 1811 rebellion involved "between 300 and 500 slaves; it alone was comparable in size to those [revolts] in the Caribbean."[35] Seizing a cache of armaments, they headed toward New Orleans, to "go to the city and kill the whites." An armed posse of eighty angry white men pursued these enslaved people from the German Coast. The city of New Orleans, upon hearing the news of the coming rebellion storm, assembled a militia, which met the enslaved rebels at a plantation where the rebels had dug in. The Black insurrectionists retreated but ran into the pursuing posse. The rebellious slaves were routed, captured, and lynched (massacred) by the posse before any federal troops could intervene. The leader of the posse, Manuel Andry, stated that his men "made considerable slaughter."[36]

Planters knew that slaves would fight against them. When the British invaded the Chesapeake Bay and the lower Mississippi Valley and began the War of 1812, slaveholders were faced with the fact that a number of their enslaved people and fugitive slaves responded favorably to British efforts to recruit them as soldiers and fought for Great Britain: "Scarlet-coated former slaves, hastily enlisted in the Colonial Marines, took part in the torching of Washington and assisted other fugitives in making their escape from bondage. When the British retreated, many of these men and women followed them to freedom in the Caribbean, Canada, and Sierra Leone."[37] The British "even assembled special battalions of fugitives (known as the Black Corps), who, they hoped, would have incentive to fight and none to desert because the enemy was likely to re-enslave them."[38]

In 1816, South Carolina (near Charleston) experienced disturbances by a band of fugitive slaves, who began, from the surrounding swamps, to attack "the planters in open day" and made attacks on the "inland coasting trade." The governor used the state militia to suppress this uprising, but it had its effect on the psyche of southern white slaveholders, including John C. Calhoun. At the same time, there was another slave insurrection conspiracy "disclosed" by a Black informant in the cotton market town of Camden, South Carolina. His allegation was deemed plausible and, under instruction of his master, he gained further information. Several Blacks were arrested, interrogated, and tortured. These confessions led to the arrest and "trial" of seventeen alleged slave rebels. The men who were perceived to be the ringleaders (five in all) were hanged (read: lynched). The Black informant was given his freedom and a yearly stipend of $50 per year for life.[39]

In 1822, the Denmark Vesey slave insurrection was planned in Charleston but was thwarted. Nearly three dozen people were executed. Erskine informed us that "thirty-five Blacks were hanged and more than forty sent to the Caribbean or to Africa."[40] Historian Lacy K. Ford added that the Vesey insurrection revitalized the "colonization movement" among Southern whites, as a possible means of colonizing free Blacks and troublesome slaves as a way to enhance white security.[41] The net effect of the Vesey revolt changed many white Charlestonians' views of management of the enslaved. As Stampp said, "After the Vesey conspiracy, Charlestonians expressed disillusionment with the idea that by generous treatment their enslaved 'would become more satisfied with their condition and more attached to whites.'"[42] In other words, enslavers ramped up greater repressive actions, dropping the paternalistic pretense that slaves were family. Berlin noted that "white supremacy mani-fested itself in every aspect of antebellum society, from the ballot box to the bedroom. Slaveholders discovered much of value in supremacist ideology. The inferiority of Black people confirmed the necessity, if not the benevo-lence, of mastership."[43]

As Delbanco informed us, "In 1826, as a 'coffle' of seventy-five slaves was being sent by flatboat down the Ohio River from Kentucky for sale in Missis-sippi or Louisiana, several of the captives rose up, killed the slave traders, sank their bodies in the river with weights, and fled north into Indiana, where they were captured and returned south and the ringleaders hanged."[44] Fear from actual events like this one and imagined ones in large measure fed the move-ment towards secession from the Union and a bloody civil war.

In August 1831, Nat Turner led his revolt in Southampton, Virginia, in the heart of the Upper South. Historians have disputed how many men were convinced by Turner to join his revolt, but the number ranged from fifty to seventy and, according to Ford, "about fifty-five whites were killed during a seventy-two-hour rampage before their insurrection was broken up by hastily assembled local patrols and militia units."[45]

According to Ford, Turner's revolt began with the killing of his master and his master's wife. The Turner revolt "took more white lives than any other North American slave insurrection."[46] Before the state militia organized by the governor could intervene, "a frenzied white reign of terror against Blacks began. Within the first six days after the rebellion broke out, whites killed at least thirty-nine Blacks, many of whom had little or no connection to the insurrection."[47] Ford described the mayhem perpetrated by white mobs, including brutal, sadistic aggression against Blacks assumed to be part of the revolt, that included maiming, cutting off body parts, burning with hot irons, beheading, and placing the Black rebels' heads on whipping posts.[48] Delbanco indicated that "at least two hundred Blacks were beaten and killed in reprisal. The frequency of such events was small, but their psychological effects were large."[49] Historian David Brion Davis added a gruesome detail to the Turner revolt: Most of the whites killed were "women and children."[50] Historian James A. Morone added additional detail to the history of the Turner revolt that explained why it created so much terror: After the original uprising left some sixty white folks dead, Turner remained at large for another two months, provoking a huge manhunt. As we know, he was eventually captured, swiftly tried, and killed.[51]

Stampp wrote that the net effect of the Turner revolt was "an event which produced in the South something resembling a mass trauma from which whites had not recovered three decades later. The danger that other Nat Turners might emerge, that an even more serious insurrection might some day occur, became an enduring concern as long as the peculiar institution survived."[52] According to Stampp, "The Turner rebellion produced an insurrection panic that swept the entire South."[53]

Nat Turner [for example] raised only about seventy enslaved insurrectionists but won fame by killing an unprecedented number of whites. "Since the previous plots and risings in Virginia had failed to draw white blood, Turner's accomplishment stood out all the more. The Gabriel Prosser and Denmark Vesey plots never had their moment but in some ways emerged as more impressive than Turner's."[54] Delbanco related Frederick Douglass's thoughts on the psychological effects of Nat Turner's rebellion: "Using Turner's full name as a mark of respect, Douglass recalled that 'the insurrection of Nathaniel Turner had been quelled, but the alarm and terror had not subsided'—good reason, he later added, to 'rejoice in every uprising.'"[55]

In this same year (1831), Samuel "Daddy" Sharpe (1801–1832) a Baptist lay preacher, led a Jamaican slave revolt called the Baptist War that involved some sixty thousand slaves. As Erskine told us, "The focus of this war was Afro-Jamaicans organizing to withdraw their labor. The focus was on the institution of the plantation."[56] Although this rebellion was initially intended as a labor strike, it became an armed rebellion. More than 200 plantations were burned or pillaged, and "in the aftermath of the Native Baptist War, 600 Afro-Jamaicans were killed by British forces."[57]

It did not take much to unleash white racist mayhem in the form of extrajudicial justice. Another slave rebellion was rumored to be rising in the summer of 1835 in Madison County, Mississippi. A committee composed of slaveholders was formed that "investigated" the rumored conspiracy by what amounted to inquisition-style interviews of suspected rebellious slaves. The committee began torturing slaves, eliciting coerced confessions. By the time it was over, the committee had put at least sixteen slaves and seven white men to death, with no pretense of a legal proceeding, as well as murdering numerous other slaves whose names were not tallied. Although there was never any real evidence that a slave rebellion was going to happen, "the fury of the mob was so out of control that anyone who expressed doubts about the process might soon find himself its victim."[58] According to Ford, "At least a dozen whites [presumed co-conspirators] and many more slaves died at the hands of 'Judge Lynch,' and most Mississippians appeared to approve."[59] In light of the slave insurrections in the South, by 1837, Calhoun began trying to unite the South around a passionate defense of slavery. Calhoun's political response—increasing the call for a vigorous defense of slavery—in light of slave rebellions, seems illogical but illustrates the palpable fear created in the masters' minds by these uprisings.

DISEASE AND OTHER NATURAL DISASTERS

On the subject of death, historian James Oakes wrote:

> To fear death in the antebellum South was to live in constant terror of the
> immediacy of one's fate. It was not a healthy place to live. Long, hot sum-
> mers and vast areas of swampland were ideal for the proliferation of disease
> bearing insects. Inadequate housing, poor diet, and simple ignorance left
> much of the South's population vulnerable. Periodic epidemics of cholera
> and yellow fever took thousands of lives, particularly in urban centers. In
> 1853, yellow fever afflicted nearly a third of New Orleans's 100,000 resi-
> dents, killing over a thousand people each week in the month of August,
> until there were more corpses than there were graves to put them in. The
> Old South suffered as well from abnormally high infant mortality.[60]

Historian William Kauffman Scarborough described yellow fever as "the
most dreaded scourge of the nineteenth-century South. From New Orleans
to Charleston, it claimed a frightful toll of victims at periodic intervals during
the antebellum period."[61]

Scarborough addressed an additional aspect of the elite slaveholders' family life that would have naturally been a continuing source of great anxiety:
the relatively high infant mortality rate. "Although the infant mortality rate
was doubtless not as high among elite families as among those of more modest economic circumstances, it was still painfully high, thus bearing eloquent
testimony to the ubiquitous incidence of disease in the rural South as well as
to the primitive state of medical knowledge in the antebellum period. The
specter of death was omnipresent, not only among infants, but among older
offspring as well."[62] Scarborough illustrated this vulnerability with several
examples: Louisiana planter David Barrow lost eight of his twelve children at
an early age. A cousin of Barrow's lost "five of his ten children before they
attained their majority. . . .Thomas Spalding of Sapelo Island, Georgia, fared
even worse, losing eleven of his sixteen children in infancy or early youth."[63]

Scarborough pointed out that the rice swamps of South Carolina created
a "deadly, miasmic atmosphere . . . from mid-April to mid-October," making it "imperative that Low Country planters leave their plantation residences
for more extended periods than was common elsewhere in the South."[64]
According to Scarborough, one of the most popular summer refuges for these
low country rice planters was the mountain community of Flat Rock, North
Carolina: "It soon became the summer colony for a host of prominent South
Carolinians."[65]

While elite planters and their families could withdraw somewhat from
these diseases, Blacks were forced to remain in disease-ridden areas and were

subject to other health issues as well. Johnson noted that malnutrition was common among the enslaved population because most slave masters did not provide either enough food or a balanced diet for their captives: "Planters used food to control their hungry slaves."[66] Oakes emphasized the threat that emanated from the poor physical condition of the slaves: "Pellagra, a disease endemic to societies where pork, corn, and molasses form the bulk of the diet, appears to have been widespread among slaves. Blacks seem to have been more susceptible to a variety of respiratory diseases."[67] According to Genovese, "The slaveholders also insisted that their slaves ate well and that, in particular, they ate more meat than laborers elsewhere could dream of. During the nineteenth century the amount of meat available to slaves did in fact increase."[68] Genovese also pointed out that eating dirt was a widespread practice among slaves, which "suggests, although it does not prove, that many suffered from wretchedly unbalanced diets and worked themselves into a stupor."[69] That enslaved people ate dirt as a desperate means of trying to stay alive is clear evidence of dietary neglect by the slave masters.

Based on his research of planters' diaries and other correspondence, Scarborough listed other environmental threats to the fortunes of the planters: "It is no accident that the two ubiquitous topics in the records and correspondence of antebellum agriculturalists were health and weather." Plantations had to contend with floods—especially those estates near the Mississippi River—severe windstorms, killing frosts, extended droughts, and infestations of worms, lice, caterpillars, and other pests.[70]

RUNAWAYS

To me, the word "runaways" is an odd word in the context of chattel slavery. It connotes an action by a child who is unhappy about life at home or rebellious about some type of institutional restraint. "Fugitive" is perhaps a better word, but it too is not quite right. A fugitive is a person fleeing from the law, and, as we shall see, in an eighteenth- and nineteenth-century antebellum context, this use of this word was correct. But what is the correct word for people attempting to escape from enslavement, who seek their right to freedom? Black men, women, and children trying to escape from enslavement and toward freedom were a direct threat to the institution of racist slavery, because it meant that the enslaved, despite what the masters claimed, were not content with their lot in life. The enslaved people were not running away from their family; they were running toward freedom. The South's fugitive slave problem stoked the slaveholders' fears.

Delbanco, in his brilliant book *The War Before the War: Fugitive Slaves and the Struggle for America's Soul from the Revolution to the Civil War*, succinctly addressed the psychological and political impact of the runaway problem:

> This book tells the story of how that composite nation came apart. There were many reasons for the unraveling, but one in particular exposed the idea of the "united" states as a lie. This was the fact that enslaved Black people, against long odds, repeatedly risked their lives to flee their masters in the South in search of freedom in the North. Fugitives from slavery ripped open the screen behind which America tried to conceal the reality of life for Black Americans, most of who lived in the South, out of sight and out of mind for most people in the North. Fugitive slaves exposed the contradiction between the myth that slavery was a benign institution and the reality that a nation putatively based on the principle of human equality was actually a prison house in which millions of Americans had virtually no rights at all.[71]

The fugitives needed to be captured, silenced, or re-enslaved at all costs. Did Marse acknowledge to himself that once the North heard repeated horror stories from fugitives running for their lives, the southern slavery empire would be exposed in glaring new ways for the brutal institution it was? That Frederick Douglass and others would emerge to tell their and other slaves' stories? Marse's fears about escaping slaves ripping open the screen undoubtedly drove the furor of capturing runaways, probably much more so than the monetary value of the capital asset he was pursuing.

FEAR OF FINANCIAL RUIN

Berlin described the financial vulnerability of slaveholders who engaged in staple crop agriculture. Periodically, there would be economic depressions

> that afflicted the nation's economy during the pre–Civil War years. They usually purchased land and slaves on credit and since most of their capital was tied up in those two assets, they had few liquid resources to call upon when prices dropped and notes came due. Consequently, some of these outwardly affluent agriculturalists suffered severely in times of economic distress, most notably in the wake of the Panic of 1837 and, to a lesser extent, during the milder recession of 1857.[72]

To put a fine point on the effects of the Panic of 1837, Berlin noted that some commercial banks were victims too: "[B]y the mid-1840s there were no commercial banks operating in Mississippi."[73]

Quoting economist Thomas Kettell from 1860, Johnson described Kettell's assessment about this important southern cash flow and its financial dynamic: "The agriculturalists who create the great wealth of the country are not in daily receipt of money. Their produce is ready but once a year, whereas they buy supplies [on credit] year round. . . . The whole banking system of the country is based primarily on this bill movement against produce."[74] Johnson relayed Kettell's contemporaneous analysis that the cotton market was stressed because of its overreliance on monetary advances. Marse carried a lot of debt and thus carried a considerable degree of financial anxiety. His slavery industrial complex required enormous amounts of financial credit. This debt anchored the cotton industry to the country's foreign money markets and financial institutions, and it also served to make Marse more creative in diversifying his holdings and ventures. The political power of the planter-class slaveholders cannot be overemphasized in looking at how Marse managed his fears about finances and his actual worries, as this power helped keep him financially solvent.

ABOLITION AND EMANCIPATION WOULD BRING ARMAGEDDON

Morone explained that it was the effects of evangelicalism that reheated the nation's conflicts over abolition, connecting the dots between slavery, evangelicalism, abolitionism, war, and Black liberation: "The first African slave stepped onto North American shores in 1619. More than two centuries later, Americans began brawling over abolition."[75] Morone asked what stoked this conflict: "What heated up the argument after all that time? Another religious revival. Evangelical fervor rolled across the United States for three decades, peaking in the 1830s. If the First Great Awakening primed Americans for their Revolution, the Second lit the long fuse to the Civil War . . . nothing struck the young United States with the force of the Second Great Awakening. People who were barred from party politics—like women and slaves—flung themselves into the business of salvation. . . . The quest for God set America on a corkscrew path toward abolition, civil war, and Black liberation."[76]

Oakes informed us that the religious fervor that ebbed and flowed out of the First Great Awakening, which began in the colonies in the 1740s, developed strong roots from a series of revivals that happened throughout the last quarter of the eighteenth century, "culminating in several spectacular camp meetings at the turn of the century—[that] transformed the culture of slaveholding more dramatically than anything thereafter, until the Civil War destroyed slavery altogether."[77] White southerners became alarmed at abolitionism because they began to see it as a conspiracy among abolitionists, Black preachers, and rebellious enslaved people.

Southern enslavers feared emancipation because of the direct threat it posed to the rewards derived from a slavery-based economy. As early as 1784, "over a thousand Virginians petitioned their legislature to cease considering a gradual emancipation bill by explicitly appealing to the rights of property that had only recently been secured by the Revolution."[78] As slavery power and white slaveholder wealth increased, and by the mid-1850s,

> slaveholders were fascinated by the phenomenal growth and prosperity of America, and they connected it in their minds to the expansion and protection of slavery. . . . It did not escape the attention of proslavery writers that the great mobility of slaveholders was largely responsible for America's remarkable expansion. "While the North has not extended her limits northward a single degree since the birth of the Constitution," D.R. Hundley wrote [in *Social Relations*] in 1860, "the South has already seized on Florida, Louisiana, and Texas, and her eagle eye is now burning with desire to make a swoop on Cuba, Central America, and Mexico."[79]

In Roman law, "emancipation" meant "the action or process setting children free from *patria potestas*," meaning protection from the power the Roman father had over his children, grandchildren, and the father's descendants. Emancipation also means "to free from restraint, control, or the power of another; *esp.*: to free from bondage."[80] The possibility of the emancipation of Black enslaved people was viewed by the master as an apocalyptic horror. Even in the abstract, the very idea of setting the slaves free from the institution of slavery was an enormous threat. In the slaveholder's mind, emancipation meant chaos and financial ruin. Oakes continued,

> By the 1850s, slaveholding politicians were so accustomed to resting the greatness of American society upon the protection and expansion of the slavery economy that the prospect of abolition provoked images of unparalleled horror. The purity of white society was jeopardized, the very basis of individual advancement was threatened, national greatness would be subverted. The consummate defense of slavery, then, was the one that assumed the highest place and the broadest significance of Black bondage. Its destruction foreshadowed nothing less than global economic calamity.[81]

This vision, as we know, led to secession from the Union and a bloody civil war. The deeply tragic irony is that what turned out to be an apocalyptic horror was the American Civil War itself.

Levine quoted Tennessee slave master Oliver P. Temple, who offered his judgment about slaveholders' vigilance: "'The supersensitiveness of slaveholders was not unnatural,' he wrote. Because of the 'inherent weakness of the institution,' they 'had to guard it against attack, whether from without or within, with the utmost vigilance.' They could therefore tolerate no open 'opposition to it, without danger of the most serious consequences.'"[82] Levine continued:

> Masters' concerns about controlling their human property lay squarely at the root of the escalating North-South conflict that finally erupted in war. To more firmly hold and work their slaves profitably, they strove to keep their Black laborers and servants uneducated, uninformed, isolated from dangerous influences, closely watched, intimidated, and convinced that enslavement was their permanent, immutable condition. To accomplish all that required confronting slaves with overwhelming force. It also required that the white population be dependably and visibly united in support of Black servitude—and ready to enforce it.[83]

Oakes illustrated the racist slaveholder logic in arguing against abolition by quoting proslavery journalist James D. B. De Bow, who wrote in an 1851 edition of *De Bow's Review* that the profits of cotton have "gradually enveloped the commercial world, and bound the fortunes of American slaves so firmly to human progress, that civilization itself may almost be said to depend on the continual servitude of Blacks in America."[84] As Oakes summarized it, "Thus did every expression of the slaveholders' gospel of prosperity become an implicit defense of slavery."[85]

The Upper South and the Lower South often "differed about many matters related to slavery," and among these matters was the issue of emancipation, although there were differences in the degrees of anxiety that the notion of emancipation elicited in the slave master's mind.[86] The issue here is what frame of mind did the anticipation—the threat—of emancipation create in Marse's mind?

Consider the frightening impact of the preeminent antebellum abolitionist William Lloyd Garrison's words, published on September 3, 1831, in Garrison's abolitionist newspaper, the *Liberator*, after the death of Nat Turner. Garrison linked two of the slaveholders' worst fears, slave rebellion and emancipation:

> "What we have so long predicted . . . has commenced its fulfillment . . . The first drops of blood are but the prelude to a deluge." You may have quelled Nat Turner's rebellion, he wrote, but "you have seen . . . but the beginning of your sorrows . . . Wo to this guilty land, unless she speedily repent of her evil doings! The blood of millions . . . cries aloud for redress! Immediate Emancipation can alone save her from the vengeance of heaven and cancel the debt of the ages."

Genovese related a story about an enslaved individual named Anne Miller who "watched her master go mad when emancipation came. He left the area, screaming that he would not live in a country in which Blacks were free. A year later, he committed suicide."[87]

Genovese and Fox-Genovese informed us that in the late 1850s, the captain of the schooner *Ontario* "reported to antislavery relatives in Virginia that emancipated Blacks [who had been sent to Haiti and the British West Indies] were veering back toward barbarism."[88] Genovese related another incident described by Robert Falls of Tennessee, another freed slave. After his master told his slaves, including Falls, that they were free, his master lamented, "'I am an old man, and I can't get along without you. I don't know what I'm going to do.' Well, sir, it killed him. He was dead in less than ten months."[89]

FEAR OF GOD

Historian Paul D. Escott connected the planters' general fears to the planters' occasional doubts about carrying out God's perceived mandate to the South about slavery. Escott articulated some of the most troublesome emotional and cognitive dissonance experienced by southern slaveholders:

> Despite being aggressively self-righteous and confident, they knew occasional fears and insecurities that they tried to hide from themselves. Although deeply religious and reassured by the Bible, they sometimes questioned their own zeal in doing God's will toward the slaves. Theirs was a world in which past and present, home and surroundings, internal and external realities did not meld completely. . . . Thus, in regard to slavery, Southern culture depended on habits of mental avoidance. External denial and internal reassurance were required for slaveholders' self-image and the perceived health of their society.[90]

Where did the slaveholders find a source for "external denial and internal reassurance"? Oakes pointed to evangelical Protestantism as the answer to this question:

> Evangelical Protestantism attracted most of the religiously inclined slaveholders. Episcopal orthodoxy remained strong in eastern Virginia and lowcountry South Carolina. A significant Catholic tradition persisted among the slaveholding descendants of the Maryland colonists and the French and Spanish settlers of Louisiana. And there were ethnic and regional variations as well. But the slaveholders who expressed religious convictions were overwhelmingly Protestant and practiced their faith in the

diverse evangelical styles of Baptists, Methodists, Presbyterians, and some Episcopalians.[91]

Quoting the written word of a traveler through Georgia and South Carolina, Oakes wrote, "men talk in public places, in the churches, and in bar-rooms, in the stage-coach and at the fireside, of their personal and peculiar relationship with the Deity."[92]

Consider for a moment the phrase, "He's a God-fearing man." Marse developed a personal relationship with God, and (as was argued in chapters 5 and 6) as a slaveholder, he had a divine duty to properly attend to the Black slaves who had been given to him by God. Marse not only followed the admonitions of his God, but also was righteously fearful of God's wrath. Marse's Protestant Christian God ruled through divine Providence, which meant that his God has his hands in every moment of life. Marse was power-less. God was believed to control all events on earth, and humans were helpless before his powers. While there is no question many evangelical slaveholders found peace and solace in their God and their relationship with Jesus, they also knew the Lord was an avenging God. Marse may have had a complex relation-ship with his God, but a large measure of the Protestant Christian enslaver's relation to Jehovah was fear.

Censer further elucidated the slave masters' view of their Christian God:

Baptist, Methodist, Presbyterian, and Episcopalian planters might disagree on many matters of religious doctrine and practice but their outlook was similar. They believed in a close personal God who held them strictly accountable. He was a jealous taskmaster who demanded intense com-mitment and who directly intervened in human affairs to aid, reward, or chastise. Methodist Henry G. Williams saw God's hand in his family's good health during an epidemic, and Presbyterian Isaac T. Avery similarly attrib-uted his mother's rescue from a fire to Divine Providence. Planters also saw deaths of spouses, beloved friends, and relatives as ordained by God.[93]

For many slaveholders, death was viewed as divine retribution: "Even the deaths of innocent children were seen by slaveholding parents as a punishment from God. When Mary Carmichael's son died, she wrote in her diary entry for May 26, 1844, he 'left his aged father and mother to mourn over the delight of their eyes—*But God took* him for he saw he was our idol.'"[94]

Religious historian Hector Avalos posited an ironic relationship between many Protestant Christians and God: "What most Christian apologists still overlook is that Christianity is itself modeled on a slave-master paradigm. God is the ultimate slave master, and Christians routinely call themselves 'slave,' or 'servants' of God." Quoting Philo, a Hellenistic Jewish philosopher (25 BCE), Avalos wrote, "To be a slave of God is the highest boast of man, a treasure more precious not only than freedom, but than wealth and power and all that mortal cherish' (cf. Lev. 25: 42)."[95] In Leviticus, the third book of Moses, when God is speaking to Moses, these verses appear in chapter 25 to fuse fear of God with sanctioned slavery:

> I am the LORD your God, which brought you forth out of the land of Egypt, to give you the land of Canaan, *and* to be your God (verse 38). . . . For they *are* my servants, which I brought forth out of the land of Egypt: they shalt not be sold as bondmen (42). Thou shalt not rule over him with rigour, but shalt thy fear thy God (43). Both thy bondmen, and thy bond-maids, which thou shalt have, *shall be* of the heathen that are around about you; of them shall ye buy bondmen and bondmaids (44).

In the New Testament book of Acts, St. Peter makes a chilling observation about God: "Then Peter opened *his* mouth, and said, Of truth, I perceive that God is no respecter of persons: But in every nation he that feareth him, and worketh righteousness, is accepted with him" (10:34–35).

Calling upon a panoply of psychological defense mechanisms—composed of both adaptive and maladaptive coping strategies—as well as marshaling every resource the South had at its disposal, Marse conquered his fears and doubled down on the value of defending and depending on the institution of racist slavery. In 1860, the secessionist drum beats began loudly in the deep South: Mississippi, Alabama, South Carolina, and Georgia sent secessionist commissioners—the "Apostles of Disunion"—into neighboring states to spread the secessionist message.[96] Notes Charles B. Dew, "In all some fifty-two men served as secession commissioners in the critical weeks just before the Civil War."[97] These commissioners accomplished two tasks: they stoked Marse's fears about possible slave emancipation and allayed his fears about the outcome of the South's decision to secede from the Union.

· 8 ·

The Slave Masters' Methodologies

OVERCOMING A CONUNDRUM

As I wrote this book, I occasionally came upon a few friends and associates who, upon learning of the subject of my writing endeavor, expressed the opinion that "not all slave masters were bad." These expressions, I noted, were often made by fellow Southerners, whose family histories may or may not have had any connection to slaveholding but that I knew included a strong Southern identity. I usually tried to avoid any public confrontation about this issue, so as not to upset the event or offend someone. But I generally attempted to highlight the fact that slaveholders had control over their slaves—by way of ownership as property—no matter how well the slaves might have been treated. It would be inaccurate to suggest or imply that American slaveholders from 1619 (when the first enslaved people were brought to Jamestown, Virginia) through the end of the Civil War always employed harsh, if not sadistic methods to manage their slaves, for they did not. Paternalism (discussed in chapter 4), for example, had an ameliorating effect on the harshness of punishments slaveholders used.

Regardless of how slave masters treated their slaves, historian Kenneth M. Stampp summarized the masters' management of slaves—toward developing the ideal slave—as follows: (1) establish and maintain strict discipline, seeking "unconditional submission"; (2) implant in the bondsmen themselves a consciousness of personal inferiority so they would know how to keep their "place"; (3) awe the slaves with a sense of their master's enormous power, based on the "principle of fear"; (4) persuade the bondsmen to take an interest in the master's enterprise and to accept his standards of good conduct; and (5) "the final step was to impress Negroes with their helplessness, to create in them a 'habit of perfect dependence' upon their masters."[1] All white slaveholders saw each enslaved person as an inferior. Black slaves could never be equal to whites. Black slaves were only bodies that could be used and abused, "a vehicle for labor and capital accumulation."[2] White safety required inerrant control. White slaveholders stood at the apex of a caste system, which had to be carefully and strategically managed with the various methods and tools available to Marse.[3]

THE RACIST PENAL SYSTEM

Because the institution of racist slavery was a crime against humanity, there is no benefit in trying to describe behaviors of slave masters who, for a multiplicity of reasons, may have tried to treat their enslaved people kindly. Such an effort represents a whitewash of the reality of racist slavery. Kindness, even when a Christian kindness, is corrupt within the institution of slavery. When a white planter "owns" another human being, he or she gets no credit for being kind. He or she gets no credit for simply being a product of the mores of his or her time. Racist slavery, as it developed in the American colonies and ultimately rooted itself as the cornerstone of the Southern antebellum economy, was a horror. As *New York Times* columnist Charles Blow wrote in 2020, "On the issue of American slavery, I am an absolutist: enslavers were amoral monsters. The very idea that one group of people believed that they had the right to own another human being is abhorrent and depraved. The fact that their control was enforced by violence was barbaric."[4]

My goal here is to distill a picture of the contours of the management styles, techniques, and philosophies used by elite planters to run the human engine of slavery. Racist slavery was a penal system and its prisoners were coerced people who had committed no crime. The prison wardens also happened to run our American government. As historian Andrew Delbanco succinctly framed it, "In this sealed world, the hierarchy was clear. Regardless of temperamental differences among slave masters, or the relative severity or benignity of living conditions among slaves, everyone was either a guard or an inmate."[5]

The story of our nation's democracy often begins with our first president, although his story usually does not include details about his being a slaveholder. George Washington as a child had inherited ten slaves from his father. By the 1770s, Washington owned more than one hundred enslaved people. At the end of the day, Washington freed his slaves, although he freed them after his death through his will. Some slaveholders had a change of heart, and perhaps Washington did as well, but he was still a slave master. Delbanco gave us an unflattering detail about our first president and his slaves: "Among female slaves Washington had a taste for the 'fat and lusty.' Among males he looked for 'straight-limbed' specimens 'with good teeth and good countenances.'"[6] The fact that he let his slaves go did not change Washington's personal history. If at any point a white person claimed total authority and property rights over another human being because of the color of his or her skin, this came from the diseased heart of a slaveholder. One of our nation's Founding Fathers, Patrick Henry, is most famous for his demand, "Give me liberty or give me death." Less well known is that he owned more than one hundred slaves.[7]

Delbanco highlighted the penal aspects of slavery. He noted that it contained a dynamic of fear on both sides of the equation. Slaveholders had their fears (described in chapter 7) and the enslaved lived in omnipresent fear: "Fear—sheer, chronic, irrepressible fear—had always been endemic to slave culture, and with slaves 'crowding into the far South and increasing faster than whites,' [fear] was growing fast on both sides of the color line. It is hideously expressed in artifacts from the penal world in which slaves were confined not only by law and custom but by shackles, manacles, and chains."[8]

The power and influence of the Southern elite slaveholder is graphically illustrated by the events emanating out of the 1787 Constitutional Convention. As historian Edward Ball pointed out,

> Arguing about population counts for the purpose of taxes based on density, Southern delegates claimed that slaves were not chiefly people but property, like livestock, and therefore should not be counted. When the issue was the apportionment of seats in the new House of Representatives, however, Southerners fought to put Black workers in the category of human beings, because doing so gave the landlords more influence. Northern delegates ridiculed the double standard, but the Southern landlords would not move.[9]

Consequently, the Southern slaveholders were able to force the "three-fifths" rule into the United States Constitution, meaning that in matters of both taxes and representation, a Black enslaved person counted as 60 percent of a white person.

Ball continued: "Two years later, when the First Congress was seated, slavery appeared first on the agenda. When antislavery groups petitioned the legislature, the skittish new lawmakers coughed up another compromise. This time they issued a report that recommended Congress take up the subject—but only in twenty years, after everyone had cooled off."[10] The net effect of this level of power and influence was that two more decades of life were breathed into the American slave industry and it went full speed ahead until the United States abolished slave trading, but not slaveholding, in 1808. The most profound impact of this three-fifths compromise was that it gave the elite politicos of the slaveholder caste a third more seats in Congress and a greater number of votes in the Electoral College. Some say this leaves a bit of stench even today on the Electoral College.

A Senate speech in 1858 by James Henry Hammond, one of South Carolina's most affluent slave masters and politicians, illustrated America's enchantment with the power and influence of slaveholders: "We, the slaveholders of the South, took our country in her infancy, led it to independence, and have since then continued 'ruling her for sixty of the seventy years of her existence.'"[11]

Power, control, domination, humiliation, violence, and exploitation were key elements for a successful slavery-based economy. Slaveholders governed the United States for six decades. America remained impressed with the power and influence of slaveholders. Psychologically, the slaveholder had power not only over the enslaved but, more importantly, over the governance of the entire country. The maintenance of slavery required significant political influence. The passivity and deference to the political power of the antebellum planter class in American history is profound. Significantly, it seems, there are echoes of this passive, deferential stance operating today in our nation's governance.

AN ENDLESS SUPPLY OF BOUND LABOR

The racist slave labor system quite obviously required an endless supply of Black people who were abducted from their ancestral homes, traded for, or purchased and forced into slavery. It is beyond the scope of this book to detail all the horrors of human trafficking and the acquisition of slaves, but a few points need telling. Prior to the official end of the importation of slaves into America in 1808, slave traders and "Negro speculators" from 1787, "citizens of the new nation had dragged 100,000 more people from the African coast. . . . As of 1807, four out of every five people who came from the Old World to the New had come from Africa, not Europe; chained in the belly of a ship, not free on the deck. . . . Ten million Middle Passages of African captives had shaped the New World and its interactions with the Old."[12]

To some white slaveholders, slave trading was an inconvenient truth. There were political and moral skirmishes about slave trading, especially the African slave trade, until the US government abolished it in 1808, having stamped slavery as "immoral." Great Britain also abolished slave trading in the British Empire in 1807. Once American slavery states had enough Blacks in bondage (to the point of becoming profoundly fearful of their sheer numbers), slave traders were seen in an increasingly negative light. An argument can be made that Marse treated his slave sources like a modern man might treat his drug dealer. A certain amount of discretion and privacy were required, but for Marse, this carefulness was directly related to managing his reputation and image, not because of any legal concerns. He could tolerate a certain brand of dealer. Marse developed certain tastes in types of enslaved humans.

Slave trading had two sides to it, however. There was the trade that involved the plunder, purchase, or abduction of people from their native homelands (e.g., Africa), and there was the "domestic trade," the buying and selling of American-born Blacks. Proslavery advocates of the international, transatlantic trade justified it because it had the virtue of bringing so-called heathens to be Christianized. The domestic trade, on the other hand, dealt in a majority of enslaved Blacks who were already Christian.

Documentary historian Willie Lee Rose provided us with a Scotsman's written account of his observations of a slave auction in Richmond, Virginia, in 1853. William Chambers was from the lowland area of Scotland and was visiting the South. The account of his observations is lengthy, so here is a summary of one of its most poignant parts: the sale of a Black man on the auction block. Chambers's account says he was drawn to the markets of Richmond in his role as a printer and publisher and because "Richmond is known as the principal market for the supply of slaves for the south—a circumstance understood to originate in the fact that Virginia, as a matter of husbandry, breeds negro labourers for the express purpose of sale." Chambers describes the white male buyers examining a Black male slave: The man was instructed to stand behind a screen and remove all his clothes,

> which he did without a word. . . . About a dozen gentlemen crowded to the spot where he was stripping . . . and as soon as he stood on the floor, bare from top to toe, a most rigorous scrutiny of his person was instituted. The clear black skin, back and front, was viewed all over for sores from disease; and there was no part of his body left unexamined. The man was told to open and shut his hands, asked if he could pick cotton, and every tooth in his head was scrupulously looked at. The investigation was at an end, he was ordered to dress himself; and having done so, was requested to walk to the block.[13]

Using the written work of a slave trader, historian Howard Zinn described an example of the conditions of captured Black Africans who were taken or purchased from the African interior to slave cages on the Gold Coast. After a forced march from the inland in shackles, they were put in cages until Europeans showed up to inspect them and decide their fate. The ship's surgeon examined each part of each one. All the captives, men and women and children, were naked. The ones perceived to be good and sound were then branded on the breast with a red-hot iron, imprinting the mark of the purchasing company. Thus branded, they were returned to the cages to await their shipment, "sometimes 10–15 days."[14]

Implicit in this horrible scene described by a slave trader is how much fear was induced and how much violence was required to bring Blacks from Central Africa to the American South. The primary, central initiation rite for the freshly enslaved was fear-inducing violence. Even today, white America has not come to grips with the fact slavery was founded on unadulterated white-on-Black violence and terror. Slavery was a special variant of international and domestic violence, driven by money and greed. It matters not that the term "domestic violence" was not to be really understood until the late twentieth century in America. In retrospect, it still applies accurately to chattel slavery. The central reality of the masters' methods was palpable fear. The creation of fear was the mother of all slaveholding methods. Fear was the "polar star" of slavery. It was the fear of omnipresent, unpredictable violence—physical, sexual, and psychological.

Historian Diane Miller Sommerville began her book *Aberration of Mind: Suicide and Suffering in the Civil War-Era South* with a quote from historian C. Vann Woodward: "The theme of violence runs deep in the life and legend of the South."[15] Quoting Woodward, she continued, "Violence in myriad forms—dueling, eye gouging, whippings, insurrections, lynching, rebellion—pervaded the region from its earliest settlements through the modern era. Indeed, it would not be an exaggeration to identify violence as a defining feature of the South, as Sheldon Hackney did decades ago: 'A tendency toward violence has been one of the character traits most frequently attributed to Southerners.'"[16]

By the 1830s, the United States had acquired enormous landholdings that became wide-open to pillage, land speculation, and cultivation, especially of King Cotton. As historian Walter Johnson explained, slaveholders and the United States military expanded the size of the country through "the Louisiana Purchase, the defeat of the Creek nation at Horseshoe Bend in 1814 and of the British at New Orleans in 1815, the Spanish cession of the Florida Parishes, and the Choctaw land cessions at Doaks's Stand in 1820 and Dancing Rabbit Creek in 1830."[17] The land needed clearing and the cotton needed growing, most particularly in the expansive Mississippi Valley. The demand for enslaved labor accelerated in America. Marse needed to see his dealer frequently. Dealers stepped out from the shadows in the 1830s and began to enjoy and bring substantial profits. A "slaveocracy" began to dominate not only the US economy but also the world economy. Once the US westward expansion of slavery began, domestic slaves were forcibly moved from the eastern (e.g., Chesapeake Bay region) and upper South (e.g., Virginia and the

Carolinas), in torturous, inhuman ways. They were often made to walk in chained gangs called coffles for hundreds of miles. Johnson pointed out that "between 1820 and 1860 as many as a million people were sold 'down the river' through the internal slave trade [into the Mississippi Valley]."[18]

An Englishman, George Featherstonhaugh, traveling through the South in 1844, published his observations of a slave coffle: "It was a camp of negro slave-drivers, just packing up to start; they had about three hundred slaves with them, who had bivouacked the preceding night *in chains* in the woods; these they were conducting to Natchez, upon the Mississippi River, to work the sugar plantations in Louisiana." Standing in front of the line were about two hundred male slaves, "in double files . . . *manacled and chained to each other* . . . to perish in the sugar mills of Louisiana, where the duration of life for a sugar-mill slave does not exceed seven years!"[19]

In support of racist slavery, the slave masters' Christian evangelicals were constantly moving from the back of the slavery drama stage to the forefront. For example, three years into the war, "[i]n 1864 a special committee of the Presbyterian church in the Confederacy considered providential the transportation of pagans to Christian America, but added that 'God's inscrutable plan' provided no excuse to reconstitute the [international] trade on a plea that good can come from evil. It pleaded for humanization of the slave codes while reiterating support for slavery as scriptural."[20] The supporters of this committee's position argued that the biblical model supported patriarchal, domestic slavery, but a renewed international trade would bring in "savages" who would have to be severely disciplined. This immensely self-congratulatory position sent an implicit message: We have been (or are on the verge of becoming) successful in the Christianizing of the generations of slaves already here. This scriptural position gives slavery a reason for being. Thus, the external trade of bringing enslaved people from other countries to Christian America went further underground, and the practice of internal, domestic buying, breeding, selling, and bequeathing became the norm.

SLAVE BREEDING

In addition to domestic slave trading and slave stealing, another method for acquiring slaves was, quite simply, the forced breeding of slaves. This sordid dimension of slaveholding is hard to imagine. In my research about slavery, the issue of "slave breeding" seems to prefer a position in the shadows. Addressing the question of slave breeding, historians Ned Sublette and Constance C. Sublette, in their work *The American Slave Coast: A History of the Slave-Breeding Industry*, stated: "A generation of scholarly research has turned up no confirmed documentation of plantations devoted exclusively to breeding slaves, and some scholars have concluded they do not exist."[21] Despite the impracticality of trying to raise slaves from babies to working adults—because of the length of time it would take and the high infant mortality rate—apparently some planters tried it. Economist Richard Sutch published research data in 1972 in which he identified forty-seven "suspected slave breeding farms" in 1860 in the Deep South "on which enslaved women and children substantially outnumbered enslaved men."[22] Regarding Sutch's research, the Sublettes conclude that, as suggestive as Sutch's research and data are, they "remain within the realm of speculation."[23]

Modest support for the existence of slave breeding does come from other sources. In a letter dated August 19, 1837, New Orleans resident Jacob Barker wrote,

> So far as the absolute necessities of life are concerned, the females of *child bearing* age, in Delaware, Maryland, northern, western, and middle Virginia, the upper parts of Kentucky and Missouri, and among the mountains of east Tennessee and western North Carolina, are in general tolerably well supplied. The same remark, with some qualifications, may be made of the slaves generally, in those parts of the country where the people are slaveholders, mainly, that they may enjoy the privilege and profit of being *slave-breeders.*[24]

Several people gave testimony about slave breeding to Theodore Weld's committee. The history and findings of Weld's committee are discussed below. Addressing the emigration of enslaved people from Virginia to other slaveholding states, some of the strongest written testimony on slave breeding comes from Charles Dew, who wrote in 1831, "This emigration becomes an advantage to the state, and does not check the Black population as much as, at first view, we might imagine—because it furnishes every inducement to the master to attend to the negroes, to ENCOURAGE BREEDING, and to cause the *greatest number possible to be raised.* &c . . . *Virginia is, in fact, a negro-raising state for other states.*"[25]

The Sublettes defined the slave-breeding industry "as the complex of businesses and individuals in the United States who profited from the enslavement of African children at birth."[26] A logical, profit-driven method eventually surfaced among certain planters, especially in regions in the South where the mortality rates among the enslaved were high. Some planters decided that breeding or raising their labor was simply smart business. At its most abstract level, the African enslaved people were seen as capital: "African American bodies and childbearing potential collateralized massive amounts of credit, the use of which made slaveowners the wealthiest people in the country. When the Southern states seceded to form the Confederacy, they partitioned off, and declared independence for, their economic system in which people were money."[27]

Breeding and domestic slave trading were capital-driven responses to the 1808 prohibition of the forced importation of Black people. Breeding was a business practice that was also—from a humanitarian perspective—a "capital" offense. As historian Caitlin Rosenthal pointed out, "More recently, scholars have argued for a broader definition of 'breeding' that incorporates experiences recounted by former slaves. A broader definition would account for the myriad ways that masters violated enslaved people, including rape, rules about marriage practices, and family separation. In the space between outright breeding and adequate respect for private lives, planters constantly intruded."[28]

One such example comes from a 1937 Federal Writers' Project interview of Ida Blackshear Hutchinson, enslaved in Alabama in 1865: "My grandfather on my father's side . . . was a 'stock' Negro . . . six feet four inches tall and near two hundred fifty pounds. . . . [He] was the father of fifty-six children and was known as the GIANT BREEDER. He was bought and given to his young mistress in the same way you would give a mule or colt to a child. Although he was a stock negro, he was whipped and drove just like the other Negroes."[29]

The child of an enslaved woman was the master's property, and usually the child's ultimate capital value was greater than the cost of raising the child. A slave girl could, from midadolescence through her midtwenties, be made to breed perhaps as many as fifteen children. The masters saw the advantage of their slaves becoming parents (one out of three children born into slavery died before reaching his or her first birthday), because children increased the enslaver's holdings.[30]

Black children were useful workers. Historian Bruce Levine explained:

> Children's labor fit strategically into the overall choreography of plantation production. Planters considered their tiny hands superior for the performance of certain tasks. Thomas Roughley claimed that the "supple hand of the negro child is best calculated to extract the weeds and grass." Working among young [sugar] canes, children left "few breakages" because they were "more light and cautious." Not only did enslaved youth perform a wide array of jobs, but by working at lighter tasks, they freed up field hands to work at heavy ones. Perhaps most important, sending children into the fields introduced them to the strenuous patterns of labor that would govern their lives, accustomizing them to constant work.[31]

Despite their supposed value, most slave children were inadequately clothed. As a child in Maryland, Frederick Douglass "was kept almost in a state of nudity; no shoes, no stockings, no jacket, no trousers, nothing but coarse sack-cloth or two-linen, made into a sort of shirt, reaching down to my knees."[32]

Some slave owners became very invested in breeding slaves. Contemplate the role of the slave breeder. An image of a cold, calculating businessman driven by profit comes to mind. Then contemplate a man who established an enterprise on his property that set aside and controlled the impregnating of enslaved girls and women and the birth of slave children for profit. This section of Marse's estate was essentially a stable. Most often, the poor enslaved girl or woman had no say in who impregnated her. It was the master's call. The master himself may have been the one who bedded the unfortunate girl or woman. Such an action by the slave master would constitute both rape and breeding. Rape and sexual assault of slaves by masters, by the master's children, or by employees of the master—such as the overseer—were common and frequent.

Approaching an aspect of the sexual exploitation of slaves from an angle rarely discussed, historians Eugene Genovese and Elizabeth Fox-Genovese pointed out: "The more well-to-do slaveholders sent their sons to distant academies and colleges in part to get them away from the sexual temptations of plantation life."[33] For example, the parental fear of homosexuality, they state, was "enmeshed in silence." If the adult white master could sexually exploit his slaves, could not the master's child exploit the slave children? Could not the white child expect and demand submission from the Black children who were his or her playmates?

A fruitful slave woman who could bear many children was seen as a property-bearing machine, a moneymaker: "When the profitability of slaves as capital became that great, as it did early on, the market economy came to intrude deeply into the most intimate of human relationships."[34] Slave breeding was a severe form of emotional, physical, and sexual abuse. Making a woman have one baby after another so that her offspring could be monetarily valued and then enslaved, sold, or both, was profoundly cruel and immoral.

WHAT PRECISELY DID SLAVE MANAGEMENT REQUIRE?

To manage the racist slavery system, Marse had to live in the midst of a paradox. While he consciously and actively ran the system—and many ultimately fought and died for it—he was unconsciously run by the system. Writing in his autobiography in 1849, former slave J. W. C. Pennington stated, "You cannot constitute slavery without the chattel principle—and with the chattel principle you cannot save it from these results. Talk not about kind and

Christian masters. They are not masters of the system. The system is master of them."³⁵

Successful slave management demanded compliance from the enslaved. Slaves had to remain in perfect agreement with their master. Marse could sell a slave down the river in a heartbeat. The threat of sale kept many slaves psychologically in check. The master's view of the perfect slave was one who was subservient, without a murmur, to the master's will. The perfect slave was always to relieve the master as much as possible of any burden. Slavery was viewed as a rational solution to all the inherent ills of the free-labor market. Some masters convinced themselves that punishment of a slave tended to "win his attachment and promote his happiness and well-being."³⁶

If a master used an incentive such as hope to motivate his slaves, it might be the hope of a monetary reward or extra time off or a plot of land on which to have a personal garden. It was never the hope of freedom. All other forms of incentives were secondary to the power to punish. The slave master's power essentially was unlimited. The slave master made every effort to achieve a state of learned helplessness among the enslaved. Learned helplessness is the state in which a human finds him- or herself when held captive and experiencing a total loss of personal power. The presence of a debilitating fear can often render a human totally powerless.

Compliance was achieved by the application of a wide-ranging array of control, torture, and punishment methods and techniques. The installation of an ever-present fear was paramount. The "principle of fear" became the number one motivator. The master or his agent could enact unannounced, periodic searches of slave cabins and personal possessions for weapons and stolen goods. It was a "lawful" search and seizure. The enslaved's door could be kicked in at any time.

Despite efforts by slaveholders to apply a paternalistic philosophy—such as "We are all one family"—and to Christianize the enslaved, in the eighteenth-century South, "coercion lay at the heart of successful slave management and should be used as frequently and forcefully as needed to render the slaves' obedience complete. The pre-paternalist emphasis on coercion as the foundation of slavery grew in part from the eighteenth-century white fear of African slaves as robust warriors."³⁷

It was common among antebellum planters to develop guidebooks on slave management for themselves and fellow planters. As an example, between 1836 and 1846, Bennet H. Barrow, a wealthy Louisiana slaveholder, wrote a diary in which he opined on the "strict" rules of running his Highland Plantation. According to historian Eric Foner, "Barrow considered himself a model of planter paternalism who, by his own standards, treated his slaves well. . . . The rules illustrated that even the most well-intended owners claimed

complete authority over the lives of their slaves. Inadvertently, the rules also revealed planters' fears about disobedience and resistance among their slaves."[38]
Here is a summation of Barrow's slave management rules:

- No Negro could leave the planation without his permission.
- No Negro could marry outside of the plantation, which would run the risk of the slaves developing some dangerous independence.
- No Negro could sell anything to anybody without Barrow's permission.
- A slave had no time that was his own; he was subject to immediate beck and call by the planter, who had exclusive right over the slave's time.
- While trying to make the slave relatively comfortable, always create in the slave a "perfect dependence."
- Never let any man talk to the Negroes, "nothing more injurious."[39]

What's obviously missing from Barrow's rule book are the forms and methods of punishment to be used should things not always go according to plan. Historian Bertram Wyatt-Brown noted a shaming incident between Barrow and one of his slaves: "Bennet Barrow, a Louisiana planter, once threatened to put an offending slave on a scaffold in the yard, wearing a red cap."[40] Describing Barrow's response to one of his slave's possibly feigning blindness, historian James Oakes wrote: "'& after I Whiped him.' One slave claimed to have lost his eyesight and refused to work for months until Barrow 'gave him 25 cuts yesterday morning & ordered him to work Blind or not.' The next day the slave 'run off.'"[41]

THE METHODS

Slave masters had at their disposal a wide range of control and punishment implements, devices, actions, and structures from 1619 until emancipation in 1863. The following is a list of verified cruelties I have developed over the years of research leading up to this book, although it is by no means an exhaustive list:

- Scant feeding and malnourishment[42]
- Scant (or no) clothing
- Generally discouraging or preventing from learning to read or write
- Maiming
- Beating to death
- Torturing with thumbscrews and pincers

- A slave "driver" cracking his whip throughout the day at unpredictable intervals
- Binding an individual for punishment (usually a severe whipping), which took place in front of the enslaved's family members
- Burning alive
- Castrating
- Murdering
- Hanging
- Imprisoning in "nigger boxes"
- Throwing to the dogs
- Chasing runaways for sport
- Dragging by horse
- Wrapping in barbed wire
- Drowning
- Branding
- "Pushing," a system that increased the number of acres each enslaved was supposed to cultivate to abusive levels; if an enslaved fell behind his expected goal, he was punished severely, even shot, in front of other bound workers
- "Mob control," or mob psychology, forming the basis for judgment about racist murders (lynchings)
- Coercing "confessions" (inquisition style) out of enslaved persons suspected of plotting insurrection
- Purchasing specific female slaves to be their forced concubines with female, "fancy" mistresses often costing five times the median cost of a similar but ordinary house slave
- Buying their slaves to treat them as sadistic victims
- Giving full physical, naked exams of slaves, which was, for many buyers, an erotic experience
- Forcing one of the most brutal dislocations of people in human history
- Insuring some enslaved people as property through the purchase of insurance policies
- Identifying many enslaved as property by slave deeds registered in the courthouse
- Shooting and beheading the leaders of an unsuccessful slave revolt and placing their heads on poles alongside the main road for all to see
- Lynching[43]
- Kidnapping
- Using the enslaved as subjects of medical experiments
- Considering "Negroes" as pieces of money

- Slave buyers walking along side one another in the slave pens, talking about and joking about the slaves exhibited before them
- Publishing journals about "how to" manage slaves, covering such topics as proper diet and discipline
- Utilizing a group of men known as "breakers," whose skills (usually with a whip) entailed breaking the spirits of difficult enslaved people, with other slaves as the intended audience; "slave breaking was a technology of the soul"[44]
- Purchasing slaves as gifts for his wife and children
- Considering slave ownership a status symbol as well as a necessity for success
- Utilizing the enslaved as stepping-stones for slaveholders to buy their way into the planter class
- Cruelly keeping the enslaved under chronic emotional torture in a system based on power and fear, forcing them to find a place between being a person and being a thing[45]
- Examining a slave at market, and trying, as an astute buyer, to tell a slave's history by looking at his back
- Believing that slave buying created slaveholder skills in the meaning of different skin tones
- Bequeathing chattel enslaved people to others through wills, comparable to giving a child a treasured piece of furniture
- Buyers showing a palpable interest for young (below fifteen), light-skinned females
- Forbidding the enslaved to talk with one another while imprisoned
- Separating enslaved family members from one another; often done by deceit on the part of the slave master, a sudden event with no time for enslaved families to tell one another goodbye
- Controlling and forcing marriages
- Raping and sexually assaulting
- Coercing pregnancies
- Breeding of enslaved people
- Making slave trading often simply the buying and selling of children and teens
- Skinning alive
- Developing slave labor camps, where one of every three Black children died before his or her first birthday[46]
- Whipping enslaved people to make them sing, often when being separated, to divert them from any expression of sorrow or rage
- Emasculating

- Marching the enslaved in coffles, where they were chained two-by-two, with chains around the wrists, waists, and ankles
- Making them eat their food without utensils, just with their fingers
- Creating conditions that led to abject despair, self-mutilation, and suicide among the enslaved
- Whippings (According to Edward E. Baptist, many enslaved people considered the bull whips of the southwest to be the whips bringing the most brutal effects. An overseer could develop dexterity with his whip, so that not only could he inflict a laceration, but also could tear out a small piece of flesh with his lash.)[47]
- Ear cropping
- Preaching a biased, proslavery form of scripture to the enslaved
- Instilling fear and dread of the absolute power of the slave master
- Not allowing Black men to act fully as men in any traditional sense
- Most likely killing an enslaved person who tried to fight back against a punishment
- Imprisoning, building slave prisons
- Keeping the enslaved in pens at the slave yards; "commonly fifty to a hundred people were held in a space the size of a home lot," awaiting examinations in the next-door showrooms[48]
- Developing the skills of slave buying and selling to gain the admiration and attention of one's male white men friends and associates
- Publicly examining enslaved persons' whole bodies in front of others, as if they were horses
- Thinking themselves clever for sometimes giving their enslaved classical names, such as Plato, Aristotle, or Artemis
- Treating enslaved people as less-than-human heathens
- Selling an enslaved person easily and quickly between the buyer and seller, and then later recording the sale
- Forcing Christianity on them
- Controlling them around the clock
- Making unannounced raids on the slaves' quarters
- Turning a blind eye sometimes to his own overseer's treatment of the master's enslaved
- Building such inhumane conditions aboard the slave ships that many enslaved died in the passage or threw themselves overboard to escape the horrid conditions and avoid their enslaved future
- Slave trading turned the enslaved to "it" instead of "her" or "him"
- "Fattening up" and packaging the enslaved before putting them on the market
- Robbing the enslaved of their heritage

- Selling
- Buying
- Trading
- Developing public slave yards, where a slave, viewed by the master to deserve punishment, could be sent to or dropped off, and where the enslaved person would be whipped by a public official who earned a fee, keeping the slave master's hands clean
- Placing a sadistic neck device on an enslaved, usually made of iron, designed to cause maximum discomfort and humiliation
- Putting a monetary value on the enslaved person
- Creating work conditions that were inherently lethal, such as in massive rice plantations
- Creating an institutionalized fiction that the enslaved individual was not a person but a piece of property
- Convincing the enslaved that God Almighty gave them to white people to serve the master and his family
- Dr. Samuel Cartwright bizarrely fabricating the so-called Black diseases, such as *Drapetomania*, which caused running away, and *Dysthesia Ethiopica*, a disease that caused resistance
- Economically exploiting the enslaved

THE THEODORE WELD DATA

Table 8.1 sets out a different perspective on the wide range of punishment, torture, and lynching methods, in greater detail and specificity, used by many (not all) white racist slave masters against their enslaved. The list contains approximately one hundred and thirty-five examples derived from selections taken from Theodore Weld's remarkable book *American Slavery as It Is: Testimony of a Thousand Witnesses*, published in 1839. As Weld wrote in the book's opening section, "A majority of the facts and testimony contained in this work rests upon the authority of slaveholders, whose names and residences are given to the public, as vouchers for the truth of their statements. That they should utter falsehoods, for the sake of proclaiming their own infamy, is not probable."[49]

Some of the "testimony" published in Weld's book was taken from newspaper advertisements placed in slave state newspapers. Many of these statements were, in effect, newspaper advertisements placed by slaveholders in their pursuit of fugitive slaves. The ads are highly self-incriminating, because not only do they explicitly connect the runaway slave being sought with the particular slaveholder, but they also offer excruciating detail about the punishment, branding, disfigurement, and flogging marks on the individual slave's body to be used as identifying detail for slave hunters, slave catchers, and other interested parties.

Additionally, Weld's book contains statements from slaveholders' papers, periodicals, books, and letters. His book also contains testimony—often in the form of letters (nineteenth-century equivalents to affidavits) given to Weld's investigative committee—from persons who "have resided in slave states, many of whom are natives of those states, and have been slaveholders." While this latter category may be considered hearsay in twenty-first-century legal terms, their admission into evidence was perfectly acceptable in the process and context of Weld's task. The manner in which it was collected and recorded more than 180 years ago makes it inherently reliable as a contemporaneous summary of what Weld's committee heard and read about Marse's treatment of his slaves. Statements about character accompany many of the letters Weld received from other persons who knew and vouched for the integrity of the writer.

Table 8.1.   Punishment Methods

Method of Punishment	Alleged Offense(s)	Victim(s)	State Location	Perpetrator	Outcome	Page No.
attempted rape; flogged	resistance	female	NC	master	gave in to master's lust	15
beaten	not working enough or some cooking mistake	female named Piney	KY	mistress	severe beatings	50
beaten about her head for serving too much molasses	minor mistake	female	SC	master	unknown	26
beaten almost to death	stealing 5 dollars	unidentified male	VA	constable called by the master	severely beaten	62
beaten and chained	resistance	male	AL	master	sold	49
beaten to death with a whip	runaways	mostly males	GA	masters	died	21
beaten with paddle with holes dipped in hot water	runaway	all slaves	IL	master	severely beaten	46
beatings with rawhide	running away	multiple slaves	VA	master	permanent scars from beatings	52
beheaded	runaway	male	SC	unknown	death	23
blow to back of head	meanness	all slaves	NC	overseer	survived	14

(continued)

Table 8.1. *(Continued)*

Method of Punishment	Alleged Offense(s)	Victim(s)	State Location	Perpetrator	Outcome	Page No.
blow to head	not working fast enough	female	NC	overseer	survived	14
bound and flogged	runaway	male	NC	master	survived	16
branded by hot iron	some offense	slaves	GA	masters or agents	scarred for life	21
branding, maiming, gunshot wounds, hunted by dogs, ears and toes cut off, eyes knocked out, bones dislocated	unidentified runaways	slaves in general	various slave states	various	descriptions of slave runaways with marks of torture and injuries	77
buried in ground with only his head above ground	runaway	male	NC	overseer	survived	15
cancer; no medical attention	old age	male	NC	master	presumed died	23
cat-hauling: while holding a cat, draw the cat's claws across the slave's bare back	some offense	slaves	GA	masters and agents	horrible tearing of skin; poisons the flesh	21
chained	runaways	slaves, mostly male	GA	masters or agents	hobbled	21
collars or yokes around their necks	runaways	mostly males	GA	masters or agents	hobbled, confined	21
committed to jail, had a large neck iron with a huge pair of horns and a large band of iron on his left leg	runaway	"negro boy"	TN	master	runaway advertisement	73
cruelty is the rule, kindness the exception	unidentified	slaves in general	AL	master	general cruelty	61
died from flogging wounds	staying too long with their wives	3 males	KY	master	death	50

Method of Punishment	Alleged Offense(s)	Victim(s)	State Location	Perpetrator	Outcome	Page No.
drowning of baby	drowning	slave infant	NC	baby's older sister	died	12
ears pinched with hot tongs, hot embers thrown on child's legs	child had an unidentified infirmity	6-year-old female child	VA	master and mistress	torture	85
ears slit	petty theft	female	SC	mistress	physical damage	23
eye knocked out by a maul	unknown	male	VA	master	lacerations and loss of eye	27
feet hacked off with broad axe; then legs chopped off at knees; body chopped to pieces, thrown into flames	accidental breaking of vase	17-year-old male	KY	master	sadistic dismemberment	93
female made to work naked, then murdered	unidentified	female adult	TN	master	murder	93
flogged	accidental pin prick	female	NC	other slave	unclear	13
flogged	premature death of slave baby	female mother	NC	master	survived	16
flogged	tardiness	male	NC	overseer	survived	14
flogged in the presence of other slaves	some offense	slaves	GA	masters as means of creating fear	unknown	21
flogged in work-house, made to walk tread mill, ankles chained	uncertain	18-year-old slave	SC	master was also a reputable M.D.	crippled, sadistic medical treatment	55
flogged	pig stealing	male	NC	mistress and overseer	survived	12
flogged to death	traveling without a pass	male	AL	2 unidentified white men	murdered	47
flogging	unknown	all slaves on plantation	AL	overseer named Tune	unknown	45
flogging	unknown	pregnant slave beaten so severely she delivered a dead child	AL	overseer named	murder of unborn child	46

(continued)

Table 8.1. *(Continued)*

Method of Punishment	Alleged Offense(s)	Victim(s)	State Location	Perpetrator	Outcome	Page No.
forced cohabitation	no offense	2 females	NC	local merchant	merchant died from stabbing	16
forced nakedness	no offense	male	NC	master	survived	16
given unnecessary medication	suspicion of malingering	unknown	NC	overseer	unknown	14
half-naked and half starved	unidentified	slaves in general	GA	master	neglected	60
handcuffs, manacles, blood-stained cowhide	uncertain	slaves in general	unidentified	unidentified	savage cruelties	58
hanged for killing his master	master had whipped slave's mother to death	male	KY	unidentified	hanged	64
head crushed by ax "helve"	insulted her mistress	female	IL	master	murdered	46
head shaved to disgrace him and whipped so severely he could hardly walk	uncertain	small boy	SC	master and mistress	crippled	55
heads laid open by beatings, jaws broken, teeth knocked out, ears cropped, sides of the cheeks gashed out; eye put out	some offense	all slaves	GA	masters and agents	range of physical and emotional damage	20
hot brine and turpentine poured into lash wounds	unidentified	slaves in general	unidentified	unidentified	general cruelty	62
hung up by hands, tied, beaten, wounds washed with salt	unidentified	slaves in general	TN	master	tortured	60
hunted	runaways	slaves	GA	master and slave catchers	dead or alive	21
imprisoned	alleged poisoning	female girl	AL	Mrs. H.	put in jail	47

Method of Punishment	Alleged Offense(s)	Victim(s)	State Location	Perpetrator	Outcome	Page No.
in response to rumored slave rebellion, suspects were jailed, whipped, thumb screws used to extract confessions	rumored insurrection	multiple slaves	NC	authorities	torture; false confessions, whippings	51
in stocks for 6 weeks; not allowed to join wife	runaway to join wife	male	SC	master	unknown	23
inadequate clothing	general neglect	all	NC	master	neglect	13
interrogated for being Black	all	slaves	GA	white men	varies	21
iron band around his head, locked with a padlock; in the front, where it passed the mouth, there was a projection inward of an inch and a half into the mouth	runaway, alleged "addicted to running away"	male	MS	overseer	torture instruments kept on all the time so that if he ran away, he couldn't eat and would starve to death	74
jailed and whipped cruelly	multiple reasons	all in this vicinity	GA	jailers and constables	unknown	20
jailed as a runaway	runaway	Martha, 17-18 years old	TN	jailer	imprisonment	62
kept naked or poorly clothed in winter	unidentified	slaves in general	unidentified	master	neglected	59
kidnapping	slave market	free slaves and runaways, including children	across slave states	slave traffickers	kidnapped and sold	140

(continued)

Table 8.1. *(Continued)*

Method of Punishment	Alleged Offense(s)	Victim(s)	State Location	Perpetrator	Outcome	Page No.
knocked down, some have eyes beaten out, arm or leg broken	uncertain	slaves in general	unidentified	slave drivers	general mistreatment and cruelty	58
locked in stocks and placed on a table	unsure	13-year-old female house slave	SC	mistress	found dead after falling off the table	54
made to stand on one foot and hold the other up	unknown	male	SC	mistress	unknown	23
made to walk until dead	unidentified	male	VA	master	torture, death	92
made to wear chains, handcuffs, fetters, iron clogs, bars, rings, and bands of iron on their limbs, iron masks on their faces, iron gags in their mouths	unidentified	slaves in general	unidentified	various	tortured and humiliated	72
made to wear heavy iron yoke on his neck, the two prongs twelve to fifteen inches long	runaway	male	AL	master	tortured	47
mangling, imprisonment, every species of torture	unidentified	slaves in general	KY	master	general cruelty	61
medical neglect	ill	male	NC	master	died	12
multiple rapes	situational	multiple females	NC	surrogate of master	unknown	16
mutilation of teeth, cropping (cutting off) usually the ears	runaways	slaves in general	various slave states	various	descriptions of slave runaways with marks of torture and injuries	84
neglect; whipped	old age	female	SC	master and mistress	presumed died	24

Method of Punishment	Alleged Offense(s)	Victim(s)	State Location	Perpetrator	Outcome	Page No.
ordered to Charleston work-house	runaway	female	SC	master and mistress	death	24
paddles called "pancake sticks" used to punish house slaves; verbally abused	flogged every day for every trifling offense	house slaves in Charleston	SC	mistress	scars, from whippings and scolding; constant fault-finding	53
rubbing with salt and red pepper is very common after a severe whipping	deficiencies in work	slaves in general	MS	master	general cruelty	61
running dogs	runaways	slaves	GA	masters	varies	21
75 lashes for visiting another slave	socializing	male	SC	master	unknown	25
severe beating	accidental boat drift	male	NC	overseer	unknown	14
shackled	resistance	male	NC	master	sold	13
shot	pig stealing	male	NC	overseer	survived	11
shot	runaway, weapon stealing	male	NC	master and slave catcher	killed	15
shot and beheaded	runaway	male	NC	slave hunters	killed	15
shot through the head	disappointed slave master's sexual advances	female	AL	unidentified white man	killed and buried in log heap	47
shot to death	ran into a white man in the woods	male	AL	shot by assailant because the slave refused to stop	murdered	46
shot to death accidentally	ran out of cabin too fast carrying a knife	male	MS	overseer	killed	46
skull caved in with axe	refusal to be flogged	male	AL	overseer	murdered	47
slave fastened to a log then beaten on bare skin with board paddle full of holes	some offense	all slaves	GA	master and agents	severe tearing of skin	20

(continued)

Table 8.1. *(Continued)*

Method of Punishment	Alleged Offense(s)	Victim(s)	State Location	Perpetrator	Outcome	Page No.
slave stretched out face down, tied to four stakes, in form of St. Andrew's cross, beaten	slave judged guilty of serious faults	slaves in general	unidentified	"negro" driver	severely beaten	59
slave trading: gags and thumb screws used	demand	slaves in general	MD, VA	trader	buying and selling	60
slave "wench" tied to a peach tree and beaten	disappointed the master	female	AL	master	sores from whippings	48
slave's daughter chained to her neck	prevent her from running away	female	NC	mistress	burden, humiliation	51
slaves sent to jail to be whipped	multiple reasons	all in this vicinity	GA	plantation mistress	some died	20
stabbed	consorting with a female slave	male	AL	Mr. Mosely	severely wounded	47
staked out and beaten, pinched, and bitten	failure to interpret mistress' wish	slaves in general	unidentified	white creole women	severely beaten	59
starved to death	unknown	female	SC	mistress	death	23
stocks/flogging	runaway	male	NC	master	survived	11
stocks whipped	unclear	male	NC	overseer	sold	12
stripped, beaten, then wounds rubbed with salt, water, and pepper	unknown	male	IL	master	beaten severely	46
stripped naked, stretched over barrels, beaten	unidentified	slaves in general	TN	master	severely beaten	60
stripped naked, suspended by their hands, then cruelly whipped	taking a hen's egg	both sexes	VA	farmer and slave trafficker	beatings	49
strung up with feet barely touching the ground; slashed and tortured	multiple reasons	all in this vicinity	GA	overseer	barely survived	20

Method of Punishment	Alleged Offense(s)	Victim(s)	State Location	Perpetrator	Outcome	Page No.
suicide	being trafficked	male	KY	farmer and slave trafficker	death by drowning	50
task made harder	27 slaves	presumably male	SC	overseer	driven to exhaustion	26
39–100 lashes on bare back	multiple reasons	all in this vicinity	GA	master and agents, including constables	unknown	20
threatened for not breeding	not breeding	multiple females	NC	master	survived	15
300 stripes given	unknown	17 house servants	SC	mistress	unknown	25
tied and beaten	unknown	male	VA	2 unidentified men	unknown	27
tied and lashed 500 times	alleged theft	male	VA	master	unknown	27
tied and paddled by board with holes for a full day	acting too leisurely	brick mason slave	AL	master	severe cuts	46
tied to a tree and lashed 100 times	robbing a hen roost	male	GA	master	wounds from severe lashing	50
tied to tree and flogged while master's guests watched and played cards	unknown	male	VA	master	beaten as form of entertainment	46
tied to tree and whipped; heavily ironed	resistance	male	SC	master	died of old age	22
tied up in tortuous posture	some offense	all slaves	GA	masters and agents	range of damages	20
tied to tree and whipped to death	attempted runaway	two males	VA	overseer	murdered	64
tied to tree, flogged, and burned to death	unknown	male	VA	overseer	lynched; perpetrator was tried and convicted	26
tied up, thumb screwed, tortured with pinchers, beaten	a trifling neglect of duty	slaves in general	unidentified	Christian master	savage cruelties	58

(continued)

Table 8.1. *(Continued)*

Method of Punishment	Alleged Offense(s)	Victim(s)	State Location	Perpetrator	Outcome	Page No.
toenail pulled out	runaway; burned his master's barn; murdered 2 of the master's children	male	IL	master	shot and hanged	46
tooth knocked out by hammer	toothache	female	NC	overseer	tooth removed	13
tortured	unidentified offense	young boy	VA	master	died	26
tortured by iron collars, with long prongs or "horns," sometimes with bells on them	unidentified	slaves in general	unidentified	various	tortured and humiliated	72
trial of 1 Black and 1 white slave	unknown	1 white and 1 Black woman	SC	unknown	unknown	25
twenty, twenty-five, forty, fifty or one hundred lashes	slave judged guilty of serious faults	slaves in general	unidentified	the manager, master, or driver	cruelties	59
whipped	not completing task	female with child	GA	master	survived	18
whipped	some offense	children	GA	masters	unknown	20
whipped	uncertain	10-year-old house slave	SC	master	blinded in one eye during severe whipping	54
whipped and jailed; heavy iron collar with long prongs; strong front tooth extracted	same runaway as above	mulatto female	SC	master and mistress	permanent physical damage	22
whipped at Charleston work-house	runaway	mulatto female	SC	master and mistress	cuts	22
whipped for professing belief in God	Christian piety	male	SC	master	death from his lashings	24
whipped in Charleston work-house	uncertain	multiple slaves	SC	master	master watched them being whipped	55

Method of Punishment	Alleged Offense(s)	Victim(s)	State Location	Perpetrator	Outcome	Page No.
whipped to death	for "grabbling" a potato hill	female	AL	One Jones	murdered	47
whipped to death	not done as much work as expected	male	VA	same master Harris	slave cut off his own hand; murdered	26
whipped to death by white family	some offense	male	VA	family members of white-owned company	death	27
whipped to death, while wife burned her with an iron		slave girl, age 15	VA	master Benjamin James Harris and wife	murdered	26
whipped until they miscarried	some offense	pregnant females in this vicinity	GA	overseers and drivers	death of fetus	20
whipping	being off plantation without pass	male	NC	slave patrol leader	survived	14
whipping, kicking, beating, starving, cat-hauling, loading with irons, imprisoning, torture	witness observation of general treatment of slaves	all in this vicinity	GA	master and agents	unknown	20

The reader of entry after entry of table 8.1 is no doubt left with increasing feelings of disbelief, horror, and profound sadness, for even those of us who thought we understood the nature of southern slavery cannot truly fathom that the individual and collective cruelty set out in those entries occurred on our soil not that many generations ago. Our slaveholding forefathers and foremothers engaged in heinous crimes against humanity, and the brutality of it all should continue to resonate with us as we today contemplate Black Lives Matter issues and beyond.

PSYCHOLOGICAL CONTROL

Racist slavery was a parent-child relationship ultimately founded on paternalism. Historically, the three pillars of paternalism were the church, the monarchy, and the aristocracy. Many American slaveholders considered themselves as masters of tradition, although they, of course, had thrown off the chains of the monarchy while both consciously and unconsciously becoming monarch-like themselves. White male masters were already paternalistic with white women and children. Being thus so with Black people was a natural progression. The slavery system was in its essence a process of infantilization.[50]

Slave masters fancied themselves as astute psychologists: "The successful master was often a keen student of human psychology. Those who discussed the problem of managing slaves advised owners to study carefully the character of each chattel."[51] This dynamic led masters to develop a set of rules that governed their private domain. These rules became the "law" of the plantation. Slavery was perceived as a "good, a positive good."[52] Thomas Jefferson unhappily (and ironically) acknowledged in 1787 that masters exercised "the most unremitting despotism" over their slaves that gave free rein "to the most boisterous passions [in the masters]."[53]

THE PROBLEM OF RUNAWAYS

Despite the typical slave master's delusional wish or belief that his slaves were content, especially as the ideology of paternalism took root in slave management, there was the problem of runaways, a subject discussed in chapter 7. Addressing the fate of most enslaved runaways, Delbanco wrote, "In fact, most runaways never made it out of the South, where chronic offenders were sometimes mutilated—tendons cut, faces branded—as warnings not to try it again, and to others not to try at all."[54] He added,

> As for those who tried against the odds to run away, repeat offenders might be rendered immobile by having their insteps split or Achilles tendons cut. Henry Bibb, who escaped from Kentucky in 1842, reports that after a previous escape attempt, an "iron collar [was] riveted on my neck with prongs, extending above my head, on the end of which there a small bell" designed to sound an alert if he strayed. In incorrigible cases, the offender might be stripped and beaten with a paddle specially designed with numerous holes in order to raise blisters that could be shredded by a later beating or splashed with salt water to prolong the pain.[55]

The slave master did not brook any challenge to his authority. From a power and control perspective, slavery was and is domestic violence. Slavery became state-sanctioned domestic violence. No matter how kindly or benevolent a master wanted to be toward his slaves, "a human master's impulse to be kind to his slaves was severely circumscribed by the inescapable problem of control."[56] Without the power to punish, which the state conferred upon the

Common mode of whipping with the paddle. *Photograph of woodcut. Library of Congress*

master, bondage could not have existed. On large plantations, such as Colonel Edward Lloyd's, described below, which were kingdoms or realms all of their own, the master or his surrogate was the judge, jury, and executioner. If there was any local law enforcement, it usually turned a blind eye to the management of the enslaved by the master.

Douglass described the cruelty of slaveholder Lloyd, a man who kept from three to four hundred slaves on his home plantation, the Great House Farm. Douglass lived on one of Lloyd's plantations with Douglass's master, who was a clerk and overseer for Lloyd, who owned approximately twenty plantations or farms and was said to own a thousand slaves. Displeased one day with the way one of his horses was responding to his commands, Lloyd blamed the slave for the horse's behavior. Douglass wrote, "I have seen Colonel Lloyd make old Barney, a man between fifty and sixty years of age, uncover his bald head, kneel down upon the cold, damp ground, and receive upon his naked head and toil-worn shoulders more than thirty lashes at a time."[57]

Delbanco wrote a superb analysis of the struggle for our country's soul caused by the slaves' almost immediate (upon being enslaved) efforts to break the chains of bondage.[58] The runaway slave dynamics, in Delbanco's words, lit a long fuse in America that culminated in the Civil War. As Delbanco pointed out, when Lincoln delivered his Gettysburg Address in November 1863 and spoke reverently about "that all men are equated equal," Lincoln knew at the time what he said was not true and that even he did not believe it.

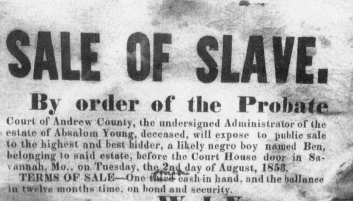

"Sale of a Slave." *Library of Congress*

"A Negro Hung Alive by the Ribs to a Gallows." *Engraving by William Blake for the book* Narrative, of Five Years' Expedition, against the Revolted Negroes of Surinam *by John Gabriel Stedman (1796)*

White southern racist elite slaveholders developed management rules designed to create and control the perfect slave. For the southern master, slavery had been in existence and was a natural continuation since the beginning of civilization. All civilizations rested on a hierarchy in which one inferior level of beings supported the superior level of beings. To the southern elitist slave master, it was a system created by God.

The elite masters instituted a massive penal system with fear as its cornerstone. Black Africans were legislated into being two-thirds of a person. Power, control, domination, humiliation, violence, and exploitation were the mixture of the grease

Detail of Enslaved Man in Coffle. *Enslaved statuary group by Kwame Akoto-Bamfo, National Memorial for Peace and Justice, Montgomery, AL. Photograph by the author*

that made the slavery industrial machine run relatively smoothly. Some masters attempted to convince their slaves that the master was God: If a slave disobeyed the master, the slave was disobeying God. Slaves never really bought into this egotistical lie. The master was largely unaware that slavery ran the master.

Slavery required a boundless supply of Black human beings. The number of enslaved people in America reached around 11 million men, women, and children. Slave trading and slave breeding helped to bolster the supply. As our nation's land holding expanded, slavery and cotton production increased with it. Between 1820 and 1860, a million slaves were moved into the Mississippi Valley.

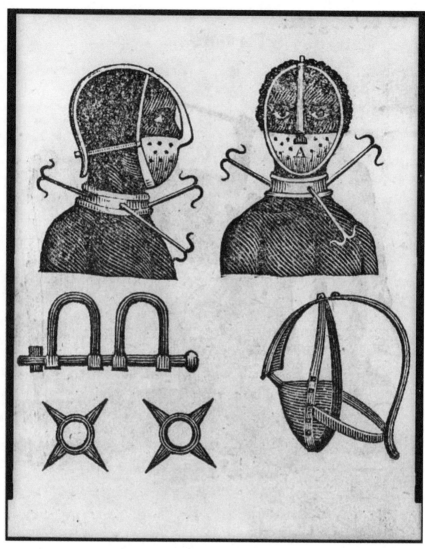

Torture Devices. *Photograph of woodcut by Samual Wood, 1807. Library of Congress*

A vast range of punishment techniques and methods, many of which fall along a sadistic continuum, reinforced power and fear. While it needs to be said again that not all slaveholders were cruel or sadistic, all slaveholders were complicit in their support of a dehumanizing system of bondage.

· 9 ·

The Slave Masters' Laws and Social Policies

THE POLITICAL POWER OF SLAVEHOLDING

Massive numbers of laws and policies adhered to the maintenance and defense of slavery, not only in the southern states, but also in the nation as a whole. I do not address them with any comprehensive specificity but do underscore that southern slaveholders held elite positions of power and influence in the early governance of America. They were able to create both a legal and social policy framework designed to ensure slavery's success by laws and policies promoting the domination of Black slaves and the systematic suppression of their human rights.

From the American Revolution through early 1849, while in office eight US presidents (Washington, Jefferson, Madison, Monroe, Jackson, Tyler, Polk, and Taylor) owned enslaved people. Two other presidents (Van Buren and Harrison) also owned slaves, but not while in office. Neither John Adams nor John Quincy Adams owned slaves, as they were both antislavery. Nine men out of these twelve presidents were Southerners. Six of these nine hailed from Virginia.

The significance of the foundation and role of white southern racist slavery in our American democratic experiment cannot be overemphasized. Quoting Karl Marx from 1861, historian Matthew Karp wrote, "In the foreign, as in the domestic policy of the United States, the interest of the slaveholders served as the guiding star."[1]

From a psychological perspective, this fact helps us understand the depth of racist slavery ideology in white America's psyche, especially in the South. Returning to Wendell Berry's formulation of the largely unconscious "hidden wound" experienced by Black and white Americans (addressed in chapter 1), racist slavery settled into the initial fabric of our national psyche[2] and most uniquely into the psychological makeup of the white southern slave master. Its traumatic effects are now roaring to the surface in our country in the twenty-first century.

NECESSARY CONTROL MEASURES

To state the obvious, if you forcefully seize and imprison people for life to be your eternal slaves held as human property solely because of the color of their skin, then you must set up an effective system to control and dominate people who would rather be free, not chained and under the lash, and living in their own country of origin or living wherever and however they want to live. The development of rules, regulations, codes, social policies, laws, institutions, and other racist control mechanisms regarding slavery began early in the colonies. As historians Elizabeth Fox-Genovese and Eugene Genovese accurately summarized, "The ultimate horror of slavery lay not in the extent of its physical abuse but in the extent and depth of the enforced subordination."[3] Domination was the ultimate goal of southern slavery policies and laws. Under the mantle of these repressive laws and policies, every master developed psychological and behavioral methods for carrying out that goal.

It is important to keep in mind the psychological linkage between southern slaveholders' generalized fears of slaves and the masters' comprehensive installation of laws and policies created to dominate and repress Black Africans and native-born African Americans. Black folks terrified most white folks—slaveholders and nonslaveholders.

In the late 1660s, Virginia, New York, and Maryland passed decrees insuring that baptizing an enslaved person did not change his bondage status. In 1664, the General Assembly of Maryland enacted a law that made being a slave a "service for life" (*Durante Vita*).[4] Taking their lead from the English Parliament of 1667, these colonial decrees foreshadowed what was to become a central part of the domination and control of Black African slaves. Slaveholders were encouraged to attend to saving the slaves' souls but had the absolute power and authority "only with strict severity" over their captives' bodies.[5]

Rich planters learned it was wise to separate poor whites from enslaved Blacks. In 1680 in Virginia, the legislature determined that only a white person could be called a Christian. As historian James Oakes informed us, "Long before the American Revolution, the dehumanization of the slaves was institutionalized in law . . . it was not until 1705 [in Virginia] that the first comprehensive legal code explicitly defined slaves as property. . . . The South Carolina slave code of 1740 declared that unless they were born free or manumitted, 'All Negroes, Mulattos, Indians and Mustees [*sic*] shall be deemed Slaves and Chattels personal in the Hands of their Owners.'"[6]

These codes were more than "labor laws"; "they were also public declarations that Black people, by virtue of their skin color, were slaves for life, and that their status was that of laborers held as property. Bondsmen and all of their descendants would enter the wills of their deceased masters and be passed from generation to generation along with houses, land, furniture, and livestock."[7]

Louisiana passed its slave code—the Louisiana Code of 1824—derived through the French *Code Noir*, detailing the control of slaves in that state. The Louisiana Code circumscribed that Black slaves were entirely subject to the will of their master and were without any legal ability to enter into a contract, that everything slaves possessed belonged to the master, that slaves could not hold public office, nor could they be witnesses in a civil or criminal matter.[8] Alabama developed one of the South's most comprehensive (read: dominating) slave codes in 1852. Although the basic humanity of a slave was recognized in these Alabama codes, "the restrictions on slave testimony made enforcement difficult."[9] In other words, in actual practice, the enslaved had few protections in circumstances where it was the slave's word against a white master or other white man or woman. This code went into great detail about the establishment of mandatory slave patrols, made up only of white men, with enormous extrajudicial power and authority to punish.

ANCHORING WHITE SUPREMACY

Blacks became fair game for any white person. Further, historian Ibram X. Kendi elaborated, "all Whites now wielded absolute power to abuse any African person. By the early eighteenth century, every Virginia county had a militia of landless Whites 'ready in case of any sudden eruption of Indians or insurrection of Negroes.' Poor Whites had risen into their lowly place in slave society—the armed defenders of planters—a place that would sow bitter animosity between them and enslaved Africans."[10] Here, we have a plausible explanation—if not a touching of the root—of the resentment antebellum poor whites felt about Black people. An argument can be made that the self-identification that many whites feel about themselves—that they for generations have been, and remain, the rightful protectors of white dominance—goes a long way toward explaining twenty-first-century white militia violence.

The elite white southern planters and local authorities found a useful place for these poor whites, essentially deputizing them as members of local communities' slave patrols, "which served as the eyes and ears of the white community by nightly monitoring slave after-hours activity."[11] Vigilance committees were formed to monitor slaves and abolitionist activities. Out of this group of whites devolved the "slave catchers," men who often possessed one of the significant symbols of power among white slaveholders: a horse. Horses were teamed with slave catchers, a wing of the slave patrols. As historian Walter Johnson clarified,

> The words "slave patrol" summon to mind a vision of white men on horseback, an association so definitive that it elides the remarkable fact that the geographic pattern of county governance in the South emerged out of the circuits ridden by eighteenth-century slave patrols. These circuits were themselves materially determined by the character of the landscape and the distance a man on horseback could cover in the span of a single night.[12]

These mounted slave patrols were precursors of the Ku Klux Klan, which emerged in 1865.

The need to surveil Black people on a twenty-four-hour, seven-days-a-week basis and the need for increasingly harsh power and control mechanisms became the emotional baseline of the white southern racist slaveholder: "Lynch law, vigilantism and charivaris were the ultimate expressions of [Southern] community will. They established the coercive lines between acceptable and unacceptable behavior for all members of the Southern social order. . . . By such means individual slaves, and sometimes whites affiliated with them, were made sacrifices to a sacred concept of white supremacy."[13]

THE EFFECTS OF ABOLITIONISM

As the profits of slavery deepened their hold on America, the South increasingly found it necessary to develop the proslavery political strength to withstand the abolitionists' onslaught. Constitutional issues of slavery became a major focus of concern in the country in the 1830s. Over time, as America wrestled with the morality of slavery, the American antislavery movement found its way into national and regional politics.[14]

Most of our country's Founding Fathers—the framers—were from the South and they, as historian Peter Kolchin pointed out, "were most often wealthy planters. This undeniable fact is tremendously important—that most of our country's Founding Fathers—men of great political stature and wisdom—were implicitly biased in favor of slaveholding, even though a few great statesmen like John P. Chase described the 'Framers' of our Constitution as 'anti-slavery,'" Kolchin continued, "An extraordinary generation of planter-politicians—historian Clement Eaton termed it the 'great generation'—led the American states to independence, created a new government, and dominated that government during its early years."[15] Prominent among these men were George Washington, Thomas Jefferson, James Madison, and Patrick Henry—"all among the largest slave owners of their day."[16] There is some recent emerging scholarship, released by the Schuyler Mansion State Historic Site about another Founding Father—Alexander Hamilton—entitled "As Odious and Immoral a Thing: Alexander Hamilton's Hidden History as an Enslaver" by Jessie Serfilippi, a researcher at the Schuyler Mansion. Her research concludes that, among other things, Hamilton, known for his abolitionist efforts, was also a slaveholder who "purchased enslaved people for himself."[17]

In his 1899 treatise *Slavery in the State of North Carolina*, John Spencer Bassett stated that prior to 1831, the general condition of the enslaved population in North Carolina was more humane than after that date.[18] This was not generally true throughout the slaveholding states, as there was a wide variation in the range, types, and humanity (or not) in the laws and policies of the various states pertaining to racist slavery.

For example, the restrictive laws passed in South Carolina were the result of increased fear due to Gabriel's Rebellion in Virginia in 1800.[19] Gabriel and his band of enslaved men, who numbered between five and six hundred, planned to capture the city of Richmond and take Virginia's governor prisoner. Despite the fact that Gabriel's Rebellion was thwarted by slave informants, terribly inclement weather, and swift white intervention, the details of the intent of Gabriel's revolt seriously frightened South Carolina whites. Slave patrols were increased, authorized by the state's governor to forcibly search "negro homes" for weapons, break up all meetings of Black folks unless white people were present, and detain slaves away from "home" who did not have proper passes.[20] The 1800 South Carolina legislature ultimately expanded the so-called Negro Acts into a "draconian new Black code. In addition to limiting the rights of slaves and free Blacks to assemble, it also included tough new laws concerning three other critical matters: the regulation of the interstate slave trade, the strengthening of the slave patrol system, and limitations on a master's ability to voluntarily free his or her own slaves."[21]

Two events in 1831 led to less humane conditions for the South's enslaved population. One, the northern abolitionists flooded the South with antislavery literature. This effort was intensified by William Lloyd Garrison's postal campaign in 1835, in which he swamped southern post offices with antislavery literature. Garrison was one of sixty-two abolitionists who met in Philadelphia in 1833 to form the American Anti-Slavery Society. Prior to 1831, even though slavery existed in the South, a number of its population were neutral on the subject of slavery, or even antislavery, but when this abolitionist tsunami hit the South, the majority felt offended. Bassett suggested that an increase in repressive antislave laws was an unintended consequence of the abolitionist "propaganda" assault on the South.[22] The South had already felt attacked by abolitionists decades earlier. In the late eighteenth century, Congress made decisions affecting where slavery could exist, such as in the Northwest Ordinance of 1789, which banned slavery from this territory.

The South also reacted angrily to the Quakers' efforts to submit petitions seeking to end slavery to the American Congress. Quoting South Carolinian Thomas Tucker, historian Lacy K. Ford wrote: "[Tucker] suggested prophetically that while the abolitionists might 'expect a general emancipation of slaves by law,' the southern states would never submit to such action 'without a civil war.'"[23]

The second event in 1831 that shook the South—particularly the Upper South—was Nat Turner's Rebellion in Virginia. Turner's revolt, in which at least fifty whites died, stoked a deep fear in the psyche of the white South, among slaveholders and nonslaveholders alike. Just as racist whites saw all Blacks as inferiors, whites imagined that a Black slave insurrection would view all white people as targets. A "free" (read: unchained) Black was increasingly perceived as a threat.

As historian Andrew Delbanco informed us,

> In an effort to prevent such horrors, laws were imposed throughout the South making it a crime to teach slaves—or for that matter, free Black people—to read or write, lest they learn and spread seditious ideas about rebelling or running away. . . . In North Carolina, patrols searched "every negro house for books or prints of any kind," and if any were found, including "Bibles or hymn books," the offender was subject to "whipping . . . until he *informed who* gave them to him." Every "slaveholding community," [Frederick] Douglass observed, had "a peculiar taste for ferreting out offenses against the slave system."[24]

Bertram Wyatt-Brown offered two alternating states of mind in the normally rational planter that explain why he would succumb to his fears of slave rebellion: (1) apathy or (2) horror. He drew a brilliant parallel: "The [Southern] slave insurrection scares were analogous to the heresy trials of the Reformation era, the anti-peasant outbreaks that produced the English Black Laws, or the 'great fear of 1789,' when France was convulsed with worries about vagabonds and rogues."[25] Likewise, slaveholder fears fed their behaviors in ferreting out any potential slave insurrection plans, demonstrating the parallels between the coerced confessions of alleged witches and alleged Black insurrectionists. Burning a witch was, after all, a lynching.

ONLY SLAVERY COULD PROVE THE
SECESSIONISTS' SUPREMACY

The southern slave master was determined to keep all enslaved individuals subordinate because slavery provided the only evidence to prove the secessionists' white supremacy. Many psychological conundrums surface in any analysis of the institution of racist slavery. One of the most complicated is the slave master's view of himself as a man who would fight tyranny and oppression at any cost coupled with the fact that he became a tyrant and oppressor over Black Africans. He somehow managed to believe that "requiring obedience and subordination was not oppression,"[26] yet the master would not and could not succumb to becoming the target of tyranny and oppression. This perception requires a selective denial system: What was good for the goose was not good for the gander. Standing on the necks of the Black enslaved, the racist white southern slaveholders cried out against the perceived efforts of oppression from the North. As historian Kenneth M Stampp informed us, a North Carolina planter, Charles Pettigrew, wrote to a family member, "It is a pity . . . that agreeable to the nature of things Slavery and Tyranny must go together and that there is no such thing as having an obedient and useful slave, without the painful exercise of undue and tyrannical authority."[27]

Literally, slaveholders had life-or-death control over the lives of their slaves. Even though this was true, the slave master was able to convince himself that slaveholding and its associated discipline and control measures were not "crimes." Laws were developed from legal decisions to protect slavery *within* the South. For example, see the 1823 decision, *State v. Hale* (9 N.C. [2 Hawks] 582 [1823]), in which it was decided that no slave is protected by criminal law; see the 1829 decision, *State v. Mann* (13 N.C. [2 Dev.] 263 [1829]), in which it was decided that no law restricts a slave owner's power to chastise or render the submission of a slave. In the 1857 US Supreme Court decision *Dred Scott v. Sandford* (60 U.S. [19 How.] 393 [1856]), Chief Justice Roger B. Taney "found that under the Constitution Blacks 'had no rights which the white man was bound to respect.'"[28] In other words, Blacks were not recognized as American citizens and not even fully human.

NO LICENSE REQUIRED

Slaveholders were not vetted by anyone. There were no laws regulating slave ownership or slaveholding behavior. Stampp observed, "No southern state required masters to be tested for their competence to rule slaves. Instead, they permitted slaves to fall willy-nilly into the hands of whoever inherited them or had the cash or credit to buy them. As a result, bondsmen were owned [at times] by persons of unsound minds. . . . It would be pointless to catalogue the atrocities committed by psychopaths."[29] I catalogue many of these atrocities, which underscore that some slave masters and their overseers were psychopathic in their treatment of slaves, in chapter 8. In chapter 6, I argue that "psychopathy" was one of the slaveholder's defense mechanisms. Otherwise "normal" people became corrupted by the extraordinary power that slavery conferred on them, and they exhibited a wide range of behaviors, sometimes driven by whims, moods, racist hatred, and lack of self-control in relating to the enslaved. They succumbed to what psychologist Phillip Zimbardo described as overwhelming situational forces.[30]

CRUEL CRIMES AND PUNISHMENTS TO ENFORCE THE LAW

The branding of slaves was common in colonial days, although less so in the nineteenth century: "In the late 1600s, some slaves in Charleston had two letters—DY—burned into their flesh. The inscription was the mark of King James II, known before his ascension to the throne as the Duke of York. As a principal in the Royal African Company, the Duke controlled most of the traffic of Africans sold into South Carolina, and every person was branded with his title."[31] Branding remained a frequent torture method throughout the antebellum period. Theodore Weld offered two examples, the details of which come from advertisements placed by slaveholders pursuing their runaways. One, an advertisement from Mr. Micajah Ricks of Nash County, North Carolina, in 1838: "Ranaway, a negro woman and two children; a few days before she went off, *I burnt her with a hot iron,* on the left side of her face, *I tried to make the letter M."* A second advertisement, this one in 1832 from Mr. R. P. Carney of Clark County, Georgia: "One hundred dollars reward for a negro fellow Pompey, 40 years old, he is *branded* on the *left jaw."*[32]

Some white Virginians surmised that what partially fueled the slave Gabriel's 1800 insurrection and anger—other than wanting his freedom—was that, as a result of his fighting with and biting off part of a white man's ear a year earlier, he had been found guilty, lashed thirty times, and had his thumb branded, "as was then the common practice, to indicate to all that he was no longer entitled to invoke benefit of clergy," which he had successfully used at his trial.[33]

The hunting of runaway slaves, with the hunters on horseback and the enslaved pursued by hunting dogs, was seen by some as a sport comparable to fox hunting. A few slaveholders built private jails on their premises.[34] Some

used stocks, some chains and irons. The whip was the most common instru-
ment of punishment. Delbanco offered commentary on the ubiquity of the
whip: "Anywhere in the South, a slave could be whipped for any infraction
ranging from theft or flight to failure to pound the hominy long enough to
make grits soft enough to please her master or mistress at breakfast."[35]

Historian Edward Ball described a horrible place in the port of Charleston, South Carolina, known as the Charleston Work House, where Marse
could take an enslaved person who, in Marse's eyes, deserved punishment that
Marse had neither the time or stomach for, and could leave the poor person
for a flogging, purchased for a fee, by a civil servant: "The Work House was
used by slave owners who wished to punish their workers when in Charleston.
The contract beatings ensured that the master did not dirty his trousers with
blood."[36]

The certainty, not the severity, of punishment was always in the air. No
matter what the outward appearance of a master's relationship to his slaves,
physical punishment was always a possibility: "Even the best masters accepted
whipping as essential to the maintenance of discipline."[37] If a master shunned
the use of the whip, he likely had an "overseer" or favorite slave to do his dirty
work, or, as mentioned above, he could hire out the punishment.

The slaveholder dictated the basic needs of the slaves: food, clothing, and
shelter. Some slaves lived in abject neglect and some were better provided for
by the master. These outward factors did not change their status: They were
enslaved forever. Stampp cited Affleck's *Cotton Plantation Record and Account
Book*, which contains some printed instructions about relating to and handling
slaves: "Never be induced by a course of good behavior on the part of the
negroes, to relax the strictness of your discipline. . . . The only way to keep a
negro honest is not to trust him. This seems a harsh assertion; but it is unfortunately, too true."[38]

THE ENSLAVED HAD LITTLE TO NO LEGAL PROTECTION

A male slave could not protect his wife or daughters from the unwanted
advances of the slaveholder or his overseers or any of the offspring of either
of these two. Enslaved parents could not protect their children from sexual
exploitation. If an enslaved person challenged the authority and decisions of
the slave master, the consequences were usually dire, if not fatal. The use and
exercise of the slave trader's and the slave master's power to break up a slave
family through a sale instilled a great fear in the slave family. The economics
underneath this were simple: Individual slave sales brought a higher combined
profit than did the sale of a group or family.

A Slave Father Sold Away from His Family—"Family Ectomy." *Photograph from Woodcut. Library of Congress*

The essential problem seeking a solution of American slavery was this: The country was founded on the doctrine "all men are created equal," ironically penned by Thomas Jefferson, a slave master. The American Revolution took place, in large measure, because the colonists felt that "Great Britain had reneged on its reciprocal obligations,"[39] and that the British were trying to take away their liberty and property rights. In order to achieve some measure of emotional harmony within themselves, slaveholders and proslavery individuals had to believe that Black people were not human, and thus not deserving of liberty or equality: "The racist defense of slavery emerged from the interaction of such hostile predispositions with the dehumanizing effects of plantation discipline and slaveholding capitalism. . . . The equality of all human beings could be widely proclaimed as long as it was understood that Blacks were, somehow, less than human. It was no accident that the first systematically racist analysis of Black slaves was written by the master who wrote the Declaration of Independence."[40]

As historian Nicholas E. Magnis stated,

> Throughout his life, Jefferson maintained that if freed, the former slaves
> must be colonized outside of North America to Africa or the Caribbean
> Islands. He based this imperative on his belief that Blacks "are inferior to
> the whites in the endowment both of body and mind" (Jefferson, 1787).
> . . . In addition, soon after writing the Declaration of Independence, Jef-
> ferson participated in political activity that clearly indicated his unwavering
> belief that Blacks, if emancipated, must not live as freemen in Virginia.
> Lastly, a consummate political strategist, Jefferson did almost nothing to
> advance abolition during his 40 years in the turbulent political arena of
> Virginia and the new republic.[41]

Chattel slavery fused in the mind of the slaveholders a self-defeating,
omnipotent belief. According to historian Bruce Levine, "Owning other
human beings outright shaped the very core of the typical planter's personality. . . . They dominated those who labored for them not only economically
but also legally and politically. . . . [E]very Southern plantation was a kingdom
unto itself in which 'the master was armed with magisterial power, by the laws
alike of God and man.'"[42] The slave system fostered the development of a narcissistic personality in the elite planter, based on claimed principles of entitlement. The planters became "'a race of haughty and waited-upon people' who
expected to have their way in all things." [43]

The entitlement, the grandiose sense of self-worth and superiority,
instilled in the southern planter a perception of unassailable white privilege:
"In ethico-religious terms, antebellum Americans were rarely called to make
direct choices between submission to social roles and individual autonomy,
between personal sacrifice and collective reward, or between traditional values
and material progress."[44] Southerners developed and clung to a fierce stance
of self-reliance and independence: "The moral principle of self-government
spoke to Southerners of all classes and denominations and made any act of
independence appear as natural and irresistible as the setting of the sun."[45]

THE FUGITIVE SLAVE ACT

The political power of white southern slave masters was powerfully demonstrated in 1850, when the US Congress passed the controversial Fugitive Slave
Act, a federal law that applied to the entire country. This act mandated that
fugitive slaves anywhere in the country had to be returned to their masters.
All US citizens were compelled to assist in the capture and return of runaway
slaves. The act "was meant to be a remedy and salve [to the country], but it

turned out to be an incendiary event that lit the fuse that led to civil war. It was an act without mercy. . . . Everything about the Fugitive Slave Act favored the slave owners."[46]

This act denied runaway slaves the right to challenge the legality of their enslavement, and it "disallowed all forms of exonerating evidence, including evidence of beatings, rape, or other forms of abuse while the defendant had been enslaved. It criminalized the act of sheltering a fugitive [by anyone in any state] and required local authorities to assist the claimant in recovering his lost human property. . . . If the accused could be shown to have belonged to the claimant according to the laws of the state from which she had fled, she was ordered back to captivity."[47] The terrorizing effect of this act and the racist manner in which it was enforced meant that even free Black people, with no history of ever being enslaved, could be seized anywhere in the country on the assumption that they once belonged to someone because of their skin color.

Although the act was intended to mollify the South and preserve the Union, its net effect was just the opposite. The act generated a national clash and crisis between the dictates of the law favoring the white slaveholders and the ethics and morality of antislavery Americans who were expected to uphold a law that was abhorrent to them.

Delbanco described the effects of this law:

> Intended to secure the Union, the fugitive slave law made it less secure. It clarified just how mutually hostile North and South had become. . . . It made the possibility of disunion, once an extremist idea, seem plausible. . . . Before the fugitive slave law, northerners could pretend that slavery had nothing to do with them. After the fugitive slave law, there was no evading their complicity. The most famous fugitive in America, Frederick Douglass, acknowledged as much when he said that "the fugitive slave bill has especially been of positive service to the anti-slavery movement."[48]

The fugitive slave act was so abhorrent to Harriet Beecher Stowe that she wrote *Uncle Tom's Cabin*, "whose most memorable scene made visible the terror of an enslaved mother leaping from ice floe to ice floe across the Ohio River with her baby in her arms, just ahead of a slave-catching posse."[49]

The codes, laws, and policies pertaining to slavery were *in toto* aimed at dominating Blacks and ensuring whites' safety and false sense of racial superiority. American racist slavery, as established in the South, ensured white supremacy and drilled institutional racism into the American democratic experiment. Southern racist slavery laws, codes, and policies were designed to keep Black people positioned as inferior and in bondage for life. The dehumanization of the enslaved was institutionalized into law, which ensured that Black slaves had no rights at all. The dominant threat of punishment and death underpinning racist slavery laws, codes, and policies created palpable fear and oppression. Paradoxically, the southern elite slave master who despised tyranny and oppression developed an elaborate racist institution founded on tyranny and oppression, and then hung the fate of the South on it. Although our country ostensibly was founded on the premise that "all men were created equal," this was a big lie.

"Whipping a Slave, Virginia, 1850s." Captioned, The Last Daughter. Slavery Images: A Visual Record of the African Slave Trade and Slave Life in the Early African Diaspora. *http://www.slaveryimages.org/s/slaveryimages/item/1230*

• *10* •

Money Talks

Slavery Was Just Business

SERIOUS MONEY

Historian Caitlin Rosenthal wrote that while he was campaigning for the presidency in March 1860, "[Lincoln] reflected that even 'our wisest men' under-rated the conflict between North and South because they had not properly estimated its magnitude. 'What is the difficulty?' he asked. 'One sixth of the population of the United States is a slave. One man of every six, one woman of every six, one child of every six, is a slave. Those who own them look upon them as property, and nothing else.'" And, Rosenthal added, "The monetary value of this property was immense: 'at a moderate estimate, not less than $2,000,000,000. [having such an amount of property has a] vast influence upon the minds of those who own it. The 'slaveholders battle any policy which depreciates their slaves as property. What increases the value of this property, they favor.'" Rosenthal noted that Lincoln's moderate estimate of the monetary value of the enslaved "was indeed too conservative. Economists have estimated that the nearly four million slaves who lived in the United States on the eve of the Civil War had a combined market capitalization of between $3.1 and $3.6 billion."[1] Those market assets provided great wealth to a small number of white Southern elite slaveholders. They were capitalists to the bone, but ironically, were reluctant to trumpet their own financial success in defense of slavery.

Proslavery advocates constructed an effective, comprehensive sales pitch, though curiously omitting how incredibly profitable slave labor was. As historian Kenneth M. Stampp put it:

> In searching for evidence to justify their cause, southern proslavery writers showed remarkable resourcefulness. In persuasive prose their polemical essays spun out religious, historical, scientific, and sociological arguments

to demonstrate that slavery was a positive good for both Negroes and whites—that it was the very cornerstone of southern civilization. But they rarely resorted to the most obvious and most practical argument of all: the argument that the peculiar institution was economically profitable to those who invested in it.[2]

How many Southerners are we talking about? Stampp reminded us that the truly great wealth (including the property values of their bondpeople) was in the hands of a relatively small group of southern slaveholders. The "extremely wealthy families who owned more than a hundred slaves numbered less than three thousand, a tiny fraction of the southern population." This elite cohort of enslavers, not surprisingly, owned the vast majority of slaves. Stampp added an important point: "That the majority of slaves belonged to members of the planter class, and not to those who owned small farms with a single slave family, is in fact of crucial importance concerning the nature of bondage in the antebellum South." The "crucial importance" Stampp alludes to is "that the preservation of slavery was fundamental to the economic future of the South."[3] Offering an economic defense of slavery, Virginian Colin Clarke wrote on the eve of secession, slavery was to be protected because it was "a property which depends upon our social & economic happiness, our [indu]strial wealth, & which is worth some $200,000,000."[4]

A WORLDWIDE STAGE

Most Americans today are not likely to have an accurate picture of the magnitude—the global scope—of the wealth of the elite slaveholder. The elite Marse was more than gratified with the economic and political stage he commanded. His profits and the efficiency of his plantations and other commercial ventures assured him he was an astute businessman. He was applying scientifically based management techniques to his crop-based ventures, and it was paying off: "Cotton, tobacco, rice, sugar, naval stores, and other slave-cultivated exports, [New York journalist and economist Thomas] Kettell calculated in 1851, added up to nearly $100 million in a total trade of $135 million. 'It is apparent,' he concluded, 'that 75 per cent of the exports of the union are the product of slave labor.'"[5]

Southern white racist slaveholders figured out how to make the slavery-based money machine work. Rosenthal painted a clear picture of the elite slaveholders' moneymaking machine: "Many of the agro-businesses built by southern planters were incredibly successful. In 1860, more millionaires lived in the slave South than in the rest of the United States. . . . Surveying cotton fields and seeing humans as inputs of production seems to have stimulated management innovation in ways that were difficult in free factories plagued with turnover."[6]

Cotton had indeed been crowned king. Brimming with financial success, the elite slave masters were proud of what they had developed: "Spiking global demand for cotton, meanwhile, left them flush with wealth and ecstatic about the dependence of the entire industrial world on a commodity that only American slaves could produce with profit. . . . In an international context, slaveholding power and slaveholding confidence [in the 1850s] seemed at their zenith."[7] The pride, the self-congratulatory nature of the slaveholders' economic success, and, yes, the perceived majesty of the bound labor system, caused a self-defeating moral and ethical blindness. History professor Sven Beckert described the magnitude and impact of the South's cotton economy: "By the time shots were fired on Fort Sumter in April 1861, cotton was the core ingredient of the world's most important manufacturing industry. The manufacture of cotton yarn and cloth had grown into 'the greatest industry that ever had or could possibly have ever existed in any age or country,' according to the self-congratulatory but essentially accurate account of British cotton merchant John Benjamin Smith."[8] Beckert continued, "The industry that brought great wealth to European manufacturers and merchants, and bleak employment to hundreds of thousands of mill workers, had also catapulted the United States onto center stage of the world economy, building 'the most successful agricultural industry in the United States of America which has ever been contemplated or realized.'"[9]

HUMAN MACHINES

At bottom, slavery was a cold-hearted business. The slaveholders' drive for profits transformed their slaves, in the masters' worldview, into profit-making machines. Rosenthal's description captured the military flavor of the cotton industry: "Slave labor and capital were deployed in search for new markets, new crops, new production processes, and new information systems to coordinate production. Control aided planters in the pursuit of new seeds, new manures, and new lands. Slavery enabled capitalists to build machines made of men, women, and children, and also to regear this machinery on command."[10] Beckert echoed Rosenthal's portrayal of the cotton industry's militarization quality: "The Industrial Revolution in Europe also actively influenced the evolution of slavery in the American South. Gang labor, by no means new but never so prevalent as on cotton plantations, exemplified the new rhythm of industrialized labor, or what one author has called 'military agriculture'.

. . . Slave owners secured these productivity gains by taking almost total control of the work process—a direct result of the violent domination of their workers."[11]

South Carolinian James Henry Hammond serves as a prime example of the elite southern master planter. In her book about Hammond, historian Drew Gilpin Faust described his dedication to taking control of the plantation Silver Bluff, which he had gained through marriage in 1831. On that estate prior to his arrival, 147 enslaved persons had been living there without a master in permanent residence. Hammond determined immediately that he needed to assert control.[12]

Faust wrote,

> To force them to acknowledge their own weakness and his power, he would destroy the autonomy of the slave community and bring its members under his direct and total domination. Over the next several years, he developed a carefully designed plan of physical and psychological control intended to eliminate the foundations of Black solidarity. Yet at the same time he sought despotic power over his slave force. Hammond from the first cherished a conception of himself as a beneficent master whose guidance and control represented the best of all possible worlds for the uncivilized and backward people entrusted to him by God. His need both to dominate and be loved would pose insurmountable difficulties within his evolving system of slave management.[13]

Not surprisingly, Hammond found this group of slaves resistant to his efforts at control, leading him to frequent public floggings "as the most effective representation of his control."[14] This vignette also illustrated that the well-intended elite planter, out of perceived necessity, almost always resorted to using the whip, as he fine-tuned his profit-generating human machines.

Although a real invention and not a dramatic contrivance, the cotton gin invented by Eli Whitney dropped into the marketplace in 1793 like a deus ex machina. Its force was profound, as the economic impact of this machine's invention was felt in the global marketplace. No matter what type of cotton was grown, separating its fiber from the seed was laborious. With the invention of the cotton gin, cotton production, beginning with a much more rapid separation of the seed from the fiber, took off. Beckert captured the influence of this machine, "Overnight, his machine increased ginning productivity by a factor of fifty. . . . As a result, in what can only be described as a 'cotton rush,' land on which cotton grew allegedly trebled in price after the invention of the gin."[15]

The regions of South Carolina and Georgia, where upland cotton thrived, swelled with settlers, who brought thousands of enslaved laborers with them:

The Mode of Flogging Slaves. *Photograph of engraving. Library of Congress*

In the 1790s, the slave population of the state of Georgia nearly doubled, to sixty thousand. In South Carolina, the number of slaves in the upcountry cotton growing districts grew from twenty-one thousand in 1790 to seventy thousand twenty years later, including fifteen thousand Black humans newly brought from Africa. . . . All the way to the Civil War, cotton and slavery would expand in lockstep, as Great Britain and the United States had become the twin hubs of the emerging empire of cotton.[16]

Historian Walter Johnson offered some intriguing details about Whitney, shedding a questionable light on the inventor's integrity: "Although there was (and still is) a long-running dispute about whether or not Eli Whitney had actually invented the gin himself or had claimed credit for the invention of another (in some tellings, from a slave), there was little doubt about its effect." By the time this machine had been utilized for approximately a quarter of a century, efficiently separating the cotton seeds from the cotton bolls, "high prices for cotton, especially in the early 1830s, produced the greatest economic boom in the nation's history." Even though there was a depression in 1837 that negatively affected the slavery business, especially in the Mississippi Valley, "by the 1850's," Johnson informed us, "the economy was booming again." In 1859, the two states of Mississippi and Louisiana produced 864 million pounds of cotton.[17]

Historian James Brewer Stewart added another dimension to the overall impact of the cotton gin. For a good while, it took the wind out of the sails of the abolitionist movement that had begun in the states in the 1790s: "By 1810, as Eli Whitney's cotton gin opened vast new opportunities for the planter class to adapt slave labor to a new and extraordinarily profitable commodity, militant abolitionism in white America had run its course."[18]

A LABOR FORCE EASILY REPLACED AND RELOCATED

The reality of the magnitude of the slave trade is staggering. As historian Andrew Delbanco pointed out, "When delegates from the former colonies of Great Britain convened at Philadelphia in May 1787 with the aim of forming a common government, slavery had been an essential part of colonial life for nearly three hundred years."[19]

In his remarkable work *Slaves in the Family*, Edward Ball painted a disturbing picture:

> According to a conservative estimate, during the centuries of the slave trade, nearly 9.5 million people were carried from Africa to European colonies in the Western hemisphere. Of these, a little under 450,000 went to the territory that would become the United States . . . between 1701 and 1775, forty-six percent of the Black people entering the British mainland colonies came by way of South Carolina. . . . During a single generation, from 1735 to 1775, 1,108 slave ships arrived with their cargoes in Charleston harbor.[20]

Rosenthal captured the drumbeat of the South bound-labor system and further clarified the cold economics of the slavery capitalist system:

> Underlying all these business practices was the fundamental flexibility of the slave system. From the perspective of planters, humans proved a complex and dynamic form of both labor and capital. As labor, enslaved people could be allocated and reallocated from task to task with comparatively little negotiation. They could be driven to labor in unpleasant jobs or moved thousands of miles to fertile soils. As capital, they multiplied—the price of slaves rose, and women bore children. Higher prices and larger communities meant more capital, and this capital became collateral for the purchase of more slaves, land, and tools.[21]

As soil exhaustion occurred due to lack of crop rotation, planters moved westward. By the end of the 1830s, Mississippi produced more cotton than any other southern state.[22] By 1860, three-fourths of all cotton grown in the United States came from states and territories west of South Carolina and Georgia.

Given that southern slaveholders defined the productivity of slave labor in cotton rather than currency, it is telling that by 1860, there were 331,726 slaves in Louisiana and 436,631 in Mississippi. These numbers also provide evidence of the relationship between the slave labor force and productivity. Johnson vividly described the economic interplay between the acquisition of more slaves and the planters' wealth: "In the years 1820–1860, a sevenfold increase in the [Mississippi] Valley's slave population produced a fortyfold increase in its production of cotton."[23]

Johnson put a fine point on the largely cotton-fueled growth of the Mississippi Valley, comparing data about the number of steamboats in New Orleans in 1820 as compared with 1860: "In 1820 it was still possible to publish a detailed list of the nearly 200 steamboats arriving at the levee in New Orleans in the space of three pages, whereas in 1860 there were more than 3,500 such arrivals. Taken together, those boats represented some 160,000 tons of shipping and $17 million of capital investment, annually carrying something like $220 million worth of goods (mostly cotton) to market."[24]

By 1857, the United States was producing "about as much cotton as China. . . . What distinguished the United States from virtually every other cotton-growing area in the world were planters' command of nearly unlimited supplies of land, labor, and capital, and their unparalleled political power."[25] Cotton became the king. The United States had itself an agricultural monarchy.

SLAVERY UNIFIED CAPITAL AND LABOR

The economic premise is clear: "The use of slaves in Southern agriculture was a deliberate choice (among several alternatives) made by men who sought greater returns than they could obtain from their own labor alone, and who found other types of labor more expensive."[26] Southern elite Grandees relished in their self-congratulatory position that bound labor was smart, lucrative business: "During the eighteenth century it cost Southerners, including slaveholders, nothing to be theoretically antislavery. They explained their reluctance to emancipate slaves in the commonly accepted language of the day: It was business."[27] Slavery unified capital and labor. Beckert informed us, "The slave markets in New Orleans and elsewhere boomed as cotton did. . . . Indeed, by 1830 fully 1 million people (or one in thirteen Americans) grew cotton in the United States—most of them slaves."[28] By 1860, 85 percent of all cotton picked in the South was grown on parcels of land larger than a hundred acres, owned by elite planters who owned 91.2 percent of all slaves.[29]

PLANTER CAPITALISM

Defining planter capitalism, historian William Kauffman Scarborough quoted Charles Sellers, who declared that planter capitalism is "production for a competitive world market with commodified slave labor."[30] In its stark reality, the slavery system was a criminal horror. Beckert addressed the dual horrors of slave-based capitalism: "Cotton demanded quite literally a hunt for labor and a perpetual struggle for its control. Slave traders, slave pens, slave auctions, and the attendant physical and psychological violence of holding millions in bondage were of central importance to the expansion of cotton production in the United States and of the Industrial Revolution in Great Britain."[31]

In her work analyzing the complex relationship between capitalism and slave labor, Rosenthal highlighted the plantation journal of Thomas Walter Peyre, a South Carolina planter, which he began in December 1834 and which she says "looks like a lab notebook."[32] Peyre practiced what came to be known as "scientific agriculture," based on empiricism that careful recordkeeping and data analysis would lead to increased output and greater profits.[33] According to Rosenthal, "Slaveholders left behind thousands of volumes of account books. These extensive archives have been widely studied, but rarely as business records."[34] Rosenthal stated that "a portrait that emerges from plantation records is that of a society where precise management and violence went hand in hand . . . the soft power of quantification supplemented the driving force of the whip."[35] Here we have a poignant summation of the South's racist slavery system: the combination of precise management and violence.

Rosenthal summarized the elite planter's aim for perfection and what it took to achieve such perfection:

> Yet if there was an ideal to which slaveholders aspired, it took form in the literature of plantation management that flourished in the South in the three or four decades before the Civil War. Articles appeared in the agricultural press advocating the systematic management of everything from hogs and cattle to overseers and slaves. The ideal plantation was a model of efficiency. Its premise was Black inferiority, its organizing principle was the absolute control by the master, and its structure was bureaucratic. It was governed by rules that were enforced by persuasion if possible, by force if necessary.[36]

As we know, pride was a central feature of the antebellum southern mind and adds texture to the psychological portrait of the slaveholder. He was proud of his management techniques, for "[a]t a minimum, slaveholders (and those who bought their products) built an innovative, global, profit-hungry labor regime that contributed to the emergence of the modern economy."[37]

Marse's investments went well beyond land and slaves, and his profits came from multiple sources, including banking; commerce; railroading; mining; steamboats; manufacturing; land speculation; corporate, state, and federal stocks and bonds; and ironworks. The largest slave force in Tennessee during the decade of the 1850s was the Cumberland Iron Works in Stewart County.[38] Marse also made a few dollars on the side, selling or trading enslaved humans to doctors, clergy, lawyers, bankers, and other professionals, who wanted to benefit from the elevated status of owning a few "servants" who could attend to their every need.

It is no surprise that the elite slave masters had few tax burdens. Stampp informed us that direct taxes on the slave industry were generally "so low as to be almost negligible. Masters generally paid no state tax on slave children or on the aged and infirm; the annual tax on able-bodied slaves was usually between fifty and seventy-five cents. In 1833, a Georgia planter paid a tax of $29.21 on 330 acres of land and 70 slaves; in 1839, a South Carolina planter paid a tax of $136.55 on 10,000 acres of land and 153 slaves."[39] This latter tax figure derives from the Manigault Plantation records of Henry James Hammond. Stampp provided some painful data about the attention given to the health and welfare of the slaves: "The yearly charge for support [including medical treatment, food, and clothing] of an adult slave seldom exceeded $35.00, and was often considerably less than that."[40]

In 1828, the firm of Franklin and Armfield was organized. It became the largest slave-trading enterprise in the South, operating out of Alexandria, Virginia. Before they retired, each partner had accumulated fortunes in excess of a half million dollars.[41] Franklin and Armfield was both a practical and clever firm: "The firm purchased its own dedicated ships—primarily manufactured in places like Haddam, Connecticut—and sailed on a regularized schedule. In addition to moving [enslaved] people, these ships moved currency, transporting bank notes back to their point of origin on the eastern seaboard and cycling funds generated in the New Orleans slave market back to Maryland and Virginia to purchase yet more slaves."[42]

Delbanco described the staggering increase of cotton-based wealth in a short period of time:

> There was much more cotton in 1836 than there had been in 1828. Over eight years of seedtime, the US government, the states, banks, private citizens, and foreign entities had collectively invested about $400 million, or

Representation of the brig *Vigilante*, a slave trading vessel, from Nantes.
Library of Congress

one-third of the value of all US economic activity in 1830, into expanding production on slavery's frontier. This includes the price of 250,000 slaves moved, 48 million new acres of public land sold, the costs of Indian removals and wars, and the massive expansion of the southwestern infrastructure.[43]

As Delbanco informed us, "Slavery became the 'flywheel' driving not only the southern and American but also the global economy. . . . In 1844, as estimated by one anti-slavery newspaper, 'twelve hundred million dollars worth of human beings' was held 'by two hundred thousand slaveholders.'"[44]

Slave trading required the transportation of slaves, and as we have seen, a common method was driving the slaves on forced walks in chains and manacles hundreds of miles, say, from the eastern shores of Maryland to the slave pens of Mississippi and Louisiana. It would be an error to think that after 1808, slave-carrying ships had disappeared into history. Some slave traders were much more sophisticated, such as the firm of Franklin and Armfield, whose common method was the utilization of sleek, fast, and heavily armed slave-running ships, stacked to the brim with imprisoned slave captives. But there were others: "By the 1850s the largest coastal slaving vessels were the steamships plying the Gulf of Mexico owned by Charles Morgan, Henry R. Morgan, and Israel C. Harris of New York. These massive ships carried first-class passengers, the U.S. mail, and slaves between New Orleans and Texas, generating revenue for an international transportation conglomerate."[45]

MASSIVE WEALTH

The elite slaveholders were among the wealthiest businessmen of their time. They became, as historian James Oakes described them, "the ruling race."[46] Massive fortunes were made from sugar in the eighteenth century. Cotton's profits ultimately surpassed sugar and indeed became king, as it drove the development of the textile industry, which became the leading industry of the Industrial Revolution. Slaveholders took out mortgages, insurance policies, and slave deeds on their bound labor, all elements of control that helped them manage their enterprises with great precision. The figure on page 220 is page 1 of a deed of trust, executed on February 26, 1845, held by a North Carolina slaveholder, in which he refers to the sale of certain of his slaves to another slaveholder. The enslaved property listed begins as "1 negro man named Hartwell, aged about 50 years, 1 woman Irma about 20, the three children Sandy about 6 years old, and Tom 2 years old, and Josephine 1 year old." This document, though difficult to read because of its script, lists approximately five more slaves who were sold, and further lists additional properties included in the sale, such as furniture, a saddle, and barrels of oats.[47]

Rosenthal described the sophisticated and advanced accounting methods many slaveholders developed for their slave-based enterprises: "Slavery became a laboratory for the development of accounting because the control drawn on paper matched the reality of the plantation more closely than that of almost any other early American business enterprise."[48] Planters with successful, well-controlled plantations were smug in their view that they did not have the management problems employers had with wageworkers. Southern elite slaveholders, generating massive amounts of wealth, thumbed their noses at northern employment practices. Although there were problems with slave management too, slaves could not quit, "and planters blended information systems with violence—and the threat of sale—to refine labor processes, building machines made of men, women, and children."[49] Human misery permeated the success. The slave master looked past the human cost, measured in death rates among enslaved people, especially in the sugar and rice growing areas. Marse's focus was the bottom line. Death and violence were the costs of doing business.

Using common plantation accounting methods in the British West Indies as her template, Rosenthal described a sophisticated plantation management hierarchy, especially with "absentee" planters who owned multiple

"Receipt for $500 payment for Negro man, January 20, 1840." *Library of Congress*

plantations.[50] A typical structure might have the absentee owner on top, the second in command a local or on-site attorney (or manager), and the "overseer" the third-tier manager. She describes as examples—although certainly not the norm—the multiple holdings of Simon Taylor and John Tharp, who owned 2,990 and 2,228 slaves, respectively, by the early nineteenth century.

THE OVERSEER CHIEF OPERATING OFFICER

As Scarborough informed us, "No figure occupied a position of greater importance in the managerial hierarchy of the southern plantation system than did the overseer. It was this agent who, in great measure, determined the success or failure of planting operations on the larger estates devoted to the production of staple agricultural products."[51]

Pulling from 1850 census data derived from a study of more than fifteen hundred overseers in seventeen sample counties in the South, Scarborough paints the following statistical composite portrait of this group:[52]

- Their average age was 33.
- 59 percent were married.
- 6 percent were illiterate.
- 52 percent owned personal property.
- 9 percent owned substantial property.[53]
- 14 percent owned slaves.

Scarborough added to the overseer picture: "Slave discipline was clearly the decisive factor in the success or failure of an overseer."[54] Most masters attempted to put restraints on the type and severity of punishments used by their overseers. The on-site planter could more easily watch over the management exhibited by his overseer, but what about the circumstances when the master was absent, sometimes for extended periods of time? Although the historiography on the subject of the overseers' general use of punishment suggests that they, as a group, treated slaves fairly well, there were obvious brutal exceptions. The master's "second" or "third" (depending on the size and applied management hierarchy), the overseer, might not have the master's humanity or restraint, and might exercise a great deal of severe cruelty to keep the slaves in line. And there was, of course, the harsh reality of sexual exploitation. It goes without saying that the slave could not "rat out" the behavior of the overseer, especially in plantation situations where the owner was only part-time in residence. For obvious reasons, it would be almost impossible for a slave to raise allegations against the master's second in command. It would be a classic his word against mine situation. "The typical overseer seemed to have little confidence in the use of incentives as a method of governing slaves; he had a decided preference for physical force." Think of the agonizing torture the overseer used in the film *Twelve Years a Slave*, as Platt turned on his toes in the mud with a secure noose around his neck. The only person who could come to Platt's rescue, without reprisal, was Marse.[55]

Realistically, however, if a sadistic or even psychopathic overseer's management style brought profit to the master, the master probably would tolerate the overseer's behavior. A master's wish for benevolence toward his slaves and his greed created a conflict for him. Stampp, quoting a slave master, wrote, "My great desire is to have my Blacks taken care of. . . . I would be content with much less . . . cotton if less cruelty were exercised. I fear I am near an abolition[i]st. But I should never consider myself an unjust and unfeeling man if I did not have a proper regard for those who are making me so much money."[56] Stampp concluded, "Southerners who were concerned about the welfare of slaves found it difficult to draw a sharp line between acts of cruelty and such measures of physical force as were an inextricable part of slavery."[57]

RETROSPECTIVE ON SLAVERY CAPITALISM

Protestant Christian slave masters—the majority being Presbyterians— believed they were stewards of God's plan to utilize bound labor not only for the enslaveds' benefit but for the glory of the South. This group was the historical equivalent of our nation's twenty-first-century 1 percent—the insanely rich billionaires who control and influence much of the economic and political power of our country. Cotton became the foundation for an empire, an empire the South determined could successfully become its own nation—the Confederate States of America—a Slave Power country. Slavery was just business.

Historians Ned and Constance C. Sublette concluded their book *The American Slave Coast: A History of the Slave Breeding Industry* with a poignant quote from the Reverend Dr. Martin Luther King Jr. (see figure on page 223) that captures, with fierce clarity, the central conclusion of this chapter:

Free! *Photograph of drawing by Henry Louis Stephens, c. 1863. Library of Congress*

Dr. Martin Luther King Jr. Memorial, Washington, DC. *Photograph by the author*

Again, we have deluded ourselves into believing the myth that capitalism grew and prospered out of the Protestant ethic of hard work and sacrifice. The fact is that capitalism was built on the exploitation and suffering of Black slaves and continues to thrive on the exploitation of the poor—both Black and white, both here and abroad.

—Martin Luther King Jr., "Three Evils of Society" speech, August 31, 1967

· *11* ·

The Throughline

I have painted a conceptual theory of the psychology of the American white southern elite slave master, a deceased man called "Marse," a nineteenth-century synonym for "master," a man of a previous time (1830–1861). Because this book is not about one particular man but is a psychological examination of a cohort of American southern white elite slave masters, there is no concluding psychological diagnosis of Marse. This portrait is composed of elements from the collective, not from any one individual. This retrospective portrait of Marse, based on his psychological autopsy, renders the following conclusion.

There is a distinct throughline originating with American southern slavery that runs through American history for more than four hundred years; that throughline—the connecting thread—is racist white supremacy.

Some people might argue that the term "white supremacy" implicitly includes "racist" in its definition. White supremacy means the whiteness of a person's skin is supreme, on top, the best in a hierarchy of nature's human skin tones. My counter argument is that as the term "white supremacy" developed in the antebellum South at the time Black African slavery was flourishing, it was paired with the notion that Black people were subhuman and thus inferior. Black individuals were not perceived as simply being one rung down on the ladder; racist white supremacists view people with nonwhite skin coloration to be inferior, less than human, and threatening.

In a 2020 *New York Times* editorial, Michael Powell wrote that the term "white supremacy" has become a contentious term.[1] There is apparently an emerging debate among historians, scholars, and activists about whether or not the term is losing its effectiveness because it is so frequently used to describe too many different things. In the context of the psychology of the white elite southern planter slaveholder, I argue that it remains an effective, accurate, and powerful phrase, particularly when the adjective "racist" is attached to it. When you cut into the core of white dominance that defined the antebellum South's "peculiar institution," racist white supremacy is what is culled out and rendered.

In analyzing Marse's personality and behaviors, it was impossible to avoid the conclusion that many of his psychological features, traits, characteristics, and actions tragically remain relevant in the twenty-first century. The antebellum white slave master may be a relic of our past, but Marse's racist psychopathology has managed to survive—and often thrive—through the generations. The antebellum slaveholder is gone, but all Americans continue to suffer, to this day, from traumatic wounds inflicted by Marse and his slaveholding world. Marse dragged racist white supremacy and its traumatic wounds into the twenty-first century, where they seem to be enjoying a pathological rejuvenation.

We can see these wounds in the yawning racial gaps in education, income, housing, mortality, health, and incarceration, as well as toxic partisan politics. We can note that American society has made advances—often astounding advances—in integration, voting rights, and civil rights, but we must also accept that white resistance—as covert and overt racist white supremacy—often impedes progress or brings it to a grinding halt. This white resistance often reflects the thinking and actions of Marse.

I want to reiterate briefly the ways in which the slaveholding South justified slavery. The masters put forth many justifications, on top of which they erected multiple proslavery rationales. One of their foundational justifications was that slavery, in one form or another, had been in existence since the beginnings of civilization. Based on this retrospective, historical view, the rationale for slavery was thus: There must be a subordinate class to do the menial tasks so that the elite class can lead the way to progress, refinements, and civilization. Even though most Southerners did not own slaves, most Southerners, unless they fought against the institution, were complicit and did accept slavery.

There was also another justification: the white privilege card. The wealthy minority of elite slaveholders falsely held out the promise of equality to all whites because of their skin color. White equality was and is a myth. Within the caste system of white supremacy, the white elite has never been interested in white equality. Whiteness, on the other hand, became a social construct, which developed a correlation between race and privilege. Citing the powerful book *Between the World and Me* by Ta-Nehisi Coates, trauma therapist Resmaa Menakem pointed out that Coates convincingly argues that "white body supremacy" has created an inherited trauma embedded in all Americans that remains destructive, particularly the destruction of the Black body.[2] A poignant reality emanating from this white privilege issue: white parents have no equivalent conversations about social dangers and risk avoidance strategies in America that Black parents must have with their children.

A third justification was built on the Protestant Christian masters' scriptural bedrock belief that racist slavery was a gift from God. Slave masters and religious divines found multiple biblical passages to defend and justify slavery, but the granddaddy of all the proslavery verses was Genesis 9:18–27 in the Old Testament: the story of Noah after the flood.

An insidious fourth rationale for southern racist slavery was the masters' firm belief that Black Africans were subhuman, a belief and assumption upon which they justified their treating Black individuals with contempt, domination, and enslavement.

Southerners referred to the South's brand of slavery as its "peculiar institution." It was special. But what did this term really mean? Although the word "peculiar" in modern usage typically means "strange" or "unusual," its origins take us to other applied definitions. *Webster's Dictionary of Word Origins* offers the following: "The sense 'strange' developed naturally from the earlier sense 'exclusively one's own, distinctive.'"[3] When used as an adjective, "peculiar" is defined as "characteristic of only one person, group, or thing: distinctive; different from the usual or normal: special, particular; odd, curious, eccentric."[4] It is not difficult to imagine that from the perspective of wealthy, entitled, and proud slave masters, claiming their brand of slavery as exclusive, distinctive, or special would seem entirely accurate and self-satisfying.

However, the application of "peculiar" used as an adjective to modify southern slavery is apt for another inherently racist reason. Many white slave masters saw, branded, and counted their slaves as chattel property, as beasts of service, accounting for them in the same manner as they would tally their cattle. The word "peculiar" derives from the Latin word *peculiaris*, which meant "of private property," "special," "peculiar." At its root, *peculiaris* is derived from the Latin word *pecus*, meaning "cattle." The word *pecus* was further defined in Latin as "a head of cattle, beast, brute, animal, one of a herd."[5] Seeing their slaves as subhumans on a par with animals gave the masters the fundamental reason for treating them as inferior—*as something dehumanized*. As a result, white racist slaveholders declared that Black Africans and African Americans were their chattel property, along with their farm animals and personal possessions.

The South's brand of slavery was peculiar for another reason as well: Unlike the many manifestations of slavery stretching back over the course of many civilizations, Southern slavery was based on skin color. Black people were abducted, enslaved, dominated, and exploited because of the color of their skin. Black Africans were considered "barbarians who therefore needed to be kept in bondage."[6] Today, Black people refer to the color of their skin in pleading with America to makes their lives matter as much as white lives.

There was yet a sixth racist justification embraced by southern white slaveholders: The South's elite slaveholders formed a society in which *owning* other humans as property was morally acceptable and socially desirable. Despite the fact that the manner in which slaveholders treated their enslaved people ran along a continuum from humanitarian care and Christian kindness to cruel, sadistic, and brutal actions, I nevertheless have concluded that, regardless of the slaveholder's attitudes and behaviors, all slaveholders were bound together by the justification of ownership. It is the *ownership*—the proclaimed property rights—that links the best master with the worst master. There is no legitimate or defensible continuum differentiating types of slaveholders among racist white supremacy slavery. It's a complex epic crime scene with major psychopathological features.

This psychological autopsy coalesces the evidence into a clear finding that the American Southern white elite slave master committed egregious crimes. Slavery inflicted a profound trauma on the individual enslaved human, his or her family, their places of origin, and our nation as a whole. The institution of chattel slavery in the South traumatized the white slaveholder and nonslaveholder alike. Without question, slavery qualified as a trauma, which is defined clinically as the effects of an event or series of events that are life-threatening and/or emotionally damaging, and that are outside the range of normal human experience. For the abducted, traded, inherited, or purchased Black Africans, the trauma began when the slave master forced the enslaved individuals into a helpless state of dehumanization, such as cramming his captures like piles of wood into slave ships, or "death ships" as historian Andrew Delbanco called them.

The American southern elite white slave master's peculiar institution of racist slavery was a crime against humanity, despite the master's good and bad qualities as a human being, despite the kindnesses he might have provided to people he imprisoned, despite his prowess in founding and governing our nation, and despite his actions as a slaveholder being sanctioned by biblical scripture, contemporary laws, and policies. The wounds left by his crime continue to fester and infect our current national discourse about racial issues. This psychological portrait of the American Southern elite white slave master can help clarify the contents and profound effects of our past and current American slavery wound.

Beyond rationales based on history, the Bible, a racial hierarchy, the subhumanness attributed to Black enslaved people, the election of masters to high offices, and the proclaimed justifiable property rights of white human beings, slave masters developed and held assumptions and beliefs about Black Africans and African Americans that can only be described as delusional, such as slave masters claiming to see and hear contentment as a primary emotional state among the enslaved. This was delusional—a delusional reverie—because the master thus had to deny the enslaved people's palpable anguish, grief, and understandable rage.

Slavery was thus twisted to generate a false, alleged psychological freedom for the American southern white elite slaveholder. This emotional stance became deadly—suicidal—as Southerners, led by Marse, clamored for war against a much larger, more industrialized opponent. The ultimate, tragic posture of self-deception was the vast portion of the Confederacy who rode or marched into battle certain that God was on the side of the South. As historian Stephanie McCurry pointed out, "In retrospect it is easy to view the Confederate cause as doomed from the start. But that makes it difficult to explain how it held on for four years. Nevertheless the challenges were considerable. The North had ten times the South's manufacturing capacity, and the Confederate population of 9 million was dwarfed by the Union's 22 million. But even that understates the problem, because in addition 40 percent of adult men in the Confederate states were enslaved and unavailable for military service."[7]

Four years later, many of the Rebel soldiers who managed to survive returned to devastated fields and towns with a crushed, abandoned sense of self and feeling betrayed by God. It was truly delusional for an intelligent Southerner to have convinced himself that God was for the Confederacy and that God had no positive, spiritual connection with the Union.

We've seen how Marse read Genesis and other biblical texts to reassure him that God and Jesus were not against slavery. In our twenty-first-century forensic examination that does not hold up well, but at the time it was a reasoned argument. Then, as surging abolitionists targeted slavery on moral grounds, the masters and their preachers began to contort Protestant Christianity to promote and defend slavery as a positive good. The masters proclaimed the positive elements to include, for example, baptizing enslaved people, feeding and clothing them, and being benevolent and "nice." This so-called positive good was fraudulent. Many masters and their overseers did not treat their slaves well, and emphasizing the positives—while denying or ignoring the negatives—was delusional, because the realities of racist slavery included the abducting, buying and selling, breaking up slave families, sexual exploitation, administering regular—often violent—punishments and killings, relentless pursuit of fugitive slaves, denying enslaved individuals any rights, segregating churches, and codifying laws against the education of enslaved people. As discussed in chapter 10, slavery linked "precise management and violence."

Although slaveholders became adept at impression management, to make their peculiar institution appear to be a positive good and to function efficiently, slave masters developed and employed, out of necessity, a vast range of conscious and unconscious psychological defense mechanisms. Objectively, managing an economy that was based on a massive scale of bound labor was stressful for the white masters, an effect they went to great lengths to hide or deny to themselves and the rest of the world.

Holding millions of people against their will necessitated the development of what amounted to a massive penal system. American racist slavery, as established in the South, ensured white supremacy and drilled institutional racism into the American democratic experiment. The institutionalization of this antebellum system of incarceration against Black people remains profoundly present in our nation's penal system.

As any effective penal system would, the southern slavery institution needed to develop an armamentarium of domination, control, and punishment methods. An examination of the methods and instruments of control, punishment, torture, and murder of enslaved people is a journey through a chamber of horrors. As described in chapter 8, slaveholders used many implements and methods of control and punishments—the arsenal of the trade—to manage their bound people, often with great cruelty.

Because of their positions of power and political influence in the early governance of America, Southern enslavers created a massive legal and social policy framework around and within a slave-based labor system that was brutally efficient. These laws and social policies were set up to dominate Black people, thwart or eliminate any efforts at Black freedom or equality, and protect the physical (but not financial) well-being of all whites, while ensuring the financial well-being of elite whites. The gestalt of the laws and social policies developed by Southern slaveholders led to the creation of a systemic institution designed to rob Black individuals of their human rights, one from which most Americans continue to suffer.

The peculiar institution of southern, skin-color-based, white supremacist slavery attempted to murder by fear and domination the souls of millions of Black slaves. While the institution of slavery was successful in maiming, branding, mutilating, and murdering the bodies of slaves, it was unsuccessful in its individual and systemic efforts at Black soul murder. The souls that slavery did successfully kill were those of the slave masters. Understandably, the psychological effects of slavery on our country were and are collectively—for Black and white alike—traumatizing. Menakem centered the wounds of slavery in our bodies and identifies this vestigial effect as "racialized trauma."[8] Menakem's construct parallels what Wendell Berry described in his 1989 book, *The Hidden Wound*, as the "historic wound" of slavery left in all Americans.[9]

This "wound" of slavery is America's legacy—our lingering trauma. Part of this trauma is the degree to which many Southerners have not let go of the "lost cause." The defeat of the South and the economic devastation clearly left many former slaveholders bitter, depressed, and angry. Many Southerners still carry their ancestors' scars, their ancestors' rage, and the grudges of the war.

Some colloquialisms remain today that provide evidence that the defeat of the South still does not sit well with some folks: "The South Will Rise Again!" "Forget, hell!" "Damn Yankees!" There are manifest behaviors in the South along these lines, too. Confederate battle flags are reappearing with increasing frequency, and not just in the South. There is an apparent resurgence of the Klan, but it is not hiding its face. An argument can be made that a strong element in the so-called nativist alt-right is continuing to reprosecute the Civil War.

For example, in October 2017, an African American attendee asked Alabama GOP senatorial candidate Roy Moore at a campaign rally in Florence, Alabama, when was the "last time" America was great. "I think," Moore responded, "it was at the time when families were united. Even though we had slavery, they cared for one another. . . . Our families were strong. Our country had direction."[10] The throughline is clear: "The collapse of the Confederacy and the end of slavery did not obliterate or even seriously challenge white Southerners' views of the moral superiority or justice of their cause. Indeed the war strengthened these convictions."[11]

Many Americans—especially whites—are now seeing one of slavery's effects in real time. We have been witnesses to frighteningly frequent brutal slayings of Black men and women by white law enforcement. The throughline of violence from slavery is that Black bodies have been—and are still today—frequent objects of physical violence at the hands of whites.

This psychological autopsy of the white male American southern elite slave master clearly confirms two facts: One, Marse is not dead. He is alive, but not well. Two, features and behaviors of this historical class of slaveholders exist today in many Americans and are the overt evidence of the hidden wounds and trauma left by American slavery, an awareness of which is creating a seismic shift in our national consciousness.

America is beginning to realize that Black slaves built much of this country's infrastructure—government buildings, dams, roads, bridges, public and private schools, colleges, churches, and universities. Black enslaved labor was initially an acceptable means for many whites—not only Southerners—to build our republic. The interests of the peculiar institution of racist slavery were the guiding star of our country for the first seven decades of its existence. In large measure, America was founded—literally and figuratively—on racist slavery. The white male politician-planters, beginning with George Washington and the other Founding Fathers, ran the nation's government and economics on the backs of racist slavery. America is waking up to that fact as a reality.

Fortunately, a moral reckoning about racial injustice and institutional racism is occurring in America. This conscious reckoning—a phenomenon many describe as being "woke"—may, over time, become something analogous in terms of profound, uplifting effects on our national psyche to the Great Awakenings in eighteenth-century America. Even though the two Great Awakenings were essentially spiritual revivals, our current protests and unrest may lead to a transformation of American democracy. I am guardedly optimistic. The national voting results of our 2020 presidential and state elections vividly illustrate just how divided our nation is.

I wrote this book to try to explain *how*, psychologically, Marse did what he did. Slave masters weren't conforming to the dictates of a monarch or centralized church. In spite of their own European ancestral histories, wherein many battles over centuries were waged against tyranny, persecution, and oppression by powerful white, political and religious forces, many American southern slave masters ironically became tyrants. The reality that America, founded in large measure by subversive, terrorist actions against the king and Britain's economy, was supported and built largely by the subjugation and domination of Black people, seems a part of our history a great number of Americans find difficult to admit or remember.

Slave masters created a powerful system of bound labor that made them—a minority of white elites—enormous amounts of money. The slaveholders in the midnineteenth century served a king—King Cotton—that made them millions of dollars. The heart of southern racist slavery was greed. Slavery made a small number of white people very wealthy.

The data culled from this psychological examination can be helpful in informing our personal and collective efforts to understand the roots—individual as well as institutional—of our American racism. The data illustrate that slaveholders inflicted prodigious, traumatic psychological damage on themselves, their region, and their country through the process of slaveholding. How did they contend with the loss of the war and their shattered belief that God would be on the South's side? Their assumptions about Black Africans, their fears, and their need to dominate and control certainly did not disappear once the South lost. Their feelings about Black individuals as subhumans did not magically vanish once the formerly enslaved were living "free" around them. Slave masters had deluded themselves about the honor of slaveholding, a narcissistic position—"moral entitlement"—a delusion that took them and the South down the road to perdition and lingered long after the South's defeat.[12] Racist southern whites did not psychologically humanize Blacks just because they lost the war. Reversing the dehumanization of Black slaves and Black freepeople by whites is a multigenerational task that is still underway.

In the final analysis, the throughline of white supremacist racism is alive, but not well, in America. The slavery-specific delusional—and at times psychotic—beliefs and assumptions spawned by southern elite slaveholders have maintained traction for hundreds of years and contribute to the basis of the current racist white supremacy resurgence in our nation. Black lives *don't* matter to white supremacists because they remain in the grip of delusional beliefs that Blacks are inferior and subhuman. Many whites in America (and in other parts of the world) remain afraid of Black people and other people of color. His need to dominate, assert his legal authority to control, and hide his fear probably led that Minneapolis police officer to lethally leverage his knee on George Floyd's neck for more than nine minutes. Floyd's killing was a brutal, public (fortuitously filmed) twenty-first-century lynching fueled by the same assumptions and beliefs that fed the lynchings of enslaved people and freedmen in America in previous centuries.

Witness the recent discovery of the alleged white supremacist plan to kidnap Governor Gretchen Whitmer of Michigan and hold a vigilante trial of her for treason. Recent media information reported that this group of white supremacist terrorists planned to execute her. The allegations suggested the planning of a twenty-first-century lynching. Joe Biden, then the Democratic presidential candidate, responded to this terrorist threat: "There is a throughline from President Trump's dog whistles and tolerance of hate, vengeance, and lawlessness to plots such as this one. He is giving oxygen to the bigotry and hate we see on the march in our country."[13]

I proclaimed at the beginning of this book that Marse as a slaveholder is dead. I also said that this book was about estimating how much life is left in Marse. Racist white supremacy has kept Marse on life-support. This psychological autopsy of Marse underscores that the throughline that carries the woundedness of Marse marches and slithers into the twenty-first century. Many white Americans, myself included, have deluded ourselves into thinking our psychological makeup bears little resemblance to the morally corrupt psychological framework of the southern racist slaveholder described in this book. Most, if not all, white folks have been complicit in pretending Marse is dead. We whites continue to enjoy the benefits derived simply from having white skin and Black people continue to fear and feel the vestiges of many of the attitudes, beliefs, and behaviors deeply ingrained in our white ancestors, whether they were slaveholders or not.

The truth is that Black people and white people, to great degrees, are afraid of each other. Fear of Black slaves was the antebellum slaveholders' most difficult emotional state to address, a psychological state they went to great lengths to deny and conceal. Marse frequently resorted to violence and cruelty to address his fear of Black slaves. Many whites' worst fears underlie the contemporary white supremacist movement. These fears are percolating in and driving their views and behaviors in today's climate of renewed, openly racist words and actions. Fear of losing their presumed supreme status of being the dominant race in America is driving many white boys and men carrying long guns openly and driving in trucks amidst peaceful Black Lives Matter protests. The Proud Boys are under orders, standing by and weighing in.

Former attorney general William Barr, in a public statement, likened some states' lockdown of public venues as preventive measures against COVID-19 as analogous to the imposition of slavery on America, demonstrating a distorted, absurd, and profound lack of understanding of the horrors of racist slavery and the repercussions of it today. Blacks' fears, legitimate fatigue and trauma from slavery and racism, and hopes are driving the BLM movement—hope inspired by such leaders as Martin Luther King Jr., John Lewis, Al Sharpton, William Barber II, and Alicia Ganza (the latter being one of the founders of Black Lives Matter).

In what ways do the actions of racist antebellum slaveholders to psychologically justify their behaviors to own and maintain chattel slavery relate to how white supremacists justify their racist behavior today? While there are many troubling parallels, some of the more salient ones are racist assumptions that people of color are inferior, that people of color want to control and dominate the white race, that seeking a reconciliation of the systemic causes of social injustice and frequent law enforcement brutality is really an effort to overthrow the assumed legitimate rule and enforcement of white power, and that the 2020 election results were rigged, corrupted and manipulated by illegitimate and fraudulent votes from nonwhite voting districts.

As an institution, southern racist slavery devoured the slaveholders. The slave master ruled and was ruled. The psychological cost to the slave master, to the South, and to our nation as a whole was immense, a tragedy of epic proportions.

American democracy is at a crucial crossroads. As the results of our 2020 election concluded, we had a sitting president who was stoking divisions in our country, many of these divisions falling along racist lines. Many white supremacists were aligning and arming themselves against not only Black people and other people of color, but also against followers of the Jewish faith and authority figures these supremacists resent. And as many feared, there was increased violence between the election in November 2020 and the inauguration of Joe Biden as president at noon on January 20, 2021. My fervent hope is that America will develop a deeper understanding of the roots of racism, so it can move toward healing the individual and collective wounds created in all of us by racist slavery. We have much work to do to stop white racist brutality. Where do we start?

As I bring this book to a close, I am forced to contemplate the relevance of my personal history. I am a direct ancestor of white supremacist slaveholders. Only three generations removed from slaveholding, I am the great-great-grandson of a man, after whom I am named, who owned thirty slaves or more on the eve of the Civil War. He was a proud advocate of North Carolina's movement to secede from the Union. Several of his sons fought for the Confederacy. I carry his blood and his psychological wound, an emotional trauma I assume he could not identify and therefore could not dwell on. Writing this book has helped me come to terms with the existence of this generational wound in me.

As a white man with ancestral slaveholding roots and as a man who, because of the color of my skin, has benefitted from the claimed and accorded privilege of being white, it seems clear to me that the healing conversation about the effects of racist slavery must occur, in large measure, between and among white folks. It is we who have to dismantle the false premise that whites are better than people of color. We whites have to stop projecting the debilitating notion that Black folks and other people of color threaten our well-being. White folks have to make meaningful emotional reparations among ourselves. We must come to terms with the utterly horrible truth about racist slavery and what it did to the heart and soul of our country. We must then do what it takes to truly humanize all persons in this country, and maybe then, we can talk about equality for all.

Epilogue

$\mathcal{I}$ completed this book through chapter 11 a few days after the presidential election of November 3, 2020. By law, Donald Trump had the keys to the White House until high noon on January 20, 2021. The two and a half months between those dates would prove catastrophic for our democracy. The momentous and tumultuous events since November 3, 2020—including a national emergency at the US Capitol on January 6, 2021, and the first time in history a sitting president faced a second impeachment—compelled me to write some final thoughts. As postelection events roiled our nation and became disturbingly dramatic and traumatic, an epilogue seemed necessary. *Merriam Webster's* defines "epilogue" as "a concluding section that rounds out the design of a literary work . . . the final scene of a play that comments or summarizes the main action."[1] The main action appeared to be a near-death experience of American democracy perpetrated by agents of the legacy of white supremacy. America remains in our nation's critical care unit.

Donald J. Trump is not a man who could accept losing something he valued or felt entitled to have. He never thought he would win the 2016 presidential election. He apparently was surprised he won, but how and why that came about is not the subject of this book. Once he had control of the American presidency, despite being a man who did not imbibe alcohol, he became drunk on the power of the office. Over four years, his overt, rage-infused, intimidating behavior illustrated what many people in the addiction field would call a "dry drunk." I am not opining or offering any diagnosis of Trump, but I am commenting on his public behaviors. Technically, "dry drunk" is a term that describes an individual who suffers from the disease of alcoholism but manages sobriety "without the psychological and social components and benefits of a recovery program. The person is, therefore, likely to exhibit dysfunctional behaviors associated with alcoholism such as anxiety, depression, and a range of mood instability and fluctuation such as disproportionate anger."[2] I believe there is sufficient evidence to support the finding that Trump meets many of his needs through addictive behaviors. His niece, Mary L. Trump, offered commentary on her uncle's personality features and behaviors, including raising the allegation that he drinks "upward of twelve Diet Cokes a day" and may therefore suffer "from a substance- (in this case caffeine-) induced sleep disorder."[3]

Trump displays behaviors that make him look like a dry drunk. The most prominent behavioral characteristic is his being an enraged bully. Over the course of his four years as president, we watched him appear to enjoy abusing his subordinates—often cruelly. His targets make up a long list: John Dowd, Michael Flynn, Paul Manafort, Anthony Scaramucci, John Bolton, Steve Bannon, Kirstjen Nielsen, H. R. McMaster, James Mattis, Mick Mulvaney, Andrew McCabe, Reince Priebus, Sean Spicer, Rod Rosenstein, Michael Cohen, Rex Tillerson, James Comey, Sally Yates, Christopher Wray, William Barr, Jeff Sessions, and, last but not least, Vice President Mike Pence. Bob Woodward described a moment when Trump demeaned other important subordinates: Speaking to the National Security Council—a group of military and civilian advisors—he said, "'The soldiers on the ground could run things much better than you. . . . They could do a much better job. I don't know what the hell we're doing.' It was a 25 minute dressing-down of the generals and senior advisors."[4]

Most often, despite his crafted, television image reputation as a man who could forcefully fire people, his preferred method of terminating people from their jobs was through passive-aggressive public tweets. When he ultimately turned on his vice president, he described Pence to the January 6, 2021, "Stop the Steal" rally attendees as someone who appeared to be disloyal to Trump and Trump's so-called patriots by not helping Trump overturn the presidential election results. Based on erroneous legal advice, Trump wrongly declared that the vice president had the power to do such: "According to the [*New York*] *Times*, [retired North Carolina Chief Supreme Court Justice Mark] Martin advocated [to Trump] a 'radical' constitutional interpretation giving Vice President Mike Pence the authority to reject any state election returns he deemed fraudulent—a theory that legal scholars across the political spectrum dismissed as nonsensical and which even Pence, one of Trump's most loyal allies, refused to embrace."[5]

In Trump's world, disloyalty to him was the ultimate sin. Trump's demand for extreme loyalty from everyone created a common analogy that compared him to a mafia boss. This extreme loyalty and solidarity with the mafia "don" is called *omerta*, the violation of which is punishable by death.

Prior to the assault on the Capitol, Neal Katyal, offering commentary on Trump's behavior during the infamous telephone call on January 2, 2021, with Georgia Secretary of State Brad Raffensperger, described the manner in which Trump spoke with Raffensperger as "the way people in organized crime rings talk."[6] Trump's proclaimed disloyalty by Pence turned a volatile cohort of this crowd into a lynch mob, with an expressed, focused intent to "hang Mike Pence." In Trump's world, Pence, a man who had been steadfastly loyal to him for more than four years, had violated *omerta*. In cataloguing Trump's characteristics, reporters Philip Rucker and Carol Leonnig described in great detail twenty-five troublesome behaviors.[7] One of the more troubling behaviors was that "the universal value of the Trump administration was loyalty—loyalty not to the country but to the president himself. Some of his aides believed his demand for blind fealty—and his retaliation against those who denied it—was slowly corrupting public service and testing democracy itself."[8] Michael Cohen, Trump's former personal attorney, offered his account of what happened when he was perceived as not loyally standing by his boss and the subsequent punishments he received from Trump in his book *Disloyal*.[9]

Rucker and Leonnig stated accurately that Trump was addicted to the media. In describing Trump's aides who were either forced out or who left out of self-preservation, they wrote, "They lament a president who nursed petty grievances, was addicted to watching cable television news coverage of himself, elevated sycophants, and lied with abandon."[10] Combined with his pathological narcissism, Trump hungered for praise and recognition. He appeared to get a "fix" from the adoration he sucked from his rallies and so-called briefings. At times, he became giddy at the anger he stirred in his crowds. Like a dry drunk, he became notorious for his impulsivity, keeping many people in his orbit and across the world on edge, worried about what he might say or do next.

As president, he naturally became the "master" of the White House, found himself almost romantically attracted to other tyrants who ran their countries with iron fists, and treated almost everyone else around him as subservient to his whims and impulses. With the exception of other autocrats, whom he adored and mistakenly thought adored him, Trump perceived he had no equals. The power of the presidential office gave him, as he saw it, unlimited license to let his bully nature run full tilt. What the majority of Americans did not bargain for was that with the election of Trump, America renewed the historic thread of installing *another* white supremacist in the Oval Office. As reporter Karen Grigsby Bates stated, "But when it comes to calling Trump the *most* racist president, it's tough to make such a definitive characterization. After all, racism was baked into the founding of the United States, a country built on the genocide of Native American people and slavery; 12

of the first 18 presidents actually owned slaves."[11] Racist attitudes and policies that marginalized Blacks and other people of color were exhibited by a number of US presidents, including Theodore Roosevelt, Rutherford B. Hayes, William McKinley, Woodrow Wilson, Franklin D. Roosevelt, Andrew Jackson, Richard Nixon, and Ronald Reagan. Although famous for many things, including the Emancipation Proclamation, Abraham Lincoln did not believe in the equality of Blacks and whites. As reporter Touré stated, "The roots of modern American racism were put down by those early European colonizers: the road to Trump begins in America's first years."[12] This statement is a succinct summary of the racist white supremacy throughline.

We also did not bargain for the magnitude of his desire to bring a fool's gold–plated wrecking ball to the American democratic experiment. Trump attracted millions of his followers by acting as if he were a revolutionary, framed in his campaign mantra, "draining the swamp." The sad irony is Trump hijacked the Republican Party and populated Washington, DC, with vast numbers of humanoid alligators, crocodiles, and other vindictive swamp creatures. Underneath it all, he is a racist authoritarian who cares only for his own interests. His four-year term was one long, excruciating reality show, and it unfortunately still has airtime.

The notion that he might lose his reelection in 2020 sent him into a panic. The show would be over. To defend against this panic, he dropped into a mindset that became an infantile fantasy—an autistic fantasy. He convinced himself and his supporters that the only way he could lose would be if he were the victim of foul play. He tied his alleged victimization to multiple conspiracies. For more than a year he forecast that if he suffered a loss, it would be because the election was stolen from him. This became popularly known among his critics as the Big Lie.

There are really three lies that need to be addressed: (1) the COVID-19 virus lie; (2) the stolen election lie, the so-called Big Lie; and (3) our national racist white supremacy lie. The Big Lie regarding the alleged stolen election appears to deserve a position secondary to the virus lie. While we could debate the relative damaging effects of lie number 1 and lie number 2, Trump's lie about the lethality of COVID-19 put a massive torpedo through the hull of our ship of state. As of this writing, more than half a million people have died of COVID-19 in the United States.

Trump's use of an autistic fantasy to defend himself against a potential defeat was the psychological equivalent of southern slave masters for a time convincing themselves that their enslaved people were content with their lot in life—that their bound people were members of their extended families. Trump created a myth about himself, around which his supporters could be nurtured and assured of his power. The Trumpian myth became a balm to

Trump's panic. The theft—the "steal"—became a target for his supporters. They swallowed the Big Lie whole. The definition of "myth" helps explain the relevance of myth making for former president Trump. A myth is "an unfounded or false notion . . . a person or thing having only an imaginary or unverifiable existence."[13] Trump and his followers are breathing and touting an imaginary, unverifiable experience—that he won the election.

In a brilliant analysis of the Big Lie—that former president Trump's victory was stolen from him—associate professor of religious studies Bradley Onishi argued that since Trump's defeat on November 3, 2020, Trump "has cultivated the myth that the election was stolen," even though there is absolutely no legal basis for this claim. The establishment of this myth, now believed by millions of his followers, "became the basis for contesting the fact." As Onishi explained, "A myth becomes reality through ritual, when its story is dramatized and its adherents brought to collective participation in it."[14] Trump spent months in rallies, tweets, and public appearances predicting the certainty that if he lost, it could only be understood as a conspiratorial grand theft perpetrated by his enemies, and when he did lose, he relentlessly pursued and promoted the grand theft myth.

Onishi's analysis anchored Trump's election lie into the muck and mud of antebellum racist white supremacy. Onishi further argued that Trump's myth about losing the 2020 election—his claims that he lost by fraud and theft—can be understood by grasping an earlier white supremacy myth, the "Lost Cause"—the revisionist belief espoused by Southerners after losing the war that the South was a victim of "Yankee vandals," whose motives had nothing to do with slavery, but were an immoral "political and economic power grab." The Lost Cause myth is built upon the belief that Southerners occupied "the moral high ground in the conflict—a class of honorable and loyal families who defended their soil and way of life in the face of undue Northern aggression." The claims that Trump was victimized and the election was stolen from him and that the antebellum South was the victim of Yankee aggression make for an apt, fascinating parallel—although each is historically untenable. Onishi further stated, "As Charles Reagan Wilson, a Southern historian, has shown, Lost Cause mythology was enacted through the rituals of Confederate civil religion: the funerals of Confederate soldiers, the celebration of Confederate Memorial Day, the pilgrimages made to the hundreds of Confederate monuments that had been erected by the dawn of World War I.[15] The rituals and symbols instilled in the younger generation the nobility of the Confederacy and the moral vacancy of its enemies. Together, they supported a religious myth that for many Southerners supplanted the historical record. The men who died in battle became its martyrs. The generals became its patron saints." Although Donald Trump is far from being a southern Confederate general, psychologically and behaviorally, he displays many characteristics of an elite southern slave master whose power and control were founded on racist white supremacy. Many of his supporters pull their rage and anti-government hostility and violence from Lost Cause distortions.

An argument can be made that Trump and his supporters have instituted a twenty-first-century Lost Cause—coalescing around the myth that Trump actually won the 2020 presidential election. Such mythmaking by the Trump party uses the very same defense mechanisms that the South employed at the end of the Civil War. As historian Bertram Wyatt-Brown informed us, "Out of the weakness that military and racial overthrow had created in 1865, Southern whites gradually constructed a fabric of nostalgia for the Lost Cause. When coupled with the notion of 'Redemption' from allegedly evil Republican and Black rule, this means of interpreting the late war offered the concept of victimization, not abject military defeat."[16] Defeated Confederates blamed anyone and everyone except themselves for their loss. With the help of massive denial, a refusal to admit defeat, a personal and political reality founded on mendacity and an apocalyptic vision, and a repetitive droning of his pitiful victimization, Trump has successfully convinced millions of Americans that he didn't lose. Trump's Lost Cause myth has become militant, dangerous, and violent and likely will get worse. His followers feel that they too have been cheated and victimized, and many are consumed with resentment and rage, denying to themselves just how fearful they are about the changes taking place in the social and political fabric of our nation. They experience a strong, omnipresent danger that, like a riptide, pulls them into maelstroms of paranoid conspiracies and reality-bending propaganda. Historian Carol Anderson cut to the heart of white supremacist rage: "The trigger for white rage, inevitably, is Black advancement."[17] Trump's militia—which is how they see themselves— are emerging in greater numbers, "to save and cleanse the nation, to preserve for themselves [and their master] that abstraction which some would later call the American dream."[18]

Another one of Trump's prominent characteristics is his incapacity for empathy. His apparent psychopathy (as distinguished from sociopathy) renders him unable to develop empathy. The white supremacy throughline that traces backward from the Trump tenure as president to the personality characteristics of nineteenth-century slaveholders (as introduced in chapter 1) leads to nineteenth-century criticisms of slaveholders: They exhibited a "certain haughtiness," they were seen as "vain and imperious," lacking the "elegance of sentiment." Like Trump, the white slaveholder exalted his own being. Trump's self-view is succinctly captured in a Trump biography by Rucker and Leonnig, using as its title Trump's proud self-appraisal *A Very Stable Genius*.[19] Historian David H. Bennett, quoting Richard Hofstadter, offered a description that seems to fit Trump: "The paranoid spokesman in politics tends to be overheated, oversuspicious, overaggressive, grandiose, and apocalyptic."[20]

Although his claim that the election was stolen from him has adhered itself like a cancer into the fabric of our democracy, and has gained the epithet the Big Lie, it is not the biggest lie he told the nation. The biggest and worst by far was his repetitive lie about the lethality of COVID-19. During his eighth interview with Woodward, on March 19, 2020, Trump's dominant narcissism shone through as he told Woodward, "This thing is nasty—it's a nasty situation." As Woodward reported,

> In our interview, the president spoke with pride about his leadership. He blamed China and President Obama and continued to accept no responsibility. . . . Just two days before, at the [coronavirus] task force briefing, Trump had gone so far as to claim, "I've always known this is a—this is a real—this is a pandemic. I've felt it was a pandemic long before it was called a pandemic. . . . I wanted to play it down . . . I still like playing it down, because I didn't want to create a panic. . . . And one day, this thing came in and we had a choice to make. . . . Close everything up and save potentially millions of lives—you know, hundreds of thousands of lives— or don't do anything and look at body bags every day being taken out of apartment buildings."

To this last point, an incredulous Woodward asked, "Who told you that?"

"'It was me,' Trump said. 'I told me that.'"[21]

I was gobsmacked when I read this exchange between Woodward and Trump. Could a more brazen example of Trump's operating within his own silo be located? I doubt it. Trump's lies to the nation about the virus and his cowardly inaction cost us hundreds of thousands of lives, crushed the economy, and disrupted the psychosocial fabric of our nation. To me, this was—*is*—the Big Lie, of all the lies, and the one that infected the legacy of his presidency. The enormity of the virus and the responsibility it required of the president scared Trump to his core. Trump went AWOL on any competent response to COVID-19 and tossed any and all responsibility to facing it to the individual fifty states. On February 22, 2021, in the United States—a country comprising only one-fifth of the world's population—we reached the grim milestone of more than 500,000 COVID-19-related deaths—more than any other country on the planet.

Our forty-fifth president was not known for telling the truth, but he was clear and truthful about the storm he was inviting to break in Washington, DC, on January 6, 2021. He purposefully chose that date because it was the day the US House and Senate were to assemble in the Capitol to count and certify the Electoral College votes that would confirm Joe Biden and Kamala Harris as winners of the 2020 election. He was clear and unequivocal about his conspiracy-based victim wail that his 2020 election victory was stolen from him by Democrats, Republicans in name only (RINOS), socialists, communists, and Satanists. For months, he set the stage for a "Rally to Save America" and an unpermitted "march" for that day, to be attended by any and all true patriots to save his presidency. Thousands of his supporters, intoxicated by his repetitive, false claims, massed on Freedom Plaza the day before. The attendees were Americans ranging from everyday folks to armed insurrection-ists prepared to commit violence. Trump was their common ground. He promised his people that his rally and march to the Capitol would be "wild." As a result of his exhortation, as well as similar stoking of mistrust and rage by his political allies and at least one member of his family, a march to the Capitol morphed into a predictable, prepared, and hell-bent violent mob that overran the Capitol, breached its inexplicably meek defenses, and sacked the interior. His supporters swallowed whole his claim that Wednesday, January 6, 2021, was the last chance to "fight like hell" and "stop the steal"—to stop the certification of the electoral college votes that would confirm Biden and Harris's victory. A violent element of his rally and march attendees heard what their dark lord president extolled as a "battle cry," armed themselves, and ral-lied like orcs. Trump's disgraced personal attorney, Rudy Giuliani, reinforced the combative nature of the rally, calling for "a trial by combat." As the *New York Times* described it, "A mob overran the nation's Capitol, as lawmakers hid in fear. Wholesale vandalism. Tear gas. Gunfire. A woman dead; an officer dead; many injured. Chants of 'U.S.A.! U.S.A.!'"[22] The death toll rose to five people. Approximately 140 police officers were injured.

Trump and his supporters, across the board, mixed up a mesmerizing, stultifying, you-can-get-high-on-this concoction distilled mainly from the Big Lie. Drinks were on the house. On top of the Big Lie, he laid out the truth—for months—in plain sight. It's not hard to imagine Trump's train of thoughtless, divisive impulses: "You people have stolen the election from me and my people, so on January 6th, my people are coming to set things right." Voldemort had run out of options. An insurrection by the true patriots of his white nation was coming to town. Trump told us this. He told the world this. Clearly, not all who came to the January 6 rally were intent on violence, but there were some bad actors in the mix. Trump's rallies had become a ritual for him and his base, where everybody's rage found its happy place. They were never presidential interactions with a cross section of the diversity of our nation's population. They were antigovernment, white supremacist campaign events. Trump began campaigning for his 2020 reelection almost immediately after taking office in 2016. The rally in DC on January 6, 2021, was differ-ent. It was not a rally. It was a staged, brewing storm, and within its eye was a roaring cauldron of rage, hatred, militancy, denial, fear, and sedition. As Woodward noted, during an interview with Woodward and Robert Costa on March 31, 2016, Trump said, "*I bring rage out. I do bring rage out. I don't know if that's an asset or a liability, but whatever it is, I do.*"[23] Marsha Coats, wife of Dan Coats (who had served sixteen years as a Republican senator from Indiana and for a time served as Trump's first director of national intelligence), said in a letter supporting Trump to her fellow Indiana Republicans, "I truly believe the office will change Donald Trump. I believe it will humble him. And I think that even Donald will be impelled to turn to God for guidance."[24] Mrs. Coats later said to an associate, "He's the kind of person that would inspire crazy people."[25]

Did the many levels of law enforcement (including the US Justice Department) and US government security not believe him? Were they intimidated by the president, as seems has been the case—over the better part of four years—for hundreds of people in Trump's orbit? Did they think this threat of a riot was just another of Trump's thousands of lies? Did they think this was going to be a raucous but mainly peaceful rally and march? The evidence was all over the place, in plain sight, cascading, commanding, and careening across various social platforms—including Twitter, Instagram, and Facebook—about potential and planned violence for Trump's rally and march, synced with the precise date of the formal meeting of the Electoral College imprimatur by the two houses of Congress. The drums of war were loud. The *New York Times* reported that "the term 'Storm the Capitol' was mentioned 100,000 times in 30 days preceding Jan. 6, according to Zignal Labs, a media insight company."[26] *New York Times* reporter Kathleen Gray cogently laid the evidence out in a piece entitled, "If You Didn't See Invasion Coming, You Weren't Watching Michigan."[27] Gray is, of course, referring to the quasi take-over by armed men of the Michigan State Capitol in April 2020. Michigan law allows people to openly carry guns in the Capitol. As I wrote in chapter 11, during this same time period, Governor Gretchen Whitmer of Michigan was the alleged target of a kidnapping-murder plot. As Gray pointed out, even though the spring 2020 event in Michigan never turned violent, it must be seen as a precursor of what happened January 6, 2021, in DC.

There were other precursor events, not the least of which was the "Unite the Right" rally in Charlottesville, Virginia, on August 11–12, 2017, where white nationalists came to violently protest a decision to remove a statue of Confederate general Robert E. Lee. Primarily a white nationalist group, they carried guns and chanted racist and anti-Semitic slogans. A man intentionally drove a car into the crowd, killing Heather Heyer, who was attending the counterprotest march, and injuring dozens of other protestors. The fact that this alt-right rally was held in Lee Park, named after Lee himself, arguably the principal patron saint of the Lost Cause, shows how deeply the defense of the Confederacy and Lost Cause sentiments are woven throughout the fabric of America's contemporary domestic terrorists. There was also another Michigan precursor event. On December 6, 2020, armed protestors surrounded the home of Michigan secretary of state Jocelyn Benson, threatening violence after the results of the presidential election. There appears to be a hot white supremacist fire burning in Michigan and other states. Georgia secretary of state Brad Raffensperger reported that he and his family received death threats after he refused to comply with Trump's demands.

Who are these white nationalists, these homegrown domestic terrorists? What was the composition of the insurrectionists who stormed the Capitol on January 6, 2021? Their flags, symbols, clothing, gear, hats, and patches offer substantial evidence of some of their identities and political affiliations.[28] The following is a partial list:

- An individual wearing a T-shirt that read "Camp Auschwitz" on the front and "Staff" on the back
- Swastikas
- Trump flags and "MAGA" hats in great abundance. At one point in the insurrection, the American flag flying over the Capitol was taken down and replaced by a Trump flag.
- Confederate battle flags. During the Civil War, there were two Confederate flags flown in battle, both similar in design. One was the flag of the Army of Northern Virginia (a square design issued in November 1861) and the flag of the Army of Tennessee (issued in 1864).[29] It appears that the Tennessee design, with its rectangular shape, has become most popular among white supremacists, who argue that it represents not hatred or racism, but states' rights and southern heritage.[30] Wyatt-Brown offered an opposing view: "The Rebel banner," he wrote, "was the emblem of a sacralized determination to keep African Americans underfoot."[31] Internationally, it is seen as a symbol of white supremacy. It is also known as the "Dixie" flag, but it was never the official flag of the Confederacy. The flag officially used by the Confederate government was known as the "Stars and Bars."
- QAnon symbols and slogans: "Q," "Trust the Plan," "Save the Children," "The children cry out for justice"
- The neo-Nazi group "NSC-131." NSC means "National Social Club"; the 131 indicated the NSC "crew" originating from New England. According to the Anti-Defamation League website, the NSC

"is a neo-Nazi group with small, autonomous regional chapters in the US and abroad . . . they see themselves as [white] soldiers at war with a hostile, Jewish-controlled system that is deliberately plotting the extinction of the white race."[32]

- An individual wearing a T-shirt reading "6MWE," meaning "six million weren't enough" (a reference to the number of Jewish people killed in Nazi concentration camps during World War II)
- A noose hanging outside the Capitol
- Flags with the phrase "When tyranny becomes law, rebellion becomes duty," a phrase Laura E. Adkins and Emily Burack report is "dubiously attributed to Thomas Jefferson"[33]
- The Roman numeral III, which is the logo of the Three Percenters, an antigovernment militia founded after the election of President Barack Obama. A Three Percenter is "someone who advocates for a strict interpretation of the Second Amendment of the US Constitution, strongly believing in armed rebellion against perceived government overreach, especially with respect to gun laws. . . . The name *Three Percenters* is based on a false theory that, during the American Revolution, only 2.8 percent of the US population actually served in George Washington's army."[34]
- The Gadsden flag, which shows a coiled snake and the phrase "Don't Tread on Me." This flag, as used contemporaneously, stands for "gun rights" and "individual liberties."
- Hawaiian shirts or camouflage worn by the Boogaloo Bois, an armed antigovernment group who aspire to a second civil war
- The Oath Keepers, an antigovernment group whose membership is made up of former military and law enforcement. Their view is that the federal government is trying to strip American citizens of their rights.
- The Proud Boys, "a violent far-right group" that former president Trump told to "Stand back and stand by" in a September 2020 presidential debate. Some members of the Proud Boys at the January 6 rally and Capitol assault were photographed wearing shirts displaying the phrase "Stand Back and Stand By." The Proud Boys describe themselves as "a pro-Western fraternal organization for men who refuse to apologize for their creating the modern world; aka Western Chauvinists."[35]
- Crusader crosses, medieval-style helmets, Templar crosses, and Norse horned helmets
- The Punisher, a bastardization of a Marvel comic book character dressed in "a black shirt with a distinctive stylized white skull on it"[36]

- "Intactivists," a group dedicated to banning all forms of circumcision. Signs were seen at the Capitol that read, "Circumcision is the mark of the beast Satan" and "Outlaw Satan's circumcision."

Reporter Emma Rose offered additional commentary on the symbols present among the rioters at the Capitol on January 6, 2021.[37] Describing the various flags that day, Rose wrote, "a sea of appropriated historical flags, altered stars and stripes, and conspiracy theory symbolism"; the Three Percenters' flag is a Betsy Ross flag and the group's insignia is a Roman numeral III, "with or without the percent symbol"; the Confederate battle flag, connecting the modern movements "with white supremacy and white nationalist movements"; and the Gadsden flag. According to Paul Bruski, a faculty member of the School of Graphic Design and Human Computer Interaction at Iowa State University, the Gadsden flag predates the American Revolution. It may originate from a design in 1754 by Benjamin Franklin, showing the colonies as a divided snake, with the words "join or die." Flags in the colonies often had snakes on them, particularly the rattlesnake, "a distinctly American creature believed to strike only in self-defense." The colonies' "Navy Jack" flag had thirteen stripes and a rattlesnake with thirteen rattles, and the words, "Don't Tread on Me." Christopher Gadsden was a South Carolina slave trader and slaveholder, who according to Bruski, created the yellow flag with coiled rattler and the words "Don't Tread on Me."[38] Also included were Oathkeeper flags, patches, and decals, identified by the word "Oathkeeper," often in yellow; "Q" on clothing and flags, standing for QAnon, and the motto "Where we go one, we go all" or WWG1WGA.

The militant element of Trump's base is obviously composed of diverse groups with different emphases and ideologies. Made up mainly of white males, the glue that toxically binds them together is racist white supremacy. Although I cannot claim to understand the totality of their positions and grievances, the ones that stand out are:

1. Trump, as he says, was cheated out of his election.
2. The congressional leaders who fostered the theft of Trump's victory deserve to be terrorized or worse.
3. They have erroneously been labeled as domestic terrorists, while denying their own threatening nature and simmering resentment. They see themselves as true patriots, with guns, bombs, and anti-government rebellion as their calling cards.
4. They are enraged about the Black Lives Matter movement and are threatened by the voting success of "colored" cities, such as Atlanta, Detroit, Milwaukee, and Philadelphia. They are deeply fearful that

their America, as a Christian white nation, indivisible, with liberty and justice for all white people, is being eroded.

5. They are deeply afraid of a successful assault on their Second Amendment rights.

6. Their patriotism is embedded into their view of their First Amendment rights, which justified their assault on the Congress, whom they see as traitors.

7. Largely made up of white males, they are driven in large measure by white male entitlement.

8. They are driven by fear that their king, Donald Trump, will be successfully banished from his rightful place as the leader of the true American party and as a defender of keeping Lost Cause statues unmolested and the Confederate names assigned to many of America's military bases.

9. Many have swallowed the lie that the COVID-19 virus was not a big deal and that wearing masks is a sign of weakness.

10. Many of them are against being "forced" to take the COVID-19 vaccine.

11. Some of the subsets of Trump's base appear, curiously, to be antipolice.

12. Many are stimulated by false information and conspiracy theories, some of which are so bizarre, they border on being paranoid delusional, such as the crazy mosaic composing the QAnon conspiracies. One of the features of the QAnon belief system is that Trump has a plan (the "Storm") to save alleged abducted children from cannibalistic, pedophilic elements of the Democratic Party.

I practiced forensic psychology for thirty-five years. Many of my cases were within the family court system. I was frequently appointed by the court to help sort out what might be in the best interests of children whose parents and extended families were waging an all-out war against one another in what was euphemistically called a "high-conflict divorce." Every so often, I would be taken by surprise when one of the litigants did something during the course of a comprehensive forensic evaluation that was floridly self-defeating. The litigant's actions did not help his or her case. After this happened in a few cases, I remained bewildered. Why would someone do something to undermine his or her case? Then, one day, I stumbled upon a concept called "narcissistic immunity."[39] The narcissism exhibited by the litigant who was sabotaging his or her own best interests was generally obvious, but then it dawned on me. These litigants exhibited a type of narcissism that magically, in the recesses of their own minds, made them bulletproof. They saw themselves as omnipotent and unassailable. They were convinced that the normal rules governing others did not apply to them. They were immune and occupied a space above the rules. They lived above conventionality. Laws governing separation, divorce, child custody—these did not apply to them. They saw themselves as omniscient. They were surprised when they were challenged about their self-injurious behavior.

In 2016, Trump boasted, "I could stand in the middle of Fifth Avenue and shoot somebody and I wouldn't lose any voters." What in a person's psychological makeup would give him permission to boast something like that? Opinion writer Robert Reich called this outlandish stance "Trump's Fifth Avenue principle."[40] It appears we can also call it "narcissistic immunity." Reich accurately pointed out there are many startling examples of Trump's success with his Fifth Avenue principle: the *Access Hollywood* tape, Special Counsel Robert Mueller's findings that Trump obstructed justice, his bizarre friendship with Russian president Vladimir Putin, the "perfect" call with the president of Ukraine, his overt racism, his first impeachment, and now his second impeachment. On January 6, 2021, Trump stood at a podium and incited an insurrection, after which he went home and watched his riotous handiwork unfold on television. The president of the United States consciously and deliberately inciting a riot and insurrection on live television is not plausible, unless the president sees himself as "narcissistically immune" from any negative consequences. The US Senate's acquittal of Trump a second time at the end of his impeachment on February 13, 2021, reinforced his "narcissistic immunity" one more time: "From Florida the former president immediately issued a statement, praising his hastily gathered legal team and gleefully decrying 'yet another phase of the greatest witch hunt in the history of our Country.' He also vowed further political activity, saying his movement 'has only just begun.' In his telling, the trial amounted to an attempt to 'transform justice into a tool of political vengeance.'"[41]

But what about the self-sabotaging dimension of narcissistic immunity? On January 6, 2021, Trump and his minions screwed up. They gave our nation and millions of people across the globe a George Floyd event on steroids. They strolled free as birds down the street from the rally to the Capitol. In real-time, live television coverage, there was almost no evidence of any law enforcement. What became clear is the gift Trump and his people gave America. As the rioters stormed the Capitol steps, brushing by the meager, totally unprepared and overwhelmed police presence, bursting into the hallowed halls of the building, and threatening the government occupants, most people watching were stunned by the apparent ease with which they captured the building. My guess is the rioters were also surprised. As I watched with my wife, we both were astonished that there was little to no effective resistance, no protection, and little defense (although as witnesses via television, we had almost no knowledge of the totality of what was taking place inside the Capitol). As more video footage became available, we now know of course that the riot was bloody and more like medieval hand-to-hand combat. Proudly waving Trump, Gadsden, QAnon, and Confederate flags, Trump's people took control of large areas inside the Capitol. If this had been a Black Lives Matter march, or any march composed mainly of people of color, the numbers of police and military (including national guard) would have been profoundly visible, controlling, and intimidating. We got to see a hostile, violent cadre of Trump supporters—the majority of whom appeared to be white males—get a free pass. They looted, hunted, and vandalized the Capitol and there were few, if any, obvious arrests during the two to three hours of the insurrection.

The gift given to white America is that we got to see again, that white violence gets treated differently than Black nonviolence. We got to see the clear split in our law enforcement system. White rallies and marches get a different, more compassionate—certainly more restrained—response from security forces than do Black rallies and marches. Black folks have known this for hundreds of years. Are we white folks getting this? Could it be any clearer?

Some of Trump's people were not at the Capitol to play. Various news agencies reported that two pipe bombs were found near the Capitol (perhaps as a diversionary tactic). The *New York Times* reported that these were "live devices that would have been exploded if they had not been defused."[42] They brought Molotov cocktail materials, plastic wrist ties, guns, crowbars, metal poles, hockey sticks, baseball bats, and a gallows and noose. Several rioters brought what looked like large pieces of bamboo to use as battering rams. During and shortly after the January 6 assault, five people ultimately died; there were an untold number of injuries, including brain and spinal trauma. One rioter was shot and killed by Capitol police and another rioter reportedly was trampled to death. A police officer reportedly succumbed to the toxicity of bear spray used on him. In this same piece, the *New York Times* reported that "in the 20 days since rioters stormed the Capitol, the F.B.I. has received over 200,000 digital media tips and has opened cases on over 400 suspects."

As the days passed after this assault, more details emerged that indicated it could have been far worse. By barring the doors of the House and Senate with benches, couches, and whatever else might help establish a barricade, the Capitol Police and Secret Service held the breach. Evidence has emerged that some of the rioters sought to hang—lynch—Vice President Mike Pence. Another insurrectionist was arrested carrying evidence that he planned to kill House Speaker Nancy Pelosi. It seems reasonable to assume that if this mob had gotten to the congressional chambers, we may have been witness to vicious deaths and maybe even a hostage situation.

Two days after the assault, reporter Amanda Taub questioned the accuracy of calling the assault a "coup."[43] She wrote, "But the violent, anti-democratic attack on the Capitol doesn't fit the technical definition of a coup even though the president incited and encouraged it." Taub argued that these events are a part of a larger, more generalized "anti-democratic backsliding." Well, it certainly was that, but what we witnessed was a lynch mob, jacked up and stoked by racist white supremacy. As more evidence unfolds, we may learn that this was a poorly planned coup d'état attempt that transpired with some collusion from some government and law enforcement officials.

As a word by itself, "coup" means "a brilliant, sudden, and usually successful stroke or act." "Coup d'état" means "a sudden, decisive exercise of force in politics, especially the violent overthrow or alteration of the existing government by a small group."[44] There seems to be no question that these insurgents planned to "alter" the existing government by mayhem and murder. Some of the more rabid Trump supporters were trying to stop the ratification process of the Electoral College results. Trump lied to his base at the rally preceding the march, telling them he would march to the Capitol with them—which he of course did not do—and then retreating to the White House to watch the fire he started. Some presidential observers remarked that he appeared to enjoy the destruction in his name as he watched on television. Trump's statement to his rally attendees that he would march with them really translated as "You're on your own," and was itself a lie of huge proportions. Trump demands and expects loyalty, but he is never loyal.

Coup d'état or not, this was certainly a twenty-first-century lynching attempt. "Lynch" means "to put to death (as by hanging) by mob action without legal sanction."[45] A lynching is a noun derived from lynch and it means an act in which one or more persons are killed by an unlawful mob, typically a vigilante mob. George Floyd was lynched right before our eyes. The white supremacist members of Trump's mobsters came to lynch, bringing a gallows and rope with them and yelling, "Hang Mike Pence" as they breached the Capitol.

The fact that the rioters who stormed the Capitol constituted a lynch mob dramatically links the events of January 6, 2021, back to the racist white supremacy of American slavery and post-Reconstruction violence of the Jim Crow era in American history. Historian Eddie S. Glaude Jr. gave us a disturbing statistic about the "dreaded American ritual of lynching." Between 1887 and 1906, an African American in the South was lynched every four days.[46] For a disturbing account of an 1898 coup d'état perpetrated by white supremacists against African Americans in my native state of North Carolina, see David Zucchino's book *Wilmington's Lie*.[47]

I look to another work by Glaude for his sage analysis of lie number 3. Trump's so-called Big Lie (lie number 2) was not so large when compared to the history of "*the lie*" Glaude described in his book about the work of James Baldwin. As he guided us to the lie undergirding white supremacy, "*the lie,*" Glaude informed us, is "more properly several sets of lies with a single purpose." First of all, "*the lie* is a broad and powerful architecture of false assumptions . . . that support the everyday order of American life, which means we breathe them like air. We count them as truths. We absorb them into our character."[48] What composes this architecture of lies?

There are three components of *the lie*, Glaude told us. One set of lies is those that debase Black people. Blacks are inferior beings; they are less than human. They are stereotypes. A second component of *the lie* is the distortions and untruths we have been fed about American history. For example, the real truth about the horrors of American slavery is just now entering the mainstream of white American consciousness and states are actively seeking to suppress it. This second component of *the lie* is that America sees itself as fundamentally good and innocent. One big piece of this particular self-delusion is that "all men are created equal." The heart of Jefferson's words was "all *white* men were created equal." And, as we know, even this has never been true. There has never been equality among white people. Except when they are providing him with his insatiable need for admiration or giving him money, Trump has never cared a whit about his base. He wasn't about to put himself at risk—physically or politically—by marching to the Capitol. He has no plans for "saving the children," as QAnon adherents believe.

A third piece of *the lie*, as Glaude stated, is that America has lied to itself and never managed an honest assessment of how the nation's view of itself as "a divinely sanctioned nation called to be a beacon of light and moral force in the world" is a lie. "Taken as a whole, then, the lie is the mechanism that allows and has always allowed America to avoid facing the truth about its unjust treatment of Black people and how it deforms the soul of the country. The lie cuts deep into the American psyche. It secures our national innocence in the face of the ugliness and evil we have done."[49] Although there are some Black folks who count themselves as Trump supporters, it would seem reasonable that they have not quite grasped that they support a racist white supremacist who sees no value in them. Their value is how much admiration they shower on Trump and how much money they give.

On February 1, 2021, the *New York Times* published a comprehensive piece of investigative reporting, detailing seventy-seven days of former president Trump's efforts to subvert the 2020 presidential election.[50] This piece contains a huge amount of material, but several facts stand out as vitally important toward an understanding of where we are and where we may be going as a democratic nation:

- Trump's "Big Lie" (lie number 2) "lives on in a divided America."
- Although it would appear that the majority of the rioters who stormed the Capitol on January 6, 2021, were white males, it appears that white women played (and continue to play) key roles in supporting Trump's claim that his victory was stolen from him.
- First of all, a group called "Women for America First," which bills itself as a twenty-first-century suffrage movement, was fundamental in organizing the momentum that led to the events of January 5 and 6 in Washington, DC. It was founded by Amy Kremer, one of the original Tea Party organizers. As the *Times* reporters wrote, "As it crossed the country [in an organized bus tour] spreading the new gospel of a stolen election in Trump-red buses, the group helped build an acutely Trumpian coalition that included sitting and incoming members of Congress, rank-and-file voters and the 'de-platformed' extremists and conspiracy theorists promoted on its home page." Women for America First was instrumental in starting one of the first "Stop the Steal" Facebook groups—"shut down within 22 hours for posts that the platform said could lead to violence."
- Two of the five people who died during the Capitol assault were women—one who was shot dead by a Capitol police officer and another who was trampled to death by the mob.
- The language used by various Trump supporters who reinforced Trump's denial of his loss and his cry of victimization was bellicose and accusatory in tone:
  ° Newt Gingrich on Fox predicted that Trump supporters would "erupt in rage."
  ° Representative Kevin McCarthy on Fox said, "Everyone who's listening, do not be quiet, do not be silent about this. We cannot let this to happen before our very eyes."
  ° Senator Lindsay Graham on Fox said, "They can all go to hell as far as I am concerned—I've had it with these people. Let's fight back. We lose elections because they cheat us."
  ° Senator Marsha Blackburn of Tennessee, via a beamed video appearance, stoked the crowd at a DC Trump rally on December 12, 2020, "Hey there, all of you happy warrior freedom fighters, we're glad you're there standing up for the Constitution, for liberty, for justice."
  ° Trump adviser Michael Flynn "publicly raised the notion that the president should use martial law to force a revote in swing states."
  ° As the Women for America First organized another multiple state bus tour, on December 19, 2020, Kylie Jane Kremer (Amy

Kremer's daughter) tweeted to Trump that the calvary "is coming, Mr. President."[51]

° At the Tactical Response Marksman Training Center in Nashville, Tennesee, Kylie Kremer and Jennifer Lawrence helped the owner of the training center develop a Facebook video "of themselves cradling assault weapons and flanking [Dustin] Stockton, who narrated, 'See, in America, we love our Second Amendment like we love our women: strong. Isn't that right, girls?'"

° Couy Griffin, founder of Cowboys for Trump, stated, "We need our president to be confirmed through the states on the 6th. And right after that, we're going to have to declare martial law."

° On January 6th, Rudy Giuliani took the stage, backed by the Village People's track "Macho Man," and said, "If we are wrong, we will be made fools of. But if we are right, a lot of them will go to jail. So let's have trial by combat. . . . I'm willing to stake my reputation, the president is willing to stake his reputation on the fact that we're going to find criminality there."

° At the January 5 rally at Freedom Plaza, Cindy Chafian, a former organizer for Women for America First, said, "What we are doing is unprecedented. We are standing at the precipice of history, and we are ready to take our country back. We heard your call [Mr. President]. We are here for you. I stand with the Proud Boys, because I am tired of the lies."

° Another speaker, Pastor Greg Locke of Tennessee, spoke of a fight between "good and evil."

° Author and journalist Mab Segrest reported on the threatening words of Congressman Madison Cawthorn from North Carolina, who spoke at the January 6, 2021, rally/march: He "urged listeners to tell members of Congress, 'You know what? If you don't start supporting election integrity, I'm coming after you, Madison Cawthorn is coming after you. Everybody is coming after you.'" Segrest also reported that "Representative Cawthorn has stated that he was 'armed' while on the House floor on January 6."[52]

• By the time the bus tour reached West Monroe, Louisiana, on New Year's Day, Trump had tweeted five times over that day about the rally at the Ellipse in DC on January 6.

• The January 6 rally became "a White House production. . . . The president discussed the speaking lineup, as well as the music to be played." "Gloria," a 1982 song by Laura Branigan and an apparent favorite of Trump's, was played in the background before Trump took the stage. Curiously, the music set included tracks one might hear at a funeral: Celine Dion's "My Heart Will Go On," Linkin Park's "In the End," Elton John's "Funeral for a Friend," Pink Floyd's "Brain Damage," Linkin Park's "I Tried So Hard," and Elton John's "Candle in the Wind" and "Goodbye Yellow Brick Road." Giuliani took the stage to the Village People's "Macho Man." It's difficult to imagine this was Trump's playlist.

- The rally "had taken on new branding, the 'March to Save America.' Its policy wing, the Rule of Law Defense Fund, sent out a robo-call that said, 'We will march to the Capitol building and call on Congress to stop the steal.'"[53]
- Once the president was involved, several speakers were bumped from the January 6 rally to the January 5 evening rally at Freedom Plaza.
- The former president took the stage shortly before 1:00 p.m., "calling on the tens of thousands before him to carry his message to the Republicans in the Capitol: 'You'll never take back our country with weakness.'"[54]

On Tuesday, February 9, 2021, the US Senate began Trump's second impeachment, based on an article of impeachment from the US House of Representatives. Trump was charged with "inciting violence against the government of the United States." Five days later, the Senate voted to acquit Trump, thus effectively sounding the death knell of the Republican Party. Trump will metastasize throughout the party, branding it further as a racist, Trump-centric, white supremacist party. It will be a party that worships a personality who keeps opening up the wound slavery left on Black and white America. Trump's nonconviction vote will have disastrous effects on our country. Trump's base will dwell in the delusion that he cares about them as people. Their resentment and rage will grow because they remain convinced that Trump's reelection was stolen from him. Trump's loyalty will remain totally to himself. Rucker and Leonnig pointed out a profound truth: Trump's presidency was "powered by solipsism. From the moment Trump swore an oath to defend the Constitution and commit to serve the nation, he governed largely to protect and promote himself. . . . Trump's North Star was the perpetuation of his own power, even when it meant imperiling our shaky democracy. Public trust in American government, already weakened through years of polarizing political dysfunction, took a body blow."[55]

When Trump's behavior is compared with the known behavior of white male racist slave masters, how does he stack up? How does Trump and his party compare to the collective Marse? Let me count the ways.

- He sees himself as a member of the "master" race—the ruling race.

- He embodies the legacy of racist white supremacy intertwined in American politics since the founding of our nation.
- He is devoid of empathy.
- He lives in moral isolation.
- His lack of intellectual curiosity will keep him forever from contemplating the chronic, traumatic effects of American slavery on Black (and other people of color) and white people, including himself.
- He fraudulently garners support from the American Christian right, proclaiming that America is a white Christian nation only.
- He does not lose any sleep over separating families of color from one another.
- He sees himself and his party as the defenders of white America because they fear that "whiteness" and its inherent purity is in jeopardy.
- The militant wings of the Trump party see themselves as the defenders of white dominance.
- He views people of color through a dehumanizing lens.
- As the *Hollywood Access* tape illustrated, he feels entitled to see women as sexual objects.
- He is committed to policies that suppress the Black vote.
- He sees people of color as hostile people and denies his own intense fear of Black people.
- He supports the use of militant terror as a means of controlling his enemies.
- Psychologically, he swims in a sea of swirling conspiracies, most of which are delusional projections. He believes the election was stolen from him because that's what he tried to do in 2016. Conspiracies work for Trump and his supporters because they provide a place (a construct) upon which to project their fears and delusions.
- He has a profound paranoid streak: "There's dynamite behind every door," he told Bob Woodward.[56]
- He employs "splitting" frequently, simplistically dividing his world into "good" and "bad" people, or, said another way, "red" and "blue," or "loyal" or "not loyal."
- As an aspiring tyrant, he has no guilt.
- If asked, he would probably say that slavery was an acceptable way to build our republic.
- He sees himself as a revolutionary, although it is more a "role" for him than anything genuine.
- He sees no particular problem with Black bodies being a continued site of violence.

- He supports the maintenance of a massive penal system that mostly controls people of color.
- He finds personal advantage in promoting Lost Cause ideology, even though he probably couldn't explain the concept if asked.
- He considers making money vitally important and depends on keeping society unjust and unequal.
- As the riot at the Capitol demonstrated, he is not above trying to instill terror in others to achieve his ends. The signature method by white supremacists throughout American history has been an unrelenting campaign to control others through fear, intimidation, and terror.
- If push comes to shove, he will hang his base out to dry, claiming that he did not encourage or call them to DC on January 5 and 6, 2021. It was their own doing. He was just an innocent bystander who got blindsided by their decisions and actions.
- To save his skin, he will show no loyalty to anyone and will throw under the bus anyone or any group he wants to disengage from. In December 2020 at the second "Million MAGA March," a man named Nick Fuentes shouted through a bullhorn, "At the first Million MAGA March, we promised that if the G.O.P. would not do everything in their power to keep Trump in office that we would destroy the G.O.P." The crowd's response: "Destroy the G.O.P.! Destroy the G.O.P.!"[57]

Trump Cuddling Confederate Battle Flag. *Noncaptioned editorial cartoon by Kevin Siers, July 18, 2019. Reprinted by permission of the Charlotte Observer.*

On February 12, 2021, the US Senate voted to acquit Donald J. Trump on a bogus technicality, despite a compelling and successful prosecution. The rich irony is that the technicality used by a minority of senators to avoid convicting Trump is that the Senate did not have jurisdiction over Trump because he had become a private citizen. This in effect meant that these forty-three Republican senators, by their not guilty vote, asserted that Trump was no longer president, despite his claim (lie number 2) that he had won. The impeachment trial outcome was not a surprise. Trump's ownership of the party remains strong and he and it will wreak havoc on the United States for many years. Given that many of his supporters see both the Republican and Democratic parties as not serving their interests, Trump's loyal followers may well come after members of either party. The insurrectionists, incited by Trump, targeted anyone and everyone they saw as traitors—members of the so-called surrender caucus—to their president. As Ted Lieu of California, one of the House impeachment managers, stated during the second impeachment trial, the president "wasn't just coming [to the Capitol] for one or two people. Or Democrats like me. He was coming for you, for Democratic and Republican senators. He was coming for all of us. Just as the mob did, at his direction."[58] I would add that the video evidence of the Capitol attack showed that the rioters were coming for anyone—Capitol and DC Metropolitan police included—who tried to defend the Capitol and its occupants from their onslaught. They aimed vicious racist slurs at Black officers and called the police "traitors" as they pummeled them brutally.

In his self-centered head, Trump remains steadfast that he won the election, remaining a maligned, victimized target of election fraud. Michelle Goldberg reported that "according to a new survey by a project of the American Enterprise Institute, 66 percent of Republicans believe that Biden's victory was illegitimate. Thirty-nine percent of Republicans agree with the statement, 'If elected leaders will not protect America, the people must do it themselves even if it requires violent actions.'"[59] What does this mean? It means that, even though Trump betrayed America by ignoring and downplaying COVID-19, by falsely claiming he won the election, and by inciting an insurrection against the US Congress, his own vice president, and the Capitol building itself, Trump will continue his toxic victimization stance and millions of his followers will continue to believe him and question (and challenge) the legitimacy of the Biden-Harris administration. It means that Trump will attempt to lead a vendetta against the seven Republican senators who voted for his conviction. It means that a dangerous, militant wing of the Trump base will feel empowered to defend Trump and attack those people and institutions perceived as his enemies. Our country is at a dangerous crossroads. Evidence of the danger our country is in: There were "22 million guns sold in the US in 2020, up 64 percent from 2019."[60]

Many establishment members of the Republican Party may not truly understand the militancy fueling the white supremacist faction of Trump's base, but they need to. Their exoneration of Trump has reinforced his claimed false legitimacy of remaining in the office of the presidency. CNN reported statements made January 20, 2021, on the website Infowars by Stewart Rhodes, the national leader of the Oath Keepers: "'You gotta declare this regime to be illegitimate. You got to declare everything that comes out of King Biden's mouth as illegitimate—null and void from the inception because he is not a legitimate president.'" According to this same CNN report, "Rhodes is still peddling the falsehood that the election was illegitimate. He says Biden's administration and supporters in Congress should be seen as an occupying enemy force and issues warnings about what he claims are 365 million armed patriots ready to 'rise up . . . There is going to be resistance. The only question is what will be the spark,' Rhodes said in a January 30 interview on Infowars. 'They [leftists] keep pushing . . . That is why it's important . . . Let them be the ones who draw first blood. Then you defend.'" CNN also reported that "as early as July 2019, Rhodes told Alex Jones on Infowars that if Trump was not re-elected 'we won't accept the results' and will have 'no choice but to fight.'"[61]

Even though many Republican officials reportedly loathe Trump, many remain fearful of him and his base. Others, like Republican congressmen Paul Gosar, Mo Brooks, Josh Hawley, Ted Cruz, and Andy Biggs, sit tall in the saddle for Trump. Goldberg accurately labels these pro-Trumpers his "enablers."

Despite his not being convicted and thus not disqualified from ever again seeking office in the United States, as a private citizen, Trump is now a legitimate subject for civil and criminal investigations, in federal as well as various states' jurisdictions. As David Frum wrote, "But if justice failed, democratic self-preservation is working. Trump lost the presidency, and that loss held despite his attacks on the vote and the counting of the vote. His party split against him on this second round of impeachable offenses. He has lost his immunity to civil suit and his impunity against federal indictment. The world is crashing down on his head."[62]

I do not share Frum's confidence about the world crashing down on Trump's head—at least not politically. His nonconviction by the US Senate, for the time being, effectively legitimized the former president's direct role in the January 6, 2021, insurrection. Trump got a pass. His entitlement, impunity, and narcissistic immunity were pathologically reinforced. White supremacy will remain a weapon in his hands. He will proclaim that he is heir apparent to his distorted view of himself as a savior, a revolutionary. The militant wing of his base will continue to seethe about its perceived goal to eliminate a corrupt, incompetent government that defrauded Trump out of his reelection. By the conclusion of the Conservative Political Action Conference (CPAC), held February 25–28, 2021, in Orlando, Florida, Trump rose up like the ghost of Marse, hailed as the grand kingpin of his party. It is now *his* party. In front of an adoring crowd, he proclaimed, "We have the Republican Party." *Omerta* was confirmed among the attendees and implicit orders went out about who—because of their brazen disloyalty—needs a serious lashing or worse. Among his targets were Representative Liz Cheney and Senator Mitch McConnell. If any policies came out of the CPAC meeting, high on its agenda were ways to ramp up voter suppression across the nation, with the primary goal being to make it harder for people of color to vote. According to the *Economist*, "He continued to insist he had actually won the presidential contest. Emboldened by a party that has thrown its lot in with a rejected president (anomalous in the modern political era), Mr. Trump continues to reiterate, without any new evidence, that his defeat was fraudulent. The commitment to this belief is complete."[63] The success with which Trump and his enablers maintain the election lie (lie number 2) will remain a corrosive effect on our democratic experiment and on the very nature of truth itself.

By the time this book is published, much more will have come to light about who was involved and why in the deadly insurrection of January 6, 2021. Perhaps our nation will have experienced more political violence. The Republican Party will most likely continue to shuffle in an awkward political dance as the "Trump Party," fueled by an imaginary and delusional white utopia. There remains the potential for the emergence of a third political party. The 2022 election campaigns will be gearing up. As I contemplate where America is likely to be a year from now, let us not lose sight of the continued throughline of racist white supremacy from 1619 forward and the striking similarities between the behaviors, assumptions, and psychological makeup of the antebellum southern white slave masters and the former president and his minions, who are almost as openly racist as Marse was in his day. Their defense mechanisms have kicked into high gear as they deal with their tremendous fears of being further marginalized as free people of color around them have increasing sway over important aspects of their lives and our nation's future.

And, amid the increasing devastation of COVID-19, the cry for personal freedom from anti-vaxxers and anti-maskers adds a new dimension to Founding Father Patrick Henry's declaration, "Give me liberty, or give me death."

· *Appendix A* ·

Adaptive and Maladaptive Slaveholder Psychological Defense Mechanisms[1]

EIGHT COMMON TYPES OF ADAPTIVE DEFENSE MECHANISMS

Type one contains eight psychological defenses considered to be highly adaptive and positive. They facilitate the relatively mentally healthy person's interactions with others and society. These adaptive defenses are:

1. *Anticipation:* The individual appropriately thinks through his possible emotional reactions to future events and considers alternative responses or solutions.
2. *Affiliation:* The individual seeks help or support from others.
3. *Altruism:* The individual dedicates himself to helping others.
4. *Humor:* The individual emphasizes the humor or irony of the situation.
5. *Self-assertion:* The individual communicates his or her thoughts and feelings in a direct, noncoercive, nonmanipulative way.
6. *Self-observation:* The individual reflects on his or her internal thoughts and feelings and responds appropriately.
7. *Sublimation:* The individual puts his or her potentially maladaptive feelings or behavioral impulses into appropriate, socially acceptable behavior.
8. *Suppression:* The individual intentionally avoids thinking about disturbing issues.

TWENTY-THREE TYPES OF COMMON
MALADAPTIVE DEFENSE MECHANISMS

The second type contains twenty-three psychological defenses that are maladaptive, either by their very nature, or emerge out of the decline or compromise of one or more of the individual's adaptive defenses (e.g., a self-assertive individual becomes a bully). These twenty-three defenses are clustered under six categorical descriptors of levels—degrees of severity—of functioning. If they were shown on a Likert scale, level 1—"compromised"—would be at position one on the left end, with level 6—"failure"—escalated at number six on the right end.

> 1 Compromised—2 Minor Image-Distorting—3 Disavowal—
> 4 Major Image-Distorting—5 Behavioral Action—6 Failure

Maladaptive Defense Mechanisms

1. A "Compromised" Level
   a) *Displacement:* The individual transfers a feeling about another person or object onto a different, less threatening person or object.
   b) *Dissociation:* The individual's usually integrated functions of consciousness, memory, perception of self or the environment break down.
   c) *Intellectualization:* The individual excessively uses abstract thinking or making generalizations to control threatening issues.
   d) *Isolation of affect:* The individual separates thoughts from feelings originally held about something and loses touch with the original feelings that accompanied an event.
   e) *Reaction formation:* The individual substitutes diametrically opposed behavior, thoughts, and feelings in response to his or her unacceptable thoughts or feelings.
   f) *Repression:* The individual dispels or banishes his or her disturbing wishes, thoughts, or experiences from conscious awareness.
   g) *Undoing:* The individual says things or acts in ways that are designed to negate or make amends symbolically for his or her unacceptable thoughts, feelings, or actions.

2. A "Minor, Image-Distorting" Level
   a) *Devaluation:* The individual attributes exaggerated negative qualities to self or others.

b) *Idealization:* The individual attributes exaggerated positive qualities to others.[2]

c) *Omnipotence:* The individual acts as if he or she has special powers or abilities that are superior to others.

3. A "Disavowal" Level

a) *Denial:* The individual refuses to acknowledge some painful aspect of external reality or subjective experience.

b) *Projection:* The individual falsely attributes his own unacceptable feelings, thoughts, or impulses to another person or group.[3]

c) *Rationalization:* The individual conceals his or her own true motivations through the development of elaborate, self-serving, incorrect explanations.

4. A "Major Image-Distorting" Level

a) *Autistic fantasy:* The individual engages in excessive daydreaming as a substitute for human relationships, often leading to ineffective actions or inefficient problem-solving.

b) *Projective identification:* Unlike simple projection, the individual remains aware of his or her unacceptable thoughts and feelings, but misattributes them as being justifiable reactions to the other person or group.

c) *Splitting of self-image or image of others:* The individual experiences positive and negative feelings, thoughts, or impulses that are not integrated (i.e., a person might be all good for some period of time, and then become all bad).

5. A Behavioral "Action" Level

a) *Acting out:* This person acts with little to no input from his or her thoughts and feelings.

b) *Apathetic withdrawal:* The individual, with little to no manifest feeling, withdraws from human interaction.

c) *Help-rejecting complaining:* The individual simultaneously rejects offers of help in response to his or her chorus of ongoing complaints.

d) *Passive aggression:* The individual expresses his or her anger at another person through indirect, unassertive ways. The passive-aggressive actions are typically accompanied with a facade of overt compliance.

6. A "Failure" Level
   a) *Delusional projection:* The individual deceives himself or herself by projecting false beliefs onto another.
   b) *Psychotic denial:* The individual displays a gross impairment in reality testing by denying objective experiences.
   c) *Psychotic distortion:* The individual's reality perceptions are bizarre.

· *Appendix B* ·

Psychological Defense Mechanisms

These eleven psychological defense mechanisms derive from an applied theory that certain individuals—the so-called elite masters—dedicated to the maintenance of a bound labor system that necessitated the subjugation, domination, control, and punishment of people who were perceived as less than human and who were to be held against their will for life would generate maladaptive psychological and behavioral responses in the masters. In other words, the identification of these eleven defense mechanisms is predicated on the straightforward assumption that slaveholding would naturally be stressful for the slaveholders, who in turn would develop defense mechanisms to control, deny, or mitigate their stresses and anxieties. These eleven defenses are to be differentiated from the application of the four common, frequently used maladaptive defenses—denial, projection, delusional projection, and rationalization—identified in appendix A.

The existence of southern chattel slavery created a unique context in which it seems reasonable to assume that American southern white male elite slaveholders would develop additional, contextually specific, idiosyncratic psychological defenses to counter internal and external stressors and threats which adhered to the institution of slavery. These eleven conditions are racist, enslavement-centric terms.

ELEVEN IDIOSYNCRATIC, SLAVERY-SPECIFIC SLAVE MASTER DEFENSE MECHANISMS

- *Black stereotypes:* This is a frequently and commonly applied defense used to simplify the categories of "types" of slaves.

- *Self-deception:* This mechanism allows the master to trick or fool himself about something in the context of slave management or slave relationships that is significant, but which he cannot or will not grasp as the true nature of the situation. Self-deception usually becomes self-destructive because it is initially built upon a false narrative.
- *Splitting:* This is a very primitive, unsophisticated mechanism used to transform complicated matters into simple categories. The individual slave master distorts or reduces his self-image, or complex events, circumstances, or other people—or entire groups or nations or races of people—into simple, either/or categories, such as "good" or "bad" and "good" or "evil."
- *A profound lack of self-criticism:* When applying this defense, the master suspends his judgment and become psychopathologically blind to his own troublesome, self-defeating beliefs and behaviors. His capacity for self-appraisal is maladaptively deficient.
- *Psychopathy:* This defense is quite maladaptive because objects (including people) of his psychopathy can be harmed. Although a person can have psychopathic traits or features in his personality or character, the full-blown psychopath is a man without a conscience, a person unaffected by his emotions, unaffected by guilt, and—the hallmark of this defense—incapable of genuine empathy. He does not think societal norms apply to him and he acts as though he is narcissistically immune to social norms and legal consequences.
- *Christian comfort:* This is a religious defense that allows the believer to suspend his own morality or ethics in favor of the perceived dictates of his Protestant Christian God. The master derived a great comfort from what he accepted as the mandate of his Christian God on the matters of enslaving Black people.
- *Psychologically syntonic slaveholding:* Although highly maladaptive, this defense became creative, because it allowed the master to square and harmonize his beliefs and actions into the job of becoming a tyrant: Owning another human being as property and employing a combination of slave management techniques and violence became a condition he could live with.
- *Paternalism:* Although this descriptor historically has had no attention, as far as I know, to its being considered as a defense mechanism, it does seem to apply in the context of slaveholding. Just as the master sees the slaves as less than human and sees himself as superior because of the color of his skin, the slave master defends himself from all other people by assuming he lives on a male-dominated superior plane. His superiority is supreme. The onset of this defense began when the male of

the species assumed its dominant role. It became a defense mechanism when it was applied in all matters—physically and psychologically. As a defense mechanism, it is used as a forced social contract.

- *Alienation:* This is a defense by which the individual divorces himself from troublesome aspects of his own being. The master doesn't like a part of his makeup, which might lead to a rejection of some beliefs and behaviors that used to be a regular and predictable part of his personality. A person who was a kindhearted soul prior to becoming a slave master might alienate himself from any tendencies toward kindness. Alienation can also extend to other people, in which case the master might reject his slaves as human beings and see them only as a dehumanized piece of property with a monetary value.

- *Psychopathological entitlement:* This defense mechanism lies at the heart of slaveholding because it helps explain how individuals justify that abducting or buying another human being to be one's slave is something to which they are entitled—because of their station in life, the color of their skin, their country of origin, or how much money and power they have. If you drill into the "divine right of kings" or even "manifest destiny," you stumble into the glittering halls of psychopathological entitlement.

- *The onset of a psychotic reality:* It is generally not difficult to know when you are in the presence of a person with a psychotic disorder. When a slave master became psychotic, he was incapable of evaluating his thoughts correctly. He made incorrect inferences from objective reality.

· *Appendix C* ·

A Hypothetical Proslavery Sermon

Ebenezer Ezekiel Memorial
A Reformed Evangelical Presbyterian Church
Mecklenburg County, North Carolina
(Just south of Charlotte)
1860[1]

After the Psalm was completed, Reverend McCracken adjusted his tie and collar to lessen its chaffing of his neck. He grasped his Good Book and strode to the pulpit where it predominated the bare church on its crude, wooden dais, just ever so slightly elevated above the congregation floor level.

"It is wonderful to see everyone here this Sabbath, for these are troublesome times. Let us bow our heads.

"God, we are here today to bless, endorse, and sanctify the many rights you have bestowed upon us. We just want to thank you, Lord, for You have been generous! Our bounty is much. It is You who have blessed us, Oh God, and we are here today to consecrate. As we stand our ground, and stand we will, and affirm the rights You have given us, we lay under a spiritual siege, Oh Lord, for there are many among us in this country who reject Your Word. Reject Your Word, Lord! Northern infidels are attacking Your Word! Let us open our hearts and minds to Your Plan, which guides us in all matters. We, the children of Moses and Noah, pray for Your guidance now. In Jesus's name, Amen."

The congregants numbered about thirty. They were all blood kin. They were all white. Each household held slaves in bondage. While some slave owners and churches had made room for slaves to attend church, usually sitting on a small balcony accessed only by an outside back staircase, Ebenezer Ezekiel Memorial had dispatched with that troublesome policy in the early 1800s. The Synod had voted unanimously to exclude negroes from the

271

sanctity of the "meeting house." White masters sometimes needed to hear from the pastor some biblical guidance about slave management, and it just would not do for the enslaved negroes to be listening to spiritual imperatives well beyond their grasp.

Reverend McCracken opened the Good Book to Genesis 9. He looked at his flock and could see the proud but somewhat worried countenances of many. The congregation both needed and wanted some spiritual fire, to fuel what most thinking southern adults knew was coming.

"God has a Plan for us!" he thundered.

He paused to let the power of this bolt strike and take hold.

"The Lord speaks to us from Genesis 9, verses 18–25."

Most of the congregants opened their Bibles, without even looking, to the ninth chapter of the Bible's first book.

"God, in the Book of Genesis, through his Servant Noah, made manifest the rightful and God-given hierarchy for mankind. The Lord is not ambiguous or unclear about who shall inherit the moral and spiritual leadership of this earth!

"Let us hear God's Word!

The sons of Noah who went forth from the ark were Shem, Ham, and Japheth. Ham was the father of Canaan. These three were the sons of Noah; and from these the whole earth was peopled. Noah was the first tiller of the soil. He planted a vineyard; and he drank of the wine, And became drunk, and lay uncovered in his tent. And Ham, the father of Canaan, saw the nakedness of his father, and told his two brothers outside. Then Shem and Japheth took a garment, laid it upon both of their shoulders, and walked backward and covered the nakedness of their father; their faces were turned away, and they did not see their father's nakedness. When Noah awoke from his wine and knew what his youngest son had done to him, he said, "Cursed be Canaan; a slave of slaves shall he be to his brothers."

"Here endeth the reading of God's Word.

"All of us here know that war is coming. The abolitionists and the papists and the Northern industrialists have been stammering, spouting, spewing their inane false and specious arguments about the evils of slavery. Their arguments have sailed these contentious waters like a sailing ship with no hull. In rejecting slavery, they have rejected God's Word and God's Plan. They have sunk because they rejected the Lord's foundation—His Word!

"Man has created laws to help us govern our selves and each other. God has created his Law, which transcends, triumphs, and is unassailable!

"Noah's son, Ham, disgraced and violated his father. He surreptitiously sneaked into his father's tent, and, upon seeing him unclothed, ran out, mocking his father's nakedness. Noah's other sons, Japheth and Shem, showed the natural respect due their father, and walked into Noah's tent, without making any glance, and covered their father's state.

"Ham had no right to violate the sanctity of his father's tent. The North, with its misguided morality, has no right to violate the sanctity of the South. When Noah woke up and had become conscious of what his son had done, God spoke *through* Noah. The Almighty spoke directly and powerfully *through* Noah, who was a planter just like many of us! God directed his curse of Ham and his son Canaan and all their peoples straight through Noah, straight as an arrow! The Lord tells us later that this curse was but a part of God's larger plan, His Plan of how to repopulate the earth, after the Great Flood."

Reverend McCracken paused to see how his sermon was affecting folks. On other Sabbaths, he sometimes saw one or two sleeping, but not today. Not today. Today was about the preparation of a Holy War. Christian soldiers were marching onward. The Honor of the South and the sanctity of God's Plan were at stake.

"What the Yankee industrialists, Yankee bankers, and meddlesome abolitionists have lost complete sight of is that slavery is part of God's Plan. They are deaf, dumb, and blind to the divine wisdom and beauty of our slave system! This institution of slavery is not something we made up out of whole cloth simply because we wanted free labor!

"As the evils of abolitionism have taken its hold on thousands of weak-minded people, these victims of Satan himself have been blinded from seeing God's Truth. We see God's truth and know He is the light and the way!

"The Lord assigned Black Ham and all his issue to populate Africa . . . AND . . . to be SERVANTS, for eternity, to Shem and Japheth and all their issue. The Lord God made Ham and all his children 'a slave of slaves.' Forever. The negro has but one purpose on this earth and it is to be a slave. All Black Africans are the children of Ham. Just as our ancestors fought the tyranny of the crown, we shall not be overcome by any effort to dictate to us how we run our lives, our laws, our homes, nor our property! God will protect us from this pernicious evil!

"Thus speaketh the Lord, our God. Let us bow our heads in prayer."

Notes

PREFACE

1. Vertical file: 1860s SESSION BOOK, pg. 45, 1867, "Baptism of Coloured Infants and Adults," Sharon Presbyterian Church, Charlotte, NC. It reads, "Sam Robert, son of Sam, servt [servant] H. [Hugh] Kirkpatrick & Caroline [servant of] Dr. Ross." What this means is that Jimmie's great-great-great-grandfather and his great-great-great-grandmother were enslaved, but by two different men, Hugh Kirkpatrick and Dr. Ross, who was likely a neighbor of Hugh.

2. Figure on page xv: Image 35, Schedule 2, p. 205, listing Hugh Kirkpatrick's thirty-four enslaved holdings as recorded in the 1850 Slave Schedules taken during the 1850 census. Ancestry.com, *1850 U.S. Federal Census—Slave Schedules* [database online].

3. Charles B. Dew, *The Making of a Racist: A Southerner Reflects on Family, History, and the Slave Trade* (Charlottesville: University of Virginia Press, 2016).

4. Edward Ball, *Slaves in the Family* (New York: Farrar, Straus and Giroux, 2014).

5. Wendell Berry, *The Hidden Wound* (Berkeley, CA: Counterpoint, 2010).

6. Andrew Delbanco, *The War before the War: Fugitive Slaves and the Struggle for America's Soul from the Revolution to the Civil War* (New York: Penguin, 2019), 50.

INTRODUCTION

1. See Elizabeth Fox-Genovese and Eugene Genovese. *The Mind of the Master Class: History and Faith in the Southern Slaveholders' Worldview* (Cambridge: Cambridge University Press, 2005). See also Eugene Genovese and Elizabeth Fox-Genovese, *Fatal Self-Deception: Slaveholding Paternalism in the Old South* (New York: Cambridge University Press, 2011), and Eugene D. Genovese, *Roll, Jordan, Roll: The World the Slaves Made* (New York, Pantheon, 1974).

2. James L. Roark, *Masters without Slaves: Southern Planters in the Civil War and Reconstruction* (New York: Norton, 1977).
3. Dew, *The Making of a Racist*, 50.
4. Robert Stiles, *Four Years Under Marse Robert*, 3rd ed. (New York: Neale, 1904).
5. Stiles, *Four Years*, 19.
6. Stiles, *Four Years*, 19.
7. Stiles, *Four Years*, 325.
8. Stiles, *Four Years*, 21.

CHRONOLOGY

1. Noel Leo Erskine, Plantation Church: *How African American Religion Was Born in Caribbean Slavery* (New York: Oxford University Press, 2014), n. 14.
2. Hector Avalos, *Slavery, Abolitionism, and the Ethics of Biblical Scholarship* (Sheffield, UK: Sheffield Phoenix Press, 2013), 199.
3. Erskine, 25
4. Avalos, 2013, 198, citing Jan Rogozinski, *A Brief History of the Caribbean: From the Arawak and the Carib to the Present* (New York: Penguin Putnam, 1999).
5. Erskine, 61.
6. Peter Kolchin, *American Slavery 1619–1877* (New York: Hill and Wang, 2003), 10.
7. Erskine, 27.
8. Walter Edgar, *South Carolina: A History* (Columbia: University of South Carolina Press, 1998), 39.
9. William S. Powell, *North Carolina through Four Centuries* (Chapel Hill: University of North Carolina Press, 1989), 53. Powell informs us the boundaries of this grant ran from the Albemarle Sound, down to the St. Mary's River, on the Florida-Georgia boundary, and all the way west to the Pacific Ocean. They went back to the King and asked for even more, and received lands to the Virginia line and south to the area near Cape Canaveral, FL. This last was called "Carolina" after King Charles.
10. See Delbanco, 2019.
11. See Feely in Larry E. Tise and Jeffrey J. Crow, eds., *New Voyages to Carolina: Reinterpreting North Carolina History* (Chapel Hill: The University of North Carolina Press, 2017).
12. Kolchin, 7.
13. See Feeley, "Intercolonial Conflict and Cooperation During the Tuscarora War" in Tise and Crow, 2017.
14. Mary Norton Kratt, *Charlotte: Spirit of the New South* (Winston-Salem: John F. Blair, Publisher, 1992).
15. David Brion Davis, *The Problem of Slavery in Western Culture* (Ithaca, NY: Cornell University Press, 1966), 305.
16. Marvin L. Michael Kay and Lorin Lee Cary, *Slavery in North Carolina, 1748–1775* (Chapel Hill: The University of North Carolina Press, 1995), 10.

17. *Princeton Alumni Weekly*, November 8, 2017.

18. Kratt, 17.

19. Kratt, 14.

20. Dan L. Morrill, *Historic Charlotte: An Illustrated History of Charlotte and Mecklenburg County* (San Antonio, TX: Historical Publishing Network, 2011), 16.

21. Barry Aron Vann, *In Search of Ulster-Scots Land: The Birth and Geotheological Imagings of a Transatlantic People, 1603-1703* (Columbia, SC: University of South Carolina press, 2008), 151.

22. Morrill, 16.

23. James G. Leyburn, *The Scotch Irish: A Social History* (Chapel Hill: The University of North Carolina Press, 1962).

24. Fox-Genovese and Genovese, 71.

25. Erskine, 181–82.

26. Avalos, 2013, 260.

27. Kolchin, 79.

28. Howard Zinn, *A Peoples History of the United States* (New York: HarperCollins, 2003), 171.

29. Morrill, 20.

30. Avalos, 2013, 277.

31. Erskine, 154.

32. Morrill, 20.

33. Erskine, 65.

34. Ray A. King, *A History of the Associate Reformed Presbyterian Church* (Charlotte, NC: Board of Christian Education of the Associate Reformed Presbyterian Church, 1966), 85.

35. Ned Sublette and Constance C. Sublette, *The American Slave Coast: A History of the Slave Breeding Industry* (Chicago: Lawrence Hill, 2016).

36. Delbanco, 2019.

37. Kenneth M. Stampp, *The Peculiar Institution: Slavery in the Ante-Bellum South* (New York: Vintage, 1989), 265.

38. Davis, 231.

39. Greenwood, 22.

40. Karen F. McCarthy, *The Other Irish: The Scots-Irish Rascals Who Made America* (New York: Sterling, 2011), 186.

41. Delbanco, 2019.

42. King, 112–13.

43. John Patrick Daly, *When Slavery Was Called Freedom: Evangelicalism, Proslavery, and the Causes of the Civil War* (Lexington: University Press of Kentucky, 2002), 77,

44. McCarthy, 191.

45. Sharon Presbyterian Church, *Sharing Our Heritage* (Charlotte, NC: Jostens, 2006), 19.

46. Morrill, 17.

47. Janette Thomas Greenwood, *Bittersweet Legacy: The Black and White "Better Classes" in Charlotte, 1850–1910* (Chapel Hill: University of North Carolina Press, 1994), 21.

48. Carol Anderson, *White Rage: The Unspoken Truth of Our Racial Divide* (New York: Bloomsbury, 2016), 18.

49. Zinn, 187.

50. See Charles B. Dew's monograph, *Apostles of Disunion: Southern Secession Commissioners and the Causes of the Civil War* (Charlottesville: University of Virginia Press, 2001).

51. Dew, 2001, 19.

52. Ted Widmer, ed., *Disunion: A History of the Civil War* (New York: Oxford Press, 2016), 30.

53. Kolchin, 95.

54. Anderson, 11.

55. Widmer, 40.

56. Bruce Levine, *The Fall of the House of Dixie: The Civil War and the Social Revolution That Transformed the South* (New York: Random House, 2014), 4.

57. Zinn, 171.

58. Erskine, 65.

59. Morrill, 17.

60. Stampp, 30.

61. Kolchin, 94.

62. Levine, 2014, 3.

63. As explained in greater detail in the book, the commonly attributed definition of the term "planter" linked by the Federal census Bureau to persons owning at least twenty slaves is likely not accurate.

64. Morrill, 17.

65. Levine, 2014, 5.

66. Levine, 2014, 5.

67. Levine, 2014, 6.

68. Levine, 2014, 7.

69. Levine, 2014, 8.

70. Dew, 2001, 23.

71. Delbanco, 2019.

CHAPTER 1

1. James Oakes, *The Ruling Race: A History of American Slaveholders* (New York: Norton, 1998), x.

2. Oakes, *The Ruling Race*, 43.

3. Levine, *The Fall of the House of Dixie*, 4.

4. Stephanie McCurry, *Masters of Small Worlds: Yeoman Households, Gender Relations, and the Political Culture of the Antebellum South Carolina Low Country* (New York: Oxford University Press, 1995).

5. McCurry, *Masters of Small Worlds*, 46.

6. Oakes, *The Ruling Race*, 51.

7. Kolchin, *American Slavery*, 30.

8. Kolchin, *American Slavery*, 30.

9. Stampp, *The Peculiar Institution*, 29–30, n. 8.

10. Levine, *The Fall of the House of Dixie*, 4–5, n. 9.

11. Stampp, *The Peculiar Institution*, 30–31.

12. Roark, *Masters without Slaves*, ix.

13. *Merriam-Webster's Collegiate Dictionary*, 11th ed. (Springfield, MA: Merriam-Webster, Incorporated, 2020), 1452.

14. *Merriam-Webster's*, 1171.

15. Oakes, *The Ruling Race*, 52.

16. Oakes, *The Ruling Race*, 10.

17. Chalmers Davidson, *The Last Foray: The South Carolina Planters of 1860: A Sociological Study* (Columbia: University of South Carolina Press, 1971).

18. Kolchin, *American Slavery*, xii.

19. Levine, *The Fall of the House of Dixie*, 4, n. 8.

20. Personal communication with Dr. Thomas Cole, Librarian, Robinson-Spangler Carolina Room, Charlotte-Mecklenburg Main Library, Charlotte, NC, November 12, 2020; see US Census Bureau, *Measuring America: The Decennial Censuses from 1790 to 2000* (Washington, DC: US Census Bureau, 2007), https://www.census.gov/history/pdf/measuringamerica.pdf.

21. Jane Turner Censer, *North Carolina Planters and Their Children 1800–1860* (Baton Rouge: Louisiana State University Press, 1984), xix.

22. Levine, *The Fall of the House of Dixie*, 4.

23. William Kauffman Scarborough, *Masters of the Big House: Elite Slaveholders of the Mid-Nineteenth-Century South* (Baton Rouge: Louisiana State University Press, 2003), 429.

24. Scarborough, *Masters of the Big House*, 475.

25. Scarborough, *Masters of the Big House*, 1–2.

26. Scarborough, *Masters of the Big House*, 1.

27. Levine, *The Fall of the House of Dixie*, 7.

28. Levine, *The Fall of the House of Dixie*, 43, n. 55; see also Dew, *Apostles of Disunion*.

29. Oakes, *The Ruling Race*, 39.

30. Edward E. Baptist, *The Half Has Never Been Told: Slavery and the Making of American Capitalism* (New York: Basic Books, 2014), see table 7/1, 246.

31. Oakes, *The Ruling Race*, 3–4.

32. Christopher Leslie Brown, *Moral Capital: Foundations of British Abolitionism* (Chapel Hill: University of North Carolina Press, 2006), 122, n. 24.

33. Bertram Wyatt-Brown, *Southern Honor: Ethics in the Old South* (Oxford: Oxford University Press, 2007).

34. Fox-Genovese and Genovese, *The Mind of the Master Class*.

35. Genovese, *Roll, Jordan, Roll*, 5.

36. Genovese, *Roll, Jordan, Roll*, 93.

37. Genovese, *Roll, Jordan, Roll*, 94, quoting Dr. Francis Lieber at n. 23.

38. Genovese, *Roll, Jordan, Roll*, 95, n. 25.

39. Scarborough, *Masters of the Big House*, 1.

40. Genovese, *Roll, Jordan, Roll*, 96–97.

41. Genovese, *Roll, Jordan, Roll*, 94. Genovese notes that he believes this diary entry was most likely written in 1861, not 1855.

42. Daly, *When Slavery Was Called Freedom*, 7.

43. Fox-Genovese and Genovese, *The Mind of the Master Class*, 490.

44. Harry S. Stout, *Upon the Altar of the Nation: A Moral History of the Civil* War (New York: Penguin, 2006), xxi.

45. Greenwood, *Bittersweet Legacy*, 26.

46. Daly, *When Slavery Was Called Freedom*, 13.

47. Daly, *When Slavery Was Called Freedom*, 13.

48. In my family, these close relatives were affectionately referred to as "kissing cousins."

49. Scarborough, *Masters of the Big House*, 19.

50. Michael O'Brien, ed., *All Clever Men, Who Make Their Way: Critical Discourse in the Old South* (Fayetteville: University of Arkansas Press, 1982), 1.

51. O'Brien, *All Clever Men*, 20.

52. O'Brien, *All Clever Men*, 21.

53. Daly, *When Slavery Was Called Freedom*, 89.

54. Fox-Genovese and Genovese, *The Mind of the Master Class*, 7.

55. Fox-Genovese and Genovese, *The Mind of the Master Class*, 7.

56. Fox-Genovese and Genovese, *The Mind of the Master Class*, 370.

57. Walter Johnson, *Soul by Soul: Life inside the Antebellum Slave Market* (Cambridge, MA: Harvard University Press, 1999), 13.

58. Johnson, *Soul by Soul*, 13.

59. See Michael Tadman, *Speculators and Slaves: Masters, Traders, and Slaves in the Old South* (Madison: University of Wisconsin Press, 1996).

60. Walter Johnson, *River of Dark Dreams: Slavery and Empire in the Cotton Kingdom* (Cambridge, MA: Belknap Press, 2013), 14.

61. Harriet Beecher Stowe, *Uncle Tom's Cabin: Life among the Lowly* (1852; Lexington, KY: Black & White Publications, 2015).

62. Edward Ball, *Slaves in the Family*, 56. See his conversation with relative Dorothy, 50–63.

63. Willie Lee Rose, *A Documentary History of Slavery in North America* (Athens: University of Georgia Press, 1999), 151.

64. See Daly, *When Slavery Was Called Freedom*.

65. Diane Miller Sommerville, *Aberration of Mind: Suicide and Suffering in the Civil War–Era South* (Chapel Hill: University of North Carolina Press, 2018), 6.

66. Paul Babiak and Robert D. Hare, *Snakes in Suits: When Psychopaths Go to Work*. New York: HarperCollins, 2009, Kindle, 408–14.

67. Stampp, *The Peculiar Institution*, 14.

68. Fox-Genovese and Genovese, *The Mind of the Master Class*, 201.

69. Scarborough, *Masters of the Big House*, 287, n. 21.

70. Daly, *When Slavery Was Called Freedom*, 307.

71. Ball, *Slaves in the Family*, ix.

72. Fox-Genovese and Genovese, *The Mind of the Master Class*, 103.

73. Wyatt-Brown, *Southern Honor*, 3.

74. Wyatt-Brown, *Southern Honor*, 5.

75. Wyatt-Brown, *Southern Honor*, 14.

76. Drew Gilpin Faust, *A Sacred Circle: The Dilemma of the Intellectual in the Old South, 1840–1860* (Baltimore: Johns Hopkins University Press, 1977), 112.

77. Paul Finkelman, *Defending Slavery: Proslavery Thought in the Old South: A Brief History with Documents* (Boston: Bedford/St. Martin's, 2003), 61.

78. Edmund Ruffin, *The Political Economy of Slavery; or, The Institution Considered in Regard to Its Influence on Public Wealth and the General Welfare* (Washington, DC: Lemuel Towers, 1853); reprinted in Paul Finkelman, *Defending Slavery: Proslavery Thought in the Old South. A Brief History with Documents* (Boston: Bedford/St. Martin's, 2003), 76.

79. Larry E. Tise, *Proslavery: A History of the Defense of Slavery in America, 1701–1840* (Athens: University of Georgia Press, 1987), 344–45.

80. Genovese and Fox-Genovese, *Fatal Self-Deception*, 5.

81. Sven Beckert, *Empire of Cotton: A Global History* (New York: Vintage Books, 2014), 100.

82. Beckert, *Empire of Cotton*, 104, 105.

83. Beckert, *Empire of Cotton*, 105, 106.

84. Beckert, *Empire of Cotton*, 110.

85. Delbanco, *The War before the War*, 26–27.

86. Delbanco, *The War before the War*, 210.

87. Oakes, *The Ruling Race*, 12.

88. Tadman, *Speculators and Slaves*, 12.

89. Baptist, *The Half Has Never Been Told*, 179.

90. Ira Berlin, *Many Thousands Gone: The First Two Centuries of Slavery in North America* (Cambridge, MA: Belknap Press, 1998), 96, 99.

91. Matthew Karp, *This Vast Southern Empire: Slaveholders at the Helm of American Foreign Policy* (Cambridge, MA: Harvard University Press, 2016), 4.

92. Roark, *Masters without Slaves*, x.

93. Berry, *The Hidden Wound*.

94. Genovese, *Roll, Jordan, Roll*, 96–97.

CHAPTER 2

1. Ibram X. Kendi, *Stamped from the Beginning: The Definitive History of Racist Ideas in America* (New York: Nation Books, 2016), n. 3, referencing Washington, *Anti-Blackness*, and quoting from Silverman, *Life and Times of Cotton Mather*, 59.

2. David Livingstone Smith, *Less Than Human: Why We Demean, Enslave, and Exterminate Others* (New York: St. Martin's Press, 2011), 107, 114.

3. Kendi, *Stamped*, 291.

4. Johnson, *River of Dark Dreams*, 372.

5. Johnson, *River of Dark Dreams*, 373; see n. 15.

6. Jonathan M. Metzl, *Dying of Whiteness: How the Politics of Racial Resentment Is Killing America's Heartland* (New York: Basic Books, 2019), 270.

7. Zinn, *A People's History*, 72.

8. Smith, *Less Than Human*, 1–2.

9. Kendi, *Stamped*, 50, 51.

10. Kendi, *Stamped*, 48.

11. Smith, *Less Than Human*, 2. In this book, Smith brilliantly articulates his theory of "dehumanization."

12. Smith, *Less Than Human*, 26.

13. Genovese, *Roll, Jordan, Roll*, 93.

14. This belief belies an interesting corollary to how and why many privileged white people believe that the poor and people of color should not be helped.

15. McCarthy, *The Other Irish*, 73.

16. Genovese, *Roll, Jordan, Roll*, 165.

17. Genovese, *Roll, Jordan, Roll*, 165.

18. King, *A History*, 111.

19. King, *A History*, 112.

20. Oakes, *The Ruling Race*, 195.

21. Genovese and Fox-Genovese, *Fatal Self-Deception*, 25.

22. See Tadman, *Speculators and Slaves*.

23. Genovese and Fox-Genovese, *Fatal Self-Deception*, 31.

24. Genovese and Fox-Genovese, *Fatal Self-Deception*, 27.

25. Daly, *When Slavery Was Called Freedom*, 16.

26. Kendi, *Stamped*, 41.

27. Kendi, *Stamped*, 43.

28. Diane Miller Sommerville, *Rape and Race in the Nineteenth-Century South* (Chapel Hill: University of North Carolina Press, 2004), 65.

29. Genovese and Fox-Genovese, *Fatal Self-Deception*, 58.

30. Delbanco, *The War before the War*, 240.

31. See John E. B. Myers, *Child Protection in America: Past, Present and Future* (New York: Oxford University Press, 2006).

32. Sommerville, *Rape and Race*, 65.

33. Wyatt-Brown, *Southern Honor*, 307.

34. Wyatt-Brown, *Southern Honor*, 296–97.

35. Wyatt-Brown, *Southern Honor*, 299.

36. Fox-Genovese and Genovese, *The Mind of the Master Class*, 382.

37. Kolchin, *American Slavery*, 89.

38. Tadman, *Speculators and Slaves*, xxi.

39. Stampp, *The Peculiar Institution*, 329.

40. Peter N. Moore, *World of Toil and Strife: Community Transformation in Backcountry South Carolina* (Columbia: University of South Carolina Press, 2007), 39, quoting Davies.

41. Moore, *World of Toil and Strife*, 39.

42. Fox-Genovese and Genovese, *The Mind of the Master Class*, 225.

43. Fox-Genovese and Genovese, *The Mind of the Master Class*, 27.

44. Fox-Genovese and Genovese, *The Mind of the Master Class*, 159.
45. Martin E. P. Seligman and David L. Rosenhan, *Abnormality* (New York: Norton, 1997), 270.
46. Daly, *When Slavery Was Called Freedom*, 121.
47. Daly, *When Slavery Was Called Freedom*, 6.
48. Stephen R. Haynes, *Noah's Curse: The Biblical Justification of American Slavery* (Oxford: Oxford University Press, 2002), 9.
49. Stampp, *The Peculiar Institution*, 20–21.
50. This pairing of the certainty that God would not allow a believer to become selfish with the companion certainty that self-interest was a proper course has relevance to our contemporaneous national divisiveness, where many people reject the wearing of masks in the name of self-interest ("liberty").
51. Daly, *When Slavery Was Called Freedom*, 29.
52. Oakes, *The Ruling Race*, 22.
53. Genovese and Fox-Genovese, *Fatal Self-Deception*, 26.
54. Lucia Stanton, *"Those Who Labor for My Happiness": Slavery at Thomas Jefferson's Monticello* (Charlottesville: University of Virginia Press, 2012), 153.
55. Genovese and Fox-Genovese, *Fatal Self-Deception*, 131.
56. Edgar, *South Carolina*, 312.
57. Edgar, *South Carolina*, 313.
58. Stampp, *The Peculiar Institution*, 425.
59. Levine, *The Fall of the House of Dixie*, 86.
60. Levine, *The Fall of the House of Dixie*, 87.
61. Oakes, *The Ruling Race*, 218.
62. Roark, *Masters without Slaves*, 97.

CHAPTER 3

1. Fox-Genovese and Genovese, *The Mind of the Master Class*, 391. David Ruggles is also the same abolitionist referred to by Frederick Douglass as a man whose "vigilance, kindness, and perseverance, I shall never forget." See Frederick Douglass, *Narrative of the Life of Frederick Douglas, an American Slave, Written by Himself* (1845; New York: Barnes & Noble Classics, 2003), 94.
2. Scarborough, *Masters of the Big House*, 92, quoting Elizabeth Fox-Genovese.
3. McCurry, *Masters of Small Worlds*, 80–81.
4. Elizabeth Fox-Genovese, *Within the Plantation Household: Black and White Women of the Old South* (Chapel Hill: University of North Carolina Press, 1988), 43.
5. Kolchin, *American Slavery*, 181, citing the research of historian James Oakes.
6. Oakes, *The Ruling Race*, 50.
7. Oakes, *The Ruling Race*, 50.
8. Anne Firor Scott, *Making the Invisible Woman Visible* (Urbana: University of Illinois Press, 1984), and *The Southern Lady: From Pedestal to Politics, 1830–1930* (Chicago: University of Chicago Press, 1970).

9. Catherine Clinton, *The Plantation Mistress: Woman's World in the Old South* (New York: Pantheon, 1982), 35.

10. Clinton, *The Plantation Mistress*, 231.

11. See Bertram Wyatt-Brown's review titled, "Plantation Women in the Slave South," *Reviews in American History* 11, no. 4 (Dec. 1983): 515–20; Rachel N. Klein's review, "Plantation Mistresses," *Journal of Southern History* 50, no. 1 (Feb. 1984): 123–25; Marianne Buroff Sheldon's review in *Virginia Magazine of History and Biography* 93, no. 1 (Jan. 1985): 101–102.

12. Wyatt-Brown, "Plantation Women in the Slave South," 518, 519.

13. Clinton, *The Plantation Mistress*, 187, n. 21.

14. Clinton, *The Plantation Mistress*, 187.

15. Clinton, *The Plantation Mistress*, 187–88.

16. Clinton, *The Plantation Mistress*, 188.

17. Clinton, *The Plantation Mistress*, 188.

18. Fox-Genovese, *Within the Plantation Household*, 44.

19. Fox-Genovese, *Within the Plantation Household*, 47.

20. See Kathleen C. Berkeley's review, "Within the Plantation Household: Black and White Women of the Old South," *North Carolina Historical Review* 66, no. 3 (July 1989): 361–62.

21. Scarborough, *Masters of the Big House*, 91.

22. Scarborough, *Masters of the Big House*, 91.

23. Stephanie E. Jones-Rogers, *They Were Her Property: White Women as Slaveowners in the American South* (New Haven, CT: Yale University Press, 2019), 61, n. 9.

24. Scarborough, *Masters of the Big House*, 95.

25. Scarborough, *Masters of the Big House*, 97.

26. Karp, *This Vast Southern Empire*, 2.

27. Karp, *This Vast Southern Empire*, 2, 4.

28. See Richard C. Lounsbury, ed., *Louisa S. McCord: Selected Writings* (Charlottesville: University Press of Virginia, 1997); C. Vann Woodward and Elizabeth Muhlenfeld, eds., *The Private Mary Chesnut: The Unpublished Civil War Diaries* (New York: Oxford University Press, 1984).

29. Fox-Genovese and Genovese, *The Mind of the Master Class*, 383.

30. Fox-Genovese and Genovese, *The Mind of the Master Class*, 389.

31. Rose, *A Documentary History*, 168–72.

32. Jones-Rogers, *They Were Her Property*, 2019.

33. Johnson, *Soul by Soul*, 89.

34. Johnson, *Soul by Soul*, 90.

35. Jones-Rogers, *They Were Her Property*, 83.

36. Jones-Rogers, *They Were Her Property*, 83.

37. Roark, *Masters without Slaves*, 48.

38. Baptist, *The Half Has Never Been Told*, 287.

39. Jones-Rogers, *They Were Her Property*, xvii.

40. Wyatt-Brown, *Southern Honor*, 227.

41. Stockholm syndrome "refers to the reaction of a woman held hostage in a Stockholm bank who became enamored of one of her captors and remained faithful

to him during his prison term." This syndrome is considered a type of persecution reaction. Robert Jean Campbell, *Psychiatric Dictionary*, 7th ed. (New York: Oxford University Press, 1996), 784.

42. Lounsbury, *Selected Writings*.

43. Karp, *This Vast Southern Empire*, 139.

44. Lounsbury, *Selected Writings*, 16–17.

45. Lounsbury, *Selected Writings*, 47.

46. Jones-Rogers, *They Were Her Property*, 62.

47. Jones-Rogers, *They Were Her Property*, 11.

48. William L. Andrews, *Slavery and Class in the American South: A Generation of Slave Narrative Testimony, 1840–1865* (New York: Oxford University Press, 2019), 114, n. 127.

49. Jones-Rogers, *They Were Her Property*, 32.

50. Andrews, *Slavery and Class*, 108.

51. Jones-Rogers, *They Were Her Property*, xvii.

52. The WPA interviews are the slave narratives. See Federal Writers' Project and Library of Congress, *Born in Slavery: Slave Narratives from the Federal Writers' Project, 1936–1938* (Washington, DC: Library of Congress, 2001), http://hdl.loc.gov/loc.mss/collmss.ms000008.

53. WPA interview number 320002, conducted by Marjorie Jones, Bates stamp 139.

54. Fox-Genovese, *Within the Plantation Household*, 25.

55. See Oakes, *The Ruling Race*.

56. See Clinton, *The Plantation Mistress*; Fox-Genovese, *Within the Plantation Household*; Jones-Rogers, *They Were Her Property*.

57. Jones-Rogers, *They Were Her Property*, 68, n. 28.

58. John Chester Miller, *The Wolf by the Ears: Thomas Jefferson and Slavery* (New York: Free Press, 1977), 42.

59. Andrews, *Slavery and Class*, 226.

60. Douglass, *Narrative*, 34.

61. Douglass, *Narrative*, 34.

62. Douglass, *Narrative*, 42.

63. Censer, *North Carolina Planters*, 147.

64. Theodore Weld, ed., *American Slavery as It Is: Testimony of a Thousand Witnesses* (New York: American Anti-Slavery Society, 1839), 87.

65. Harriet Jacobs, *Incidents in the Life of a Slave Girl* (Mineola, NY: Dover, 2001), 33.

66. Jones-Rogers, *They Were Her Property*, 146.

67. *Merriam-Webster's*, 301.

68. Smith, *Less Than Human*, 218.

69. Jones-Rogers, *They Were Her Property*, 69.

70. Lillian Smith, *Killers of the Dream* (New York: Norton, 1994), 138–39.

71. Smith, *Killers of the Dream*, 151.

72. Smith, *Killers of the Dream*, 120.

73. Johnson, *Soul by Soul*, 114–15, n. 95. See C. Vann Woodward, ed., *Mary Chesnut's Civil War* (New Haven, CT: Yale University Press, 1981).

74. Campbell, *Psychiatric Dictionary*, 77.

75. Leigh Fought, *Southern Womanhood and Slavery: A Biography of Louisa S. Mc-Cord, 1810–1879* (Columbia: University of Missouri Press, 2002), 112.
76. Fought, *Southern Womanhood*, 113.
77. Douglass, *Narrative*, 19.
78. Douglass, *Narrative*, 19.
79. Douglass, *Narrative*, 43.
80. Jones-Rogers, *They Were Her Property*, 204.

CHAPTER 4

1. American Psychiatric Association, *Diagnostic and Statistical Manual of Mental Disorders*, 4th ed. (Washington, DC: American Psychiatric Association, 1994), 751.
2. American Psychiatric Association, *DSM IV*, 765; American Psychiatric Association, *Diagnostic and Statistical Manual of Mental Disorders*, 4th ed., text revision (Washington, DC: American Psychiatric Association, 2000), 807–9.
3. American Psychiatric Association, *DSM IV–TR*, 807–9.
4. *Merriam-Webster's*, 717.
5. Drew Gilpin Faust, *James Henry Hammond and the Old South: A Design for Mastery* (Baton Rouge: Louisiana State University Press, 1982), 94–95.
6. Faust, *James Henry Hammond*, 95.
7. Rose, *A Documentary History*, 345.
8. Rose, *A Documentary History*, 354.
9. Faust, *James Henry Hammond*, 85, n. 26.
10. Faust, *James Henry Hammond*, 87.
11. American Psychiatric Association, *DSM IV–TR*, 765.
12. David Brion Davis, *Inhuman Bondage: The Rise and Fall of Slavery in the New World* (New York: Oxford University Press, 2006), 197.
13. See O'Brien, *All Clever Men*; Michael O'Brien, *Conjectures of Order: Intellectual Life and the American South, 1810–1860*, 2 vols. (Chapel Hill: University of North Carolina Press, 2004).
14. Karp, *This Vast Southern Empire*, 3, n. 9.
15. Eugene D. Genovese, *The Slaveholders' Dilemma: Freedom and Progress in Southern Conservative Thought, 1820–1860* (Columbia: University of South Carolina Press, 1992), 1, 2.
16. O'Brien, *All Clever Men*, 2.
17. O'Brien, *Conjectures of Order*, 879. See Caitlin Rosenthal, *Accounting for Slavery: Masters and Management* (Cambridge, MA: Harvard University Press, 2018), for her brilliant analysis of slave masters' development of astute business practices.
18. Davis, *Inhuman Bondage*, 197.
19. Kolchin, *American Slavery*, 181.
20. Karp, *This Vast Southern Empire*, 1, n. 2.
21. Karp, *This Vast Southern Empire*, 2.
22. McCurry, *Masters of Small Worlds*, 93–94.

23. Rosenthal, *Accounting for Slavery*, 190.

24. American Psychiatric Association, *DSM* IV–TR, 752.

25. Seligman and Rosenhan, *Abnormality*, 42.

26. John D. Davis and Henry Snyder Gehman, *The Westminster Dictionary of the Bible* (Philadelphia: Westminster Press, 1944), 312.

27. Daly, *When Slavery Was Called Freedom*, 84.

28. American Psychiatric Association, *DSM* IV, 751–57.

29. Dinesh D'Souza, "Ignoble Savages," in *Critical White Studies*, ed. Richard Delbanco and Jean Stefancic (Philadelphia: Temple University Press, 1997), 56.

30. Phillip Zimbardo, *The Lucifer Effect: Understanding How Good People Turn Evil* (New York: Random House, 2008), 4–5.

31. Zimbardo, *The Lucifer Effect*, 5.

32. Johnson, *River of Dark Dreams*, 171, i.

33. Kolchin, *American Slavery*, 57–58.

34. Kolchin, *American Slavery*, 59.

35. Stampp, *The Peculiar Institution*, 28.

36. Karp, *This Vast Southern Empire*, 3–4, n. 11.

37. Lacy K. Ford, *Deliver Us from Evil: The Slavery Question in the Old South* (New York: Oxford University Press, 2009), 524.

38. Baptist, *The Half Has Never Been Told*, xxi.

39. Sublette and Sublette, *The American Slave Coast*, xiii.

40. Oakes, *The Ruling Race*, 27.

41. Mitchell Snay, *Gospel of Disunion: Religion and Separation in the Antebellum South* (Chapel Hill: University of North Carolina Press, 1993), 83–84.

42. Snay, *Gospel of Disunion*, 85, n. 10.

43. Bonnie Martin, "Neighbor-to-Neighbor: Local Credit Networks and the Mortgaging of Slaves," in *Slavery's Capitalism: A New History of American Economic Development*, ed. Sven Beckert and Seth Rockman (Philadelphia: University of Pennsylvania Press, 2016), 113.

44. Dew, *Apostles of Disunion*, 79, n. 8.

45. Faust, *James Henry Hammond*, 360.

46. A quotation attributed to Hammond in 1858, inscribed on the wall of the National Museum of African American History and Culture, Washington, DC.

47. John Blassingame, *The Slave Community: Plantation Life in the Antebellum South* (New York: Oxford University Press, 1979), 133–34.

48. George Fredrickson, "White Images of Black Slaves (Is What We See in Others Sometimes a Reflection of What We Find in Ourselves?)" in *Critical White Studies*, ed. Richard Delbanco and Jean Steancic (Philadelphia: Temple University Press, 1997), 39.

49. Fredrickson, "White Images," 40.

50. Fredrickson, "White Images," 42.

51. Haynes, *Noah's Curse*, 10.

52. David Stefan Doddington, *Contesting Slave Masculinity in the American South* (Cambridge: Cambridge University Press, 2018), 138–39, n. 47.

53. Genovese, *Roll, Jordan, Roll*, 353.

54. Alison M. Parker, "When White Women Wanted a Monument to Black 'Mammies,'" *New York Times*, February 6, 2020, https://www.nytimes.com/2020/02/06/opinion/sunday/confederate-monuments-mammy.html.

55. Kendi, *Stamped*, 172.

56. Genovese and Fox-Genovese, *Fatal Self-Deception*, 73, 89, 91, 134, 138, 142, 145.

57. Matthew Estes, *A Defence of Negro Slavery, As It Exists in the United States* (Montgomery: Press of the *Alabama Journal*, 1846), 128.

58. Lawrence W. Levine, *Black Culture and Black Consciousness: Afro-American Folk Thought from Slavery to Freedom* (New York: Oxford University Press, 1977), xiii.

59. Malcom X, *The Autobiography of Malcolm X* (New York: Grove, 1965), 274.

60. Rose, *A Documentary History*, document 74, 372.

61. Jones-Rogers, *They Were Her Property*, 22.

62. Stampp, *The Peculiar Institution*, 86.

63. T. W. Hoit, *The Right of American Slavery* (St. Louis, MO: L. Bushnell, 1860), 21, http://name.umdl.umich.edu/ABJ1322.0001.001.

64. Smith, *Less Than Human*, 1.

65. Woodward, *Mary Chesnut's Civil War*, 260.

66. Oakes, *The Ruling Race*, 45.

67. Oakes, *The Ruling Race*, 23.

68. Baptist, *The Half Has Never Been Told*, 347.

69. See Slave Rebellion Web Site, "A Map of STOPPED Slave Revolts in the United States," http://slaverebellion.info/index.php?page=maps

70. See Kevin M. Levin, *Searching for Black Confederates: The Civil War's Most Persistent Myth* (Chapel Hill: University of North Carolina Press, 2019).

71. Colin Edward Woodward, "Free to Fight: The Confederate Army and the Use of Slaves as Soldiers," in *Marching Masters: Slavery, Race, and the Confederate Army during the Civil War* (Charlottesville: University of Virginia Press, 2014), 155–79.

72. Stephanie McCurry, "The Confederacy," in *Disunion: A History of the Civil War*, ed. Ted Widmer (Oxford: Oxford University Press, 2016), 205–6; see also Delbanco, *The War before the War*; David S. Cecelski, *The Fire of Freedom: Abraham Galloway and the Slaves' Civil War* (Chapel Hill: University of North Carolina Press, 2012).

73. Genovese, *Roll, Jordan, Roll*, 155.

74. Stout, *Upon the Altar*, 309–10.

75. American Psychiatric Association, *DSM* IV, 753.

76. Campbell, *Psychiatric Dictionary*, 682.

77. Snay, *Gospel of Disunion*, 192–93.

78. *South Carolina Encyclopedia*, "Palmer, Benjamin Morgan," www.scenclyclopedia.org/sce/entries/palmer-benjamin-morgan/.

79. Snay, *Gospel of Disunion*, 177–78.

80. O'Brien, *Conjectures of Order*, 877.

81. O'Brien, *Conjectures of Order*, 888.

82. James Hervey Smith, "Sismondi's Political Economy," in *All Clever Men, Who Make Their Way: Critical Discourse in the Old South*, ed. Michael O'Brien (Fayetteville: University of Arkansas Press, 1982), 32.

83. Smith, "Sismondi's Political Economy," 937.

84. Babiak and Hare, *Snakes in Suits*, 406–13.

85. See Dana Kay Nelkin, "Psychopaths, Incorrigible Racists, and the Faces of Responsibility," *Ethics* 125, no. 2 (2015): 357–90.

86. See Hervey M. Cleckley, *The Mask of Sanity* (1941; St. Louis: Mosby, 1976).

87. Christopher J. Patrick, "Getting to the Heart of Psychopathy," in *The Psychopath: Theory, Research, and Practice*, ed. Hugues Herve and John C. Yuille (Mahwah, NJ: Lawrence Erlbaum Associates, 2007), 209.

88. See Nelkin, "Psychopaths," 364, n. 18.

89. Fox-Genovese and Genovese, *The Mind of the Master Class*, 520.

90. Snay, *Gospel of Disunion*, 78.

91. Genovese and Fox-Genovese, *Fatal Self-Deception*, 27, n. 6.

92. Catherine M. Herba et al., "The Neurobiology of Psychopathy: A Focus on Emotion Processing," in *The Psychopath: Theory, Research, and Practice*, ed. Hugues Herve and John C. Yuille (Mahwah, NJ: Lawrence Erlbaum Associates, 2007), 254.

93. Hugues Herve and John C. Yuille, *The Psychopath: Theory, Research and Practice* (Mahwah, NJ: Lawrence Erlbaum Associates, 2007), 31.

94. See Hugues Herve, "Psychopathy across the Ages: A History of the Hare Psychopath," in *The Psychopath: Theory, Research, and Practice*, ed. Hugues Herve and John C. Yuille (Mahwah, NJ: Lawrence Erlbaum Associates, 2007), 32–44.

95. See R. D. Hare, "Psychopaths and Their Nature: Implications for the Mental Health and Criminal Justice Systems," in *Psychopathy: Antisocial, Criminal, and Violent Behavior*, ed. T. Millon, E. Simonson. M. Burket-Smith, and R. Davis (New York: Guilford Press, 1998), 188–212.

96. Miller, *The Wolf by the Ears*, 62.

97. Kendi, *Stamped*, 130.

98. Miller, *The Wolf by the Ears*, 105.

99. Annette Gordon-Reed, *The Hemingses of Monticello: An American Family* (New York: Norton, 2008), 15–16.

100. Stephen Greenblatt, *Tyrant: Shakespeare on Politics* (New York: Norton, 2018), 53.

101. O'Brien, *Conjectures of Order*, 1093–4.

102. Daly, *When Slavery Was Called Freedom*, 14.

103. Daly, *When Slavery Was Called Freedom*, 138.

104. O'Brien, *Conjectures of Order*, 956.

105. Genovese and Fox-Genovese, *Fatal Self-Deception*, 146.

106. Snay, *Gospel of Disunion*, 67, is quoting from James Warley Miles, *The Relation Between the Races in the South* (Charleston, SC: Evans and Cogswell, 1861).

107. Snay, *Gospel of Disunion*, 68.

108. *Merriam-Webster's*, 908.

109. *Merriam-Webster's*, 909.

110. Oakes, *The Ruling Race*, 4.

111. Oakes, *The Ruling Race*, xii.

112. Oakes, *The Ruling Race*, 201.

113. Fox-Genovese, *Within the Plantation Household*, 64.

114. Genovese and Fox-Genovese, *Fatal Self-Deception*, 89.

115. Stout, *Upon the Altar*, 1.

116. Kendi, *Stamped*, 193–94.

117. See L. Gunsberg and P. Hymowitz, eds., *A Handbook of Divorce and Custody: Forensic, Developmental, and Clinical Perspectives* (Hillsdale, NJ: Analytic Press, 2005).

118. David Brion Davis, *Homicide in American Fiction 1798–1860* (Ithaca, NY: Cornell University Press, 1957), xiv.

119. See Berry, *The Hidden Wound*. This powerful book identifies the traumatic wound racist slavery inflicted on white and Black America, though its target audience is white America.

120. Delbanco, *The War before the War*, 9.

121. Faust, *James Henry Hammond*, 326.

122. Faust, *James Henry Hammond*, 326.

123. Daly, *When Slavery Was Called Freedom*, 121.

124. Daly, *When Slavery Was Called Freedom*, 121, citing Foner.

125. There appear to be ample data to support a finding that many slaveholders lost their capacity for using a balanced self-observation (an adaptive defense mechanism) because of the highly destructive effects of self-deception (a maladaptive defense mechanism).

126. Karp, *This Vast Southern Empire*, 233.

127. Karp, *This Vast Southern Empire*, 233.

CHAPTER 5

1. Avalos, *Slavery*, 4.

2. Avalos, *Slavery*, 4.

3. Paul Harvey, "Religion, White Supremacist," in *The New Encyclopedia of Southern Culture*, ed. Thomas C. Holt, Laurie B. Green, and Charles Reagan Wilson, vol. 24 (Chapel Hill: University of North Carolina Press, 2013), 142–46.

4. Erskine, *Plantation Church*, 25.

5. By 1700, there were a million Scotsmen in Ireland, most of whom migrated from lowland Scotland.

6. Daly, *When Slavery Was Called Freedom*, 133.

7. Daly, *When Slavery Was Called Freedom*, 17.

8. Richard Furman (1755–1825) was an influential southern Baptist evangelist and slaveholder.

9. Ford, *Deliver Us from Evil*, 262.

10. Fox-Genovese and Genovese, *The Mind of the Master Class*, 225.

11. Finkelman, *Defending Slavery*, 26.

12. Daly, *When Slavery Was Called Freedom*, 15.

13. Richard Furman, *Exposition of the Views of Baptists* (Charleston, SC: A. E. Miller, 1822), 3, 17.

14. Daly, *When Slavery Was Called Freedom*, 6.

15. Daly, *When Slavery Was Called Freedom*, 134.

16. Daly, *When Slavery Was Called Freedom*, 132.
17. Snay, *Gospel of Disunion*, 5–6.
18. Snay, *Gospel of Disunion*, 7; see n. 12. E. Brooks Holifield's work is entitled *The Gentlemen Theologians: American Theology in Southern Culture: 1795–1860*.
19. Roark, *Masters without Slaves*, 96.
20. Moore, *World of Toil and Strife*, 39.
21. Daly, *When Slavery Was Called Freedom*, 44.
22. Snay, *Gospel of Disunion*, 27.
23. Finkelman, *Defending Slavery*, 10.
24. Finkelman, *Defending Slavery*, 97, 105. Holmes's essay was published in Holland N. Mctyeire, ed., *Duties of Masters to Servants* (Charleston, SC: Southern Baptist Publication Society, 1851).
25. Finkelman, *Defending Slavery*, 31.
26. Davis and Gehman, *The Westminster Dictionary of the Bible*, 503.
27. William G. Brownlow and A. Pryne, *Ought American Slavery Be Perpetuated? A Debate* (Philadelphia: Lippincott, 1858), 94.
28. Daly, *When Slavery Was Called Freedom*, 53.
29. Douglass, *Narrative*, 72.
30. Zimbardo, *The Lucifer Effect*. Philip Zimbardo, a social psychologist, is perhaps most famous for his Stanford prison experiment.
31. Zimbardo, *The Lucifer Effect*, vii.
32. Stampp, *The Peculiar Institution*, 16.
33. Fred A. Ross, *Slavery Ordained of God* (Middletown, DE: Author, 1857). I obtained a paperback edition by this title from Amazon.com. It has no publisher or copyright identification. It simply says "Middletown, DE 24 June 2015." In *Slavery, Abolitionism, and the Ethics of Biblical Scholarship*, Avalos references this work as: Ross, Fred A., *Slavery Ordained of God* (repr., New York: Negro University Press, 1969 [1859]). Thus, it appears we can safely say this was a self-published work by the author circa 1859. As Ross says in his preface, "The book I give to the public, is not made up of isolated articles. It is one harmonious demonstration—that slavery is part of the government ordained in certain conditions of fallen mankind . . . I give it to the North and South—to maintain harmony among Christians, and to secure the integrity of the union of this great people." (1).
34. Ross, *Slavery*, 1.
35. Ross, *Slavery*, 1.
36. Ross, *Slavery*, 1.
37. Ross, *Slavery*, 2.
38. Ross's point on this issue is well taken. As history shows, one of the largest and wealthiest slave-trading enterprises was run by the De Wolfe family out of Rhode Island. See Katrina Browne, Jude Ray, Alla Kovgan, dir., *Traces of the Trade: A Story From the Deep North* [film] (POV Documentary, 2008).
39. Ross, *Slavery*, 2.
40. Ross, *Slavery*, 3.
41. Ross, *Slavery*, 16.
42. Ross, *Slavery*, 17.

43. Ross, *Slavery*, 18.

44. Erskine, *Plantation Church*, 85.

45. Erskine, *Plantation Church*, 75. Whitfield is sometimes alternately spelled White-field.

46. Fox-Genovese and Genovese, *The Mind of the Master Class*, 232.

47. Albert Barnes, *An Inquiry into the Scriptural Views of Slavery* (Philadelphia: Perkins & Purves; Boston: B. Perkins, 1846), 21.

48. Fox-Genovese and Genovese, *The Mind of the Master Class*, 506.

49. Fox-Genovese and Genovese, *The Mind of the Master Class*, 510.

50. See Ford, *Deliver Us from Evil*, n. 88.

51. Ford, *Deliver Us from Evil*, 472.

52. The Canaanites were direct descendants of Canaan, Noah's grandson, who was the inexplicable target of Noah's curse in chapter 9 of the book of Genesis: "We must remember that Noah's curse declared that Canaan shall be a [forever] slave of slaves to his brothers."

53. Fox-Genovese and Genovese, *The Mind of the Master Class*, 511.

54. Avalos, *Slavery*, makes a compelling argument that God's overarching paradigm with his chosen people was a master-slave relationship.

55. Ross, *Slavery*, 15.

56. Ross, *Slavery*, 15.

57. Galatians 3:26–29: "For ye are all the children of God by faith in Christ Jesus. For as many of you as have been baptized into Christ have put on Christ. There is neither Jew nor Greek, there is neither bond nor free, there is neither male nor female: for ye are all one in Christ Jesus. And if ye *be* Christ's, then are ye Abraham's seed, and heirs according to the promise."

58. Jennifer A. Glancy, *Slavery in Early Christianity* (Minneapolis: Fortress Press, 2006), 129.

59. Avalos, *Slavery*, 374.

60. Glancy, *Slavery in Early Christianity*, 127.

61. Glancy, *Slavery in Early Christianity*, 102.

62. Glancy, *Slavery in Early Christianity*, 103.

63. Glancy, *Slavery in Early Christianity*, 103, n. 13. Keith Bradley is the author of "The Problem of Slavery in Classical Culture," *Classical Philology* 92 (1997): 273–82.

64. Delbanco, *The War before the War*, 38.

65. Delbanco, *The War before the War*, 38.

66. Snay, *Gospel of Disunion*, 15; see also James Brewer Stewart, *Holy Warriors: The Abolitionists and American Slavery* (New York: Hill and Wang, 1996).

67. Snay, *Gospel of Disunion*, 24.

68. Avalos, *Slavery*, 285, n. 1.

69. Snay, *Gospel of Disunion*, 54–55.

70. David M. Goldenberg, *The Curse of Ham: Race and Slavery in Early Judaism, Christianity, and Islam* (Princeton: Princeton University Press, 2003), 199.

71. Fox-Genovese and Genovese, *The Mind of the Master Class*, 508.

72. Avalos, *Slavery*, 14; de Ste. Croix was one of the most prominent Marxist scholars of ancient Greece.

73. Avalos, *Slavery*, 23.
74. Fox-Genovese and Genovese, *The Mind of the Master Class*, 510.
75. Avalos, *Slavery*, 23.
76. Avalos, *Slavery*, 27–37.
77. Finkelman, *Defending Slavery*, 27.
78. Browne et al., *Traces of the Trade*.
79. See Tadman, *Speculators*.
80. Daly, *When Slavery Was Called Freedom*, 16.
81. Fox-Genovese and Genovese, *The Mind of the Master Class*, 565.
82. Mark A. Noll, *The Civil War as a Theological Crisis* (Chapel Hill: University of North Carolina Press, 2006), 76.
83. Snay, *Gospel of Disunion*, 214–15.
84. Daly, *When Slavery Was Called Freedom*, 143, n. 35.
85. This scriptural reference may be to the Old Testament book Proverbs 18:5, which reads, "It is not good to accept the person of the wicked, to overthrow the righteous in judgment."
86. Noll, *The Civil War*, 77–78, n. 6.

CHAPTER 6

1. Davis, *Inhuman Bondage*, 64.
2. Linda Murray, *The High Renaissance* (New York: Praeger, 1967).
3. Murray, *The High Renaissance*, 50.
4. Murray, *The High Renaissance*, 80.
5. Murray, *The High Renaissance*, 53.
6. I don't think it fair or accurate to say these were "white" men; Michelangelo painted them as light skinned. His models, if he used any, likely would have been Italian, with a darker than white complexion, a people historian Matthew Frye would call *Whiteness of a Different Color*. See Brent Staples, "How Italians Became White," *New York Times*, October 12, 2019, https://www.nytimes.com/interactive/2019/10/12/opinion/columbus-day-italian-american-racism.html.
7. Ascanio Condivi, *The Life of Michelangelo*, ed. Helmut Wohl, trans. Alice Sedgwick Wohl (University Park: Pennsylvania State University Press, 1999).
8. Dr. John Pinto, October 13, 2014, personal communication. Dr. Pinto was formerly chair of the Art History Department at Princeton University.
9. Murray, *The High Renaissance*, 90.
10. Goldenberg, *The Curse of Ham*, 1.
11. Haynes, *Noah's Curse*, 6.
12. Haynes, *Noah's Curse*, 7.
13. Haynes, *Noah's Curse*, 7.
14. Haynes, *Noah's Curse*, 7.
15. Haynes, *Noah's Curse*, 177.

16. Haynes, *Noah's Curse*, 178; see also Don Cameron Allen, *The Legend of Noah: Renaissance Rationalism in Art, Science and Letters* (Urbana: University of Illinois Press, 1963), 73.

17. Haynes, *Noah's Curse*, 178.

18. Haynes, *Noah's Curse*, 178–79, n. 11.

19. Haynes, *Noah's Curse*, 181.

20. Haynes, *Noah's Curse*, 181; see Samuel Sewall, *The Selling of Joseph: A Memorial*, ed. Sidney Kaplan (Amherst: University of Massachusetts Press, 1969).

21. Haynes, *Noah's Curse*, 185.

22. Davis, *Inhuman Bondage*, 55–56.

23. Haynes, *Noah's Curse*, 7.

24. Davis, *Inhuman Bondage*, 66–67, citing Goldenberg at n. 60.

25. O'Brien, *Conjectures of Order*, 1082.

26. David M. Goldenberg, *Black and Slave: The Origins and History of the Curse of Ham* (Berlin: De Gruyter, 2017); see also, David M. Goldenberg, www.bibleinterp.com.

27. Quoted in David M. Goldenberg, "Black and Slave: The Origins and History of the Curse of Ham," August 2017, https://www.bibleinterp.com/PDFs/Hampdf.pdf.

28. Goldenberg, *Black and Slave*, 5–6.

29. Fox-Genovese and Genovese, *The Mind of the Master Class*, 522–23.

30. Fox-Genovese and Genovese, *The Mind of the Master Class*, 522.

31. H. Hirsch Cohen, *The Drunkenness of Noah* (Tuscaloosa: University of Alabama Press, 1974), 1.

32. Haynes, *Noah's Curse*, ix.

33. Cohen, *The Drunkenness of Noah*, 8.

34. The version of the Bible I used for this book says "younger" son (verse 24). *The Holy Bible, Containing the Old and New Testaments: Translated out of the Original Tongues; and with the Former Translations Diligently Compared and Revised* (New York: American Bible Society, 1881).

35. Davis and Gehman, *The Westminster Dictionary of the Bible*, 223.

36. Cohen, *The Drunkenness of* Noah, 13.

37. Cohen, *The Drunkenness of Noah*, 13.

38. Ross, *Slavery*, 1.

39. Ross, *Slavery*, 12.

40. Fox-Genovese and Genovese, *The Mind of the Master Class*, 521.

41. Fox-Genovese and Genovese, *The Mind of the Master Class*, 506.

42. Haynes, *Noah's Curse*, 8.

43. Haynes, *Noah's Curse*, 5.

44. *Vade mecum*: this phrase literally means "Go with me," but I think it's safe to say that Noah's curse and prophecy as they were interpreted and shaped to support slavery meant *vade mecum* was something the proslavery supporter "never left home without."

45. Haynes, *Noah's Curse*, 11.

46. Haynes, *Noah's Curse*, 12.

47. Daly, *When Slavery Was Called Freedom*, 85.

48. Roark, *Masters without Slaves*, 96.

49. Douglass, *Narrative*, 19.

50. See Finkelman, *Defending Slavery*, 121–28. See also E. N. Elliott et al., *Cotton Is King and Proslavery Arguments: Comprising the Writings of Hammond, Harper, Christy, Stringfellow, Henry, Bledsoe and Cartwright* (Augusta, GA: Pritchard, Abbott & Loomis, 1860), an 1860 work that contained influential proslavery arguments by James Hammond, Thornton Stringfellow, Samuel Cartwright and others.

51. Finkelman, *Defending Slavery*, 123.

52. Finkelman, *Defending Slavery*, 123.

53. Cohen, *The Drunkenness of Noah*, 4.

54. Davis, *Inhuman Bondage*, 67.

55. Robert Alter, *The Five Books of Moses: A Translation with Commentary* (New York: Norton, 2004).

56. Goldenberg, *The Curse of Ham,* 157.

57. See Cohen, *The Drunkenness of Noah*, 1–30, for a discussion of this question.

58. Gaston Bachelard, *The Psychoanalysis of Fire* (London, 1964).

59. Cohen, *The Drunkenness of Noah*, vii.

60. Cohen, *The Drunkenness of Noah*, vii.

61. Cohen, *The Drunkenness of Noah*, vii.

62. Cohen, *The Drunkenness of Noah*, 1.

63. Cohen, *The Drunkenness of Noah*, 8.

64. Cohen, *The Drunkenness of Noah*, 12.

65. Cohen, *The Drunkenness of Noah*, 13.

66. Cohen, *The Drunkenness of Noah*, 15.

67. Cohen, *The Drunkenness of Noah*, 15.

68. Campbell, *Psychiatric Dictionary*, 348.

69. Cohen, *The Drunkenness of Noah*, 16.

70. Cohen, *The Drunkenness of Noah*, 17.

71. Cohen *The Drunkenness of Noah*, 18.

72. Cohen, *The Drunkenness of Noah*, 19.

73. Cohen, *The Drunkenness of Noah*, 23.

74. Cohen, *The Drunkenness of Noah*, 30.

75. Avalos, *Slavery*, 70, n. 29.

76. Avalos, *Slavery*, 182.

77. Avalos, *Slavery*, 288.

CHAPTER 7

1. Campbell, *Psychiatric Dictionary*, 52.

2. Campbell, *Psychiatric Dictionary*, 52. Zygmut A. Piotrowski developed a method for analyzing the Rorschach test. He published his method in his work *Perceptanalysis* in 1957.

3. Delbanco, *The War before the War*, 195.

4. Levine, *The Fall of the House of Dixie*, 89.

5. Censer, *North Carolina Planters*, 144.

6. Wyatt-Brown, *Southern Honor*, 405.

7. William Kauffman Scarborough, *The Overseer: Plantation Management in the Old South* (Athens: University of Georgia Press, 1984), 515, referenced this term under the subject of "racism." Genovese and Fox-Genovese, *Fatal Self-Deception*, 1, 98, 115–16, described "negrophobia," ironically, as a derisive label hurled by Southerners about racist attitudes toward Blacks exhibited by Northerners, particularly abolitionists.

8. Levine, *The Fall of the House of Dixie*, 28.

9. Levine, *The Fall of the House of Dixie*, 87.

10. Levine, *The Fall of the House of Dixie*, 88.

11. Delbanco, *The War before the War*, 196.

12. Fox-Genovese and Genovese, *The Mind of the Master Class*, 139.

13. Oakes, *The Ruling Race*, 24.

14. Berlin, *Many Thousands Gone*, 151.

15. Edgar, *South Carolina*, 318.

16. Delbanco, *The War before the War*, 198.

17. Censer, *North Carolina Planters*, 88.

18. Delbanco, *The War before the War*, 198.

19. Johnson, *River of Dark Dreams*, 5.

20. Levine, *The Fall of the House of Dixie*, 88, n. 141.

21. John Spencer Bassett, *Slavery in the State of North Carolina*, Studies in Historical and Political Science (Baltimore: Johns Hopkins University Press, 1899; reproduced London: Forgotten Books, 2018).

22. *Merriam-Webster's*, 1187.

23. Delbanco, *The War before the War*, 198.

24. Delbanco, *The War before the War*, 195.

25. Avalos, *Slavery*, 277.

26. Erskine, *Plantation Church*, 154.

27. Delbanco, *The War before the War*, 195.

28. Stampp, 1989, 135.

29. See BlackPast.org; most historians agree that the appropriate title of this rebellion should be Gabriel's Rebellion, for Prosser was Gabriel's master's name.

30. Rose, *A Documentary History*, 107–8.

31. Bassett, *Slavery in the State of North Carolina*, 94.

32. Bassett, *Slavery in the State of North Carolina*, 95.

33. Kolchin, *American Slavery*, 63

34. Stampp, *The Peculiar Institution*, 25.

35. Genovese, *Roll, Jordan, Roll*, 588.

36. Ford, *Deliver Us from Evil*, 130, 131. Although it generally is true that lynchings were rare in the antebellum South, this German Coast history serves as a notable exception.

37. Berlin, *Many Thousands Gone*, 362, n. 12.

38. Delbanco, *The War before the War*, 110.

39. Ford, *Deliver Us from Evil*, 176, 177.

40. Erskine, *Plantation Church*, 151.

41. Ford, *Deliver Us from Evil*, 67.

42. Stampp, *1984*, 135, n. 1.

43. Berlin, *Many Thousands Gone*, 363.

44. Delbanco, *The War before the War*, 195.

45. Ford, *Deliver Us from Evil*, 338.

46. Ford, *Deliver Us from Evil*, 297.

47. Ford, *Deliver Us from Evil*, 342.

48. Ford, *Deliver Us from Evil*, 342, n. 65.

49. Delbanco, *The War before the War*, 196.

50. David Brion Davis, *Challenging the Boundaries of Slavery* (Cambridge, MA: Harvard University Press, 2003), 74.

51. James A. Morone, "South: The Pro-Slavery Argument," in *Hellfire Nation: The Politics of Sin in American History* (New Haven, CT: Yale University Press, 2003), 135.

52. Stampp, 1984, 134.

53. Stampp, 1984, 136.

54. Genovese, *Roll, Jordan, Roll*, 592–93.

55. Delbanco, *The War before the War*, 196.

56. Erskine, *Plantation Church*, 92.

57. Erskine, *Plantation Church*, 94.

58. Johnson, *River of Dark Dreams*, 55.

59. Ford, *Deliver Us from Evil*, 491.

60. Oakes, *The Ruling Race*, 110.

61. Scarborough, *Masters of the Big House*, 149.

62. Scarborough, *Masters of the Big House*, 19.

63. Scarborough, *Masters of the Big House*, 19, n. 3.

64. Scarborough, *Masters of the Big House*, 35.

65. Scarborough, *Masters of the Big House*, 35.

66. Johnson, *River of Dark Dreams*, 179.

67. Oakes, *The Ruling Race*, 110–11.

68. Genovese, *Roll, Jordan, Roll*, 62.

69. Genovese, *Roll, Jordan, Roll*, 638–39.

70. Scarborough, *Masters of the Big House*, 146–47, n. 63.

71. Delbanco, *The War before the War*, 2.

72. Berlin, *Many Thousands Gone*, 139.

73. Berlin, *Many Thousands Gone*, 224.

74. Johnson, *River of Dark Dreams*, 259. Thomas Kettle published his book *Southern Wealth and Northern Profits* in 1860.

75. Morone, "South," 123, nn. 1, 2, and 3.

76. Morone, "South," 135.

77. Oakes, *The Ruling Race*, 97.

78. Oakes, *The Ruling Race*, 32.

79. Oakes, *The Ruling Race*, 149, n. 58.

80. *Merriam-Webster's*, 405.

81. Oakes, *The Ruling Race*, 149.

82. Levine, *The Fall of the House of Dixie*, 29, n. 5.
83. Levine, *The Fall of the House of Dixie*, 29.
84. Oakes, *The Ruling Race*, 149–50, n. 59.
85. Oakes, *The Ruling Race*, 150.
86. Ford, *Deliver Us from Evil*, 4.
87. Genovese, *Roll, Jordan, Roll*, 109, n. 24.
88. Genovese and Fox-Genovese, *Fatal Self-Deception*, 98.
89. Genovese, *Roll, Jordan, Roll*, 110.
90. Paul D. Escott, *"What Shall We Do with the Negro?" Lincoln, White Racism, and Civil War America* (Charlottesville: University of Virginia Press, 2009), 145, 146.
91. Oakes, *The Ruling Race*, 96.
92. Oakes, *The Ruling Race*, 98, n. 5.
93. Censer, *North Carolina Planters*, 6.
94. Censer, *North Carolina Planters*, 112, n. 33.
95. Avalos, *Slavery*, 286.
96. See Dew's monograph *Apostles of Disunion*.
97. Dew, *Apostles of Disunion*, 19.

CHAPTER 8

1. Stampp, *The Peculiar Institution*, 144–47.
2. Jason R. Young, *Rituals of Resistance: African Atlantic Region in Kongo and the Lowcountry South in the Era of Slavery* (Baton Rouge: Louisiana State University Press, 2007), 13.
3. For an excellent analysis of America's caste system, see Isabel Wilkerson, "America's Enduring Caste System," *New York Times*, July 5, 2020, https://www.nytimes.com/2020/07/01/magazine/isabel-wilkerson-caste.html.
4. Charles Blow, "Yes, Even George Washington," *New York Times*, June 28, 2020, https://www.nytimes/2020/06/28/opinion/george-washington-confederate-statues.html.
5. Delbanco, *The War before the War*, 31.
6. Delbanco, *The War before the War*, 51–52.
7. Stewart, *Holy Warriors*, 11.
8. Delbanco, *The War before the War*, 194.
9. Ball, *Slaves in the Family*, 252.
10. Ball, *Slaves in the Family*, 252.
11. Levine, *The Fall of the House of Dixie*, 8.
12. Baptist, *The Half Has Never Been Told*, 40, 41, 42.
13. Rose, *A Documentary History*, 143, 148.
14. Zinn, *A People's History*, 28.
15. Sommerville, *Aberration of Mind*, 1.
16. Sommerville, *Aberration of Mind*, 1, n. 2.
17. Johnson, *River of Dark Dreams*, 4.

18. Johnson, *River of Dark Dreams*, 5.

19. George W. Featherstonhaugh, *Excursion through the Slave States, from Washington on the Potomac to the Frontier of Mexico: with Sketches of Popular Manners and Geological Notices* (New York: Harper, 1844), 36–38, 46–47, 141–42.

20. Fox-Genovese and Genovese, *The Mind of the Master Class*, 512.

21. Sublette and Sublette, *The American Slave Coast*, 27.

22. See Richard Sutch, *The Breeding of Slaves for Sale and the Westward Expansion of Slavery* (Berkeley: Institute of Business and Economic Research, University of California, 1972).

23. Sublette and Sublette, *The American Slave Coast*, 28.

24. See Weld, *American Slavery*, 143.

25. Weld, *American Slavery*, 182.

26. Sublette and Sublette, *The American Slave Coast*, xiii.

27. Sublette and Sublette, *The American Slave Coast*, xiii.

28. Rosenthal, *Accounting for Slavery*, 131.

29. Sublette and Sublette, *The American Slave Coast*, 28, n. 23.

30. Levine, *The Fall of the House of Dixie*, 12.

31. Rosenthal, *Accounting for Slavery*, 34.

32. Stampp, *The Peculiar Institution*, 291, quoting Douglass.

33. Genovese and Fox-Genovese, *Fatal Self-Deception*, 17.

34. Oakes, *The Ruling Race*, 26.

35. James W. C. Pennington, *The Fugitive Blacksmith; or, Events in the History of James W. C. Pennington* (Westport, CT: Negro Universities Press, 1971), iv–vii, quoted in Johnson, *Soul by Soul*, 218.

36. Stampp, *The Peculiar Institution*, 171, quoting Olmstead.

37. Ford, *Deliver Us from Evil*, 163, n. 81.

38. Eric Foner, *Voices of Freedom: A Documentary History*, 3rd ed. (New York: Norton, 2011), 205.

39. Bennet H. Barrow, *Rules of Highland Plantation, Plantation Life in the Florida Parishes of Louisiana, 1836–1846 as reflected in the diary of Bennet H. Barrow*, ed. Edwin Adams David (New York: Columbia University Press, 1943) quoted in Foner, *Voices of Freedom*, 205–6.

40. Wyatt-Brown, *The Shaping of Southern Culture*, 25.

41. Oakes, *The Ruling Race*, 189.

42. The reader is referred to Theodore Weld's powerful 1839 edition, *American Slavery As It Is*. See table 8.1 for a cross-sample of the Weld data.

43. I think it is fair to say that many people think the word "lynching" means "hanging." Lynching in fact refers to any manner of murder of a person (usually a Black man) or a white sympathizer, generally committed by several people, constituting a mob, as a public display of punishment. Lynchings were considered public teaching tools.

44. Johnson, *Soul by Soul*, 107.

45. Johnson, *Soul by Soul*, 164.

46. Baptist, *The Half Has Never Been Told*, 122.

47. See Weld, *American Slavery*, 58, citing from the 1791 testimony of President Edwards, the Younger.

48. Johnson, *Soul by Soul*, see illustration 9.
49. Weld, *American Slavery*.
50. Stampp, *The Peculiar Institution*, 327.
51. Stampp, *The Peculiar Institution*, 143.
52. Levine, *The Fall of the House of Dixie*, 17, a turn of phrase attributed to John C. Calhoun.
53. Levine, *The Fall of the House of Dixie*, 20.
54. Delbanco, *The War before the War*, 3.
55. Delbanco, *The War before the War*, 33.
56. Stampp, *The Peculiar Institution*, 162.
57. Douglass, *Narrative*, 2005.
58. Delbanco, *The War before the War*, 2019.

CHAPTER 9

1. Karp, *This Vast Southern Empire*, frontispiece.
2. Berry, *The Hidden Wound*.
3. Fox-Genovese and Genovese, *The Mind of the Master Class*, 3.
4. William Hand Browne, ed., *Archives of Maryland: Proceedings and Acts of the General Assembly of Maryland, January, 1637–September, 1664* (Baltimore: Baltimore Maryland Historical Society, 1883), 533–34.
5. Kendi, *Stamped*, 49.
6. Oakes, *The Ruling Race*, 27. A "Mustee" is the offspring of a white person and a quadroon, the latter being a person who is one-fourth white.
7. Oakes, *The Ruling Race*, 27–28.
8. *Civil Code of the State of Louisiana Preceded by the Treaty of Cession with France, the Constitution of the United States and of the State* (1825), 90–94.
9. Rose, *A Documentary History*, 179.
10. Kendi, *Stamped*, 54.
11. Ford, *Deliver Us from Evil*, 58.
12. Johnson, *River of Dark Dreams*, 222.
13. Wyatt-Brown, *Southern Honor*, 402. "Charivaris" in this context means a mocking directed toward a Black slave.
14. Foner, *Voices of Freedom*, 73.
15. Kolchin, *American Slavery*, 70.
16. Kolchin, *American Slavery*, 70.
17. Jennifer Schuessler, "Alexander Hamilton, Enslaver? New Research Says Yes," *New York Times*, November 9, 2020, www.nytimes.com/2020/11/09arts/alexander -hamilton-enslaver-research.html.
18. Bassett, *Slavery in the State of North Carolina*, 1899.
19. Although some historians refer to this 1800 rebellion as the Prosser Rebellion, Prosser was Gabriel's master's name.
20. Ford, *Deliver Us from Evil*, 86.

21. Ford, *Deliver Us from Evil*, 89.
22. Bassett, *Slavery in the State of North Carolina*.
23. Ford, *Deliver Us from Evil*, 21, n. 12.
24. Delbanco, *The War before the War*, 197.
25. Wyatt-Brown, *Southern Honor*, 406.
26. Fox-Genovese and Genovese, *The Mind of the Master Class*, 366.
27. Stampp, *The Peculiar Institution*, 141.
28. Finkelman, *Defending Slavery*, 35.
29. Stampp, *The Peculiar Institution*, 181–82.
30. See Zimbardo, *The Lucifer Effect*.
31. Ball, *Slaves in the Family*, 41.
32. Weld, *American Slavery*, 77.
33. Ford, *Deliver Us from Evil*, 49.
34. Stampp, *The Peculiar Institution*, 172.
35. Delbanco, *The War before the War*, 194–95.
36. Ball, *Slaves in the Family*, 56.
37. Oakes, *The Ruling Race*, 24.
38. Stampp, *The Peculiar Institution*, 148.
39. Oakes, *The Ruling Race*, 29.
40. Oakes, *The Ruling Race*, 30–31.
41. Nicholas E. Magnis, "Thomas Jefferson and Slavery: An Analysis of His Racist Thinking as Revealed by His Writings and Political Behavior," *Journal of Black Studies* 29, no. 4 (March 1999): 491–509. For a full understanding of Jefferson's racist views on slavery, see his *Notes on the State of Virginia*, published in 1787.
42. Levine, *The Fall of the House of Dixie*, 20.
43. Levine, *The Fall of the House of Dixie*, 20.
44. Daly, *When Slavery Was Called Freedom*, 12.
45. Daly, *When Slavery Was Called Freedom*, 141.
46. Delbanco, *The War before the War*, 5.
47. Delbanco, *The War before the War*, 5.
48. Delbanco, *The War before the War*, 8, 9.
49. Delbanco, *The War before the War*, 11.

CHAPTER 10

1. Rosenthal, *Accounting for Slavery*, 152–53.
2. Stampp, *The Peculiar Institution*, 383.
3. Johnson, *River of Dark Dreams*, 13.
4. Scarborough, *Masters of the Big House*, 417.
5. Karp, *This Vast Southern Empire*, 130.
6. Rosenthal, *Accounting for Slavery*, 190–91.
7. Karp, *This Vast Southern Empire*, 125.
8. Beckert, *Empire of Cotton*, 242.

9. Beckert, *Empire of Cotton*, 243.

10. Rosenthal, *Accounting for Slavery*, 191.

11. Beckert, *Empire of Cotton*, 115.

12. Faust, *James Henry Hammond*.

13. Faust, *James Henry Hammond*, 72–73, n. 6.

14. Faust, *James Henry Hammond*, 73.

15. Beckert, *Empire of Cotton*, 102–3.

16. Beckert, *Empire of Cotton*, 103.

17. Johnson, *River of Dark Dreams*, 255–56.

18. Stewart, *Holy Warriors*, 30.

19. Delbanco, *The War before the War*, 43.

20. Ball, *Slaves in the Family*, 190.

21. Rosenthal, *Accounting for Slavery*, 190.

22. Rosenthal, *Accounting for Slavery*, 104, n. 13.

23. Johnson, *River of Dark Dreams*, 256.

24. Johnson, *River of Dark Dreams*, 6.

25. Johnson, *River of Dark Dreams*, 104–5.

26. Stampp, *The Peculiar Institution*, 5.

27. Fox-Genovese and Genovese, *The Mind of the Master Class*, 77.

28. Beckert, *Empire of Cotton*, 109, n. 22.

29. Beckert, *Empire of Cotton*, 110.

30. Scarborough, *Masters of the Big House*, 408.

31. Beckert, *Empire of Cotton*, 110.

32. Rosenthal, *Accounting for Slavery*, 1.

33. Rosenthal, *Accounting for Slavery*, 2.

34. Rosenthal, *Accounting for Slavery*, 2.

35. Rosenthal, *Accounting for Slavery*, 2.

36. Oakes, *The Ruling Race*, 153.

37. Rosenthal, *Accounting for Slavery*, 3.

38. Scarborough, *Masters of the Big House*, 218.

39. Stampp, *The Peculiar Institution*, 405–6, n. 8.

40. Stampp, *The Peculiar Institution*, 406.

41. Stampp, *The Peculiar Institution*, 265.

42. Sven Beckert and Seth Rockman, eds., *Slavery's Capitalism: A New History of American Economic Development* (Philadelphia: University of Pennsylvania Press, 2016), 22–23.

43. Baptist, *The Half Has Never Been Told*, 271.

44. Delbanco, *The War before the War*, 26.

45. Beckert and Rockman, *Slavery's Capitalism*, 22–23.

46. Oakes, *The Ruling Race*.

47. This deed of sale is approximately seven pages. It can be found in the Peoples Family Papers, mss#0575, J. Murrey Atkins Library, the University of North Carolina at Charlotte, Charlotte, North Carolina.

48. Rosenthal, *Accounting for Slavery*, 4.

49. Rosenthal, *Accounting for Slavery*, 4.

50. Rosenthal, *Accounting for Slavery*, 9–48.
51. Scarborough, *The Overseer*, xix.
52. Scarborough offers a caveat about his conclusions: There are to be expected some reliability errors in the census data affecting accuracy, as well as the care taken by the census takers.
53. This group of substantial property owners had an average age of forty-one.
54. Scarborough, *The Overseer*, 93.
55. This is a description of a scene in the 2013 film, directed by Steve McQueen, based on the autobiographical slave narrative and memoir by Solomon Northup, *Twelve Years a Slave* (New York: Derby & Miller, 1853).
56. Stampp, *The Peculiar Institution*, 191.
57. Stampp, *The Peculiar Institution*, 185.

CHAPTER 11

1. Michael Powell, "'White Supremacy' Once Meant David Duke and the Klan. Now It Refers to Much More," *New York Times*, October 17, 2020, https://www.nytimes.com/2020/10/17/us/whitesupremacy.html.
2. Resmaa Menakem, *My Grandmother's Hands: Racialized Trauma and the Pathway to Mending Our Hearts and Bodies* (Las Vegas: Central Recovery Press, 2017), 10.
3. *Webster's Dictionary of Word Origins* (New York: Smithmark, 1995), 351–52.
4. *Merriam-Webster's*, 912.
5. *Merriam-Webster's*, 912; Charlton T. Lewis, *A Latin Dictionary for Schools* (1888; New York: American Book Company, 1916), 738.
6. Stampp, *The Peculiar Institution*, 11.
7. McCurry, "The Confederacy," 204–6.
8. Menakem, *My Grandmother's Hands*.
9. Berry, *The Hidden Wound*.
10. Lisa Mascaro, "In Alabama, the Heart of Trump Country, Many Think He's Backing the Wrong Candidate in Senate Race," *Los Angeles Times*, September 21, 2017.
11. Daly, *When Slavery Was Called Freedom*, 136.
12. Paul Bloom, "The Root of All Cruelty," *New Yorker Magazine*, November 20, 2017, headline "Beastly." Paul Bloom uses the term "moral entitlement" in his discussion of the work of the philosopher Kate Manne.
13. Naomi Lim, "Biden Slams Trump 'Throughline' from Rhetoric to Whitmer's ISIS-Style Kidnap Plot," *Washington Examiner*, October 9, 2020, http://a.msn.com/01/en-us/BB19QsYD?ocid=se.

EPILOGUE

1. *Merriam-Webster's*, 420.

2. Marvin Ventrell, Chief Executive Officer, National Association of Addiction Treatment Providers, personal communication, January 26, 2021.

3. Mary L. Trump, *Too Much and Never Enough: How My Family Created the World's Most Dangerous Man* (New York: Simon & Schuster, 2020), 13.

4. Bob Woodward, *Fear: Trump in the White House* (New York: Simon & Schuster, 2018), 125.

5. Michael Gordon, "Did Ex-NC Judge Help Ignite 'Human Bomb' at Capitol? Critics Say He Should Be Punished," *Charlotte Observer*, February 7, 2021.

6. Joseph Choi, "Ex-Solicitor General Says Trump 'Talks Like a Mafia Boss, and Not a Particularly Smart Mafia Boss,'" *The Hill*, January 3, 2021.

7. Philip Rucker and Carol Leonnig, *A Very Stable Genius: Donald J. Trump's Testing of America* (New York: Penguin, 2020), 462–63.

8. Rucker and Leonnig, *A Very Stable Genius*, 3.

9. Michael Cohen, *Disloyal: A Memoir. The True Story of the Former Personal Attorney to the President of the United States* (New York: Skyhorse, 2020).

10. Rucker and Leonnig, *A Very Stable Genius*, 3.

11. Karen Grigsby Bates, "Is Trump Really a Racist?" *Code Switch*, St. Louis Public Radio, October 21, 2020.

12. Touré, "Slavery in America Reminds Us: Trump Is Far from an Aberration," *Guardian*, August 16, 2019.

13. *Merriam-Webster's*, 822.

14. Bradley Onishi, "Trump's New Civil Religion: The Storming of the Capitol Is a Creation Myth for a Political Movement," *New York Times*, January 19, 2021.

15. See Charles Reagan Wilson, *Baptism in Blood: The Religion of the Lost Cause, 1865–1920* (Athens: University of Georgia Press, 2009).

16. Wyatt-Brown, *The Shaping of Southern Culture*, 282.

17. Anderson, *White Rage*, 3.

18. David H. Bennett, *The Party of Fear: From Nativist Movements to the New Right in American History* (New York: Vintage, 1990), 1.

19. Rucker and Leonnig, *A Very Stable Genius*. Trump tweeted this self-assessment on January 6, 2018.

20. Bennett, *The Party of Fear*, 4.

21. Bob Woodward, *Rage* (New York, Simon & Schuster, 2020), 284, 285, 288.

22. Dan Berry, Mike McIntire, and Matthew Rosenberg, "Mob's Battle Cry: 'Our President Wants Us Here,'" *New York Times*, January 10, 2021.

23. Woodward, *Rage*, xi.

24. Woodward, *Rage*, 28.

25. Woodward, *Rage*, 28.

26. Barry et al., "Mob's Battle Cry."

27. Kathleen Gray, "If You Didn't See Invasion Coming, You Weren't Watching Michigan," *New York Times,* January 10, 2021.

28. This list was adapted from an article by Laura E. Adkins and Emily Burack titled "Hate on Display: A Guide to the Symbols and Signs on Display at the Capitol Insurrection," *Jewish News of Northern California*, January 7, 2021.

29. Ben Steelman, "6 Confederate Flags and How They Are Different," *StarNews Online*, June 25, 2015, https://www.starnewsonline.com/article/NC/20150625/news/605043805/WM.

30. ABC Chicago, "A Brief History of the Confederate Flag Design," June 26, 2015, https://abc7chicago.com/confederate-flag-debate-banned-buy/808079/.

31. Wyatt-Brown, *The Shaping of Southern Culture*, 295.

32. Anti-Defamation League, "Nationalist Social Club (NSC)," https://www.adl.org/resources/backgrounders/nationalist-social-club-nsc.

33. Adkins and Burack, "A Guide to the Hate Signs."

34. Dictionary.com, "Three Percenter," https://www.dictionary.com/e/politics/three-percenter/.

35. See *Hon. Bennie G. Thompson v. Donald J. Trump, Rudolph W. Giuliani, Proud Boys International c/o Jason L. Van Dyke, and the Oath Keepers, Attn: Stewart Rhodes*, a civil lawsuit filed February 16, 2021, in the US District Court for the District of Columbia. This lawsuit offers yet another link of Trump and his minions to white supremacy terrorism, as the legal precedent being used as the basis for this lawsuit is a law known as the Ku Klux Klan Act, 42 U.S.C.§ 1985 (1). This Ku Klux Klan Act, signed into law by President Ulysses S. Grant, on April 20, 1871, enforced the 14th Amendment."

36. Adkins and Burack, "A Guide to the Hate Signs."

37. This additional listing is adapted from an article by Emma Rose, "The Many Flags That Flew during the US Capitol Storming and What They Represent," *The Wire*, January 15, 2021.

38. This flag erroneously is sometimes referred to as the Gadsen flag. The US National Park Service website spells his last name as Gadsden, which appears to be the correct spelling. A portrait of Gadsden using that spelling is located in the Library of Congress. The Gadsden Wharf in Charleston, South Carolina, will be the site of the International African American Museum, scheduled to open in 2022. In 1806 the Gadsden Wharf became the official site for offloading Black Africans to be sold into slavery. See Nic Butler, "The Story of Gadsden's Wharf," Charleston County Public Library, February 2, 2018, https://www.ccpl.org/charleston-time-machine/story-gadsdens-wharf. See Paul Burski, "Yellow Gadsden Flag, Prominent in Capitol Takeover, Carries a Long and Shifting History," *The Conversation*, January 7, 2021, https://theconversation.com/yellow-gadsden-flag-prominent-in-capitol-takeover-carries-a-long-and-shifting-history-145142.

39. I am uncertain about where I first encountered this term, but I have been able to track its use in the work of forensic psychologist, Katherine Ramsland, PhD, personal communication with Dr. Ramsland, February 2, 2021.

40. Robert Reich, "Trump Said He Could Kill and Win—Covid and Cheating May Prove It," *Guardian*, October 11, 2020. Robert Reich served in the administrations of presidents Gerald Ford and Jimmy Carter and was President Bill Clinton's secretary of labor.

41. "Donald Trump's Second Impeachment Ends in Second Acquittal," *Economist*, February 14, 2021.

42. Luke Broadwater, Emily Cochrane, and Adam Goldman, "Capitol Police Admit to Failures as Pro-Trump Mob Took Place," *New York Times*, January 27, 2021.

43. Amanda Taub, "Tumultuous Day, But a Coup Attempt?" *New York Times*, January 8, 2021.

44. *Merriam-Webster's*, 286.

45. *Merriam-Webster's*, 743.

46. Eddie S. Glaude Jr., *African American Religion: A Very Short Introduction* (Oxford: Oxford University Press, 2014), 52.

47. David Zucchino, *Wilmington's Lie: The Murderous Coup of 1898 and the Rise of White Supremacy* (New York: Grove, 2020).

48. Eddie S. Glaude Jr., *Begin Again: James Baldwin's America and Its Urgent Lessons for Our Own* (New York: Crown, 2020), 7.

49. Glaude, *Begin Again*, 8–9.

50. Jim Rutenberg et al., "77 Days: Trump's Campaign to Subvert the Election," *New York Times*, January 31, 2021, https://www.nytimes.com/2021/01/31/us/trump-election-lie.html.

51. It seems most likely Kylie Kremer misspelled the word, as the context of her tweet would strongly suggest she meant the cavalry was coming.

52. Mab Segrest, "'Go There Ready for War'—Militia Organizing in North Carolina in the Context of the Insurrection at the US Capitol," *Scalawag*, March 29, 2021, 11–12. https://scalawagmagazine.org/2021/03/blueprint-nc-report/.

53. The Rule of Law Defense Fund is an arm of the Republican Attorneys General Association (RAGA).

54. Rutenberg et al., "77 Days."

55. Rucker and Leonnig, *A Very Stable Genius*, 1, 2. *Merriam-Webster's* defines "solipsism" as a "theory holding that the self can know nothing but its own modifications and the self is the only existent thing: *also*: extreme egocentrism," 1188.

56. Woodward, *Rage*, xx–xxi, 243, 260, 272, 285, 294, 386, 388, plate 3.

57. Michelle Goldberg, "Impeachment Offers Republicans Grace. They Don't Want It." *New York Times*, February 11, 2021.

58. *USA Today*, February 10, 2021.

59. Goldberg, "Impeachment Offers Republicans Grace."

60. Gail Collins, "Ready to Nag About Gun Control?" *New York Times*, February 25, 2021.

61. Mallory Simon, Sara Sidner, and Anna Maja Rappard, "Some of His Followers Are Being Sought by the FBI. It's Not Stopping the Leader of the Oath Keepers," CNN, February 15, 2021, https://www.cnn.com/2021/02/15/politics/capitol-riot-oath-keepers-stewart-rhodes-soh/index.html. This CNN report states that Rhodes incorporated the Oath Keepers in 2009, "after the group rose to prominence during the first election campaign of Barack Obama."

62. David Frum, "It'll Do. Impeachment Did Not Prevail, but Trump Still Lost," *Atlantic*, February 13, 2021.

63. *Economist*, "Donald Trump Emerges from Seclusion before an Adoring Crowd: The Second Coming," March 1, 2021, https://www.economist.com/united

-states/2021/03/01/donald-trump-emerges-from-seclusion-before-an-adoring-crowd.

APPENDIX A

1. Adapted from the American Psychiatric Association, *DSM* IV (Washington, DC: American Psychiatric Association, 1994), 751–53; American Psychiatric Association, *DSM* IV–TR (Washington, DC: American Psychiatric Association, 2000), 807–9.

2. Idealization is not the mirror opposite of devaluation because the overvaluing of oneself takes the human being down a different psychopathological road into self-absorption and narcissism.

3. I have taken the liberty of adding "group" as a target of projections and projective identification defense mechanisms, for the simple reason that humans project negative attributes to entire groups and even nations.

APPENDIX C

1. This sermon and its location are fiction and hypothetical. It was derived solely from the author's imagination. If familiar to the reader, this sermon is best read in a "fire and brimstone" tone and cadence.

Bibliography

ABC Chicago. "A Brief History of the Confederate Flag Design." June 26, 2015. https://abc7chicago.com/confederate-flag-debate-banned-buy/808079/

Adkins, Laura E., and Emily Burack. "Hate on Display: A Guide to the Symbols and Signs on Display at the Capitol Insurrection." *Jewish News of Northern California,* January 7, 2021.

Allen, Dom Cameron. *The Legend of Noah: Renaissance Rationalism in Art, Science and Letters.* Urbana: University of Illinois Press, 1963.

Alter, Robert. *The Five Books of Moses: A Translation with Commentary.* New York: Norton, 2004.

American Psychiatric Association. *Diagnostic and Statistical Manual of Mental Disorders,* 4th ed. Washington, DC: American Psychiatric Association, 1994.

————. *Diagnostic and Statistical Manual of Mental Disorders,* 4th ed., text revision. Washington, DC: American Psychiatric Association, 2000.

Anderson, Carol. *White Rage: The Unspoken Truth of Our Racial Divide.* New York: Bloomsbury, 2016.

Andrews, William L. *Slavery and Class in the American South: A Generation of Slave Narrative Testimony 1840–1865.* New York: Oxford University Press, 2019.

Anti-Defamation League. "Nationalist Social Club (NSC)." https://www.adl.org/resources/backgrounders/nationalist-social-club-nsc

Avalos, Hector. *The Bad Jesus: The Ethics of New Testament Ethics.* Sheffield, UK: Sheffield Phoenix Press, 2015.

————. *Slavery, Abolitionism, and the Ethics of Biblical Scholarship.* Sheffield, UK: Sheffield Phoenix Press, 2013.

Babiak, Paul, and Robert D. Hare. *Snakes in Suits: When Psychopaths Go to Work.* New York: HarperCollins, 2009. Kindle.

Bachelard, Gaston. *The Psychoanalysis of Fire.* London, 1964.

Ball, Edward. *Slaves in the Family.* New York: Farrar, Straus and Giroux, 2014.

Baptist, Edward E. *The Half Has Never Been Told: Slavery and the Making of American Capitalism.* New York: Basic Books, 2014.

Barnes, Albert. *An Inquiry into the Scriptural Views of Slavery*. Philadelphia: Perkins & Purves; Boston: B. Perkins, 1846.

Barrow, Bennet H. *Rules of Highland Plantation, Plantation Life in the Florida Parishes of Louisiana, 1836–1846, as reflected in the diary of Bennet H. Barrow*. Edited by Edwin Adams David. New York: Columbia University Press, 1943.

Bassett, John Spencer. *Slavery in the State of North Carolina*. Studies in Historical and Political Science. Baltimore: Johns Hopkins University Press, 1899; repr. London: Forgotten Books, 2018.

Bates, Karen Grigsby. "Is Trump Really a Racist?" *Code Switch*. St. Louis Public Radio, October 21, 2020.

Beckert, Sven. *Empire of Cotton: A Global History*. New York: Vintage, 2014.

Beckert, Sven, and Seth Rockman, eds. *Slavery's Capitalism: A New History of American Economic Development*. Philadelphia: University of Pennsylvania Press, 2016.

Bennett, David H. *The Party of Fear: From Nativist Movements to the New Right in American History*. New York: Vintage, 1990.

Berkeley, Kathleen C. "Within the Plantation Household: Black and White Women of the Old South." *North Carolina Historical Review* 66, no. 3 (July 1989): 361–62.

Berlin, Ira. *Many Thousands Gone: The First Two Centuries of Slavery in North America*. Cambridge, MA: Belknap Press, 1998.

Berry, Dan, Mike McIntire, and Matthew Rosenberg. "Mob's Battle Cry: 'Our President Wants Us Here.'" *New York Times*, January 10, 2021.

Berry, Wendell. *The Hidden Wound*. Berkeley, CA: Counterpoint, 2010.

Blassingame, John W. *The Slave Community: Plantation Life in the Antebellum South*. New York: Oxford University Press, 1979.

Bloom, Paul, "The Root of All Cruelty." *New Yorker*, November 20, 2017.

Blow, Charles, "Yes, Even George Washington." *New York Times*, June 28, 2020. https://www.nytimes/2020/06/28/opinion/george-washington-confederate-statues.html

Botsford, Edmund. *Sambo and Toney: A Dialogue in Three Parts*. Georgetown, SC: Francis M. Baxter, 1808.

Broadwater, Luke, Emily Cochrane, and Adam Goldman. "Capitol Police Admit to Failures as Pro-Trump Mob Took Place." *New York Times*, January 27, 2021.

Brown, Christopher Leslie. *Moral Capital: Foundations of British Abolitionism*. Chapel Hill: University of North Carolina Press, 2006.

Browne, Katrina, Jude Ray, and Alla Kovgan, directors. *Traces of the Trade: A Story from the Deep North* [film]. POV Documentary, 2008.

Browne, William Hand, ed. *Archives of Maryland: Proceedings and Acts of the General Assembly of Maryland, January, 1637–September, 1664*. Baltimore: Baltimore Historical Society, 1883.

Brownlow William G., and A. Pryne. *Ought American Slavery Be Perpetuated? A Debate*. Philadelphia: Lippincott, 1858.

Brundage, Fitzhugh. "A Look Back at the Peculiar Institution." *Journal of Blacks in Higher Education*, no. 15 (spring 1997): 118–20.

Burski, Paul. "Yellow Gadsden Flag, Prominent in Capitol Takeover, Carries a Long and Shifting History." *The Conversation*, January 7, 2021. https://theconversation

.com/yellow-gadsden-flag-prominent-in-capitol-takeover-carries-a-long-and -shifting-history-145142

Butler, Nic. "The Story of Gadsden's Wharf." Charleston County Public Library, February 2, 2018. https://www.ccpl.org/charleston-time-machine/story-gadsdens -wharf

Campbell, Robert Jean. *Psychiatric Dictionary*, 7th ed. New York: Oxford University Press, 1996.

Cecelski, David S. *The Fire of Freedom: Abraham Galloway and the Slaves' Civil War*. Chapel Hill: University of North Carolina Press, 2012.

Censer, Jane Turner. *North Carolina Planters and Their Children 1800–1860*. Baton Rouge: Louisiana State University Press, 1984.

Choi, Joseph. "Ex-Solicitor General Says Trump 'Talks Like a Mafia Boss, and Not a Particularly Smart Mafia Boss.'" *The Hill*, January 3, 2021.

Civil Code of the State of Louisiana Preceded by the Treaty of Cession with France, the Constitution of the United States and of the State. 1825.

Cleckley, Hervey M. *The Mask of Sanity*. 1941; St. Louis: Mosby, 1976.

Clinton, Catherine. *The Plantation Mistress: Woman's World in the Old South*. New York: Pantheon, 1982.

Coates, Ta-Nehisi. *Between the World and Me*. New York: Spiegel & Grau, 2015.

Cohen, H. Hirsch. *The Drunkenness of Noah*. Tuscaloosa: University of Alabama Press, 1974.

Cohen, Michael. *Disloyal: A Memoir. The True Story of the Former Personal Attorney to the President of the United States*. New York: Skyhorse, 2020.

Collins, Gail. "Ready to Nag About Gun Control?" *New York Times*, February 25, 2021.

Condivi, Ascanio. *The Life of Michelangelo*. Edited by Helmut Wohl, translated by Alice Sedgwick Wohl. University Park: Pennsylvania State University Press, 1999.

D'Souza, Dinesh. "Ignoble Savages." In *Critical White Studies*, edited by Richard Delbanco and Jean Stefancic, 55–65. Philadelphia: Temple University Press, 1997.

Daly, John Patrick. *When Slavery Was Called Freedom: Evangelicalism, Proslavery, and the Causes of the Civil War*. Lexington: University Press of Kentucky, 2002.

Davidson, Chalmers G[aston]. *The Last Foray: The South Carolina Planters of 1860: A Sociological Study*. Columbia: University of South Carolina Press, 1971.

Davis, David Brion. *Challenging the Boundaries of Slavery*. Cambridge, MA: Harvard University Press, 2003.

———. *Homicide in American Fiction 1798–1860*. Ithaca, NY: Cornell University Press, 1957.

———. *Inhuman Bondage: The Rise and Fall of Slavery in the New World*. New York: Oxford University Press, 2006.

———. *The Problem of Slavery in Western Culture*. Ithaca, NY: Cornell University Press, 1966.

Davis, John D., and Henry Snyder Gehman. *The Westminster Dictionary of the Bible*. Philadelphia: Westminster Press, 1944.

Delbanco, Andrew. *The War before the War: Fugitive Slaves and the Struggle for America's Soul from the Revolution to the Civil War*. New York: Penguin, 2019.

Dew, Charles B. *Apostles of Disunion: Southern Secession Commissioners and the Causes of the Civil War*. Charlottesville: University of Virginia Press, 2001.

———. *The Making of a Racist: A Southerner Reflects on Family History and the Slave Trade*. Charlottesville: University of Virginia Press, 2016.

Doddington, David Stefan. *Contesting Slave Masculinity in the American South*. Cambridge: Cambridge University Press, 2018.

Dolan, J. P. *The Irish Americans: A History*. New York: Bloomsbury, 2008.

"Donald Trump's Second Impeachment Ends in Second Acquittal." *Economist*, February 14, 2021.

Douglass, Frederick. *Narrative of the Life of Frederick Douglass, an American Slave: Written by Himself*. 1845; New York: Barnes & Noble Classics, 2003.

Dred Scott v. Sandford, 60 U.S. (19 How.) 393 (1857).

Economist. "Donald Trump Emerges from Seclusion before an Adoring Crowd: The Second Coming." March 1, 2021. https://www.economist.com/united-states/2021/03/01/donald-trump-emerges-from-seclusion-before-an-adoring-crowd

Edgar, Walter. *South Carolina: A History*. Columbia: University of South Carolina Press, 1998.

Elliott, E. N., C. Hodge, S. A. Cartwright, J. Henry Hammond, R. Goodloe Harper, T. Stringfellow, A. Bledsoe, D. Christy. *E. N. Elliott, Cotton Is King and Proslavery Arguments: Comprising the Writings of Hammond, Harper, Christy, Stringfellow, Henry, Bledsoe and Cartwright*. Augusta, GA: Pritchard, Abbott & Loomis, 1860.

Erskine, Noel Leo. *Plantation Church: How African American Religion Was Born in Caribbean Slavery*. New York: Oxford University Press, 2014.

Escott, Paul D. *"What Shall We Do with the Negro?" Lincoln, White Racism, and Civil War America*. Charlottesville: University of Virginia Press, 2009.

Estes, Matthew. *A Defence of Negro Slavery, As It Exists in the United States*. Montgomery: Press of the *Alabama Journal*, 1846.

Faust, Drew Gilpin. *James Henry Hammond and the Old South: A Design for Mastery*. Baton Rouge: Louisiana State University Press, 1982.

———. *A Sacred Circle: The Dilemma of the Intellectual in the Old South, 1840–1860*. Baltimore: Johns Hopkins University Press, 1977.

Featherstonhaugh, George W. *Excursion through the Slave States, from Washington on the Potomac to the Frontier of Mexico: with Sketches of Popular Manners and Geological Notices*. New York: Harper, 1844.

Federal Writers' Project and Library of Congress. *Born in Slavery: Slave Narratives from the Federal Writers' Project, 1936–1938*. Washington, DC: Library of Congress, 2001. http://hdl.loc.gov/loc.mss/collmss.ms000008

Finkelman, Paul. *Defending Slavery: Proslavery Thought in the Old South; A Brief History with Documents*. Boston: Bedford/St. Martin's, 2003.

Foner, Eric. *Voices of Freedom: A Documentary History*, 3rd ed. New York: Norton, 2011.

Ford, Lacy K. *Deliver Us from Evil: The Slavery Question in the Old South*. New York: Oxford University Press, 2009.

Fought, Leigh. *Southern Womanhood and Slavery: A Biography of Louisa S. McCord, 1810–1879*. Columbia: University of Missouri Press, 2002.

Fox-Genovese, Elizabeth. *Within the Plantation Household: Black and White Women of the Old South*. Chapel Hill: University of North Carolina Press, 1988.

Fox-Genovese, Elizabeth, and Eugene D. Genovese, *The Mind of the Master Class: History and Faith in the Southern Slaveholders' Worldview*. Cambridge: Cambridge University Press, 2005.

Fredrickson, George. "White Images of Black Slaves (Is What We See in Others Sometimes a Reflection of What We Find in Ourselves?)." In *Critical White Studies*, edited by Richard Delbanco and Jean Stefancic, 38–45. Philadephia: Temple University Press, 1997.

Frum, David. "It'll Do. Impeachment Did Not Prevail, but Trump Still Lost." *Atlantic*, February 13, 2021.

Furman, Richard. *Exposition of the Views of Baptists*. Charleston, SC: A. E. Miller, 1822.

Genovese, Eugene D. *A Consuming Fire: The Fall of the Confederacy in the Mind of the White Christian South*. Athens: University of Georgia Press, 1998.

———. *Roll, Jordan, Roll: The World the Slaves Made*. New York: Pantheon, 1974.

———. *The Slaveholders' Dilemma: Freedom and Progress in Southern Conservative Thought, 1820–1860*. Columbia, SC: University of South Carolina Press, 1992.

Genovese, Eugene D., and Elizabeth Fox-Genovese. *Fatal Self-Deception: Slaveholding Paternalism in the Old South*. New York: Cambridge University Press, 2011.

Glancy, Jennifer A. *Slavery in Early Christianity*. Minneapolis: Fortress Press, 2006.

Glaude, Eddie S., Jr. *African American Religion: A Very Short Introduction*. Oxford: Oxford University Press, 2014.

———. *Begin Again: James Baldwin's America and Its Urgent Lessons for Our Own*. New York: Crown, 2020.

Goldberg, Michelle. "Impeachment Offers Republicans Grace. They Don't Want It." *New York Times*, February 11, 2021.

Goldenberg, David M. *Black and Slave: The Origins and History of the Curse of Ham*. Berlin: De Gruyter, 2017.

———. *The Curse of Ham: Race and Slavery in Early Judaism, Christianity, and Islam*. Princeton, NJ: Princeton University Press, 2003.

Gordon, Michael. "Did Ex-NC Judge Help Ignite 'Human Bomb' at Capitol? Critics Say He Should Be Punished." *Charlotte Observer*, February 7, 2021.

Gordon-Reed, Annette. *The Hemingses of Monticello: An American Family*. New York: Norton, 2008.

Gray, Kathleen. "If You Didn't See Invasion Coming, You Weren't Watching Michigan." *New York Times*, January 10, 2021.

Greenblatt, Stephen. *Tyrant: Shakespeare on Politics*. New York: Norton, 2018.

Greenwood, Janette Thomas. *Bittersweet Legacy: The Black and White "Better Classes" in Charlotte, 1850–1910*. Chapel Hill: University of North Carolina Press, 1994.

Gunsberg, L., and P. Hymowitz, eds. *A Handbook of Divorce and Custody: Forensic, Developmental, and Clinical Perspectives*. Hillsdale, NJ: Analytic Press, 2005.

Hare, R. D. "Psychopaths and Their Nature: Implications for the Mental Health and Criminal Justice Systems." In *Psychopathy: Antisocial, Criminal, and Violent Behavior*, edited by T. Millon, E. Simonson, M. Burket-Smith, and R. Davis, 188–214. New York: Guilford Press, 1998.

Harvey, Paul. "Religion, White Supremacist." In *The New Encyclopedia of Southern Culture*, edited by Thomas C. Holt, Laurie B. Green, and Charles Reagan Wilson, vol. 24. Chapel Hill: University of North Carolina Press, 2013.

Haynes, Stephen R. *Noah's Curse: The Biblical Justification of American Slavery*. Oxford: Oxford University Press, 2002.

Herba, Catherine M., Sheilagh Hodgins, Nigel Blackwood, Veena Kumari, Kris H. Naudts, and Mary Phillips. "The Neurobiology of Psychopathy: A Focus on Emotion Processing." In *The Psychopath: Theory, Research, and Practice*, edited by Hugues Herve and John C. Yuille, 253–83. Mahwah, NJ: Lawrence Erlbaum Associates, 2007.

Herve, Hugues. "Psychopathy across the Ages: A History of the Hare Psychopath." In *The Psychopath: Theory, Research, and Practice*, edited by Hugues Herve and John C. Yuille, 32–44. Mahwah, NJ: Lawrence Erlbaum Associates, 2007.

Herve, Hugues, and John C. Yuille, eds. *The Psychopath: Theory, Research, and Practice*. Mahwah, NJ: Lawrence Erlbaum Associates, 2007.

Hoit, T. W. *The Right of American Slavery*. St. Louis, MO: L. Bushnell, 1860. http:// name.umdl.umich.edu/ABJ1322.0001.001

Jacobs, Harriet. *Incidents in the Life of a Slave Girl*. Mineola, NY: Dover, 2001.

Johnson, Charles. *Middle Passage*. New York: Scribner, 1990.

Johnson, Walter. *River of Dark Dreams: Slavery and Empire in the Cotton Kingdom*. Cambridge, MA: Belknap Press, 2013.

———. *Soul by Soul: Life inside the Antebellum Slave Market*. Cambridge, MA: Harvard University Press, 1999.

Jones-Rogers, Stephanie E. *They Were Her Property: White Women as Slave Owners in the American South*. New Haven, CT: Yale University Press, 2019.

Karp, Matthew. *This Vast Southern Empire: Slaveholders at the Helm of American Foreign Policy*. Cambridge, MA: Harvard University Press, 2016.

Kay, Marvin L. Michael, and Lorin Lee Cary. *Slavery in North Carolina, 1748–1775*. Chapel Hill: University of North Carolina Press, 1995.

Kendi, Ibram X. *Stamped from the Beginning: The Definitive History of Racist Ideas in America*. New York: Nation Books, 2016.

King, Ray A. *A History of the Associate Reformed Presbyterian Church*. Charlotte, NC: Board of Christian Education of the Associate Reformed Presbyterian Church, 1966.

Klein, Rachel N. "Plantation Mistresses." *Journal of Southern History* 50, no.1 (Feb. 1984): 123–25.

Kolchin, Peter. *American Slavery 1619–1877*. New York: Hill and Wang, 2003.

Kratt, Mary Norton. *Charlotte: Spirit of the New South*. Winston-Salem, NC: John F. Blair, 1992.

Levin, Kevin M. *Searching for Black Confederates: The Civil War's Most Persistent Myth*. Chapel Hill: University of North Carolina Press, 2019.

Levine, Bruce. *The Fall of the House of Dixie: The Civil War and the Social Revolution That Transformed the South*. New York: Random House, 2014.

Levine, Lawrence W. *Black Culture and Black Consciousness: Afro-American Folk Thought from Slavery to Freedom*. New York: Oxford University Press, 1977.

Lewis, Charlton T. *A Latin Dictionary for Schools.* 1888; New York: American Book Company, 1916.

Lewis, Jan. "Within the Plantation Household: Black and White Women of the Old South." *Journal of Social History* 23, no. 2 (winter 1989): 402–5.

Leyburn, James G. *The Scotch-Irish: A Social History.* Chapel Hill: University of North Carolina Press, 1962.

Lim, Naomi. "Biden Slams Trump 'Throughline' from Rhetoric to Whitmer's ISIS-Style Kidnap Plot." *Washington Examiner*, October 9, 2020. http://a.msn.com/01/en-us/BB19QsYD?ocid=se

Lounsbury, Richard C., ed. *Louisa S. McCord: Political and Social Essays.* Charlottesville: University Press of Virginia, 1995.

———. *Louisa S. McCord: Selected Writings.* Charlottesville: University Press of Virginia, 1997.

Magnis, Nicholas E. "Thomas Jefferson and Slavery: An Analysis of His Racist Thinking as Revealed by His Writings and Political Behavior." *Journal of Black Studies* 29, no. 4 (March 1999): 491–509.

Martin, Bonnie. "Neighbor-to-Neighbor: Local Credit Networks and the Mortgaging of Slaves." In *Slavery's Capitalism: A New History of American Economic Development*, ed. Sven Beckert and Seth Rockman, 107–21. Philadelphia: University of Pennsylvania Press, 2016.

Mascaro, Lisa. "In Alabama, the Heart of Trump Country, Many Think He's Backing the Wrong Candidate in Senate Race." *Los Angeles Times*, September 21, 2017.

McCarthy, Karen F. *The Other Irish: The Scots-Irish Rascals Who Made America.* New York: Sterling, 2011.

McCurry, Stephanie. "The Confederacy." In *Disunion: A History of the Civil War*, ed. Ted Widmer, 204–6. Oxford: Oxford University Press, 2016.

———. *Masters of Small Worlds: Yeoman Households, Gender Relations, and the Political Culture of the Antebellum South Carolina Low Country.* New York: Oxford University Press, 1995.

Mctyeire, Holland N., ed. *Duties of Masters to Servants.* Charleston, SC: Southern Baptist Publication Society, 1851.

Menakem, Resmaa. *My Grandmother's Hands: Racialized Trauma and the Pathway to Mending Our Hearts and Bodies.* Las Vegas: Central Recovery Press, 2017.

Merriam-Webster's Collegiate Dictionary, 11th ed. Springfield, MA: Merriam-Webster, 2020.

Metzl, Jonathan M. *Dying of Whiteness: How the Politics of Racial Resentment Is Killing America's Heartland.* New York: Basic Books, 2019.

Miller, John Chester. *The Wolf by the Ears: Thomas Jefferson and Slavery.* New York: Free Press, 1977.

Moore, Peter N. *World of Toil and Strife: Community Transformation in Backcountry South Carolina, 1750–1805.* Columbia: University of South Carolina Press, 2007.

Morone, James A. "South: The Pro-Slavery Argument." In *Hellfire Nation: The Politics of Sin in American History*, 169–82. New Haven, CT: Yale University Press, 2003.

Morrill, Dan L. *Historic Charlotte: An Illustrated History of Charlotte and Mecklenburg County.* San Antonio, TX: Historical Publishing Network, 2011.

Mullin, Michael, ed. *American Negro Slavery: A Documentary History*. New York: Harper Torchbooks, 1976.

Murray, Linda. *The High Renaissance*. New York: Praeger, 1967.

Myers, John E. B. *Child Protection in America: Past, Present and Future*. New York: Oxford University Press, 2006.

Nelkin, Dana Kay. "Psychopaths, Incorrigible Racists, and the Faces of Responsibility." *Ethics* 125, no. 2 (2015): 357–90.

Noll, Mark A. *The Civil War as a Theological Crisis*. Chapel Hill: University of North Carolina Press, 2006.

Northup, Solomon. *Twelve Years a Slave*. New York: Derby & Miller, 1853.

Oakes, James. *The Ruling Race: A History of American Slaveholders*. New York: Norton, 1998.

O'Brien, Michael, *Conjectures of Order: Intellectual Life and the American South, 1810–1860*. Vol. 1. Chapel Hill: University of North Carolina Press, 2004.

———. *Conjectures of Order: Intellectual Life and the American South, 1810–1860*. Vol. 2. Chapel Hill: University of North Carolina Press, 2004.

O'Brien, Michael, ed., *All Clever Men, Who Make Their Way: Critical Discourse in the Old South*. Fayetteville: University of Arkansas Press, 1982.

Onishi, Bradley. "Trump's New Civil Religion: The Storming of the Capitol Is a Creation Myth for a Political Movement." *New York Times*, January 19, 2021.

Parker Alison M. "When White Women Wanted a Monument to Black 'Mammies'." *New York Times*, February 6, 2020. https://www.nytimes.com/2020/02/06/opinion/sunday/confederate-monuments-mammy.html

Patrick, Christopher J. "Getting to the Heart of Psychopathy." In *The Psychopath: Theory, Research, and Practice*, ed. Hugues Herve and John C. Yuille, 207–52. Mahwah, NJ: Lawrence Erlbaum Associates, 2007.

Pennington, James W. C. *The Fugitive Blacksmith; or, Events in the History of James W. C. Pennington*. Westport, CT: Negro Universities Press, 1971.

Powell, Michael, "'White Supremacy' Once Meant David Duke and the Klan. Now It Refers to Much More." *New York Times*, October 17, 2020. https://www.nytimes.com/2020/10/17/us/whitesupremacy.html

Reich, Robert. "Trump Said He Could Kill and Win—Covid and Cheating May Prove It." *Guardian*, October 11, 2020.

Roark, James L. *Masters without Slaves: Southern Planters in the Civil War and Reconstruction*. New York: Norton, 1977.

Rose, Emma. "The Many Flags That Flew during the US Capitol Storming and What They Represent." *The Wire*, January 15, 2021.

Rose, Willie Lee. *A Documentary History of Slavery in North America*. Athens: University of Georgia Press, 1999.

Rosenthal, Caitlin. *Accounting for Slavery: Masters and Management*. Cambridge, MA: Harvard University Press, 2018.

Ross, Fred A. *Slavery Ordained of God*. Middletown, DE: Author, 1857.

Rucker, Philip, and Carol Leonnig. *A Very Stable Genius: Donald J. Trump's Testing of America*. New York: Penguin, 2020.

Ruffin, Edmund. *The Political Economy of Slavery; or, The Institution Considered in Regard to Its Influence on Public Wealth and the General Welfare.* Washington, DC: Lemuel Towers, 1853. Reprinted in Paul Finkelman. *Defending Slavery: Proslavery Thought in the Old South. A Brief History with Documents.* Boston: Bedford/St. Martin's, 2003.

Rutenberg, Jim, Jo Becker, Eric Lipton, Maggie Haberman, Jonathan Martin, Matthew Rosenberg, and Michael Schmidt. "77 Days: Trump's Campaign to Subvert the Election." *New York Times*, January 31, 2021. https://www.nytimes.com/2021/01/31/us/trump-election-lie.html

Scarborough, William Kauffman. *Masters of the Big House: Elite Slaveholders of the Mid-Nineteenth-Century South.* Baton Rouge: Louisiana State University Press, 2003.

———. *The Overseer: Plantation Management in the Old South.* Athens: University of Georgia Press, 1984.

Schuessler, Jennifer. "Alexander Hamilton, Enslaver? New Research Says Yes." *New York Times*, November 9, 2020. http://www.nytimes.com/2020/11/09/arts/alexander-hamilton-enslaver-research.html

Scott, Anne Firor, *Making the Invisible Woman Visible.* Urbana: University of Illinois Press, 1984.

———. *The Southern Lady: From Pedestal to Politics, 1830–1930.* Chicago: University of Chicago Press, 1970.

Segrest, Mab. "'Go There Ready for War'—Militia Organizing in North Carolina in the Context of the Insurrection at the US Capitol." *Scalawag*, March 29, 2021, 1–44. https://scalawagmagazine.org/2021/03/blueprint-nc-report/

Seligman, Martin E. P., and David L. Rosenhan. *Abnormality.* New York: Norton, 1997.

Sewall, Samuel. *The Selling of Joseph: A Memorial.* Edited by Sidney Kaplan. Amherst: University of Massachusetts Press, 1969.

Sharon Presbyterian Church. *Sharing Our Heritage.* Charlotte, NC: Jostens, 2006.

Sheldon, Marianne Buroff. *Virginia Magazine of History and Biography* 93, no. 1 (1985): 101–2.

Simon, Mallory, Sara Sidner, and Anna Maja Rappard. "Some of His Followers Are Being Sought by the FBI. It's Not Stopping the Leader of the Oath Keepers." CNN, February 15, 2021. https://www.cnn.com/2021/02/15/politics/capitol-riot-oath-keepers-stewart-rhodes-soh/index.html

Slave Rebellion Web Site. "A Map of Slave Revolts in the United States." http://slaverebellion.info/index.php?page=maps.

Smith, David Livingstone. *Less Than Human: Why We Demean, Enslave, and Exterminate Others.* New York: St. Martin's, 2011.

Smith, James Hervey. "Sismondi's Political Economy." In *All Clever Men, Who Make Their Way: Critical Discourse in the Old South*, ed. Michael O'Brien, 29–54. Fayetteville: University of Arkansas Press, 1982.

Smith, Lillian. *Killers of the Dream.* New York: Norton, 1994.

Snay, Mitchell. *Gospel of Disunion: Religion and Separation in the Antebellum South.* Chapel Hill: University of North Carolina Press, 1993.

Sommerville, Diane Miller. *Aberration of Mind: Suicide and Suffering in the Civil War–Era South.* Chapel Hill: University of North Carolina Press, 2018.

————. *Rape and Race in the Nineteenth Century South.* Chapel Hill: University of North Carolina Press, 2004.

South Carolina Encyclopedia. "Palmer, Benjamin Morgan." http://www.scencyclopedia.org/sce/entries/palmer-benjamin-morgan/

Stampp, Kenneth M. *The Peculiar Institution: Slavery in the Ante-Bellum South.* New York: Vintage, 1989.

Stanton, Lucia. *"Those Who Labor for My Happiness": Slavery at Thomas Jefferson's Monticello.* Charlottesville: University of Virginia Press, 2012.

Staples, Brent, "How Italians Became White." *New York Times,* October 12, 2019. https://www.nytimes.com/interactive/2019/10/12/opinion/columbus-day-italian-american-racism.html

State v. Hale, 9 N.C. (2 Hawks) 582 (1823).

State v. Mann, 13 N.C. (2 Dev.) 263 (1829).

State v. Will, 18 N.C. 121 (1834).

Steelman, Ben. "6 Confederate Flags and How They Are Different." *StarNews Online,* June 25, 2015. https://www.starnewsonline.com/article/NC/20150625/news/605043805/WM

Stewart, James Brewer. *Holy Warriors: The Abolitionists and American Slavery.* New York: Hill and Wang, 1996.

Stiles, Robert. *Four Years under Marse Robert,* 3rd ed. New York: Neale, 1904.

Stout, Harry S. *Upon the Altar of the Nation: A Moral History of the Civil War.* New York: Penguin, 2006.

Stowe, Harriet Beecher. *Uncle Tom's Cabin: Life among the Lowly.* 1852; Lexington, KY: Black & White Publications, 2015.

Sublette, Ned, and Constance C. Sublette. *The American Slave Coast: A History of the Slave Breeding Industry.* Chicago: Lawrence Hill, 2016.

Sutch, Richard. *The Breeding of Slaves for Sale and the Westward Expansion of Slavery.* Berkeley: Institute of Business and Economic Research, University of California, 1972.

Tadman, Michael. *Speculators and Slaves: Masters, Traders, and Slaves in the Old South.* Madison: University of Wisconsin Press, 1996.

Taub, Amanda. "Tumultuous Day, But a Coup Attempt?" *New York Times,* January 8, 2021.

Taylor, Elizabeth Dowling. *A Slave in the White House: Paul Jennings and the Madisons.* New York: Palgrave Macmillan, 2012.

Tise, Larry E. *Proslavery: A History of the Defense of Slavery in America, 1701–1840.* Athens: University of Georgia Press, 1987.

Tise, Larry E., and Jeffrey J. Crow, eds. *New Voyages to Carolina: Reinterpreting North Carolina History.* Chapel Hill: University of North Carolina Press, 2017.

Touré. "Slavery in America Reminds Us: Trump Is Far from an Aberration." *Guardian,* August 16, 2019.

Trump, Mary L. *Too Much and Never Enough: How My Family Created the World's Most Dangerous Man.* New York: Simon & Schuster, 2020.

US Census Bureau. *Measuring America: The Decennial Censuses from 1790 to 2000.* Washington, DC: US Census Bureau, 2007. https://www.census.gov/history/pdf/measuringamerica.pdf

Vann, Barry Aron. *In Search of Ulster-Scots Land: The Birth and Geotheological Imagings of a Transatlantic People 1603–1703.* Columbia: University of South Carolina Press, 2008.

Webster's Dictionary of Word Origins. New York: Smithmark, 1995.

Weld, Theodore, ed. *American Slavery as It Is: Testimony of a Thousand Witnesses.* New York: American Anti-Slavery Society, 1839.

Widmer, Ted, ed. *Disunion: A History of the Civil War.* New York: Oxford University Press, 2016.

Wilkerson, Isabel. "America's Enduring Caste System." *New York Times,* July 5, 2020. https://www.nytimes.com/2020/07/01/magazine/isabel-wilkerson-caste.html

Wilson, Charles Reagan. *Baptism in Blood: The Religion of the Lost Cause, 1865–1920.* Athens: University of Georgia Press, 2009.

Woodward, Bob. *Fear: Trump in the White House.* New York: Simon & Schuster, 2018.

———. *Rage.* New York: Simon & Schuster, 2018.

Woodward, Colin Edward. "Free to Fight: The Confederate Army and the Use of Slaves as Soldiers." In *Marching Masters: Slavery, Race, and the Confederate Army during the Civil War,* 155–79. Charlottesville: University of Virginia Press, 2014.

Woodward, C. Vann, ed. *Mary Chesnut's Civil War.* New Haven, CT: Yale University Press, 1981.

Woodward, C. Vann, and Elizabeth Muhlenfeld, eds. *The Private Mary Chesnut: The Unpublished Civil War Diaries.* New York: Oxford University Press, 1984.

Wyatt-Brown, Bertram. "Plantation Women in the Slave South." *American History* 11, no. 4 (Dec. 1983): 515–20.

———. *The Shaping of Southern Culture: Honor, Grace, and War, 1760s–1880s.* Chapel Hill: University of North Carolina Press, 2001.

———. *Southern Honor: Ethics and Behavior in the Old South.* Oxford: Oxford University Press, 2007.

X, Malcolm. *The Autobiography of Malcolm X.* New York: Grove, 1965.

Young, Jason R. *Rituals of Resistance: African Atlantic Region in Kongo and the Lowcountry South in the Era of Slavery.* Baton Rouge: Louisiana State University Press, 2007.

Zimbardo, Phillip. *The Lucifer Effect: Understanding How Good People Turn Evil.* New York: Random House, 2008.

Zinn, Howard. *A People's History of the United States.* New York: HarperCollins, 2003.

Zucchino, David. *Wilmington's Lie: The Murderous Coup of 1898 and the Rise of White Supremacy.* New York: Grove, 2020.

Further Reading

Akamatsu, Rhetta. *The Irish Slaves: Slavery, Indenture, and Contract Labor among Irish Immigrants*. N.p.: Author, 2010.

Alexander, Michelle. *The New Jim Crow: Mass Incarceration in the Age of Colorblindness*. New York: New Press, 2012.

Alexander, Roberta Sue. *North Carolina Faces the Freedmen: Race Relations during Presidential Reconstruction, 1865–67*. Durham, NC: Duke University Press, 1985.

Alexander, Shawn Leigh, ed. *Reconstruction Violence and the Ku Klux Klan Hearings*. Boston: Bedford/St. Martin's, 2015.

Allcott, John V. *Colonial Homes in North Carolina*. Raleigh: North Carolina Department of Cultural Resources, 1975.

Anonymous. *Kirkpatrick of Closeburn (Memoir)*. 1858.

Bailey, Fred Arthur. "Thomas Nelson Page and the Patrician Cult of the Old South." *International Social Science Review* 72, no. 3/4 (1997): 110–21.

Bartoletti, Susan Campbell. *They Called Themselves the K.K.K.: The Birth of an American Terrorist Group*. Boston: Houghton Mifflin, 2010.

Bennett, David H. *The Party of Fear: From Nativist Movements to the New American Right*. New York: Vintage, 1990.

Billingsley, Andrew. *Yearning to Breathe Free: Robert Smalls of South Carolina and His Families*. Columbia: University of South Carolina Press, 2007.

Blackwelder, Linda Lawless. *Steele Creek: An Early History of the Steele Creek Community, Mecklenburg County, North Carolina*. Pineville, NC: Steele Creek Printing and Design, 2018.

Blaufarb, Rafe. *Inhuman Traffick: The International Struggle against the Transatlantic Slave Trade*. New York: Oxford University Press, 2014.

Blethen, H. Tyler, and Curtis W. Wood Jr. *From Ulster to Carolina: The Migration of the Scotch-Irish to Southwestern North Carolina*. Raleigh, NC: Office of Archives and History, Edwards Brothers Inc., 1999.

Blythe, LeGette, and Charles Raven Brockmann. *Hornet's Nest: The Story of Charlotte and Mecklenburg County*. Charlotte, NC: McNally, 1961.

Bond, Donovan H. *The Scots-Irish in the Virginias and the Carolinas.* Loachapoka, AL: Unicorn Limited, 1995.

Boritt, Gabor S., and Norman O. Forness, ed. *The Historian's Lincoln: Pseudohistory, Psychohistory, and History.* Urbana: University of Illinois Press, 1988.

Bouie, Jamelle. "The Joy of Hatred." *New York Times,* July 19, 2019. https://www .nytimes.com/2019/07/19/opinion/trump-rally.html

Boyte, Jack Orr. *Houses of Charlotte and Mecklenburg County.* Charlotte, NC: Josten Graphics, 1998.

Breen, Patrick H. *The Land Shall Be Deluged in Blood: A New History of the Nat Turner Revolt.* New York: Oxford University Press, 2016.

Broomall, James J. *Private Confederacies: The Emotional Worlds of Southern Men as Citizens and Soldiers.* Chapel Hill: University of North Carolina Press, 2019.

Brophy, Alfred L. *University, Court, and Slave: Pro-Slavery Thought in Southern Colleges and Courts and the Coming of the Civil War.* New York: Oxford University Press, 2016.

Brown, Martha R. *Holding Sweet Communion.* Winston-Salem, NC: Author, 2012.

Budiansky, Stephen. *The Bloody Shirt: Terror after the Civil War.* London: Penguin, 2008.

Bushman, Claudia. "The Plantation Mistress: Woman's World in the Old South," *Winterthur Portfolio* 20, no. 2/3 (summer-autumn 1985): 201–2.

Cahill, Thomas. *How the Irish Saved Civilization: The Untold Story of Ireland's Heroic Role from the Fall of Rome to the Rise of Medieval Europe.* New York: Anchor, 1995.

Cameron, Christopher. *To Plead Our Own Cause: African Americans in Massachusetts and the Making of the Antislavery Movement.* Kent, OH: Kent State University Press, 2014.

Carlin, Colin. *William Kirkpatrick of Malaga.* Glasgow: Grimsay Press, 2011.

Catton, Bruce. *This Hallowed Ground: A History of the Civil War.* New York: Random House, 1956.

Chalmers, David M. *Hooded Americans: The History of the Ku Klux Klan,* 3rd ed. Durham, NC: Duke University Press, 1987.

Chestnut, Charles W. *The Marrow of Tradition.* New York: Penguin, 1993.

Claiborne, Jack, and William Price, eds. *Discovering North Carolina: A Tar Heel Reader.* Chapel Hill: University of North Carolina Press, 1991.

Clarke, Erskine. *Dwelling Place: A Plantation Epic.* New Haven, CT: Yale University Press, 2005.

Clarkson, Thomas. *An Essay on the Slavery and the Commerce of the Human Species, Particularly the African.* 1785; New York: Cambridge University Press, 2013.

Conser, Walter H. Jr. *A Coat of Many Colors: Religion and Society along the Cape Fear River of North Carolina.* Lexington: University of Kentucky Press, 2006.

Cooper, William J., Jr. *Liberty and Slavery: Southern Politics to 1860.* Columbia: University of South Carolina Press, 2000.

———. *We Have the War upon Us: The Onset of the Civil War, November 1860–April 1861.* New York: Knopf, 2012.

Countryman, Edward, ed. *How Did American Slavery Begin?* Boston: Bedford/St. Martin's, 1999.

Covington, Howard E., Jr. *Henry Frye, North Carolina's First African American Chief Justice.* Jefferson, NC: McFarland, 2003.

Crowley, J., W. J. Smyth, and M. Murphy, eds. *Atlas of the Great Irish Famine, 1845–1852.* Cork, Ireland: Cork University Press, 2012.

Cunningham, Bria. *$1000: The Price of Life and Honor in the 1834 North Carolina Supreme Court Case, State v. Will.* Honors thesis, Department of History, University at Albany, State University of New York, May 2013. https://www.albany.edu/honorscollege/files/Cunningham_Thesis.pdf

Dabney, Robert L. *A Defense of Virginia and the South.* 1867; Harrisonburg, VA: Sprinkle Publications, 1991.

Davidson, Chalmers G[aston]. *Cloud over Catawba.* Charlotte, NC: Dowd Press, 1949.

———. *The Plantation World Around Davidson: The Story of North Mecklenburg "Before the War",* 2nd ed. Davidson, NC: Mecklenburg Historical Association/Davidson Printing Company, 1973.

Davis, Susan Lawrence. *Authentic History Ku Klux Klan 1865–1877.* New York: Author, 1924.

DeGruy, Joy. *Post Traumatic Slave Syndrome: America's Legacy of Enduring Injury & Healing.* Stone Moutain, GA: Joy DeGruy Publications, 2017.

DeWolf, Thomas Norman, and Jodie Geddes. *The Little Book of Racial Healing: Coming to the Table for Truth-Telling, Liberation, and Transformation.* New York: Good Books, 2019.

Dobson, David. *Scots-Irish Links 1575–1725, Part One and Part Two.* Baltimore, MD: Genealogical Publishing, 2001.

Dolan, J. P. *The Irish Americans: A History.* New York: Bloomsbury, 2008.

Dyson, Michael Eric. *Tears We Cannot Stop: A Sermon to White America.* New York: St. Martin's, 2017.

Egerton, Douglas R. *The Wars of Reconstruction: The Brief, Violent History of America's Most Progressive Era.* New York: Bloomsbury, 2014.

Eichhorn, Neils. *Liberty and Slavery: European Separatists, Southern Secession, and the American Civil War.* Baton Rouge: Louisiana State University Press, 2019.

Elliott, Mark, and John David Smith, eds. *Undaunted Radical: The Selected Writings and Speeches of Albion W. Tourgee.* Baton Rouge: Louisiana State University Press, 2010.

Ellis, Joseph J. *The Quartet: Orchestrating the Second American Revolution, 1783–1789.* New York: Vintage, 2016.

Equal Justice Initiative. *Lynching in America: Confronting the Legacy of Racial Terror,* 3rd ed. Montgomery, AL: Equal Justice Initiative, 2017.

Equiano, Olaudah, *The Interesting Narrative.* Edited by Brycchan Carey. Oxford: Oxford University Press, 2018.

Evans, E. Estyn. *Irish Folk Ways.* London: Routledge & Kegan Paul, 1957.

Farnsworth, Paul. "Brutality or Benevolence in Plantation Archaeology." *International Journal of Historical Archaeology* 4, no. 2 (2000): 145–58.

Faust, Drew Gilpin. "Carry Me Back: Race, History, and Memories of a Virginia Girlhood." *Atlantic,* August 2019, 52–61.

———. *This Republic of Suffering: Death and the American Civil War.* New York: Knopf, 2008.

Finley, M. I., ed. *Slavery in Classical Antiquity: Views and Controversies.* Cambridge, UK: Hefner, 1964.

Fisher, Edward. *The Marrow of Modern Divinity.* Philadelphia: Presbyterian Board of Publication, 2012.

Fitzgerald, Frances. *The Evangelicals: The Struggle to Shape America.* New York: Simon and Schuster, 2017.

Fitzhugh, George. *Cannibals All! Or Slaves without Masters* (Richmond, 1857), ed. C. Vann Woodward. Cambridge, MA: Belknap, 1960.

Fogel, Robert William, and Stanley L. Engerman. *Time on the Cross: The Economics of American Negro Slavery.* Boston: Little, Brown, 1974.

———. *Time on the Cross: Evidence and Methods—A Supplement.* Boston: Little, Brown, 1974.

Foner, Eric. *Free Soil, Free Labor, Free Men: The Ideology of the Republican Party before the Civil War.* New York: Oxford University Press, 1970.

———. *A Short History of Reconstruction, 1863–1877.* New York: Harper and Row, 1990.

Forret, Jeff. *Slave against Slave: Plantation Violence in the Old South.* Baton Rouge: Louisiana State University Press, 2015.

Forret, Jeff, and Christine Sears, eds. *New Directions in Slavery Studies: Commodification, Community, and Comparison.* Baton Rouge: Louisiana State University Press, 2015.

Frankl, Victor E. *Man's Search for Meaning.* New York: Washington Square Press, 1967.

———. *The Will to Meaning: Foundations and Applications of Logotherapy.* New York: New American Library, 1969.

Freeman, Joanne B. *The Field of Blood: Violence in Congress and the Road to the Civil War.* New York: Picador Farrar, Straus and Giroux, 2018.

Gaillard, Frye. *Journey to the Wilderness: War, Memory, and a Southern Family's War Letters.* Montgomery, AL: NewSouth Books, 2015.

Gatewood, Willard B. *Aristocrats of Color: The Black Elite, 1880–1920.* Bloomington: Indiana University Press, 1990.

Genovese, Eugene C. *The Southern Front: History and Politics in the Cultural War.* Columbia: University of Missouri Press, 1995.

Gergel, Richard. *Unexampled Courage: The Blinding of Sgt. Isaac Woodard and the Awakening of President Harry S. Truman and Judge J. Waties Waring.* New York: Sarah Crichton Books, 2019.

Giggie, M. A. "Psychological Autopsies in Children and Adolescents." In *Principles and Practice of Child and Adolescent Forensic Mental Health,* ed. E. P. Benedek, P. Ash, and C. L. Scott, 431–44. Washington, DC: American Psychiatric Publishing, 2010.

Gilmore, Glenda Elizabeth. *Gender and Jim Crow.* Chapel Hill: University of North Carolina Press, 1996.

Gilmore, Glenda Elizabeth, and Thomas J. Sugrue. *These United States: A Nation in the Making, 1890 to the Present.* New York: Norton, 2015.

Gimelli, Louis B. "Louisa Maxwell Cocke: An Evangelical Mistress in the Antebellum South." *Journal of the Early Republic* 9, no. 1 (spring 1989): 53–71.

Giorgi, A. P. *Psychology as a Human Science.* New York: Harper and Row, 1970.

Gleeson, David T. *The Irish in the South, 1815–1877*. Chapel Hill: University of North Carolina Press, 2001.

Goldberg, Michelle. *Kingdom Coming: The Rise of Christian Nationalism*. New York: Norton, 2007.

Gonaver, Wendy. *The Peculiar Institution and the Making of Modern Psychiatry 1840–1880*. Chapel Hill: University of North Carolina Press, 2018.

Gordon-Reed, Annette. *On Juneteenth*. New York: Liveright, 2021.

Griffin, John Howard. *Black Like Me*. New York: Signet, 1961.

Griffin, Patrick. *The People with No Name: Ireland's Ulster Scots, America's Scots Irish, and the Creation of a British Atlantic World, 1689–1764*. Princeton, NJ: Princeton University Press, 2001.

Griffith, D. W., and Thomas Dixon. *Birth of a Nation* [film]. Los Angeles, CA: Triangle Film Corp., 1915.

Grundy, Pamela. *Color & Character: West Charlotte High and the American Struggle over Educational Equality*. Chapel Hill: University of North Carolina Press, 2017.

Hamilton, Allan McLane. *Recollections of an Alienist*. New York: George H. Doran, 1916.

Hanchett, Thomas W. *Sorting Out the New South City: Race, Class, and Urban Development in Charlotte, 1875–1975*. Chapel Hill: University of North Carolina Press, 1998.

Hanchett, Tom, Ryan Sumner, and the Levine Museum of the New South. *Charlotte and the Carolina Piedmont*. Charleston, SC: Arcadia, 2003.

Hill, Daniel. *White Awake: An Honest Look at What It Means to Be White*. Downers Grove, IL: IVP Press, 2017.

Hill, Lynda M. "Ex-Slave Narratives: The WPA Federal Writers' Project Reappraised." *Oral History* 26, no. 1 (1998): 64–72.

Hinks, Peter P., ed. *David Walker's Appeal*. University Park: Pennsylvania State University Press, 2008.

Horwitz, Tony. *Confederates in the Attic*. New York: Random House, 1998.

Ingalls, Robert P. *Hoods: The Story of the Ku Klux Klan*. New York: Putnam, 1979.

Jefferson, Thomas. *The Jefferson Bible: The Life and Morals of Jesus of Nazareth*. Boston: Beacon Press, 1989.

Jennison, Watson W. *The Expansion of Slavery in Georgia, 1750–1860*. Lexington: University of Kentucky Press, 2006.

Johnston, M. P., ed. *Songs of Zion*. Nashville, TN: Abingdon Press, 1982.

Jones, H. G. *North Carolina Illustrated 1524–1984*. Chapel Hill: University of North Carolina Press, 1983.

Joyner, Charles. *Down by the Riverside: A South Carolina Slave Community*. Urbana, IL: University of Chicago Press, 1844.

Kanigel, R. *On an Irish Island, the Lost World of the Great Blasket*. New York: Vintage, 2012.

Kennedy, Bill. *The Scots-Irish in the Carolinas*. Greenville, SC: Emerald House Group, 1997.

King, Gilbert. *Devil in the Grove: Thurgood Marshall, the Groveland Boys, and the Dawn of a New America*. New York: Harper Perennial, 2012.

King, Martin Luther, Jr. *I Have a Dream also Letter from Birmingham Jail.* Logan, IA: Perfection Learning Corporation, 1963.

Kirkpatrick, Charles. *Records of the Closeburn Kirkpatricks.* Glasgow: Grimsay Press, 2003.

Kirkpatrick, J. E. *The Kirkpatrick Families: An Historical Sketch of the Name, and the Families Bearing the Name, from the 12th to the 20th Century.* N.p.: Kirkpatrick Family Association, 1908.

Kocsis, R. N. "Psychological Autopsy." In *Applied Criminal Psychology: A Guide to Forensic Behavioral Sciences,* ed. R. N. Kocsis, 235–55. Springfield, IL: Charles C. Thomas, 2009.

Lemann, Nicholas. *Redemption: The Last Battle of the Civil War.* New York: Farrar, Straus and Giroux, 2006.

Littlefield, Daniel C. *Rice and Slaves: Ethnicity and the Slave Trade in Colonial South Carolina.* Champaign: University of Illinois Press, 1981.

Lunsford, B. *Charlotte Then and Now.* San Diego, CA: Thunder Bay Press, 2008.

Lussana, Sergio A. *My Brother Slaves: Friendship, Masculinity, and Resistance in the Antebellum South.* Louisville: University of Kentucky Press, 2016.

Lynch, Willie. *The Willie Lynch Letter and the Making of a Slave.* Long Island City, NY: African Tree Press, 2019.

MacLean, Nancy. *Behind the Mask of Chivalry: The Making of the Second Ku Klux Klan.* New York: Oxford University Press, 1994.

Martinez, J. Michael. *Carpetbaggers, Cavalry, and the Ku Klux Klan: Exposing the Invisible Empire During Reconstruction.* Lanham, MD: Rowman & Littlefield, 2007.

Martinez, Thomas, and John Guinther. *Brotherhood of Murder.* New York: McGraw Hill, 1988.

Massey, R. F. *Personality Theories: Comparisons and Syntheses.* New York: D. Van Nostrand, 1981.

McCarthy, Karen F. *The Other Irish: The Scots-Irish Rascals Who Made America.* New York: Sterling, 2011.

McIlhenny, Ryan C. *To Preach Deliverance to the Captives: Freedom and Slavery in the Protestant Mind of George Bourne, 1780–1845.* Baton Rouge: Louisiana State University Press, 2020.

McPherson, James. *The War that Forged a Nation: Why the Civil War Still Matters.* Oxford: Oxford University Press, 2015.

Meacham, Jon. *American Lion: Andrew Jackson in the White House.* New York: Random House, 2008.

Mobley, Joe A., ed. *The Way We Lived in North Carolina.* Chapel Hill: University of North Carolina Press, 2003.

Moody, T. W., F. X. Martin, and D. Keogh. *The Course of Irish History,* 5th ed. Lanham, MD: Roberts Rinehart, 2012.

Moore, Joseph E. *Murder on Maryland's Eastern Shore: Race, Politics, and the Case of Orphan Jones.* Charleston, SC: History Press, 2006.

Morrill, Dan L. *The Corner of West Trade and Mint Streets: A History of the Federal Government's Home in Charlotte.* Charlotte, NC: Warren Publishing, 2017.

Morris, Christopher. "The Articulation of Two Worlds: The Master-Slave Relationship Reconsidered." *Journal of American History* 85, no. 3 (1998): 982–1007.

———. "An Event in Community Organization: The Mississippi Slave Insurrection Scare of 1835." *Journal of Social History* 22, no. 1 (1998): 93–111.

Mullin, Michael. *American Negro Slavery: A Documentary History*. New York: Harper and Row, 1976.

National Academy Task Force on the Hymnbook Project. *Songs of Zion*. Nashville, TN: Abingdon Press, 1981.

Newton, Michael, and Judy Ann Newton. *The Ku Klux Klan: An Encyclopedia*. New York: Garland, 1991.

Owens, Joseph. *A History of Ancient Western Philosophy*. New York: Appleton, Century, Crofts, 1959.

Palmer, Parker J. *Healing the Heart of Democracy: The Courage to Create a Politics Worthy of the Human Spirit*. San Francisco: Jossey-Bass, 2011.

Parsons, Theodore, and Eliphalet Pearson. *A Forensic Dispute on the Legality of Enslaving Africans*. Boston: Printed for John Boyle for Thomas Leverett, 1773.

Paton, Alan. *Cry, the Beloved Country*. New York: Charles Scribners' Sons, 1950.

Pearson, A. F. Scott. *Presbyterian Origins in Ulster*. Belfast, Northern Ireland: Presbyterian Historical Society of Ireland, n.d.

Pegram, Thomas R. *One Hundred Percent American: The Rebirth and Decline of the Ku Klux Klan in the 1920s*. Chicago: Ivan R. Dee, 2011.

Phillips, Jason. *Looming Civil War: How Nineteenth-Century Americans Imagined the Future*. New York: Oxford University Press, 2018.

Phillips, Patrick. *Blood at the Root: A Racial Cleansing of America*. New York: Norton, 2017.

Philyaw, Deesha. *The Secret Lives of Church Ladies*. Morgantown: West Virginia University Press, 2020.

Pitts, Leonard Jr. *The Last Thing You Surrender*. Chicago: Bolden, 2019.

Powell, William S. *North Carolina through Four Centuries*. Chapel Hill: University of North Carolina Press, 1989.

———. *The Proprietors of Carolina*. Raleigh, NC: Carolina Charter Tercentenary Commission, 1963.

Raboteau, Albert J. *Slave Religion: The "Invisible Institution" in the Antebellum South*. Oxford: Oxford University Press, 2004.

Ramsey, R. W. *Carolina Cradle: Settlement of the Northwest Carolina Frontier, 1747–1762*. Chapel Hill: University of North Carolina Press, 1964.

Rediker, Marcus. *The Slave Ship: A Human History*. New York: Penguin, 2007.

Reed, John Shelton. *Whistling Dixie: Dispatches from the South*. San Diego: Harcourt, 1990.

Reid, J. B. *A Goodly Heritage: The Bicentennial History of Sardis Presbyterian Church*. Charlotte, NC: Communications Committee, 1989.

Rose, S. E. F. *The Ku Klux Klan or Invisible Empire*. New Orleans, LA: L. Graham, 1914.

Rossignol, Ken. *Klan Killing America*. N.p.: Huggins Point Publishing, 2013.

Rothman, Adam. *Beyond Freedom's Reach: A Kidnapping in the Twilight of Slavery*. Cambridge, MA: Harvard University Press, 2015.

Rothstein, Richard. *The Color of Law: A Forgotten History of How Our Government Segregated America*. New York: Liveright, 2017.

Rugemer, Edward Bartlett. *The Problem of Emancipation: The Caribbean Roots of the American Civil War*. Baton Rouge: Louisiana State University Press, 2008.

Sandburg, Carl. *Abraham Lincoln: The Prairie Years and the War Years*. New York: Harcourt Brace Jovanovich, 1954.

Sims, Patsy. *Can Somebody Shout Amen! Inside the Tents and Tabernacles of American Revivalists*. Louisville: University of Kentucky Press, 1996.

Smith, Mark M., ed. *Stono: Documenting and Interpreting a Southern Slave Rebellion*. Columbia: University of South Carolina Press, 2005.

Soapes, Thomas S. "The Federal Writers' Project Slave Interviews: Useful Data or Misleading Source." *Oral History Review* 5 (1977): 33–38. https://www.jstor.org/stable/3674886

Stampp, Kenneth M., ed. *The Causes of the Civil War*, 3rd ed. New York: Touchstone, 1959.

———. *The Era of Reconstruction 1865–1877*. New York: Vintage, 1965.

Stevenson, Bryan. *Just Mercy: A Story of Justice and Redemption*. New York: Spiegel and Grau, 2014.

Stubbs, Tristan. *Masters of Violence: The Plantation Overseers of Eighteenth-Century Virginia, South Carolina, and Georgia*. Columbia: University of South Carolina Press, 2018.

Sullivan, Shannon. *Good White People: The Problem with Middle-Class White Anti-Racism*. Albany: State University Press of New York, 2014.

Summers, Mark Wahlgren. *The Ordeal of the Reunion: A New History of Reconstruction*. Chapel Hill: University of North Carolina Press, 2014.

Swarms, Rachel L. "The Nuns Who Bought and Sold Human Beings." *New York Times*, August 2, 2019. https://www.nytimes.com/2019/08/02/opinion/sunday/nuns-slavery.html

Tarn, William, and G. T. Griffith. *Hellenistic Civilisation*, 3rd ed. London: Edward Arnold, 1966.

Taylor, Rosser Howard. *Slaveholding in North Carolina: An Economic View*. New York: Negro Universities Press, 1926.

"Thomas Leroy Kirkpatrick." Vertical File. Robinson-Spangler Carolina Room, Charlotte Mecklenburg Library, Charlotte, NC.

Thomkins, D. A. *History of Mecklenburg County and the City of Charlotte from 1740 to 1903*. Vols. 1 and 2. Charlotte, NC: Observer Printing House, 1903.

Thompson, Ernest Trice. *Presbyterians in the South: Vol. One: 1607–1861*. Richmond, VA: John Knox Press, 1963.

Tomlinson, C. *Tomlinson Hill*. New York: St. Martin's, 2014.

Trelease, Allen W. *White Terror: The Ku Klux Klan Conspiracy and Southern Reconstruction*. Baton Rouge: Louisiana State University Press, 1971.

Trent, Hank. *The Secret Life of Bacon Tait, a White Slave Trader Married to a Free Woman of Color*. Baton Rouge: Louisiana State University Press, 2017.

Truth, Sojourner. *Narrative of Sojourner Truth, a Northern Slave, Emancipated from Bodily Servitude by the State of New York, in 1828.* Edited by Olive Gilbert. Boston: Author, 1850.

Tyson, Timothy B. *Blood Done Sign My Name.* New York: Broadway Books, 2004.

———. *The Blood of Emmett Till.* New York: Simon and Schuster, 2017.

US House of Representatives' Committee on Un-American Activities. Hearings before the committee on Un-American activities, House of Representatives, Eighty-Ninth Congress, Second Session: *Activities of Ku Klux Klan Organizations in the United States,* Part 3, January 4–7, 11–14, 18, and 28, 1966.

Vance, J. D. *Hillbilly Elegy: A Memoir of a Family and Culture in Crisis.* New York: Harper, 2016.

Wade, Wyn Craig. *The Fiery Cross: The Ku Klux Klan in America.* New York: Oxford University Press, 1987.

Wagner, Bryan. *The Life and Legend of Bras-Coupe: The Fugitive Slave Who Fought the Law, Ruled the Swamp, Danced at Congo Square, Invented Jazz, and Died for Love.* Baton Rouge: Louisiana State University Press, 2019.

Wallis, Jim. *America's Original Sin: Racism, White Privilege, and the Bridge to a New America.* Grand Rapids, MI: Brazos, 2016.

Weisman, Avery D. *The Realization of Death: A Guide for the Psychological Autopsy.* New York: Jason Aronson, 1974.

Wells-Barnett, Ida B. *The Red Record: Tabulated Statistics and Alleged Causes of Lynching in the United States.* 1895; Columbia, SC: Cavalier Classics, 2015.

Wexler, Laura. *Fire in a Canebreak: The Last Mass Lynching in America.* New York: Scribner, 2003.

Wheaton, Elizabeth. *Codename Greenkil: The 1979 Greensboro Killings.* Athens: University of Georgia Press, 1987.

White, Howard, and Ruth White. *Mecklenburg: The Life and Times of a Proud People.* Brentwood, TN: JM Productions, 1992.

Whitehead, Colson. *The Underground Railroad.* New York: Doubleday, 2016.

Wilentz, Sean. *No Property in Man: Slavery and Antislavery at the Nation's Founding.* Cambridge, MA: Harvard University Press, 2018.

Wilkerson, Isabel. *Caste: The Origins of Our Discontents.* New York: Random House, 2020.

Williams, Ann. *The Rural Hill Farm Journals of Adam Brevard Davidson, 1834–1856.* Charlotte, NC: Antebellum Books, 2017.

———. *The Uncommon Bond of Julia and Rose: A Novel.* Charlotte, NC: Floating Leaf Press, 2015.

Williams, Ed. *Liberating Dixie: [An Editor's Life, from Ole Miss to Obama].* Davidson, NC: Lorimer, 2013.

Wilson-Hartgrove, Jonathan. *Reconstructing the Gospel: Finding Freedom from Slaveholder Religion.* Downers Grove, IL: InterVarsity, 2018.

Wood, Betty. *Slavery in Colonial America: 1619–1776.* Lanham, MD: Rowman and Littlefield, 2005.

Wood, Peter H. *Black Majority: Negroes in Colonial South Carolina from 1670 through the Stono Rebellion.* New York: Norton, 1974.

Wyatt-Brown, Bertram. "The Mask of Obedience: Male Slave Psychology in the Old South." *American Historical Review* 93, no. 5 (1988): 1228–52.

Young, Jason R. *Rituals of Resistance: African Atlantic Religion in Kongo and the Lowcountry South in the Era of Slavery.* Baton Rouge: Louisiana State University Press, 2007.

Zaborney, John J. *Renting Enslaved Laborers in Antebellum Virginia.* Baton Rouge: Louisiana State University Press, 2012.

Acknowledgments

$\mathcal{I}$n the sense that an acknowledgment is an expression of gratitude, I am truly grateful to many people for their encouragement and support of my writing this book. If I leave anyone out, it's my memory's fault, nothing more, nothing less. First and foremost, I extend my heartfelt appreciation to Glenda Gilmore, a scholar, mentor, and friend extradordinaire. I could not have completed this project without her guidance and encouragement. There is, of course, my brother, Jimmie Lee Kirkpatrick, who, along with our ancestors, started this project in the first place. He and his wife, Vicki, have been wonderful. I am thankful too for the support from David Martindale, Priscilla Weaver, Ted Fillette, Ellen Holliday, Tom Pettus, Cecily Hines, Jock Tonissen, and John Parker. Then there were my college roommates, Karl Rohlich and Neil Martin. Neil was masterful at helping make some chapters much more readable prose. And many thanks to Louise "Weezie" Woehrle for her vision and for maintaining the documentary throughline.

A writer needs a lot of help, and I got it from my family in many ways. A heartfelt thank-you to Mela and Brian Frye, Shelley Welton and Michael Dowdy, Anna Welton and Ross Smith, Liz Welton and Jake Baumiller, Robert and Suzanne Kirkpatrick, and Phill and Libby Wilson. Pamela Kirkpatrick's undying encouragement was always a continuing, loving inspiration. Richard Wechsler's willingness to listen to my ideas during our alleged therapy sessions was a godsend. Also, I cannot thank him enough for his photographic genius.

There was fabulous collegial support too. John Smail and John Blythe offered helpful critiques and pushed me in ways that made my scholarship and writing better. Paula Eckard was wonderful in helping me focus on the subject of slavery, and Nancy Gutierrez gave me academic support that was invaluable. Jurgen Buchenau was very gracious in reading some early drafts of my work. I am also indebted to the members of the Mecklenburg History Round-table, a fine group. Dawn Schmidt and Tina Wright were very generous in helping me navigate the wonderful world of the J. Murrey Atkins Library at UNC Charlotte. And many thanks to Tom Cole, friend, colleague, public historian, and librarian at the Robinson-Spangler Carolina Room, Charlotte Mecklenburg Library.

I remain grateful for the early project work of Carol Beebe, who helped me organize the massive amount of material I wrestled with.

There is a simple truth for which I am eternally grateful: Had it not been for the timeliness and skill of Barry Chan, I would not have been around to write this book.

I cannot express fully, for there are not enough words to say, how deeply grateful I am to my beloved wife, Katie, for her undying, loving encouragement; playful craziness; support; and tireless devotion to editing and critiquing drafts, challenging me, and being my biggest fan. I simply could not have done this without her.

Index

Note: Page numbers in *italics* refer to photos and images.

poetic license, 64–65
poison, 147
poor whites, 197–98
Porter, A. A., 112
Powell, Michael, 225
power: financial debt and, 157;
governance and, 165–66; inequality
and, 69; political and economic,
6–7, 20–24, 195–96, 198–99, 206–7,
230; profits and, 23; state power,
47. *See also* domination; fears;
punishment of slaves; slave codes;
white supremacy
pregnancies of planter women, 47
Presbyterian faith, 104–5, 108, 161, 169
presidents: election of 2020 and white
supremacists, 234; racist attitudes of,
239–40; as slaveholders, 195, 199. *See
also specific presidents*
pride, 16–17
profitability of slaveholding. *See*
economics of slaveholding; property,
enslaved as
projection, 71–72
property, enslaved as: carnal entitlement,
33–36, *34*; justification of ownership,
75, 228; legal codes defining, 196–
97; monetary value, 1–2, 209–10;
women protecting right to, 51–52.
See also dehumanization of Blacks;
sexual exploitation
Prosser, Gabriel, 149–50, 153, 199, 202,
300n19
Protestant Christian faith, 9
Proud Boys, 247
providentialism, 32
The Psychoanalysis of Fire (Bachelard),
139–40
psychological defense mechanisms:
about, 63–67; conquering fear with,
162; cost of, 95–97; delusional
projection, 72–74; denial, 70–71;
projection, 71–72; rationalization,
74–76; stressors affecting slaveholders,
67, 68–69

psychologically syntonic harmony,
90, 268
psychopaths and psychopathy, 15, 38–
40, 84–88, 95, 202, 221, 242, 268–69
public slave yards, 178
punishment of slaves: about, 174–78,
194; anger and, 79; by female
slaveholders, 51–52; hangings, *192*;
overseers and, 220–21; psychopaths
enjoying, 86; of runaways, 190–91;
testimony of slaveholders, 178–79,
179–89; torture devices, *194*; types
of, 73, 178–79, *179–89*, 189, 202–3;
unlimited power of slaveholders, 173;
whipping, *191*, 202–3, *207*, 212,
213. *See also* lynchings; separation of
enslaved families

Quakers, 149, 200

racism: Black and slave as synonymous,
141–42; moral reckoning about,
231–32; religion justifying Black
slavery, 9–10, 89, 93, 99–100, 102–
10, 222, 227; of white supremacy,
225–26, 228, 233, 240. *See also*
dehumanization of Blacks; elite
slaveholders' opinions of Blacks;
Genesis 9:18–27; January 6 (2021)
insurrection; white privilege; white
supremacy
Raffensperger, Brad, 239, 246
rapes of enslaved girls, 33, 172
rationalization, 74–76
regional character development, 12, 15
Reich, Robert, 250
reinterpretative strategy, 117
religion: Civil War defeat and, 120–21;
economics of slaveholding and, 89;
favoring slaveholders, 96; fear of
God, 160–62; hypothetical sermon,
271–73; justifying slavery, 9–10,
86, 89, 93, 99–100, 102–10, 222,
227; paternalism woven into, 91; as
psychological comfort, 89; South's